A Theory of Global Goverr   and
Contestation

A Theory of Global Governance: Authority, Legitimacy, and Contestation

Michael Zürn (WZB Berlin Social Science Center; Freie Universität Berlin)

OXFORD
UNIVERSITY PRESS

OXFORD
UNIVERSITY PRESS

Great Clarendon Street, Oxford, OX2 6DP,
United Kingdom

Oxford University Press is a department of the University of Oxford.
It furthers the University's objective of excellence in research, scholarship,
and education by publishing worldwide. Oxford is a registered trade mark of
Oxford University Press in the UK and in certain other countries

© Michael Zürn 2018

The moral rights of the author have been asserted

First Edition published in 2018
Impression: 4

Published in the United States of America by Oxford University Press
198 Madison Avenue, New York, NY 10016, United States of America

British Library Cataloguing in Publication Data
Data available

Library of Congress Control Number: 2017956299

ISBN 978–0–19–881997–4 (hbk.)

ISBN 978–0–19–881998–1 (pbk.)

Printed and bound by
CPI Group (UK) Ltd, Croydon, CR0 4YY

A Klee painting named Angelus Novus shows an angel looking as though he is about to move away from something he is fixedly contemplating. His eyes are staring, his mouth is open, his wings are spread. This is how one pictures the angel of history. His face is turned toward the past. Where we perceive a chain of events, he sees one single catastrophe which keeps piling wreckage upon wreckage and hurls it in front of his feet. The angel would like to stay, awaken the dead, and make whole what has been smashed. But a storm is blowing from Paradise; it has got caught in his wings with such violence that the angel can no longer close them. The storm irresistibly propels him into the future to which his back is turned, while the pile of debris before him grows skyward. This storm is what we call progress. (Walter Benjamin, *Theses on the Philosophy of History*)

Preface

The problem with international institutions is that they are fundamentally flawed in two respects: In view of the magnitude of global problems, what they do is not enough; yet their basis of legitimacy is too small for what they already do. The last five years have seen a banking crisis with global repercussions, a level of migration that drains the sending countries and overburdens some of the receiving ones, the final reassurance that climate change needs to be controlled in order to avoid drastic human catastrophes, a dreadful density of transnational terrorist attacks, and brand new forms of nuclear brinkmanship. Measured against these challenges, the results of global cooperation are meager at best. While the attempts to contain the banking crisis were quite effective, the new regulations to prevent repetition are insufficient. The Paris climate agreement has finally brought some results, but they are likely to be insufficient to restrict global warming. The attempts to come up with a cooperative handling of the migration crisis have failed so far, and diplomatic efforts to control current threats to security do not appear to be conclusive.

For many, international institutions are not only superfluous, but they also epitomize the political enemy. Right-wing populism has risen in all countries of Western Europe, especially in Austria and France, where it has been alarmingly close to seizing power. In Eastern Europe, the political programs of right-wing populists are implemented by two governments, namely, those of Poland and Hungary, which openly violate principles of the European Union (EU). The people of the United States elected Donald Trump as their president, representing a very special version of right-wing populism. At the same time, new despots in Russia and Turkey manage to centralize power in the name of national pride. What these political leaders and movements have in common is that they all emphasize the need to control borders, are openly nationalistic, they emphasize the so-called will of the silent majority, and downgrade universal rights and obligations. The common major enemy is the EU and global governance. Any form of governance that cannot be associated with strong national governments is duly rejected.

All of this is paradoxical. In times when the need for global governance is more obvious than ever, it is being more fervently rejected than ever. This book aims at explaining the paradox. It puts forward a theory of global governance where the core of the argument is that world politics has developed a normative and institutional structure that contains hierarchies and power inequalities, and thus endogenously produces contestation, resistance, and distributional struggles. While any explanation of social processes involves an element of understanding—in this case, making the resistance to global governance comprehensible—the normative standpoint of the exploration is cosmopolitanism: I believe in the normative necessity and the political feasibility of a global governance system that is built on democratic states and that consists of accountable and effective international institutions, open borders, and a commitment to human rights.

This is a book that draws together different projects. Each of these projects was a collaborative effort at a certain stage. There is no doubt that the book would have not been possible without my colleagues. I would therefore like to express my deepest gratitude and thanks to all the people whom I have had the honor and pleasure of working with on these projects. Some of them started on the basis of friendships, and others generated new friendships or valuable collegial relations at the very least. Some of them lasted longer than expected, all had moments of crisis, and all had to survive the unfortunate blend of impatience and tardiness with which I approached these projects from time to time. Yet all of them were successful in the end, thanks to the wonderful people who took part in them.

Let me start by mentioning the projects undertaken under the auspices of the Global Governance unit (GG) at the WZB Berlin Social Science Center. The first that deserves a mention is the project on the politicization of international institutions, in which Pieter de Wilde, Matthias Ecker-Ehrhardt, and Christian Rauh are the major players. The International Authority Database brought together Martin Binder, Xaver Keller, Autumn Lockwood Payton, and, above all, Alexandros Tokhi. The project on protecting individuals from international authority consisted of Gisela Hirschmann, Theresa Reinold, and, most importantly, Monika Heupel. Tine Hanrieder, Thomas Rixen, and Lora Viola joined the effort to transfer the concepts of historical institutionalism to international relations. Finally, especially Matthew Stephen, but also Martin Binder, Sophie Eisentraut, and Alexandros Tokhi took part in the study of rising powers in the global governance system. I would like to thank all these wonderful individuals, who were imaginative and dependable at the same time. I learned an incredible amount with and from them.

Other themes elaborated in this book were the focus of cooperation with scholars outside of the WZB. While it is impossible to list all the individuals from whom I have learned and benefitted over recent years, I want to mention the excellent collaborators whom I have published with on at least one of the themes relevant for this book. Let me start with Jonas Tallberg, with whom I worked on a long-term project of legitimacy, as well as with Mathias Albert and Barry Buzan, with whom I studied functional differentiation in world society. My work on transnational and international authority benefitted especially from collaboration with Nicole Deitelhoff and Nico Krisch. These interactions were crucial in forming my thoughts.

This book benefitted enormously from a workshop in which a number of colleagues and friends discussed a first version of the draft. The fact that the finished book now looks so different, compared to the manuscript that was debated at Schloss Blankensee, speaks volumes on how important this exchange was for me. I am indebted to the following individuals for their expertise and wisdom: Karen Alter, Benjamin Faude, Markus Jachtenfuchs, Mathias Koenig-Archibugi, Thilo Marauhn, Wolfgang Merkel, Wolfgang Wagner, Klaus Dieter Wolf, and again Mathias Albert, as well as most of the WZB colleagues mentioned above.

Equally valuable were the comments from those who have read the manuscript or parts of it: Orfeo Fioretos, Rainer Forst, Robert Goodin, Andrew Hurrell, Peter Katzenstein, Bob Keohane, Christoph Möllers, Lou Pauly, Tom Pegram, Vincent Pouliot, Jan Aart Scholte, Syd Tarrow, and Ingo Venzke. I am deeply grateful for superb comments and amazing collegiality.

Different chapters of the book were presented and discussed in many different contexts, and I am not able to list them all. I would however like to mention two master classes, one in Venice and the other at the Max Planck Institute in Heidelberg—with very special thanks to Armin von Bogdandy and Anne Peters—as well as the occasions where I discussed parts of my work while teaching doctoral students in Barcelona, Stockholm, and at the Berlin Graduate School for Transnational Studies (BTS).

I have written almost all of this book while residing at my home institute. This is apparently rare. That the WZB is a place that facilitates such scholarship makes it very special among its kind indeed. I thank all my marvelous colleagues for creating this special atmosphere of intellectual curiosity and especially the fantastic GG support team, without whom the book would not have come to existence: Editha von Colberg and Katinka von Kovatsits are enormously efficient in managing the overall process at the unit, passionate, and impeccable at the same time. As to work on the manuscript itself, there are two people who deserve the deepest gratitude of all: Barçın Uluışık, who edited the material to dispense with the "Germanisms" and all the other deficiencies in my English, and Felix Große-Kreul who, as a research assistant, was always a critical commentator, a great help in putting together the graphics as well as the bibliography, and a reliable partner in discussions about the composition of the material. Both contributions were outstanding. Let me also thank Stephen Curtis, who also helped to brush up my English in some of the chapters and, not forgetting the amazing Dominic Byatt—it is a great feeling when you know that the publisher is both competent and enthusiastic about the manuscript. Dominic also chose the reviewers, who provided me with tremendously helpful comments. Last but certainly not least, I want to thank Annette and Samuel who responded to my impositions while writing the book with a lot of patience and humor.

Contents

Contents

Contents

Figures and Tables

Figures

Tables

Figures and Tables

Abbreviations

AIIB	Asia Infrastructure Investment Bank
ALL	authority–legitimation link
ATTAC	Association for the Taxation of Financial Transactions and Citizens' Action
AU	African Union
CETA	Comprehensive Economic and Trade Agreement
CSO	civil society organization
DSB	Dispute Settlement Body
ECB	European Central Bank
ECJ	European Court of Justice
ECtHR	European Court of Human Rights
ECOSOC	Economic and Social Committee of the UN
ESM	European Stability Mechanism
EU	European Union
GATT	General Agreement on Tariffs and Trade
GDP	gross domestic product
GHGs	greenhouse gases
GMO	genetically modified organism
HI	historical institutionalism
IAD	International Authority Database
IAEA	International Atomic Energy Agency
IASB	International Accounting Standards Board
IC	international court
ICANN	Internet Corporation for Assigned Names and Numbers
ICC	International Criminal Court
ICTR	International Criminal Tribunal for Rwanda
ICTY	International Criminal Tribunal for the former Yugoslavia
IEA	International Energy Agency
ILO	International Labour Organization
IMF	International Monetary Fund
IO	international organization
IPCC	International Panel on Climate Change
IRENA	International Renewable Energy Association
IPI	international parliamentary institution
IR	International Relations
IS	Islamic State

Abbreviations

MAD	mutually assured destruction
NAFTA	North American Free Trade Agreement
NAM	Non-Aligned Movement
NATO	North Atlantic Treaty Organization
NDB	New Development Bank
NGO	non-governmental organization
OECD	Organisation for Economic Co-operation and Development
OHCHR	UN Office of the High Commissioner of Human Rights
PAEA	politically assigned epistemic authority
PISA	Programme for International Student Assessment
PPP	purchasing power parity
PR	public relations
PSI	Proliferation Security Initiative
PTT	power transition theory
R2P	responsibility to protect
SDT	Special and Differential Treatment
TFEU	Treaty on the Functioning of the European Union
TTIP	Transatlantic Trade and Investment Partnership
UN	United Nations
UNCHR	UN Commission on Human Rights
UNCLOS	UN Convention on the Law of the Sea
UNESCO	UN Educational, Scientific and Cultural Organization
UNHCR	UN High Commissioner for Refugees
UNHRC	UN Human Rights Council
UNFCCC	UN Framework Convention on Climate Change
UNGA	General Assembly of the UN
UNMIK	UN Mission in Kosovo
UNSC	United Nations Security Council
UNTAET	UN Transitional Administration in East Timor
USSR	United Soviet Socialist Republic
WHO	World Health Organization
WIPO	World Intellectual Property Organization
WTO	World Trade Organization
WWF	World Wildlife Fund

Introduction

Global Governance in Hard Times

After the faltering of the Soviet Union subsequent to the fall of the Berlin Wall, many expected the consolidation of a strong liberal world order dominated by democratic states and consisting of strong international institutions, an open international economic system, and a commitment to human rights. With the benefit of hindsight, it can be said that two events in the fall of 2001 have wrecked the liberal hopes that dominated the 1990s.

On September 11th, 2001, the attack on the World Trade Center in New York and the responses to it hit these hopes heavily. The fall of the Twin Towers demonstrated on the one hand that there is large and fervent resistance to such a liberal order, which is considered by many to be instrumental in maintaining Western dominance. On the other hand, the US government did a lot to prove this charge. In response to the attack, they turned toward unilateralism and even showed a willingness to sacrifice human rights for the purpose of combating the new enemies—as symbolized by the establishment of a detention camp at the Guantanamo Bay Naval Base. Even worse, they—together with some allies—waged a war against Iraq in the name of fighting terrorism and spreading democracy that was widely seen as unjustified, insane, and parochial.

This is not all. Less than three months after 9/11, a second strike occurred—less violent, but arguably even more consequential. Jim McNeill, at that time the chief economist of Goldman Sachs, coined the term "BRIC" and, in forecasts covering the period up to 2050, pointed to the relative decline of Western economies, especially those in Europe, and the rise of new economic powers. The original BRIC countries (Brazil, Russia, India, and China), later joined by South Africa (hence BRICS), took up the challenge and institutionalized the label "BRICS" in order to meet, coordinate, and set up mechanisms to counter Western dominance. These new powers are often seen as united in emphasizing a conventional understanding of sovereignty as the right to non-interference in domestic affairs. Arguably, this understanding constitutes the most important force opposing the movement toward human rights as universal principles and the empowerment of international institutions.

As a result, the liberal world order and international institutions appear to be much weaker than fifteen years ago. The United Nations Security Council (UNSC) now seems incapable of acting in obviously urgent cases like that of Syria, the global trade negotiations in Doha are deadlocked, and the international measures taken to avoid another financial crisis fell short of what most experts think is needed. Even worse, in 2014, Russia, an important BRIC state blatantly ignored international law, annexed the Crimea, and seemed bent on doing everything it could to divide up Ukraine in order to extend its own sphere of influence. In 2015, the Eurozone crisis brought the European Union (EU) to the brink of failure. By the end of 2016, the Islamic State (IS) had brought back violence and fear to the streets of European capitals, Great Britain had voted to leave the EU, and the people of the United States, for the first time since the 1920s, had elected a president who stands openly for an isolationist foreign policy.

Of course, there are still arguments emphasizing the persistence of a liberal world order. John Ikenberry (2001, 2011b), for instance, has always emphasized the openness and adaptiveness of the post-Second World War order, arguing that a liberal order is less vulnerable to power shifts than earlier ones. Moreover, from a legal point of view and in terms of the norms that are used as means of justification in the international realm, it can be argued that the trinity of the rule of law, democracy, and human rights still prevails, and can therefore provide the normative fodder for the constitutionalization of a liberal world (Kumm 2009). Institutionalists argue that international law and international organizations (IOs) are still strong. Overall, international institutions may have changed in the last two decades, but in general, they have not lost their relevance (Keohane 2012). While the increase in the authority of IOs may have slowed down, that authority is still at a historical peak (Hooghe et al. 2017). New and important treaties such as the Paris climate agreement are still being signed, and the outcome of some crises during the last decade was stronger, not weaker, international institutions, as exemplified by the international financial authorities (Fioretos 2016). In addition, new organizational forms—especially transnational ones—have expanded rapidly (Abbott et al. 2016).

Are these recent debates between a liberal (or institutionalist) perspective[1] on world politics and a geopolitical (or realist) one just another round in the

---

[1] In general, I use the term "liberal" to refer to a normative position and thus also as a label for a certain type of political order. To refer to theories in International Relations (IR), I use the terms "realism," "institutionalism," and "critical theories." Each of these three comes in more rationalist or more constructivist versions.

battle between the two big imaginaries of the international system? Do these debates really come back cyclically every four decades? After E. H. Carr's (1964) seminal discussion of the so-called Idealists and the self-proclaimed Realists in the 1930s and the rejection of idealism in 1939 at the latest, a renewed (and more sophisticated) discussion took place forty years later with Kenneth Waltz (1979) and Robert Keohane (Keohane and Nye 1977; Keohane 1984) as the protagonists.[2] This led to the rise of institutionalism, putting realism on the defensive. Now, another forty years on, are we back to square one? Is it the same debate being repeated with the realists again on the offensive?

Contrary to the view of a perpetual battle between two imaginaries of world politics, I will argue in this book that world politics is now embedded in a normative and institutional structure that contains hierarchies and power inequalities and thus *endogenously* produces contestation, resistance, and distributional struggles. This book therefore aims to demolish the seemingly unbreakable elective affinity between institutionalism and a cooperative reading of world politics. While it is true that the liberal optimism of the 1990s is under siege, it would at the same time be odd to explain the crisis of the EU or the rise of IS in realist terms of the distribution of power between states with sovereign equality. In addition, any theory of world politics needs to take into account that, in parallel with the decline of some global governance arrangements, there has been a further deepening of others.

This book offers a theory of global governance that enables understanding of the complex parallelism of decline and deepening in global governance. The first part of the book develops the contours of this global governance system; the second part elaborates and explores hypotheses and causal mechanisms connected with its dynamics. Altogether, the book's contribution to the sum of knowledge is fourfold. First, it reconstructs *global governance as a political system* that builds on normative principles and reflexive authorities. Second, it identifies the central *legitimation problems of the global governance system* with a constitutionalist setting in mind. Third, it explains the *rise of state and societal contestation* by identifying endogenous dynamics and probing the causal mechanisms that produced them. Fourth, it identifies the conditions under which struggles in the global governance system lead to *decline or deepening*.

Global Governance

"Global governance" refers to *the exercise of authority across national borders as well as consented norms and rules beyond the nation state, both of them justified*

---

[2] Many see the work of Ernst Haas (1964) about the European integration process and Karl Deutsch et al. (1957) about the transatlantic security community as path-breaking for the revival of institutionalism.

with reference to common goods or transnational problems. Such a definition acknowledges first that global governance is carried out in international as well as transnational institutions.[3] We speak of global governance when the strictly intergovernmental UNSC authorizes a military intervention. Yet we also speak of global governance when a private and profit-seeking organization like Standard & Poor's issues credit ratings for borrowers in the financial markets. Global governance points to a pluralization of governance actors. One may therefore conceptually distinguish among global governance by government (i.e. world government), global governance with governments (as in intergovernmental institutions like the UN), and global governance without governments (as in purely transnational regimes, such as the International Accounting Standards Board (IASB), which often regulate enterprises and indirectly also states).

Second, this understanding of global governance contains both agreed norms and the exercise of authority. David Lake (2017: 11–12) recently argued that "if the concept of global governance is to be useful, it should be limited to actors and relationships that possess at least a measure of authority that spans national borders." While Lake is certainly right in emphasizing that the exercise of authority is at the core of governance (see Chapter 2), norms and rules that are consented to by all should not be excluded. Governance therefore consists of two components: shared goals, and elements of rule (Rosenau 1995: 14–5). The Dispute Settlement Body (DSB) of the World Trade Organization (WTO) judging authoritatively against the claimant is therefore as much a component of global governance as is the Universal Declaration Against Torture.

Third, the exercise of authority and the declaration of agreed norms corresponds with a communicative act. The exercise of authority in particular comes with a claim to be rightful and to be obeyed. Global governance is what claims to be global governance. In this sense, it refers to *public* authority, independent of the question whether it is carried out by state or non-state actors. It involves an element of "publicness" (see Bernstein 2014: 125). In this sense, the Hitler–Stalin Pact is not considered global governance; being secret, there was never an attempt to justify it publicly. However, an arms control treaty between great powers that is justified by the need to secure peace is global governance. Similarly, behind-closed-doors negotiations between multinational corporations about the price of a certain product do not qualify as global governance, yet the activities of private rating agencies that are justified as means to create financial stability do. However, it does not follow from this definition that global governance activities *do* always

---

[3] The former refers to intergovernmental institutions (see Young 1994), the latter to cross-border institutions with private actors as at least one group of subjects (see Risse 2013).

serve the global common good. In many cases, public justifications do not reflect the motivations that led to a particular governance arrangement. Justification does not have to be truthful.

Fourth, this definition of governance does not prejudge the social purpose behind it. Both a state interventionist and a neoliberal political project depend on governance. A certain choice of governance always includes a choice against another form of governance. It therefore privileges the beliefs and interests of some actors over others, and it always has distributional consequences reflecting societal power constellations. Power and hierarchy are thus integral parts of the governance equation.

Finally, not all global governance arrangements need to truly apply to the globe as a whole. On the one hand, there are still parts in the world which hardly participate in any international arrangements at all. North Korea or, for a long time, Myanmar are cases in point. As a consequence, many institutions which are seen as part of global governance, such as the WTO, are not really global. On the other hand, there are good reasons to include also regional governance arrangements such as the EU or the North American Free Trade Agreement (NAFTA).

Is global governance therefore a misnomer? Should we use instead more innocent terms like transnational legal orders (Halliday and Shaffer 2015), international governance (Slaughter et al. 1998; Abbott and Snidal 2011) or transnational governance (Macdonald and MacDonald 2017), complex governance (Kahler 2016), or governance beyond the nation state (Zürn 1998)? I stick with the term "global governance" for two reasons. First, it is fairly well-established and attempts to replace it with alternatives have failed.[4] Second, the term is encompassing in the sense that it includes international, transnational, and regional governance independent of their regulatory purpose and whether it comes in the form of agreed norms or as exercise of authority, thus it allows for a comprehensive perspective.

This understanding of global governance addresses those critics who consider the concept to be elusive, technocratic, and harmonistic (see e.g. Offe 2008); as being strictly associated with neoliberalism and the Third Way (Eagleton-Pierce 2014); as mystifying American interests as common good (Scheuermann 2014); or as "yesterday's dream" (Mazower 2012: 427). The goal must be to use the potential of the governance concept without falling into the traps of technocracy, neoliberal hegemony, hiding American rule, or idealism.

---

[4] A Google Scholar count shows that global governance is used almost five times as often as international governance and thirteen times as often as transnational governance (10 February 2015). This was different in the 1990s, when international governance was the term used most often.

The Global Governance System

The idea that the international political realm is structured by shared but contested norms and rules containing at least some pockets of hierarchy is a common denominator of a third wave of global governance research (see Coen and Pegram 2015). This book contributes to current global governance research by reconstructing a *global governance system* consisting of patterns of authority relationships that endogenously produce conflict, contestation, and resistance. In such a system, the rights and duties of actors derive from their position in an emergent normative order (Bartelson 1995) rather than from their membership of an international system of sovereign equals (see Waltz 1979; Mearsheimer 2001). Whereas the latter system is mostly free of normativity, the global governance system is based on a number of general normative principles and a set of more specific prescriptive institutions. Although a global governance system contains normativity, it is, however, not necessarily just or peaceful. It embodies relations of hierarchy and rule, contains institutions that can hardly be described as fair or just, and it knows violence. It is not necessarily better than anarchy—it is simply different. The claim that normativity plays a role in world politics does not involve the claim that it is a good world.

The global governance system is more than the sum of the institutions that produce regulations in different issue areas; it is also about the interplay and the relationship between these institutions and their embedding in a normative order. It selects inputs from actors inside and outside of the system and allocates responsibility to institutions on different political levels, which then transform them into governance (Easton 1953; Almond and Powell 1978). It produces transnational and international regulations and other governance activities such as agenda setting, monitoring, adjudication, and enforcement. All of these outputs are justified with reference to global common goods and thus come with the expectation of a minimal level of compliance pull (Franck 1990) for both the involved states and their societies. Although most of these outputs are regulatory in intent, they also affect the distribution of costs and benefits between and within national societies.

Most global governance studies have so far maintained the issue area-specific focus of international regimes' analysis and added insights regarding the relevance of non-state actors or the "newness" of a specific governance arrangement.[5] A theory of global governance will go beyond that by elaborating the most important features of interactions within the system. In doing

---

[5] Most empirical studies focus on specific global governance arrangements, their participants, content, and effectiveness. See Barnett and Finnemore (2004) as a partial exception. The focus on global governance as a whole is much more common in legal (see e.g. Krisch 2010) and normative theory (see e.g. Held 1995).

so, the issue of boundaries is addressed by examining the difference between the political system and other function systems of world society.[6] While a national political system is defined primarily by its territorial borders and secondarily by the boundaries of the function system within these borders, the global governance system is primarily defined by its difference to other global function systems—such as economy, science, art, and sports—and only secondarily by the differences to national political systems (Albert 2016).

The global political system consists of three distinct but interlinked "layers": These include normative principles that are general and sector-spanning; a dense set of specific political institutions that contain different types of authority and legitimation, and, the varied interactions between different spheres of authorities within the system (see Figure 0.1).

The global governance system that emerged in the 1990s is first of all based on a *set of three distinct normative principles that qualify sovereignty*. To begin with, justifications of global governance regulations address—besides states—societal actors, including individuals. In this sense, the basic right to justification

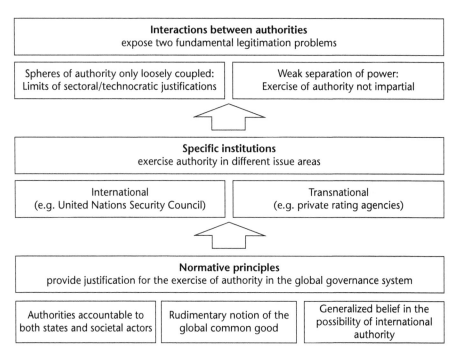

Figure 0.1. The three layers of the global governance system

Source: Thanks to David Coen and Tom Pegram

[6] In my understanding, world society refers to the development of the awareness of global transactions and the differentiation of particular functions systems within it. See e.g. Albert (2016); Reus-Smit (2013); Scholte (2002).

(Forst 2011) is at least rhetorically being institutionalized. To put it differently, the global governance system has a double constituency (see also Buzan 2004): states with conditional sovereignty and societal actors with rights to address international authorities. Moreover, global governance involves the presupposition of a rudimentary notion of the global common good. The reasons given for global regulations that reduce the autonomy of participating states and societal actors almost exclusively refer to global goals and global public goods, even in those cases in which *de facto* private goods are protected. Although many of these justifications certainly are merely strategic and hypocritical, the general practice would be meaningless if there was not the presupposition that a global common good exists. Finally, there is a generalized belief in the possibility of international authority. When states and non-state actors respect obligations that may run counter to their own stated interests, and these duties are justified with reference to the global common good and individual rights, the system is no longer anarchical. The global governance system thus contains at least some pockets of hierarchy.

The second layer of the global governance system encompasses *a set of specific institutions* that mostly exercise public authority in different spheres justified with reference to the normative principles outlined above. These institutions may be international—such as the UNSC or the International Monetary Fund (IMF)—as well as transnational—such as the IASB. Most of these institutions exercise a form of authority over at least some states and societies thus undermining the state consent principle. For instance, a UNSC resolution asking a state to stop border fights contains a prescription that is most often not consented to by the targeted state.

Authority relationships are based on deference, not on coercion or persuasion. This is true for international and transnational authorities as well. Yet authority in the global governance system is special. First of all, it is widely accepted that states strive for sovereignty and are willing to renounce it only under very special circumstances. Why should social actors that usually strive for autonomy and dominance accept an authority? Second, different to the authority relationship between some individuals and, say, clerics, global governance institutions were not prior to the birth of states; rather, it was the other way around. Third, global governance authorities target, among others, states that have considerably more resources at their disposal than any conceivable IO. Against, this background, I develop a conception of authority that is useful for the study of the global governance system. I submit that authority exercised by inter- and transnational institutions is, in the main, carried out in a reflexive manner. Contrary to conventional accounts of authority, reflexive authority is typically not internalized, but it allows a scrutiny of the effects of the exercise of authority at any time; it does not consist of commands but of demands or requests; and is embedded in sectoral knowledge orders. Those who defer in a reflexive authority relationship can—at their discretion—decide when they want to put the authority under scrutiny, carefully explore the implications of deference, and ask for changes in the authority relationship.

Moreover, inter- and transnational authority comes not only in the form of political authority—as in the case of the UNSC—but most frequently in the form of epistemic authorities that mainly produce interpretations with behavioral implications, but not necessarily decisions to which actors defer directly. A specific type of epistemic authority in the global governance system has gained special relevance: politically assigned epistemic authority. In these cases, states have delegated the competence to gather and interpret politically relevant information. For instance, the Organisation for Economic Co-operation and Development (OECD) assesses the quality of different national policies for policy fields such as labor markets or education. These assessments do not include a direct request or command, but there is an implicit expectation that their recommendations will be followed. Although authority relationships in the global governance system are mostly reflexive, they can nevertheless be highly consequential and require legitimation.

Legitimation Problems

The third layer of the global governance system consists of the *interplay of different spheres of authority*, including their relationship to the state and non-state members. Spheres of authority can be defined as problem fields that are governed by one or more authorities. The interactions between spheres of authority produce the most important systemic features of global governance. Measured by the standards of constitutionalized rule, these features point to systematic shortcomings and severe legitimation problems in the global governance system.

Inter- and transnational authorities require legitimation. For as long as the intergovernmental level was restricted by the requirement that each member state gave consent, there was contestation only by societal actors. As decisions taken at a level beyond that of the constituent members were legitimated through the (presumed) legitimacy of their representatives, delegitimation even by societal actors was rare. With the rise of inter- and transnational authorities undermining the consent principle, this has changed. International institutions now are evaluated against normative standards and they need to be justified by reference to common norms. And societal actors are no longer the only actors contesting inter- and transnational authorities: States and even IOs now employ strategies of contestation and delegitimation as well. As a consequence, inter- and transnational authorities are often subject to significant legitimation problems which are systematically produced by the features of the interplay of different spheres of authority.

To start with, different spheres of authority in global governance are only loosely coupled with each other. Inter- and transnational authorities are most often sectorally defined and responsible for a limited set of issues. While the WTO regulates international trade, the World Health Organization (WHO) is responsible for global health issues. The management of interface conflicts between different spheres of authority (e.g. between trade and health institutions) is rudimentary at best. Whereas the modern nation state has established some sites of meta-authority to handle such collisions—e.g. heads of government, parliaments, supreme courts, and public opinion—the global governance system only knows informal meta-authorities such as hegemons or the G7/20 summits, which are weak and highly exclusive at the same time. This feature of the current global governance system is responsible for a significant legitimation problem. Since spheres of authority are only loosely coupled in the global governance system, they are limited to sectoral justifications and thus introduce a technocratic bias into the patterns of legitimation. Most inter- and transnational authorities do indeed use a technocratic narrative of justification, sometimes enriched with ingredients from the legal narrative. The depth and type of authority that is exercised by many international bodies, however, increasingly overburdens such a narrative. Some of the decisions made within the global governance system cannot plausibly be based on technocratic grounds only—take, for instance, the austerity programs of the IMF or the already mentioned military interventions authorized by the UNSC.

The other central feature of the global governance system is a weakly established separation of powers, which leads to an even more severe legitimation problem. The central decision makers within international institutions are their secretariats and, more importantly, the executive representatives from the most powerful nation states. The more authority an international institution exercises, the more powerful states care about their influence within it. As a result, the most authoritative international institutions such as the UNSC, the IMF, and the World Bank contain formal mechanisms for ensuring that great power interests are given special consideration. International institutions with authority, therefore, not only introduce a hierarchy between the global and the national levels, but also stratification between different states, representatives, and their societies—i.e. they institutionalize inequality between states (see Hurrell 2007; Viola et al. 2015; Zürn 2007). This results in a weak separation of powers at the global level so that the representatives of the most powerful states sometimes combine legislative, executive, and administrative competencies in the absence of judicial supervision. The UNSC and its permanent members, for instance, assume legislative and executive functions simultaneously, when they pass resolutions that extend the meaning of threats to international peace, authorize an intervention on this basis, and then carry out the intervention—all this as "the sole judge of [their] own legality" (Zemanek 2007: 505).

The absence of a separation of powers is a second legitimation problem alongside technocratic bias. It undermines the fundamental condition for any belief in legitimacy in modernity: non-arbitrariness. The exercise of authority thus often leads to decisions and interpretations that violate the regulative idea that like cases should be treated alike. In view of these severe legitimation problems for the global governance system, it is not surprising that politicization by societal actors is rapidly increasing and that rising powers are questioning many global governance arrangements. The global governance system, therefore, is beset by struggles.

Behavioral Implications

On the basis of the layers and components of the global governance system, a set of hypotheses and causal mechanisms will be presented to explain recent and future developments in global governance. My goal is to formulate a positive theory that goes beyond negative descriptions of global governance as post-internationalist and different from the national set-up. The major claim is that the features of the current global governance system have endogenously produced contestation of international authorities. Internal tensions in the system fuel conflicts and demands for change (see Sørensen 2011), which lead to turbulence (Rosenau 1990) and possibly to gridlock in global governance (Hale et al. 2013) and its decline (Overbeek et al. 2010). At the same time, however, contestation can lead to institutional adaptation, re-legitimation, and a deepening of global governance. The model underlying this theory is sketched in Figure 0.2.

The model is based on the "authority–legitimation link" which states that international *institutions with authority require legitimation*. Growing resistance to inter- and transnational institutions is to be expected if they exercise authority but cannot build up sufficient stocks of legitimacy. The authority–legitimation link thus explains the dynamics of societal and state contestation in the global governance system.

Contestation by societal actors most often comes in the form of politicization and involves protest by non-state actors against international institutions. It takes place at the transnational level, mainly in the form of anti-globalization protests directed against neoliberal policies, or at the national level in the form of a populist backlash against open borders and public authorities beyond the nation state. But resistance is only one side of politicization. It also

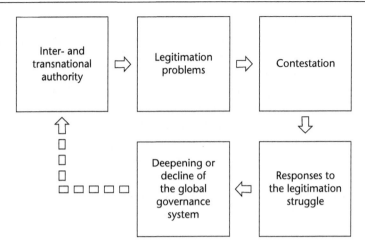

Figure 0.2. The causal model

includes the utilization of international institutions for specific policy purposes, for instance by environmental non-governmental organizations (NGOs), and direct support for more global governance. Politicization, in effect, can lead to a polarization of opinions about a particular issue handled by an international institution, mobilization for or against it, and its growing visibility. One of the more important effects of politicization is the perception on the part of the executives that the zone of agreement at the international level is shrinking.

Contestation by state actors takes place when states demand change in or the dismantling of international authorities. While states have, to a significant extent, driven the rise of international authority by delegating it to international institutions, they have done it in a reflexive manner. As a consequence, states simultaneously recognize and challenge inter- and transnational authorities. The established powers often contest the very same international institutions they have created the first time the institutions produce decisions they dislike. But their response is not—as conventional cooperation theory in the anarchy paradigm would have it—to deviate and exit. Rather, they set up new institutions closer to their current interests in order to influence or replace the old ones. This strategy has been labeled "contested multilateralism" (Morse and Keohane 2014). For reasons explained in Chapter 7, I use the term "counter-institutionalization."

Moreover, many of the states outside of the G7 world have gained power and weight during the last two decades. They increasingly contest existing institutions, deeming them biased in favor of Western interests and ideas. Although most of the rising powers challenge existing institutions, not least on the basis of a rhetoric that emphasizes "sovereignty," their position is not sufficiently well-captured by the notion of deviation or exit from the global governance system either. What is involved here is not a general rejection of international institutions, but a demand for a greater voice in existing institutions and the use of deadlocks as well as counter-institutionalization to change them.

Decline or Deepening

Contestation can lead to different outcomes. The outcomes are the result of the *delegitimation practices chosen and the respective responses by the authority holders*. Depending on the strength of the challenges, the available alternatives for challengers, and the capacity of authority holders to adapt, politicization and counter-institutionalization can lead to fragmentation and a decline of global governance. Yet, it can also create space for decisions that may, at the end of the day, deepen global governance.

Some of the international institutions confronted with delegitimation challenges respond with a *deepening of global governance* in order to regain legitimacy—in other words with an attempt at re-legitimation. Many of the international economic institutions that were the target of protests against neoliberalism and the hidden rule of multinational companies responded, for instance, by increasing transparency (Woods and Narlikar 2001). In general, increased access to IOs for transnational actors can be read as a strategy on the part of IOs to increase their legitimacy. Many see such reforms, however, as merely symbolic and in any case quite limited. Yet authority holders may also engage in more substantial revisions in response to delegitimation. The reform of voting rights in the IMF is a case in point, as is the launching of G20 summits. Similarly, analysts have interpreted some World Bank reforms—for instance, the Extractive Industries Review Process (Weidner 2013)—as substantial responses to politicization. Moreover, many IOs that were charged with violating human rights have now incorporated human rights provisions in their terms of reference to regain legitimacy (Heupel and Zürn 2017a). In other words, societal politicization and counter-institutionalization may lead to substantial reforms whose goal is to overcome institutional weaknesses and deepen global governance.

In other cases, however, contestation leads to a *decline of global governance*. Rising powers are now in a position to produce deadlocks in international negotiations. After learning how much authority the new WTO can wield through the DSB, India and Brazil in particular have insisted on a better deal above all for agricultural products. The negotiations about bilateral trade agreements between Europe and North America, the Transatlantic Trade and Investment Partnership (TTIP), and between the EU and Canada (Comprehensive

Economic and Trade Agreement (CETA)), can be seen as responses to this deadlock and thus as counter-institutionalization by the established powers. This strategy of counter-institutionalization may in turn fail due to increased politicization and, in the end, the international trade system may be significantly weakened. Similarly, as far as military interventions are concerned, a combination of counter-institutionalization by the West leading openly to double standards (the coalition of the willing), increased resistance by rising powers, and an increased politicization of the authority of the UNSC, have weakened the capacity to intervene in domestic wars even if they include drastic humanitarian disasters, such as in Syria. Again, the result is something that can be described as a decline in global governance after a phase of institutional gridlock (Victor 2011; Hale et al. 2013).

To sum up, the deficits of the global governance system point to internal tensions or contradictions that fuel conflict and demands for change. They may lead to turbulence and possibly to the decline of global governance. At the same time, authority holders may respond with substantial institutional reforms in order to ameliorate the shortcomings. The upshot is a parallelism between the deepening and the decline of global governance arrangements.

Theoretical Building Blocks and Causal Mechanisms

A theory of global governance rests on three theoretical building blocks: the notion of a functionally differentiated global political system, Weber's sociology of domination, and historical institutionalism (HI). Meta-theoretically, it is based on scientific realism, which also guides the empirical inquiries in the second part of the book.

The theory reconstructs a global political system different from other (sub) systems of world society such as economy or science. The institutional core of a political system can be grasped—to use one well-known formulation— by the "patterns of authority" (Eckstein 1973) that it displays. To achieve this, the theory makes use of Weber's sociology of domination and adapts it to the context of global governance. States then are no longer final and absolute authorities that compete with one another; they are embedded in a global governance system that has different types of public authorities that interact with one another. Patterns of public authority depend on relationships of recognition and point to the need for legitimation.

The behavioral implications of the endogenous dynamics of the global governance system are derived using concepts from HI. HI assumes that the sequence and timing of events and path dependencies are decisive elements in any explanation. The book will especially extend the concept of path dependence from self-reinforcing dynamics to self-undermining processes, i.e. institutional dynamics that challenge given institutions in reactive sequences (see Hanrieder and Zürn 2017). In this way, processes of delegitimation and contestation that result from institutional shortcomings will be brought into the realm of HI.

In meta-theoretical terms, the theory of global governance builds on scientific realism (Putnam 1966, 1981; Bhaskar 1978). Against strong versions of social constructivist meta-theories, scientific realism insists on the possibility of a reality independent of our perceptions and thus the regulative idea of science is to produce true descriptions of both the observable and unobservable aspects of this reality. In this way, it considers science as a social system that is different from other social systems such as politics. The system is geared toward the production of intersubjectively shared propositions based on certain standards and criteria. Scientific realism does not, therefore, consider scientific progress a miracle, as most postmodern ontologies need to do (see Putnam 1975: 73). At the same time, it is acknowledged that social reality is always mediated by perception and especially complicated. Social causes are of many kinds and include reasons, reflexivity, discourses, and socially constructed structures—all not known to the natural sciences (Kurki 2007: 364).

Unlike so-called positivist (empiricist and instrumentalist) meta-theories, a scientific realist understanding of explanation goes beyond the covering-law model (Hempel-Oppenheim scheme). The covering law model of an explanation requires that a particular fact (B), the explanandum, can be deduced from another fact (A), the explanans, via a general law (if A then B). Scientific realism in addition asks for mechanisms that contextualize the relationships and connect A and B in order to make us really understand what is going on (Hedström 2005; Kalter and Kroneberg 2014). These mechanisms often point to unobservables (abstract concepts) such as rationality or appropriateness that cannot be observed directly. In the realist theory of science, they are given an ontological status. They are considered as more than just instruments to derive (testable) hypotheses, but should correspond to reality as well (see also Wendt 1999: 64). While the original version of positivism denied the role of unobservables altogether, an instrumental understanding of them is typical of Popperian critical rationalism. In International Relations (IR), Kenneth Waltz (1979) and proponents of most versions of rational institutionalism see unobservables or assumptions of a theory as purely instrumental for the purpose of developing testable hypotheses. In the context of global governance theory, David Lake (2009: 3–4) has iterated this position most clearly: "All theories are based on a set of simplifying assumptions that helps render a complex reality more easily understood.... But it is important to note that these are not empirical descriptions of reality, but mere assumptions that we can accept or reject on their explanatory power." While scientific realism shares with critical rationalism the notion of a reality outside of perceptions, it gives unobservables or assumptions another status. They must be associated with reality as well in order to provide an understanding of the causal mechanisms that produce empirical correlations (see e.g. Putnam 1981; Chakravartty 2007). While, for instance, many criticisms of the implausibility of rational actors as real actors are ignored by critical rationalists ("as long as my predictions are right, I do not care"), these criticisms are right on target from the perspective of scientific realists.

Two implications for theory-building that follow from the perspective of scientific realism are important for my account of the global governance system. First, proper concepts and the modeling of complex causal relationships are enormously important. Empirical support for hypotheses is, in this view, of little value when based on sloppy conceptualization. Therefore, in order to develop the conceptual pillars of my theory with care, each of the three layers of the global governance system will be discussed in separate chapters. Second, scientific realism alludes to a move from a purely variable-based form of causal reasoning to one that focuses on mechanisms. At the most general level, a causal mechanism is defined as "recurrent processes linking specified initial conditions and a specific outcome" (Mayntz 2004: 241) or "a process by which a certain effect is produced or a purpose is accomplished" (Gerring 2008: 178).

My understanding of causal mechanisms includes both sequences of events that put relationships between social facts in a broader social context (composite mechanisms) and micro-processes that link two macro phenomena (linking mechanisms). *Composite mechanisms* refer to recurrent processes that comprise a thick sequence or a chain of events, thus reducing the distance between independent and dependent variables (see Bennett and Checkel 2015). *Linking mechanisms* refer to micro-processes via which two chain links are connected. Although each of the proximate links between two components of a composite mechanism points, at least indirectly, to a generalizable relationship between two variables, they cannot be considered as invariant (Waldner 2015). In the social world, most of these links, according to the bathtub model, refer to social choices with at least a minimal degree of freedom from constraints.[7] This means that these linking mechanisms depend on intentional or unintentional actor choices to become effective.

This use of causal mechanisms thus refers to a sequence of social phenomena linking specified initial conditions and a specific outcome as well as the micro-processes that link the steps in the sequences. These causal chains of events and choices need to be proximate enough to become intuitively compelling (Mahoney 2012: 581). Establishing causal mechanisms that consist of a sequence of events between a trigger and a final effect with probability

---

[7] I neglect the special case in which this link is provided by evolutionary mechanisms.

links between the components of the sequence, is how theoretically informed "analytical narratives" (Büthe 2002) are constructed. "Hence, the mechanism of every major social change is likely to be a combination of various kinds of mechanisms coupled together" (Bunge 1997: 417). A theory of global governance will make extensive use of this notion of causal mechanisms.

Against this backdrop, my claim in the second part of the book is that both politicization and counter-institutionalization can—via identifiable causal mechanisms—lead to either decline or deepening. Four such causal mechanisms will be discussed and empirically elaborated: two that operate through societal politicization and two that operate through counter-institutionalization. These four causal mechanisms are decisive for the theory of contested global governance. All of them are specifications of the authority–legitimation link.

The first two state that a rise in international authority leads to the rise of politicization if political opportunity structures are given. Rising politicization often involves a broadening of legitimation narratives. For instance, the rise of international authority associated with the change from the General Agreement on Tariffs and Trade (GATT) to WTO has led to street protests in Seattle. As a response, authority holders emphasized fairness and transparency of their proceedings. Whether this temporary change in legitimation narratives leads in the end to the decline or deepening of global governance depends on whether the adjustment is substantial or symbolic. Most often it is symbolic, increasing the probability of decline (undermining via politicization). If the societal challengers of inter- and transnational authority, however, find strong coalition partners within the political system (executive, legislative, or judicial), substantial reforms and the deepening of global governance can be expected (reinforcement via politicization).

State contestation, in turn, is often triggered by mismatches between the procedural rules of international institutions and power distribution between states. Counter-institutionalization is the preferred strategy in this case. International authority with a "one-state, one-vote" rule can generate counter-institutionalization if powerful states experience a loss of control. For instance, the United States formally announced in December 1983 that it intended to withdraw from UNESCO in a year's time, unless there were significant reforms. At the same time, it said that it would strengthen its participation in the United Nations and other international agencies. This type of state contestation often leads to fragmentation and decline (counter-institutionalization by incumbents). On the other hand, international institutions with institutionalized inequality will provoke contestation by disadvantaged states if the latter's power increases in the shadow of these institutions. The debate about voting rights in the IMF is a case in point. In most such cases, counter-institutionalization is the preferred strategy by rising powers and some form of institutional adaptation takes place. Counter-institutionalization, in general, points to strategies which aim at changing, not replacing, the global governance system. It is indicative of opposition, not of dissidence.

There are, to be sure, alternative accounts of the developments in world politics since the 1990s. According to one account, institutional development since the Second World War is conceived as continuous adaptation on the part of the United States and its allies—the liberal leviathan—to changing circumstances (see e.g. Ikenberry 2001). In this view, the current system continues to be essentially the same as that which emerged after the Second World War. The core of the argument advanced in this book, however, is that the 1990s brought in a new system of governance that is different from earlier ones. It is much more intrusive, with more demanding normative principles and possessing more authority and hierarchy. It is not least these new features that have been responsible for the contestation of international institutions— not only the rise of new powers. Some of the attacks on the current global governance system indeed come from within established powers, sometimes even from their governments if they fear that the institutions are slipping out of their control.

Another account emphasizes the changing distribution of power. It suggests that the post-Second World War order came to an end with the decline of the USSR. The short period of American unipolarity that followed has now been replaced by a form of multipolarity (see e.g. Layne 1993; Schweller and Wohlforth 2000). In this view, power politics has replaced an institutionalized order. I will argue instead that power struggles are embedded in the global governance system. Many critics of the status quo are non-state actors who challenge the current inter- and transnational institutions, although they accept the general idea of global governance. Likewise, many of these counterforces act within this structure, not from the outside. A theory of global governance is thus required to enable us to understand the contestation and partial roll-back of international authority and, at the same time, to account for the ongoing deepening of global governance.

The Road Ahead

Four questions need to be tackled, before we can speak of a theory of global governance. How does the global governance system function? Why did it emerge? What effects does it produce? What are the prospects for it? With these four questions in mind, the remainder of this introduction outlines the structure of the book.

The Global Governance System: The first part of the book is theoretical. It identifies the core institutional features of the global governance system and its behavioral implications. This adds up to an institutionalist theory that may explain the resistance and challengers that this global governance system has produced. These four chapters systemically develop the core features of the global governance system in order to come up with a causal model of endogenous change that is laid out in Chapter 4.

In Chapter 1, I identify the three normative principles underlying the global governance system using the method of rational reconstruction. These "unobservables" are useful for deriving testable hypotheses, but they need also to be empirically "plausible"—i.e. capable of being traced in practices of world politics. They provide the normativity that underlies the global governance system. The reader who is mainly interested in the behavioral implications of a theory may skip this chapter. The global governance system that emerged in the 1990s on the basis of these normative principles involves the exercise of authority. The key argument of Chapter 2 is that the notion of *reflexive authority* is most useful in grasping the global governance system. The interplay of these authorities is characterized by two main features: The spheres of authority are only loosely coupled and the separation of powers in this system is weak at best. This chapter provides the conceptual core of the theory.

In Chapter 3, seven different legitimation narratives are distinguished. Due to the loose coupling of the spheres of authority in the global governance system, it is argued that authority holders can only utilize the technocratic and the legal narratives. Legitimation problems are aggravated as inter- and transnational institutions undermine their perception as non-arbitrary and impartial owing to a weak separation of powers. These two deficits make the global governance system vulnerable to delegitimation efforts. In Chapter 4 then, the arguments of the preceding chapters are integrated into one theoretical framework. The authority–legitimation link and the notion of reactive sequences will be used to develop testable propositions, mainly in the form of four causal mechanisms. Chapter 4 translates the theoretical discussions of Chapters 1 to 3 into a testable theory of global governance.

The Rise of the Global Governance System: The second part of the book is empirical. It starts by asking: What made the rise of the global governance system possible? The development of the global governance system which evolved until the 1990s is—according to the argumentation in Chapter 5—the result of a process involving four components: The post-Second World War institutional set-up, established (mainly) by choices of the US government made at a critical juncture; its path-dependent self-reinforcement and resilience until the mid-1970s; the deepening of liberalization and the response to it; and finally the breakdown of the socialist bloc, an external shock that paved the way for the new system. According to this historical-institutionalist account, this sequence of developments was not accidental. The later steps in the sequence were predetermined by the earlier ones. The steps in the development of the global governance system are bolstered with data from the International Authority Database.

The Contestation of Global Governance: In the remainder of Part II of the book, propositions derived from the theory are put forward to explain societal politicization and counter-institutionalization, and how they can lead to either a deepening or a decline of global governance. Chapter 6 explores the dynamics of politicization in the global governance system. It can be shown that the rise of international authority makes its politicization likely. In turn, the politicization of international institutions most often leads to an extension of legitimation narratives. Yet, the broadening of legitimation narratives often is opportunistic and not backed up by substantial institutional reforms. In this case, the decline of global governance is likely. The chapter utilizes semi-automated content analysis.

Chapter 7 analyzes state contestations of global governance. State contestation takes place mainly in the form of counter-institutionalization. Established powers contest the same international institutions they have created and shaped the very moment these institutions produce decisions they dislike. However, the response is not state unilateralism. Instead they set up a new international institution closer to their current interests in order to influence or replace the old one. Moreover, many of the states outside the world of the G7 have gained in power and weight in the last two decades. They increasingly challenge existing institutions as biased in favor of Western interests and ideas. Instead of a general rejection of international institutions, rising powers demand a greater voice in existing institutions and use different strategies to achieve this goal. In the event of established powers reacting to these demands, a deepening of global governance is likely. The method of structured, focused comparison is mainly used in this chapter.

As Chapter 8 demonstrates, societal politicization may lead to a deepening of global governance as well. Many IOs have responded to accusations of violating human rights with institutional reforms. Efforts to bring about reforms were especially effective when societal challengers were able to create coalitions with partners inside the global governance system. In terms of methods, this chapter builds on comparative process tracing.

The Future of Global Governance: In addition to instances where global governance has been deepened, there is one more reason to believe that global governance will not necessarily disappear as a consequence of its current shortcomings. Chapter 9 takes a look at the socio-economic and socio-cultural background conditions in the current world and argues that a global normative order with cosmopolitan intent is not completely out of reach. It discusses and evaluates a subset of prominent proposals for the design of a globalized world: the intergovernmental model of democratic states, cosmopolitan pluralism, the minimal world state, and cosmopolitan democracy.

It is argued that the intergovernmental model is not the one best fitted to match the economic and social demands of the future. At the same time, although the empirical conditions presupposed by cosmopolitan pluralism and the minimal world state are still far from being realized, trends in their direction can be observed—in spite of the current backlash against cosmopolitanism in general.

In the concluding Chapter 10, the theory of global governance is recapitulated, the findings are summarized, and future areas of research are identified. It is also argued that the analysis of some of the most pressing questions requires a paradigmatic shift in IR. The cooperation paradigm, which became dominant from the 1960s by superseding the old peace and war paradigm, needs to be complemented by a global politics paradigm that moves beyond anarchy. Unlike IR theories based on state interests and beliefs as well as power distribution in an anarchical system, they will look on tensions and struggles as consequences of the features of global politics, instead of seeing the order as an epiphenomenon of struggles between independent units with differing power capacities.

From this perspective, it is no accident that right-wing populists in Europe admire Vladimir Putin, whose aim is to build a coalition of authoritarian leaders. Nor is it a surprise that Donald Trump became President of the United States as the mouthpiece for those who are not part of the political establishment. These political forces demand that national borders be closed and political authority be brought back to the national level. Cosmopolitans, conversely, ask for open borders, and demand international cooperation and authority to handle denationalized problems. This struggle may structure twenty-first-century politics for many years to come. One of the most important objects of contention in this new cleavage will be the global governance system.

Part I
The Global Governance System

"Global governance remains notoriously slippery"—so goes the rather uncordial judgment by Thomas Weiss and Rorden Wilkinson (2014: 207), two proponents of global governance studies. This slippery condition is partially due to the genealogy of global governance. The term itself resulted from a marriage between academic theory and practical policy in the 1990s. James Rosenau and Ernst-Otto Czempiel's (1992) conceptual book on *Governance without Government* was published just about the same time that the Swedish government launched the policy-oriented Commission on Global Governance (see Commission on Global Governance 1995). This interest in the concept was additionally bolstered by the rise of the concept of governance in other contexts as in administrative science or World Bank reform efforts.

Against this genealogical background, the term global governance received two different meanings from early on. One points to a prescriptive strategy to overcome the problems and costs created by interdependence and globalization.[1] In this perspective, the focus is on specific global governance arrangements and their contribution to solve particular problems. The other approach sees global governance as an analytical concept for studying world politics descriptively with theoretical ambition. The late James Rosenau (1990, 1992, 1997) has certainly been the most important proponent of this use of the term global governance in its early phase. In an attempt to move beyond Lawrence Finkelstein's (1995) formula of global governance, "IO plus," Rosenau (1997: 145) went to the other extreme and defined global governance as "all levels of human activity—from the household to the demanding public to the international organization [IO]—that amount to systems of rule in which goals are pursued through the exercise of control." While this definition may be too encompassing, it contains already a perspective that reaches beyond the analysis of issue area-specific global regulations by pointing to systems of rule and the exercise of authority.

---

[1] See Messner and Nuscheler (2003) for a clear statement in favor of the normative meaning of the term. Also see Mendlovitz (1975) and Wapner (1995).

In this book, the use of the term global governance is analytical. It is defined as consisting of consented norms and rules beyond the nation state as well as the exercise of authority across national borders justified with reference to common goods or transnational problems. Global governance takes place in a political system that is embedded in normative principles and consists of more than the sum of the institutions that produce separate regulations in different issue areas. It is also about the interplay and the relationship between these institutions and their embedding in a normative order. This notion of a global governance system aims at moving the study of global governance beyond the sectoral approach of international regimes analysis.

In the next three chapters, the global governance system will be depicted by discussing three layers: the normative principles that underlie the system; the patterns of institutionalized authority and their legitimation; and the most prominent features and deficits of the system. In Chapter 1, I elaborate the normative principles of the global governance system in which states are embedded. In Chapter 2, it will be argued that the global governance system is characterized by a special type of authority: reflexive authority. Chapter 3 goes on to examine the legitimation narratives in this global governance system and how the features of the system lead to structural legitimation problems. In Chapter 4, these ingredients are put together in a historical-institutionalist frame in order to come up with a set of hypotheses and causal mechanisms about societal and state contestation of international authorities, as well as self-undermining and reinforcing mechanisms of global governance. The goal is to formulate a positive theory of the global governance system.

1

Normative Principles

The global governance system contains normative principles that are general and sector-spanning. The actors derive their rights and duties from these principles rather than from their membership in an international system of sovereign equals. Yet talking about such normative principles has nothing to do with idealism. It neither assumes that such normative principles determine actors' behavior, nor does it say anything about the normative quality of these principles.[1] It only holds that actors have to take into account these principles, however egoistic or mean their real motivation is.

The presence of normative principles runs against the anarchy premise. It presupposes some ideational features underlying world politics that are not compatible with the notion of an international system consisting of states with exclusive sovereignty over their territory. Evidently, this is not the first attempt to challenge the concept of an anarchical international system of sovereign states based on their material capacity to control territorially delimited societies (see e.g. Bull 1977; Ruggie 1993; Wendt 1999). While I agree with the English school and with constructivists that at least some normativity has always been involved in Westphalian sovereignty, the argument put forward in this chapter contains three specific points. First, these normative principles are seen as constitutive for a political system that is different from other systems in world society (see also Reus-Smit 2013: 18; Albert et al. 2013). Second, the role normative principles play in such a system is different. While Hedley Bull (1977: 13), for instance, considers a society to be "bound by a common set of rules," the normative principles of the global governance system are primarily presuppositions that provide a normative embedding of social practices and are utilized for many different purposes (Habermas 1996).

---

[1] This use of the term "normativity" points to a double meaning. It can be used to describe the normativity predominant in a given collective (reconstruction of internal views) and it can be used to critically reflect on the normative quality of predominant norms from an external perspective (see also Forst 2015: chs 1 and 8).

Third, these normative principles and especially the more specific rules are regularly contested (see Wiener 2014).

Methodologically, the argument is built on a specific form of "rational reconstruction," which aims at laying open the normativity that underlies existing practices by identifying the implicit assumptions in social practices. These so-called presuppositions are social preconditions that must be present in order to make sense of speech acts and activities. It refers to socio-cultural conditions or social constructions of the normative. The method is often used in normative theory (see Gaus 2013; Patberg 2016). It aims at explicating the implicitly presumed normative content of real-world practices from the perspective of participants (Patberg 2016: 92). While historically the objects to be rationally reconstructed were theories, Jürgen Habermas (1996) was among the first to use the method to uncover the normative footings of social practices. Most often, normative theorists however identify such presuppositions by applying two filters: The presupposition must *a*) be found in practice and *b*) be compatible with agreements in the ideal speech situation or behind the veil of ignorance.

In the employment of the method here, only the first filter is applied. These presuppositions therefore contain (only) particles and broken bits of social reason, they primarily have a descriptive status and do not have normative dignity per se. This factual role of presuppositions is best described as the intuitive common knowledge about the normative core of practices that is necessary to allow an order to function (see similarly Adler and Pouliot 2011). In this sense, the reconstructed normativity has a factual role in understanding the working of society. Such presuppositions can be seen as part of the larger set of not directly observable theoretical concepts.

The global governance system rests on three normative principle or unobservables, each of which qualifies the Westphalian principle of sovereignty. Westphalian sovereignty denotes the idea "that there is a final and absolute political authority in the political community...and no final and absolute authority exists elsewhere" (Hinsley 1986: 26). The normative principles of the global governance system qualifies this notion of sovereignty in three respects: It questions the implicit notion that all political communities are territorially segmented by pointing to the notion of common goods, that need to be achieved together; it questions the view that political authorities are absolute by pointing to the rights of individual and entitlements of non-state actors that they have independent of being a member of a state; and it questions the notion that there are no authorities other than the state by pointing to the possibility of international authority.

The remainder of this section will discuss the content of these three presuppositions and their "empirical appropriateness." The goal is to show that the assumptions of a global governance system seem to be better suited to understand world politics in the twenty-first century than the notion of an anarchic international system or an international society.

1.1 Global Common Goods

Governance activities are by definition justified with reference to common problems and goods, but they do not necessarily serve it. A global governance activity thus comes with a normative coat in the sense that it is justified as something good for the international or transnational community (see Zürn 2008). Yet the notion of "common goods" is a contested concept, even in the context of territorially circumscribed national communities. It is considered by critical theorists as a term that hides interests of the ruling class in order to discipline the rest of the population. Claus Offe (2002) therefore pointedly asked: "Whose good is the common good?" In order to de-mystify the concept, it is helpful to think in terms of different versions of the common good and to name precisely the reference unit of the term; i.e. the community whose good we speak of.

The distinct criterion for a *global* common good is that it is ascribed to communities beyond the nation state or national societies. The reference unit has to be the collective of the members, not the interests of the single members. The notion of common good, therefore, refers to outcomes that move beyond the concept of Pareto optimality—i.e. outcomes that cannot be changed without losses for at least one of the involved parties. Rather, it requires a collectivity or identity layer to which these outcomes apply, allowing measures even against the stated interests of some members. This collectivity or identity layer does not necessarily have to be exclusive (no other identities count) or dominant (the global common good dominates the national interests); it just needs to be there (see also Risse 2015). As Jürgen Neyer (2012: 187) puts it, "supranational justifications are usually not about overcoming the nation state but about internalizing external effects."

By requiring a common good-oriented justification of norms and rules, the concept of global governance presupposes the *possibility* of a common good. Provided that international agreements are characterized as a major step to achieve goals such as global security or protection of the global environment, they refer to the notion of a global common good. Other frequently mentioned goods include international peace, global health and the eradication of global pandemics, avoiding global warming, and financial stability. While any of these specific references may be completely detached from the motivations of the justifying actors, it is still a relevant social fact that governing actors—even when they are completely selfish—use the notion of the global common good in order to hide their selfishness. The opportunistic use of specific acts of justification presupposes that there is a widespread belief in a global common good in general. The reference to such goods would hardly make sense if everyone assumes that it does not exist.

Is it plausible to assume that the presupposition of a global common good is relevant for current world politics? The development of international law since the nineteenth century has been described as moving from greater recognition and protection of state interests toward a recognition of community interests. In an influential article, Bruno Simma has identified a trend "From Bilateralism to Community Interest" (Simma 1994). For instance, the process of seeing peace as a community good arguably started only with the industrialization of war and the rise of a peace movement, leading to the Hague Conventions of 1899 and 1907. It took, however, many decades before we could speak of an institutionalization of peace as a common good. The United Nations (UN) treaty is probably the moment when peace finally achieved this status.

More generally, looking at the speeches and the documents produced at international conferences and meetings shows the dominance of the language of the global common good from the 1960s on. Analyses of speeches in the General Assembly of the UN (UNGA) are full of references to global peace, global health, and global development, and the term legitimacy is used by democratic and authoritarian states alike (Eisentraut 2013; Binder and Heupel 2015). Each international treaty, as a written output of international governance, starts with a long list of common goals that it is supposed to serve. Take, for instance, the Treaty on Principles Governing the Activities of States in the Exploration and Use of Outer Space, including the Moon and Other Celestial Bodies. This treaty is among a set of treaties about so-called "common spaces of human mankind" that are not under state control. Besides the outer space treaty, the law of the sea, and the Antarctica agreement belong to this group of agreements, which are especially good examples of the common good principle (Wolfrum 1984). The dominant reference group to which the good is ascribed is not states, but people; and they are not nations, but humankind. The treaty states in the very beginning:

The States Parties to this Treaty,

Inspired by the great prospects opening up before *mankind* as a result of man's entry into outer space,

Recognizing the *common interest of all mankind* in the progress of the exploration and use of outer space for peaceful purposes,

Believing that the exploration and use of outer space should be carried on for the *benefit of all peoples* irrespective of the degree of their economic or scientific development,

Desiring to contribute to broad international cooperation in the scientific as well as the legal aspects of the exploration and use of outer space for peaceful purposes,

Believing that such cooperation will contribute to the development of mutual understanding and to the strengthening of *friendly relations between States and peoples*...(United Nations, Treaty Series, vol. 610, No. 8843; emphases added)

This is not an atypical preamble. In their respective preambles, twenty-seven of the thirty-four international organizations (IOs)—coded in a database about international authority (see Chapter 5)—refer not only to the specific aims of the treaties, but also to broader goals which can be labeled as "common good orientations"—at least in rhetoric.[2] This means about 80 percent of the IOs refer in their founding documents to global common goods, and not only to shared interests of their member states.

Moreover, majority decision making in IOs points implicitly to the recognition of a common good. A considerable half of all IOs nowadays can vote on some issues (see Blake and Payton 2008). There would be no moral justification for majority decisions unless the concerned collective believes that it needs to achieve something that is sometimes not compatible with the interests of all its members. It is based on the belief that sometimes individual members need to make sacrifices for the common good.

The reference to global common goods comes with additional conceptual baggage; namely, the assumption of the presence of a public space in which these justifications can be put forward. Here, we will follow John Ruggie's definition of a global public domain as a potentially available

> arena of discourse, contestation and action organized around the production of global public goods. It is constituted by interactions among non-state actors as well as states. It permits the direct expression and pursuit of a variety of human interests, not merely those mediated—filtered, interpreted, promoted—by states. (Ruggie 2004: 519)

Again, indications in favor of such an assumption can be quite easily found. The media reports extensively on global conferences, and these meetings include numerous non-state actors that represent societal interests and observe the negotiations. Since 1995, around 2,000 different transnational non-governmental organizations (NGOs) have visited the ministerial meetings of the World Trade Organization (WTO), and the numbers at the UN Climate Change Conferences are much higher.

In sum, on the level of justification, global governance includes more than just simple coordination or cooperation between states to achieve a *modus*

---

[2] The keywords used as indicators for common good rhetoric were: for the total advancement of our peoples, security, stability, peace, progress, prosperity, full employment, improved standards of work, improved standards of living, (individual) freedom, political liberty, rule of law, common welfare, social development, economic development, justice, humanity, safeguarding for future generations the natural resources, environmental protection, sustainable development, civilization, education for all, promotion, and protection of health of all peoples.

vivendi of interaction and to serve the interests of the participating states. Rather, the justification of global governance presupposes common goods and some common good orientations beyond individual state interests, at least in a rudimentary form—without, of course, denying the persistence of fundamental conflicts about the precise content of these commonalities. Since international regulators often publicly claim to pursue normatively laden political goals in handling common problems of the international community, this assumption seems to be realistic—in spite of the fact that any specific justification may be purely opportunistic. The mere use of this strategy presupposes the presence of the notion of a common good and a public domain in which the justifications can be put forward. Struggles about the meaning of the common good presuppose the possibility of its existence. This presupposition seems more appropriate than the anarchy assumption, for which all the justificatory efforts in the global realm remain nonsensical. Arguably, this process started after the Second World War and became the dominant way of justifying international institutions from the 1960s on.

1.2 Individual Rights and Entitlements of Non-state Actors

The second normative principle of the global governance system that qualifies sovereign equality is the inscription of individual rights and entitlements of non-state actors. The inscriptions of rights and duties for non-state actors has both a procedural and a substantive aspect. Procedurally, the targets of justification for global governance are no longer only states and governments, but also individuals and societies. Substantially, some degree of recognition of individuals and societal groups as beneficiaries of governance has become a requirement for states to be recognized members in the global governance system.

1.2.1 Individuals and Societies as Addressees of Justification

The central move of the concept of governance in general is a separation between the product (governance) and the producer (government) (Rosenau 1992). At the same time, global governance addresses states as well as (national or transnational) societal actors including individuals. This is different from the notion of Westphalian sovereignty, in which the addressees of regulation and the actors who need to consent are states only. The development can be illustrated by contrasting, for instance, the international trade regime as a good example of a post-Second World War international institution with the global governance regime based on the WTO. Under the General Agreement on Tariffs and Trade (GATT) regime, the states were the ultimate and exclusive addressees of the regulation. They were issued with directives not to increase customs tariffs or to apply them in a non-discriminating way. The objective of the regulation was to influence state behavior in order to solve the problem (i.e. protectionism) in question. States were not only the subjects, but also the objects of regulation. This has changed over time. It is now the companies that have to change their behavior when it comes to product regulations, not the states as in the case of tariffs. This is even more obvious in international environmental agreements. The final addresses of these regulations are the consumers and the companies in the national societies. They have to change their products and their behavior in order to reduce, for instance, CO_2 emissions. While the states act as intermediaries between the international institutions and the addressees, it is ultimately societal actors such as consumers and businesses who have to alter their behavior (see Parson 2003).

Consequently, the justifications of these international authorities are also geared toward both states and societal actors. To the extent that justifications of global governance indeed speak to both governments and their peoples, it is implicitly recognized that the right to justification for the loss of autonomy—as the most fundamental of all rights (Forst 2011)—is in the case of global governance held by corporative state actors, societal groups, and individuals. The implication of this statement is that at least some rudimentary individual rights and societal entitlements are—unlike intergovernmental cooperation serving state interests only—conceptually inscribed into the notion of global governance.

It is not too difficult to show the plausibility of this "assumption." Recent research demonstrates this compellingly. Most fundamentally, Jonas Tallberg and colleagues (2013) have demonstrated the opening up of IOs for non-state actors. The Economic and Social Committee of the UN (ECOSOC) have been among the first who offered access for non-state actors. Over the years, the number of non-state actors has moved up from one in 1948 to about 3,500 in 2012 (Tallberg et al. 2013: 4). Their index for transnational access measured across a representative sample of fifty IOs has gone up from roughly 0.2 in 1959 to about 0.8 in 2010 (Tallberg et al. 2013: 6). The trend has not been reversed since then. To put it differently, the average IO, in the 1950s and up the 1980s, did not give access to non-state actors. This changed rapidly from the 1990s on. Today, the average IO provides access to non-state actors.

The change is also reflected in the communication of IOs. Matthias Ecker-Ehrhardt (2017) has analyzed public communication of IOs. He shows an increased level of IO public relations (PR) activities over time, with a significant rise of those activities after 1995. Even more telling, the targets or addressees of these PR activities are not only states, but experts and non-state actors as well. The share of non-state actors as addressees of IO activities has grown over time to about a third in 2014. This supports the notion of a double constituency of the global governance system.

Similarly, Klaus Dingwerth, Henning Schmidtke, and Tobias Weise (2018, in preparation) have studied the official annual reports from twenty cross-regional IOs. They can show very convincingly that IOs' use of democratic rhetoric has gone up significantly since the early 1990s. Arguably, it is mainly directed at societal addressees, not so much at states. Indeed, they show that especially IOs targeted by transnational protests have responded with democratic rhetoric.

The latest instance of support to be mentioned here is the nomination process of Antonio Guterres as United Nations Secretary General in October 2016. Vincent Pouliot (2018, in preparation: 1) reports in a case study: "The UN organized public hearings and town hall meetings with the dozen candidates, a website was launched to allow individuals to ask questions directly to the nominees, and the presidents of the Security Council (SC) and the General Assembly (GA) signed a rare joint letter to determine the nomination procedure in advance." An insider, Edward Luck, comments, about this change: "There really is an expectation now that the business of governance and policymaking should be carried out publicly and transparently" (cited in Pouliot 2018, in preparation: 21).

1.2.2 Individual Rights as an Element of Conditional Sovereignty

Fundamental to the development of the external recognition of states was the process of the monopolization of force in a given territory. A royal monopoly of force prevailed as a result of fierce competition between different power holders, first in France and in England. This monopolization of force was accompanied by a tax-raising monopoly, through which, in turn, the monopoly of force could be defended against aggressors from within and outside the controlled territory (see Elias 1976; Giddens 1985; Tilly 1985). The ensuing capacity to govern a certain territory was the material basis for external recognition in the Westphalian version of sovereignty. It was the foundation for a claim of final authority over a given territory, and it also laid the basis for sovereignty understood as "a social status that enables states as participants within a community of mutual recognition" (Strange 1996: 22).

The role of individual rights in world politics grew from this starting point over time. With the rise of nationalism, mainly in the eighteenth and nineteenth centuries, external recognition was in a first step supplemented by internal recognition of the territorial state as the legitimate and necessary organizational form of a political community that defines itself as a nation.

Although the territorial state was able to build upon proto-national cultures and communities, it actively contributed to the rise of national identities through harmonization policies and the symbolic representation of "imagined communities" (Anderson 1983). As a result, the notion that national boundaries and territorial state boundaries have to coincide prevailed (Gellner 1983), and the territorial state became a nation state. Modern sovereign statehood thus became linked to a double requirement: the external recognition of the capacity of the state to govern effectively, and the internal recognition that state practices are legitimate to the nation (the people's right to self-determination).

In the twentieth century, then, the basis of recognition shifted further and the capacity to govern became a secondary criterion. Effective governance by the state as the basis of recognition was progressively replaced by people's right to self-determination. As late as 1946, the British government refused to give up its colonies at short notice, arguing that these countries lacked an effective state that was able to pursue the goals of governance. The British government was able to bolster its argument by citing the League of Nations, which restricted the right to state building by establishing criteria for the "capacity for independence." Not until fourteen years later did the UN pass a resolution that the right to self-determination did not depend on the existence of the ability to govern. "Inadequacy of political, economic, social or educational preparedness should never serve as a pretext for delaying independence" (Declaration on the Granting of Independence to Colonial Countries and Peoples, Resolution 1514 [XV], 14 December 1960). While the material capacity to control a territory certainly still played some role in the background, the principle of self-determination became the decisive criterion for external recognition of states (Jackson 1987, 1990).

On a deeper level, however, two things remained unchanged up until recently: States are the subjects that recognize other states and, once recognized, states are permanent members of the club and can hardly be excluded. Arguably, with the end of the Cold War, there has been some change in this respect as well. To the extent that the fulfilment of substantial international norms and rules are increasingly decisive for the recognition of a state (Franck 1992), recognition becomes a conditional concept that is not provided any more once and forever. Moreover, one can question to what extent still only states (bilaterally) and intergovernmental organizations (multilaterally) decide on this. To a certain degree, non-state actors and societies seem to play a role as well. For instance, as the fall of the South African apartheid regime has shown, processes of external de-recognition may start with claims by non-state actors, and governments increasingly need to justify themselves if they interact with the governments of "pariah" states. International society thus has been transformed to a world society with multiple constituencies.

After 1989, the recognition of states does not, in this view, result only from state interaction, but increasingly involves transnational society as well; moreover, it is not declared eternally, but remains conditional on certain standards (see Zürn 1998: 332–3). Sovereignty can be practically suspended if drastic violations of fundamental duties take place.

The growing relevance of individuals in world politics also plays out in the form of the global spread of the norm of collective self-determination. David Armitage (2007) shows convincingly, self-determination as the organizing principle spread globally in five waves from the seventeenth century on. The process started with the establishment of sovereignty in the core of Europe with the Westphalian Treaty. It went on with the rise of sovereignty in the Americas in the late eighteenth and early nineteenth centuries leading to seventeen new sovereign states, the end of the First World War and the Versailles Treaty leading to twenty new states, the big wave of decolonization after the Second World War until the later 1960s, and the fall of the Berlin Wall in 1989 leading to sovereign states in Eastern Europe. Each of these waves was the result of struggles that led to the end of empires with differentiated entitlements for individuals. In each of these cases, the principle of sovereignty guided the struggles of the oppressed, and it was a struggle for general rights for individuals and against foreign determination. Therefore, the spread of sovereignty also points to an increased relevance of individual rights (Reus-Smit 2013).

In sum, individuals and non-state actors are inscribed into the concept of global governance. Their recognition as targets of justification for global governance points to the minimal right for justification. On the other hand, states are expected to recognize and institutionalize at least some level of individual rights protection before becoming a fully recognized member of the club. This level falls clearly short of Western notions of human rights, but points to the recognition of individuals and societies as beneficiaries of governance. To put it bluntly, the struggles over individual rights and their role in world politics have increased empirically over time to a level at which the presupposition of individual rights and societal entitlements seems a more "realistic" assumption than the notion of absolute state authority.

1.3 The Possibility of International Authority

Inherently tied to the first two presuppositions is the belief in the possibility of international authority. If there is a common good and a built-in acceptance of individual rights, then it requires international public authorities to identify, substantiate, and monitor norms and rules that foster the common good and entitlements of actors other than states.

According to Westphalian sovereignty, state parties are not subject to any external authority. Any international regulation, therefore, must be based on the consent principle, and international law remains a shallow instrument. International law is limited to the realm of coordinating states' external activities but does not intervene in domestic affairs, and it is in any case secondary to national law and constitutions. Empirically speaking, the practice of the core states of the European state system came close to this ideal at least in the eighteenth century, probably even until the end of the Second World War. IOs were introduced in the second half of the nineteenth century, primarily only as means to coordinate different national (foreign) policies. The consent principle prevailed; states were rarely asked to implement decisions that were not agreed on by consensus.

The age of embedded liberalism and the evolution of the UN system already brought in some changes. International treaties were ratified in national parliaments more often than before. Moreover, significant parts of international law now also addressed the relationship between states and their citizens, with the rise of human rights law being a case in point. International lawyers label this development as the move from coordination law to cooperation law (see e.g. Schweisfurth 2006). While the consent principle prevailed in theory, some IOs introduced the possibility of majority decisions, thus creating in practice the possible condition that (some) states were asked to implement decisions they had not agreed on. Moreover, some of the new constitutions developed in Europe after 1945 indicated a place for international law. For instance, the Italian constitution agrees, in principle, "to limitations of sovereignty" when they serve peace and justice among nations. Nevertheless, the theoretical attempt to conceptualize international institutions as instruments of the territorial state without possessing a political authority of their own still seemed defensible (see e.g. Kahler 2004).

The big exceptions were the European Communities and, later, the EU. Here, over time, strong institutions that increasingly developed a political authority of their own emerged beyond the state (Haas 1964). Although this development does not apply to the whole institutional make-up of the EU or all policy fields within it, the EU emerged as a genuine political system that made states give up their veto positions, at least in part. With the Single European Act and the Maastricht Treaty, the EU is now unquestionably seen as a site of political authority that cannot be reduced to the notion of European institutions as tools of the nation states.

The last two to three decades have brought changes that have undermined the consent principle also on the global level. One may indeed speak of the decay of consent (Krisch 2014). International institutions, in this view, have the potential, and are expected, to exercise authority to the extent that it is necessary to foster global common good and to protect some individual rights (see von Bogdandy et al. 2016).

The notion of global governance and the presupposition of the possibility of international authority can be corroborated by looking at the quantity and quality of international regulations. It shows that a dense network of international and transnational rules, prescriptions, and recommendations of unprecedented quality and quantity has arisen. The number of UN-registered international agreements grew from a total of 8,776 treaties in 1960 to 63,419 as of March 25, 2010. If we consider only the most important multilateral agreements officially drawn up and countersigned in the UN, then we obtain a comparable level of growth—namely, from 942 such agreements in 1969 to 6,154 by 2010.[3] The growth rate of these regulations, when measured in the annual ratification of multilateral treaties, for a long time far surpassed growth rates in national legislation (see Beisheim et al. 1999: 327–54).[4] These developments point to the possibility of international authority as one of the principles inscribed into the global governance system.

In sum, the concept of global governance points to practices in world politics that distinguish it from ideas about the international system based on Westphalian sovereignty. Instead of Westphalian anarchy, the global governance system rests on three normative principles that constrain the principle of sovereignty. It points to the assumption that there is a global common good, which is more than the sum of individual state interests. Otherwise, it would not make sense to justify global governance in those terms. Second, the global governance system refers to an inscription of individual rights and societal entitlements as parts of the normative structure of world politics. The right to justification—if autonomy is reduced by international institutions—applies not only to states, but also to individuals. At the same time, member states must fulfill minimal criteria internally before they are considered as recognized members. Lastly, in order to substantiate these underlying norms, the concept of global governance includes the possibility of international authority undermining the Westphalian idea of states as exclusive holders of final authority. The concept thus points to spheres of authority beyond the nation state without necessarily requiring a legal–doctrinal acceptance of the supremacy of international law (see Krisch 2010). All the three presuppositions discussed here seem to be not far-fetched, but can easily be traced as presuppositions in the current practice of world politics. This undermines the notion of Westphalian sovereignty that states are neither absolute nor final authorities—they need to acknowledge some normativity beyond them.

---

[3] See <http://treaties.un.org/Pages/Home.aspx?lang=en>.
[4] More recently, the growth rates slowed down significantly (Pauwelyn et al. 2014). This turn took place after the global governance system was established and could produce counter-effects.

2

Reflexive Authorities

In addition to underlying normative principles, a political system needs to have institutions that produce governance. This institutional core of a political system can be grasped by its "patterns of authority" (Eckstein 1973). Patterns of authority are key to the understanding of any political system. They are also used here as a central building block for developing a theory of the global governance system. When states and societal actors respect obligations formulated by trans- or international institutions that run counter to their stated interests without being forced or persuaded, then they stand in an authority relationship. These authority relationships in the global governance system are embedded in the ideational frame based on the presuppositions of a common good, individual and societal rights, and the possibility of international authority. They affect the autonomy of the constituent units and justify this with reference to a common good (see von Bogdandy et al. 2010a).

In developing authority as key concept for analyzing the global governance system, Max Weber's foundational treatment is used to capture the paradox involved in the notion of "voluntary subordination" (section 1). Building on this foundation, I develop in sections 2 and 3 the conception of reflexive authority in contrast to two other conceptions that have prevailed in International Relations (IR) so far. The argument is laid out against the background of the global governance context, one in which the authority holders (international and transnational institutions) are in many respects weaker than some actors within their constituency (states). Section 4 goes on to distinguish between two types of reflexive authority: epistemic and political authority. Finally, section 5 analyzes the interplay between different authorities in global governance in order to identify the major features of the global governance system. This system falls short when measured against a fully constitutionalized system of political rule. It is—to put it in the shortest possible form—a system of only loosely coupled spheres of authorities that is not coordinated by a meta-authority and lacks a proper separation of powers.

2.1 Public Authority as a Core Concept of the Political

The exercise of power includes all instances in which an actor A brings an actor B to think or do something that they would not have thought or done otherwise (Weber 2013a: 211). If actor A is replaced by something that encompasses not only actors but also structures, the definition becomes even more encompassing (see Barnett and Duvall 2005). In any case, power can come in different forms. Those who do something that they actually do not want to do may be forced to do so. In this version, the respective actor does something because she fears the consequences of not doing so. Power is also involved when someone is persuaded to change beliefs in a way that affects their behavior. In this case, the subordinate does something because he is convinced by the power of the argument that it is appropriate. These two logics, the logic of consequentiality and the logic of appropriateness (March and Olsen 1998) or, to put it another way, the logics of bargaining and arguing (Elster 1995, 1999), have dominated thinking about cooperation and institutions in IR in recent decades.

In contrast, the concept of authority points to the logic of deference as a form of power. It is based on the acceptance of a decision or an interpretation because it comes from a certain source. It is a belief in certain qualities of an authority which make subordinates adapt their beliefs and behavior. The exercise of authority has been central to the study of political power since ancient times. From the early treatments of the theme by Aristotle and the notion of *auctoritas* in the Roman republic, it was always the interplay between the defenders and challengers of public authorities that constituted the core of the political.[1] Although authority for a long time has received little attention in IR, a detailed examination of the concept of public authority in this context is necessary to understand global governance.

The foundational treatment of the concept in modern social sciences is probably still the one by Max Weber in his sociology of domination (see Simmerl and Zürn 2016). He defines authority and domination as the chance

> that certain specific commands (or all commands) will be obeyed by a given group of persons. It thus does not include every mode of exercising "power" or

---

[1] See Furedi (2013) for an impressive "sociological history" of authority. He traces the concept from its antique origins via the competing claims of the Church and the kings in the Middle Ages, as well as the bourgeois ambition to free itself from traditional powers in order to establish popular sovereignty, to the anarchists' struggle against any restriction on autonomy, the celebration of the Führer, and the self-critique of modernity by critical theory.

"influence" over other persons.... Hence every genuine form of domination implies a minimum of voluntary compliance, i.e. an *interest* (based on ulterior motives or genuine acceptance) in obedience. (Weber 1978 [1925]: 212)

This interest in obedience requires explanation. The paradoxical core of the concept of authority has been pointed out by many of the best-known social theorists. Max Horkheimer (1987a [1936]), for instance, talks about "affirmed dependency," while Pierre Bourdieu (1990) labels the same phenomenon the "complicity of the dominated." In the words of Georg Simmel (2009 [1908]: 130–1), authority "presupposes in large measure... a freedom of those subject to the authority; it is, even where it seems to 'crush' them, not based on coercion and pure resignation alone." The deference to commands of others sounds paradoxical and invokes theories about the sources of abnormality. Indeed, the authoritarian personality (Adorno et al. 1950) and the Milgram experiment (Milgram 1974) are still among the most often cited works on authority. Yet these seminal theories about the social origins of mindless obedience do not do much to help us understand the pervasive and partially productive role of authority relationships in many modern societies and in the global political system.

The notion of an interest in obedience becomes even more puzzling when it comes to international relations and global governance. Why should the US government have an interest in being obedient to the World Trade Organization (WTO)? And why should the Greek government be obedient to rating agencies? There are four reasons why an interest in obedience or deference strikes one as being especially peculiar when it comes to global governance. First of all, it is widely accepted that states strive for sovereignty and are willing to renounce it only under very special circumstances. Why should social actors that usually strive for autonomy and independence—as in liberalism—or for superiority and dominance—as in realism—accept their subordination without being forced, incentivized, or persuaded to do so? Second, the global governance authorities are young. By far the majority of international organizations (IOs) are the product of state interactions after the Second World War and transnational authorities developed mainly from the 1980s on. Unlike the authority relationship that exists between some individuals and, say, clerics, global governance institutions did not precede the birth of most states; rather, it was the other way around. States are not born into a pre-existing authority practice of global governance. Third, states and the societies governed by them have established numerous mechanisms of questioning any kind of obligations in the international realm—both within the government and outside in the form of expertise in the parliament, universities, and think tanks. Fourthly, global governance authorities target, among others, states that have considerably more resources at their disposal than any conceivable IO. All IOs, including the European Union (EU), have less staff than any of the big cities in Europe. This is again different from traditional authority relationships, in which the authority usually possesses more resources and capacity than the individuals deferent to that authority. It seems that the notion of "affirmed dependency" or the "complicity of the dominated" poses even more of a paradox for global governance institutions than it does in authority relationships between institutions and individuals.

2.2 Conceptions of Public Authority

Authority relationships have for a long time been only implicitly part of IR. For instance, some influential authors—loosely associated with realist thinking—see the international system as a progression of hegemonic constellations that are based on both hard and soft power (see Triepel 1938; Kennedy 1989; Modelski 1987). Classical realism—as it developed in the United States after the Second World War—also allowed for a hierarchy between states and for a role of social recognition (Carr 1964; Morgenthau 1967; Herz 1981). Yet this tradition was pushed aside by Kenneth Waltz's (1979) rigorous neorealist analysis of the international system as an anarchical one. In addition, many theories of imperialism emphasize the mutual recognition of hierarchical structures as being important within imperial settings (Doyle 1986; Münkler 2005).[2] Yet, it is only recently, and to the extent that authority relationships between international institutions on the one hand, and states, societies, and individuals on the other are analyzed, that the concept has entered the institutionalist camp of IR theory,[3] as well as of international law.[4] With the rise of global governance, it became obvious that authority in IR can take different forms.[5]

These recent contributions usually follow one of two conceptions of authority. The first may be labeled "contracted authority." It conceives

---

[2] Dependency theorists, in particular, focused on the co-optation of local elites as a necessary condition for the functioning of a system of inequality (see Galtung 1972; Senghaas 1972; and also Wallerstein 1974, 1980).

[3] Early contributions are Ruggie (1975); Bull (1977); Taylor (1978).

[4] The work of Armin von Bogdandy and colleagues has been path-breaking (von Bogdandy et al. 2010b; von Bogdandy and Venzke 2014; von Bogdandy et al. 2017; Goldmann 2015). See also, more recently, the work of Krisch (2017) and Black (2017).

[5] See Avant et al. (2010); Barnett and Finnemore (2004); Biersteker and Hall (2002); Grande and Pauly (2005); Kahler and Lake (2003); Rittberger et al. (2008); Zürn (2004); Zürn et al. (2007). Other approaches assign international and transnational organizations an independent role without calling it authority, but still see states as the principals, orchestrators, or managers in the background (Abbott et al. 2015; Cooper et al. 2008; Genschel and Zangl 2014).

authority relationships in the international realm as an outcome of a social contract between the later authority holders and their constituency. Such a relationship depends on generating benefits for both sides. A second approach to resolving the paradox can be labeled "inscribed authority." It conceives authority relationships as a result of socialization processes. On a basis of a critique of these two versions dominant in IR—the former broadly associated with a rationalist and the latter with a constructivist understanding of international institutions—I set out a third response that I label "reflexive authority." It sees authority in global governance as deriving from epistemic foundations that include the permanent monitoring of authorities.

2.2.1 Contracted Authority

On this understanding, the foundation of authorities is the making of contracts, in which fully autonomous actors agree on a treaty that is to the benefit of all who subscribe to it. This liberal conception of authority is reason-based, locates authority mainly in institutions and law, and can be traced back to Hobbes and Locke (see e.g. Enoch 2014; Schmelzle 2015). In IR, this view is mostly associated with the influential work of David Lake (2009, 2010), but also with the works authored by Alex Cooley (2005) and Liesbet Hooghe, Gary Marks, Tobias Lenz, and colleagues (2017) among others. The most important elements of this conception of authority are commands, legitimacy, and interests.

"One speaks of authority if B regards A's command as legitimate and correspondingly has an obligation to obey.... Whereas power is evidenced in its effects irrespective of their cause, authority exists only to the extent that B recognizes an obligation resting on the legitimacy of A's command" (Hooghe et al. 2017: 8). Where does the legitimacy of the commands derive from in this perspective? Given the object of study, charisma, religion, and tradition—some of the Weberian sources of legitimacy—are rejected. In this view, it is mostly "legal-rational authority" based on a codified order that needs to be studied. This means that social contracts are the source of legitimacy.

This conception of authority is based on rational interest. Lake puts it very explicitly: "Both dominant and subordinate states have to be better off in hierarchic than in strictly anarchic relations for the contract to be fulfilled" (2009: 93). This is true for the moment of negotiating the contract as well as for the compliance with it. On this view, the conferral of authority is negotiated and it allows one actor to exercise authority to the extent that it serves the interest of both sides. Authority therefore needs to be bought by the dominant actors and holds only for as long as the contract is beneficial for both sides.

Lake (2009, 2010) has analyzed the bilateral relationships between the United States and its Caribbean allies as an ideal-typical case. According to his analysis, the smaller partners recognize US leadership in certain issue areas in return for protection and the provision of collective goods. Therefore, authority expresses a right to command, which needs to be acquired, and thus results from a social contract based on well-defined interests on both sides.

Such a contractualist conception of authority has a number of advantages. First of all, it is a relational concept of authority emphasizing mutual recognition and thus avoiding any conception that considers authority as a property of an actor based on some capacities. The second strength derives from building on a clearly identified micro-mechanism. Authority, especially if understood as based on mutual recognition, is not just there as a structure that empowers and constrains actors, but is also affected by actors and their actions. The contractualist understandings therefore can account very well for both the rise of international authority and its contestation.

The original version of contracted authority was dyadic (Lake 2009), which leaves little room for the authority of international or transnational organizations. In the dyadic version, A and B are both states. The dominant state A uses contracts as instruments in order to exercise authority over B. The contracts and thus international institutions are actually epiphenomena of the state interactions. This is odd since authority has been introduced mainly to enrich the study of global governance and international as well as transnational organizations. Yet, more recent versions of this conception have moved to a triadic understanding. In the triadic version, contracts may lead to the pooling or delegation of authority to international institutions. This is most explicit in the "Measuring International Authority" project by Hooghe and colleagues (2017), as well as in David Lake's work on supranationalism (see e.g. 2017). In any case, the contractualist version of international authority does not lose sight of the interests that stand behind the establishment of third parties exercising authority. It is open to the possibility that any given IO or third party may reflect underlying power constellations.

The contractualist understanding of international authority has two important weaknesses. First, contracted authority is based on—as Vincent Pouliot (2017) puts it—excessive voluntarism. The contract view seems to assume that authority depends completely and at all times on legitimacy. As soon as legitimacy—or mutual recognition—is gone, so is authority. Sharman moves the point forward by stating "[i]f parties are free to bargain, transact or break off negotiations as best suits their individual interests, this suggests a 'horizontal' market interaction on the basis of formally equal parties, rather than one premised on super- and subordination" (Sharman 2013: 190). The contractualist notion of international and transnational authority thus becomes identical with cooperation under anarchy, losing sight of the forms of authority, dominance, and hierarchies established in and via global governance institutions.

This leads to my second objection. The social paradox of authority is solved by defining away deference. If the recognition of an authority can be explained completely as a contract with a reference to pre-defined interests, then it is the outcome of negotiations and not the authority relationship as such that is accepted. To put it differently, in this conception, actors comply content-dependently with the contract and do not defer content-independently to an authority. Deference to the authority evaporates in this concept. Such a perspective lacks the special epistemic role of the authority holder. All the classical figures of authority—the theological father, Hegel's master, or the modern judge (see Kojéve 2014)—have a cognitive component that can roughly be described as "knowing better."

2.2.2 Inscribed Authority

Socialization-based accounts of authority give priority to the social order in which individuals are situated. Authority, on this view, is a relationship in which habits are activated and reproduced by actors. Actual proponents of this view emphasize that even modern relationships are not based on free-dom and autonomy, but on socializations that reflect relations of productions, the distribution of social capital, or—to put it in Foucaultian terminology—sedimented discourses.[6] In IR, this view is associated with the influential work of Michael Barnett and Martha Finnemore (2004), Ian Hurd (1999, 2007), Deborah Avant and colleagues (2010), as well as of Emanuel Adler and Vincent Pouliot (2011; Pouliot 2016a). While I focus on these authors, some post-structuralist and postcolonial accounts can also be considered to subscribe to this view (see Simmerl and Zürn 2016 for an overview).

Michael Barnett and Martha Finnemore (2004: 5) define authority as the "ability of one actor to use institutional and discursive resources to induce deference from others" (see also Avant et al. 2010: 99). At first sight, such a definition focusing on the ability of the authority holder seems to move away from a relational understanding of authority. Yet the relation comes back when the foundation of deference is brought into the picture: legitimacy. Ian Hurd (2007: 31) is most explicit in spelling out the role of legitimacy in authority relationships. He claims that "[a] rule will become legitimate to an individual (and therefore become behaviorally significant) when the individual internalizes its content and reconfigures his or her interests according to

---

[6] Cf. Horkheimer (1987b [1936]); Adorno et al. (1950); Bourdieu (1991); Butler (1996). Hegel's analysis of the relationship between the master and the slave has been foundational for this thinking (Kojéve 1975: 48–89). In an existential struggle, the master prevails and enforces subordination of the slave. Yet the relationship remains interdependent: The master depends on the recognition and work of the slave, which in turn is a source of emancipation for the slave. This argumentative figure is as foundational for critical thinking from Marx to critical theory to post-structural reasoning as that of social contract is for liberal theory.

the rule. When this happens, compliance becomes habitual (in the sense of being the default position)..." (ibid.). In this understanding, authority is relational, based on shared understandings, and is legitimate in the sense that actors have been successfully socialized into them.

How does this internalization process happen? In the inscribed authority conception, legitimacy is learned. Actors get socialized into certain practices; they therefore know where they stand and what is expected of them, and their beliefs about right or wrong derive from the shared understandings of society. It is essentially habits and practices that pre-exist and to which actors become accustomed in order to perform them competently (see Adler and Pouliot 2011; Pouliot and Thérien 2017). These are also the mechanisms through which authority relationships and stratification reproduce themselves.

The conception of inscribed authority has important strengths. Most importantly, it does not need to reduce authority relationships to mutual interests. While there can be no doubt that many authority relationships are in the interest of both sides—the authority holder and the subordinates—the concept reaches beyond interests. While it may be true that even the relationship between master and slaves contained elements of mutual recognition and were thus not based only on coercion, it however is debatable—to say the least—whether such an authority relationship was also in the interest of the slave. The shared understanding about inequality underlying such a relationship needs to be carved out. The notion of inscribed authority aims at exactly that. Moreover, it brings legitimacy into the equation and therefore takes deference seriously.

However, for the analysis of authority relationships in global governance, such a perspective also displays weaknesses. First of all, it depends too much on habits. States and many other global governance actors were there before global governance institutions were established. States have literally invented some of those global governance institutions without first being socialized by them. When France and the United Kingdom joined the International Monetary Fund (IMF), they either believed in the need to establish a global governance authority in this area or they were forced by the United States to join. It was hardly because the structure of the international system socialized them to do so. There are good reasons to consider socialization as a consequence of, not a cause for, the rise of international institutions (Checkel 2005; Zürn and Checkel 2005). In addition, the willingness and ability of state and non-state actors to challenge international institutions in general or for what they do specifically is far too prevalent for the notion of inscribed authority. The degree of contestation of international authorities that can be observed in the international realm is too pervasive for a conception based on internalized habits (see Zürn et al. 2012a). In short, this conception does not account sufficiently for change and contestation in global governance because it is bent too much toward the structural side of the equation of social action.

The strong emphasis on internalization in the notion of inscribed authority points to a second weakness. A conception that bases deference completely on internalization seems to miss some of the features of authority relationships in global governance. Deference to reflexive transnational and international authorities is often not internalized, but permanently under observation. While states at times accept that they need guidance by IOs, they observe the IOs very closely. This does not exclude internalization per se, which is a possible long-term consequence of a relationship, but not a necessary part of the story in global governance. Yet even in those cases in which deference to the authority gets internalized over time, the norms postulated by the authority may or may not be internalized. The payment of taxes to states, for instance, is rather grudgingly accepted, without being transformed into an internalized desire to pay, even if the state, as authority, is recognized or even internalized. If the internalization is emphasized as a micro-mechanism sustaining authority relationships, it neglects the specific features of global governance institutions, and underestimates their degree of instability and contestation.[7]

2.3 Reflexive Authority

Building on the conceptions of contracted and inscribed authority and the stated criticisms, I aim at developing a conception of public authority consisting of reflexivity and requests that is based on epistemic foundations (Zürn 2017; Zürn et al. 2012a). This understanding claims that authority builds on a logic of action other than the logic of appropriateness or the logic of consequentiality. It is neither the quality of a specific argument nor a manipulation of the subordinate's preferences through incentives that leads to deference, but the recognition of the authority as worth observing. This leads to the concept of reflexive authority consisting of two types: political authorities making decisions and epistemic authorities making interpretations.

2.3.1 *Reflexivity and its Epistemic Foundations*

In general, current authority relationships in global governance do not reproduce long-standing practices. Against this contextual background, authority

---

[7] It needs to be clarified that these remarks about the insufficiency of the micro-mechanism in inscribed authority are not meant to be general. They form a contextualized statement referring to the authority relationship between global governance institutions and states as well as organized non-state actors. These remarks do not exclude the fact that many authority relationships within world society are based on internalized habits.

is conceptualized as reflexive. Reflexive authority relationships include enlightened and critical subordinates that recognize authorities because they acknowledge their own limitations. Reflexive authority thus has advantages for both the authority holders *and* the constituencies. In this respect, I follow the "service conception" of authority as developed by Joseph Raz (2006).[8]

The reflexivity in reflexive authority relationships is twofold. On the one hand, it speaks to an element of *enduring reflection about the worthiness of the authority* that runs counter to the notion of internalization. While reflexive authority involves dispensing with an exact examination of the specific judgment or decision on the side of subordinates, it is at the same scrutinized by a permanent monitoring and consideration of the standards that make an authority appealing and trustworthy. For instance, most people would believe in the climate models of a Nobel laureate without checking all the parameters and equations, which would take a long time. At the same time, the credentials and the reputation of the authority are checked continuously. Authority relationships therefore become their own theme in the sense that there is always the possibility of questioning and re-designing the relationship. Reflexive authorities are under perennial observation.

On the other hand, the recognition of an authority does not derive exclusively from a rationalist conception based on predefined interests; rather it stems from reflections about the limits of rationality. It is therefore especially in situations without predefined interests that reflexive authority plays out. By providing information and new perspectives, the authority may shape the preferences. As Frank Furedi (2013: 52) puts it, "[t]he need for a concept of authority only emerges when communities are forced to contend with uncertainty about questions who to believe, trust, follow or obey." In the case of reflexive authority, *the recognition of external authorities is based on the knowledge about the limitations of one's own rationality and information base.*[9] In turn, authorities offer either a superior or an impartial perspective, or both.[10]

Reflexive authorities depend on the epistemic constructions that identify the limits of subordinates and the realm of superiority of an authority. In contrast to the contractual notion of international authority, therefore, reflexive authority emphasizes the role of knowledge orders as constitutive background

---

[8] This also is in line with the starting point of the influential discussion in Michael Barnett and Martha Finnemore (2004: 21): "The authority of IOs...lies in their ability to present themselves as impersonal and neutral—as not exercising power but instead serving others." See also Sending (2015).

[9] Reflexive authority resembles the self-binding logic of Ulysses when confronted with the sirens that is also reflexive in the sense that it permanently monitors its own reflexivity (see Elster 1986).

[10] Joseph Raz (2009) offers five—more fine-grained—reasons for accepting an authority: The authority is wiser than the subject; it has a steadier, less biased will; it prevents self-defeating action; it reduces transaction costs; and it is better placed to make the decision.

of authority relationships and deference (see also Sending 2017; Venzke 2013). Yet the notion of reflexive authority does not depend on the assumption that those who are considered to be authorities are indeed closer to the truth. Rather it points to the relevance of the social process in which superior knowledge or an impartial perspective is established. The focus on the social processes of knowledge production highlights the role of science therein. The whole notion of "scientification" of social processes (Weingart 1983, 2008) indicates the importance of science in this process.

Science has shown its effectiveness in the course of history and, at the same time, has developed reputational mechanisms—such as the ranking of universities, citation indexes, and the like—that tell us which scientific opinion is more accurate. As a consequence, those who question authorities often need to question science as well. Critics of genetically modified food, for instance, tend not to challenge the scientific quality of studies that point to the non-hazardousness of these products. Instead, they cast doubts on whether science has properly considered the ethical implications, and whether science is able to take into account the "unknown unknowns." Most strategies that aim at questioning authority, therefore, involve epistemic challenges to the dominant knowledge order. For instance, many transnational movements challenging international institutions question neoliberal thinking at the same time.

2.3.2 Requests

Most accounts of inscribed and contracted authority place commands at the core of the exercise of authority. Weber also referred most often to commands when he talked about authority. Yet reflexive authority does not work exclusively with "commands to do x" but also includes "requests to consider y." Requests can come either indirectly, in the form of behavioral implications of interpretations, or directly, in the form of demands. In both cases, it is not possible to speak of commands. Most analysts of international authority therefore avoid statements like "The World Trade Organization (WTO) commands the government of the US to reduce tariffs" or "The World Health Organization (WHO) commands France to invest more in health."

Instead, reflexive political authorities *request* that certain action is taken as a means to pursue international or global goals. When the WHO directly requests a new vaccination, states do not take this as a command. This is especially obvious in the case of all the indirect demands that are put forward by international authorities, such as the Programme for International Student Assessment (PISA) benchmarking for the quality of high-schools. In this case, the authority of transnational and international institutions is based on what pragmatist philosophy labels "secondary reasons." It is especially in cases when one is uncertain about the primary reasons for making a decision (e.g. "Is the food good in this restaurant?") that secondary reasons (such as "If it is Michelin-starred, it must be good") become decisive.[11] This deference to the certification scheme, however, excludes neither one's own judgment afterwards ("The food was, in spite of the recommendation, mediocre") nor the possibility of shifting to another certification scheme after negative experiences have multiplied. Different reflexive authorities may thus compete with each other allowing for forum shopping on the side of the subordinates.

Moreover, in the reflexive conception of authority, it is not the perceived "duty to follow" that is decisive. One does not usually follow a restaurant guide because one feels obligated to do so. Secondary reasons do not create a "duty" to follow. Indeed, states usually follow IO prescriptions because they feel that the authority is doing a good service, not because they feel a strong duty to oblige. If states feel an obligation to follow at all, they feel a duty toward their fellow states to contribute to the public good or toward future governments not to destroy the reputation of a country.

Since the reflexive conception of authority focuses on requests, it can also include those cases in which states disregard the prescription of an IO and, at the same time, try to ensure that they still recognize the authority. In the case of labeling of genetically modified food, for instance, the EU accepts that it has to pay fines for its genetically modified organism (GMO) policy, thus affirming WTO authority, but without following the prescription to change their policy.

2.3.3 Perpetuation and Legitimation

While it is true that an authority relationship may, in some cases, emerge spontaneously—for instance, in crisis situations—the future of this relationship will not forget its spontaneous foundation. If there is a fire in a theatre, a few may put themselves forward to coordinate the safe exit of others, without any such pre-assignment. If that same group of people happened to be in an airplane when an emergency situation arose, it is likely that the passengers would look to those same people for guidance. Any authority relationship therefore has a tendency to be not just a one-off, but rather to persist, at least for a period of time. Such a transformation can take the form of either "objectification" or "institutionalization." In these ways, authority becomes a form of hierarchy.

---

[11] See Legg (2012) for a treatment of secondary reasons of the national discretion in the implementation of human rights.

An authority relationship is *objectivized*[12] if the knowledge order that underlies the relationship becomes a dominant worldview or ideology that reaches beyond the immediately involved actors to external audiences. It is then broadly accepted that the authority holder represents the "objective" "non-particularistic" perspective. Scientists with public appeal are a case in point. To the extent that they are broadly accepted by external audiences, objectification also points to social pressure and coercion. If an actor rejects insights from such an "authority" that are seen as "objective" and unquestionable, the danger of social exclusion and being seen as weird arises. The voluntariness of subordination is then reduced.

Objectivized authority can transform into indirect coercion when third parties are dependent on those who acknowledge an authority. An institution carrying out tests on consumer products, for instance, may initially only influence those consumers who are reading the journal reporting the test. Consumers often follow the recommendations of the test, although it is in no way binding. At the same time, epistemic authorities may induce deference from the producer of consumer goods indirectly via affecting the behavior of consumers. If the tester enjoys high credibility and has a significant effect on consumer choice, then its ideas about a good product become "indirectly binding" for the producer via the pressure of a third party, i.e. a large share of consumers.

The other form of perpetuation of authority is *institutionalization*. An authority relationship is institutionalized when the decisions and interpretations are a priori delegated or pooled (see Hooghe et al. 2017). Governments represent an ideal type for this form of authority perpetuation. IOs can also be seen as institutionalized authority. Since the establishment of international institutions involve sunk costs that are lost if one exits, and breaking a commitment in addition often leads to reputational losses, the voluntariness of subordinations is reduced the very moment authority is institutionalized.

When authority is objectivized or institutionalized, it turns into a form of hierarchy and there is a need for legitimation. Every authority therefore tends to legitimate its practice in order to stimulate the belief in its legitimacy (see Weber 1978 [1925]: 213; Barker 2001; Geis et al. 2012). The distinction between legitimacy beliefs and the process of legitimation points to the close relationship between authority and legitimacy, without mingling them by defining authority as legitimate power. This conception of the relationship between authority and legitimacy points to another important difference between reflexive authority on the one hand and contracted and inscribed

---

[12] "Objectivization" in this context does not mean that something becomes an objective truth, but that an authority relationship becomes generalized in the sense that many actors consider it as intersubjectively true and existent.

Table 2.1. Contracted, inscribed, and reflexive authority

	Contracted Authority	Inscribed Authority	Reflexive Authority
Commands (including enforcement) or Requests	Commands derived from contracts	Internalized commands	Requests
Logic of Action	Interest-based compliance	Socialization-based appropriateness (learned competence)	Reflected deference
Agent or Structure	Actor interests	Inscribed in structures	Actors based on epistemic foundations
Fusionist or Separate	Fusionist	Fusionist	Separate

authority on the other. Contrary to the fusionist view, which more or less equates authority and legitimacy (authority is legitimate power), it draws a distinction between perpetuated expressions of authority and the exercise of authority (see Chapter 3).

To sum up the conceptual discussion of authority: Reflexive authority is different from both the contractualist and the inscribed conceptions of authority (see Table 2.1). In reflexive authority relationships, the authority holder sends requests instead of commands to constituencies who know about their limitations, but tend to monitor the authorities closely. Reflexive authority is based on the acceptance of a knowledge order that reproduces the authority relationship. Whereas reflexive authority can—under certain conditions—transform into habituation, especially on the side of those members of the constituency that lack informational and monitoring capacities, this is not a part of the definition. The concept of reflexive authority is compatible with the idea of "liquid authority" (Krisch 2017). Whereas liquid authority mainly sheds light on the form (or the aggregate state) of transnational and international institutions, reflexive authority looks at its social foundation. The ongoing contestation of the underlying episteme of transnational and international authorities, the deliberate and permanent monitoring of these authorities, and strategies developed to maintain room for manoeuver in spite of recognizing authorities, are, in principle, the features of reflexive authority that induce liquidity.

2.4 Two Types of Authority in Global Governance

Two basic types of authority can be distinguished: the authority to make decisions and the authority to provide interpretations. The authority to make decisions can be labeled political authority whilst the authority to make interpretations can be called epistemic authority. The epistemic foundation applies to both political and epistemic authorities. The recognition of an institution as having an impartial or third perspective, that allows them to make requests in the name of a common good, depends as much on knowledge construction (i.e. political authority) as the recognition of valid information production (i.e. epistemic authority). Both types of reflexive authority are founded in epistemic constructions.

2.4.1 *Political Authority*

In the case of political authority, stipulations, rules, and norms are viewed as "binding" for a certain collective. Political authority rests on the acknowledgment that there needs to be an institution that is authorized to make collectively binding decisions in order to promote the common good and to prevent chaos. Political authorities thus have the right to make decisions that violate the particular interests of members in the short term. Political authority rests on a cognitive framework that permits a common interpretation of the common good. A political authority may have the right to enforce rules, but its influence does not rest on force alone.

On the transnational and international level, newly institutionalized political authorities especially have emerged in recent decades. The principle that a given territory is governed exclusively by the national government does not hold any longer. International institutions circumvent the consent principle by taking decisions through forms of majority voting or through the informal dominance of hegemonic powers. Majority decisions and the exercise of dominance by strong countries enhance the capacity of international institutions to act by avoiding vetoes by single states and overcoming blockades. Today, roughly two thirds of all IOs—in which at least one major power participates—have the capacity to take decisions by a majority vote (Blake and Payton 2008; Breitmeier et al. 2006). Moreover, states are increasingly delegating power directly to IOs. The authority index developed by Liesbet Hooghe and Gary Marks show a marked increase in the last decades. Their standardized delegation index for seventy-eight IOs rose from 23.5 in 1975 to 33.2 in 2010 (Lenz et al. 2015).

To the extent that the new international institutions exercise political authority, they set rules that reduce the room of manoeuver for national states and govern formerly domestic affairs either directly or indirectly. Especially powerful states aim to use such authorities to exercise influence outside of their territory; at the same time, they often try to limit the authorities' influence on their own affairs. Powerful states thus keep open the possibility of evaluation and shifting loyalty, and they even create circumstances in order to extend these options. The notions of "counter-multilateralism" (Morse and Keohane 2014) and "deliberate fragmentation" (Benvenisti and Downs 2007) point to the strategy that states recognize "multiple" authorities with overlapping competences in order to put pressure on authorities not to act against their interests and in order to keep the option of shifting loyalty.

Political authorities occasionally come with the right to enforce decisions— as in the case of the United Nations Security Council (UNSC)—but they more often come without it. Even the EU had no sanctioning capacity for a long time. While the subjects of reflexive political authority accept an inducement to defer, they keep alternatives and the exit option open, and thus keep it liquid.

2.4.2 Epistemic Authority

The other basic type of authority can be labeled epistemic authority. Epistemic authorities provide interpretations that structure the behavior of others. Epistemic authority is based on expert knowledge and moral integrity. The views and positions of an authority are adopted because they appear to be both knowledgeable and non-partisan at the same time. Epistemic authority is based on the assumption that knowledge and expertise are unequally distributed, but that there is a common epistemological framework that makes it possible to ascertain knowledge inequality. An epistemic authority need not, in all cases, convince people factually and in detail. It is, therefore, not the quality of the specific argumentation, but rather the general reputation of an institution or a person that is decisive (Haas 1992). What is involved is governance by reputation (Schuppert 2010: 94).

The significance of institutions with purely epistemic authority unquestionably plays a role in global governance. This includes, in particular, influential and "credible" non-governmental organizations (NGOs) such as Greenpeace— in the environmental area—or Amnesty International—in the area of human rights—which are active in setting as well as monitoring norms. The authority of some of these NGOs has been objectivized over time. While not all NGOs exercise authority, the growth of transnationally active NGOs has been enormous—today there are roughly eight times as many of them as there were in 1975 (United Nations Department of Economic and Social Affairs 2009). The access to IOs has increased dramatically as well, by a factor of three since 1975 (see Tallberg et al. 2013: 68). It therefore seems plausible to claim a growth of epistemic authorities in global governance in recent decades.

Epistemic authority can be institutionalized as well. In this case, an epistemic authority is officially assigned that status by other authorities. We may label this strange animal politically assigned epistemic authority (PAEA). If organizational bodies receive the mandate to authoritatively interpret facts and norms from political authorities, this means that an act of delegation of competences and the related institutionalization has taken place. PAEAs are those transnational or international institutions that do not make binding decisions, but have the competence to make often very consequential interpretations. In the context of global governance, the International Panel on Climate Change (IPCC) or the role of Organisation for Economic Co-operation and Development (OECD) in education policy (with PISA) are two examples. On the basis of the type of knowledge that constitute these PAEAs, we may distinguish among reasoning-based (courts or ethics commissions), model-based (economic councils and natural science panels), and ranking-based PAEAs (i.e. PISA, etc.). In all of these cases, the demand for legitimation increases compared to pure epistemic authority, because PAEAs objectivize and institutionalize knowledge orders.

It is this type of authority that seems to have grown especially strongly in the global governance system. At the transnational and international level, PAEAs in particular have become the focus of attention over the past two decades. The rating agencies, the International Accounting Standards Board (IASB) (Büthe and Mattli 2011; Botzem 2012), the IPCC (Beck 2012) and the international evaluation institutions in the area of environmental policy generally (Mitchell et al. 2006), the OECD in the area of educational policy (Martens and Jakobi 2010), and international courts (cf. Alter 2011, 2014) are all politically assigned institutions that have become more influential over the past two decades.

In sum, authority relationships in the global governance system are mainly reflexive. Both political and epistemic authority have grown over time.[13] In both cases, however, authority can be very consequential in spite of being permanently monitored and revisited.

2.5 The Relationships between Authorities

Conceiving global governance as a political system requires more than just an account of the relationships between authorities and their constituencies. We also need to consider the relationship of different global governance authorities with each other. While the concept of reflexive authority grasps mainly the relationship between international institutions and states, as well as other actors in world society, this final section highlights two features of the relationship between the different global governance authorities. This

---

[13] Chapter 5 will provide a much more detailed account of the development of reflexive authority based on the International Authority Database (IAD).

prepares the ground to identify the major legitimation problems of global governance institutions in the next chapter.

In general, states are embedded in a larger political system that contains normative principles and authority relationships. Their rights and duties derive from their position in an emergent normative order. The global governance system therefore is not an anarchical system, in which states stand exclusively in a segmentary relationship with each other. Yet, the global governance system is also quite different from a constitutionalized system of political rule. The current global governance system is neither anarchy nor constitutional rule, yet it contains pockets of hierarchy.

Using anarchy as a benchmark for discussing the features of an international system is broadly accepted in IR. In contrast, using a constitutionalized system of political rule as the other reference point may be criticized for being both old-fashioned and idealistic. If a constitutionalized world state were presented as a normative project, the criticism may apply. However, these accusations make little sense when the goal is to descriptively assess the features of the global governance system in comparison to other political systems. The repetitive reference to the newness and uniqueness of global governance arrangements may be fashionable but provides limited insight. Suggesting that each global governance arrangement needs to be analyzed separately overlooks the context and structure of global governance. As Mendes and Venzke (2018, forthcoming) so eloquently put it:

> Reality is certainly messy. As important as it may be to draw attention to that mess, the relentless reference to the novelty and sui generis of one government arrangement or another will not be ultimately instructive. Suggesting that each institution or regime lives on its own logic and rationality runs the risk of undermining the possibilities of critique.

It also runs the risk of undermining the possibilities of comparison, one may add. The ideal of constitutionalized rule provides a yardstick for comparison in the first place, and a measure for critique in the second (see Chapter 3). It would in fact be misleading to look within the global governance system for the same institutional arrangements that we know from constitutional states in the Western world. When comparing the global governance system to the concepts of anarchy and constitutionalized rule, we focus instead on the cognitive and normative principles on which the interaction between different authorities is based. These principles can lead to quite different institutional embodiments.

What are these principles? The ideal of constitutionalism fulfills two tasks at the same time: Constitutions constitute political rule including final authority, but at the same time they limit that very authority (cf. Krisch 2010: ch. 4). A constitutional order thus both limits political decision making and enables the creations of new institutions and laws.[14] From this double function—foundational and limitational—two criteria for identifying the major features of the global governance system can be derived.

The *foundational aspect* concerns the productive coordination between authorities. A constitutionalized political system can potentially take action on all issues and thus involves meta-authorities that make the final decision where different authorities are in conflict. It can be described, therefore, as a system of rule. Such a system-wide political rule is typically backed up by institutionalized force. Whereas political rule in this use of the term is encompassing—it is systemic and involves the recognition that force can be used in order to enforce rules—the term "authority" is more limited. It refers to specific issues and does not necessarily involve (but may include) the acceptance of rule enforcement. While a Central Bank holds authority, the modern state—with its monopoly on the legitimate use of force and its institutionalized sites of coordination—exercises meta-authority. Once meta-authorities are formed to make the final decision in cases of disagreement between various authorities, and once these meta-authorities can use force to implement their positions if necessary, we can speak of political rule. Only then do we find both "the permission to do something" and the "right to grant such permissions" (Raz 1990: 2).[15]

The *limitational aspect* of a constitutionalized system of political rule concerns the separation of powers. The separation of powers has evolved in all modern constitutional states on different tracks with dissimilar starting points (see Möllers 2013: ch. 1). Yet the meaning of the concept has converged over time. It means, at its core, that different political authorities should balance each other by separating different policy functions and, in this way, avoid unrestrained dominance. As Madison has put it, "the accumulation of all powers legislative, executive and judiciary in the same hands... may justly be pronounced the very definition of tyranny" (Hamilton et al. 1982: 293). It is part of the general program to constitute political rule by delimiting it. While the meaning of separation of powers has converged, the institutional enactments of the principle vary significantly—for instance, between presidential and parliamentary systems, between proportional and majoritarian voting systems, and between central states and federal systems (see Ackerman 2000; Linz 1994).

With these two benchmarks in mind, the current global governance system can now be described as one in which different spheres of authority are

---

[14] This represents a basic understanding of constitutionalism. See Grimm (2012: 47) for an encompassing definition consisting of seven elements. For good discussions of constitutionalism in the global context, see also Kumm (2009) and Krisch (2010).

[15] See Daase and Deitelhoff (2015)—based on Onuf and Klink (1989)—for a different distinction between rule and authority.

only loosely coupled and in which the separation of powers is only weakly developed.

2.5.1 Loosely Coupled Spheres of Authority

Spheres of authority can be defined as fields that are governed by one or more authorities. In general, the boundaries of such fields are socially constructed and are organized around a common set of institutions serving similar social purposes.[16] The rise of spheres of authority in many ways follows the logic of functional differentiation (see Fischer-Lescano and Teubner 2004). As a response to increasing complexity due to globalization, each of the function systems of world society creates its own regulatory system according to its own logic without taking into account broader concerns. Seeing institutional differentiation as a response to increasing functional differentiation and transaction density in world society contrasts with the predominant view that complains about the increasing fragmentation of international institutions and international law (see e.g. Benvenisti and Downs 2007; Raustiala and Victor 2004: 300–2; Urpelainen and Van de Graaf 2015). In contrast to the fragmentation view, it is not institutional differentiation per se, but the relationship between these different spheres of authority that is decisive for the global governance system (Zürn and Faude 2013; see also Fischer-Lescano and Teubner 2006: 66). One can distinguish four ideal types of relations.

To begin with, the different spheres of authority may be neatly separated from each other (1). In this case, each regulation produces effects only within one sphere of authority, and the different spheres can easily exist in parallel. The neat separation between different spheres of authority does not, however, exist in global governance. Most regulations produce effects in other issue areas. The WTO, for instance, has liberalized international trade without taking into account detrimental effects in areas like health and environment. Similarly, the UNSC has formulated anti-terror policies that violated basic rights of suspects. The borders of a sphere of authority are therefore blurred and contested, and at least partially determined by interaction with other spheres of authority. Interface conflicts across different spheres of authority can arise because of competing interests of involved actors, because of unclear boundaries (ambiguities), or because of a clash of recognitions and beliefs. If different spheres of authority overlap, collide, or contradict each other, then we shift from independent to interdependent spheres of authority and the need for coordination arises.

---

[16] The concept "spheres of authority" was first introduced by Rosenau (1997). See also Pauly and Grande (2005) and Zürn (1998). There are similarities to the concept of regime complexes (see Victor 2004; Keohane and Victor 2011).

Decentralized coordination (2) between interdependent spheres of authorities takes place when each of them adapts to others in a mode of self-interest and only as much as necessary. In this case, different spheres of authority are in competition with each other, each with the goal to prevail over the others and enlarge their own sphere of authority. It is a more or less "anarchical" system with spheres of authority as constituent members. Some of the conflicts between the WTO and environmental authorities are a case in point. If dominant, this form of coordination describes a system of competitive spheres of authority.

In contrast, in a system of cooperative spheres of authority (3), the authorities coordinate their actions by adjusting to each other in a non-hierarchical way (see Gehring and Faude 2014). The coordination between the Global Fund and the WHO, or the interaction between the UN and the European Court of Justice (ECJ) regarding the delisting procedures of terrorist suspects are examples.

Finally, the solution provided by a system of constitutionalized rule is the development of meta-authorities that coordinate specific authorities (4). Supreme courts, parliaments, public option, and heads of governments often coordinate specific authorities in the context of national political systems.

Against the reference point of a constitutionalized system of political rule, we can now see clearly one of the major features of the global governance system. Since the different spheres of authority are interdependent and their borders contested, interface conflicts between different spheres of authority can arise. In this sense, the different spheres of authority are certainly *coupled*. However, the current global governance system does not have an institutionalized site for the final decision about the coordination of these spheres. Meta-authorities hardly exist. The current global governance system thus is not a constitutionalized system of political rule, rather it consists of spheres of authority that are only *loosely* coupled. While it seems to be too far-fetched to talk about full-scale institutional fragmentation (Benvenisti and Downs 2007), the global governance system does have an institutional architecture that lacks centralized coordination. If spheres of authority collide, they have to resolve such a collision by themselves, either via competition or cooperation.

To sum up, it can be said that the global governance system consists primarily of loosely coupled spheres of authority. Specialized public authorities of different types have, in recent decades, increased in significance, especially at the inter- and transnational levels, as well as at the national level. They cluster in spheres of authority which are coordinated in a decentralized way. Accordingly, we move from encompassing constitutional rule, which is territorially segmented, to plural and only loosely coupled spheres of international and transnational authorities as summarized in Figure 2.1.

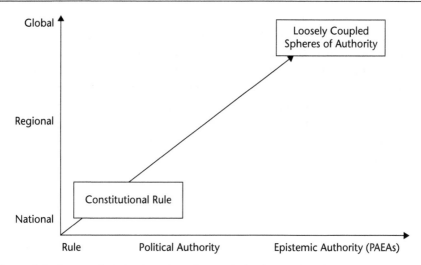

Figure 2.1. From political rule to loosely coupled spheres of authority

Source: Zürn, M. (2017), "From Constitutional Rule to Loosely Coupled Spheres of Liquid Authority. A Reflexive Approach," *International Theory*, 9/2: 261–85, 279

2.5.2 Weak Separation of Powers

The characterization of the global governance system as loosely coupled spheres of authority is based on the relationship *between* spheres. Another issue is the question of how different authorities interact *within* one sphere of authority, and whether they are able to balance each other in order to prevent unrestrained dominance in this issue area. The criteria used in this dimension are derived from the "separation of powers" doctrine that has formed the modern constitutional state (see Ackerman 2000; Möllers 2013).

The separation of powers is akin to the rule of law.[17] Both normative concepts aim at equality in two senses. First, both the executive and the legislative must be limited by law, just as any other members of the collective under question. It is against the idea of the rule of law that the law is applied to some members of the constituency, but not to others. The separation of powers is thus a means to ensure that the executive and the legislative follow their own law. Also under the rule of law, the laws must be applied consistently across cases and like cases treated alike. A separation of powers that is working well ensures equality.

There is no doubt that we see some separation of powers in the realm of global governance—most importantly, with the rise of international courts. Almost all courts—across quite different cultures—make individualized

---

[17] See Tamanaha (2004). On the international rule of law, see Zürn et al. (2012b); Hurd (2015); Nolte (2016).

decisions and interpretations and, in doing so, claim they are not making law, but protecting specific actors (Shapiro 1981; Möllers 2013: 100). Courts therefore (should) have institutional rules that protect them from "political" influence. All this applies by and large to international courts as well (von Bogdandy and Venzke 2012).

Indeed, work that has focused on international courts reports a remarkable rise in the numbers of such courts. In 1960, there were only twenty-seven quasi-judicial bodies worldwide; by 2004, this number had grown to ninety-seven.[18] These bodies are quite active (Alter 2014: 4) and they control, to some extent, the supranational rule setters. In some cases, the judgments even cross-cut spheres of authority. Most famously, the ECJ has ruled that the delisting procedure of UN suspects of terrorism are illegal. Even more importantly, international courts control national rule implementers. They do this quite often by evoking some of the normative principles standing behind the separation of powers ideas (Mendes and Venzke 2018, in preparation).

In separation of powers theory, the opposite pole to the courts acting in specific cases is the legislature, which lays down generalized rules and measures. It is this power—that of parliament—that is most closely bound to the will of the people and open to all kinds of influences. The executive is supposed to stand in between the making of individual decisions and interpretations (courts) and setting general rules (parliaments), as well as between being protected from public will-formation (courts) and being open to societal influences (parliaments) (see Möllers 2013: ch. 2). The executive needs sufficient independence to be able to be impartial, but it is accountable via elections.

In practice, however, international legislatures are dominated by executives. Most often, the assembly of member states fill the legislative function. Around a third of the world's important IOs today have international parliamentary institutions (IPIs)[19] (see Rocabert et al. 2017, in preparation), whose members are delegates of national parliaments. In both cases, the difference between authority holders and their constituencies is heavily blurred and the political process is controlled by a few national executives in collaboration with international secretariats. This leads to deviations from the idea of separation of powers.

On the one hand, the administration is not sufficiently independent of the most important objects of regulation—the states themselves. It thus lacks impartiality. Almost all rules set on the global level require the resources of the participating states to be implemented. Almost all administration of

---

[18] See <http://www.pict-pcti.org/matrix/matrixintro.html>; see also Alter (2009); von Bogdandy and Venzke (2014).
[19] IPIs are "public, transnational, and collegial bodies consisting of either directly or indirectly elected members" (Rocabert et al. 2017, forthcoming: 1).

international norms is therefore biased. Even in the exceptional cases where there is a chance to coerce and implement global norms from above—as in the case of the UNSC—resources from member states are necessary to carry them out. The permanent members of the UNSC (P5) are the most significant actors when it comes to providing the military resources for any intervention based on chapter seven of the charter. This fusion of authority holders with *some* authority takers makes it unlikely that like cases are treated alike. On the other hand, the executive arms of the very same states also play a decisive role in setting the norms on the international level. Most negotiations about new treaties and any norm development in the UN context are mostly dominated by a few strong states, while the UNGA is weak and plays no serious political role. The process of legislations, therefore, is most often dominated by the same states that also control the executive implementation process.[20]

Overall, it seems appropriate to speak of a weak and incomplete separation of powers in the global governance system. While it is not completely absent, as indicated by the rise of international courts and the presence of formal assignment, within most sectoral arrangements, there is very little *de facto* separation between rule setters and rule implementers. In most instances, the representatives of the most powerful states play the decisive role.

2.6 Conclusion

In summarizing this exploration of the patterns of authority in the global governance system, three aspects can be highlighted. First of all, reflexive authority is the major mechanism by which global governance plays out. It is a form of authority that is different from the notion of a "right to command," but can still be highly consequential. It produces requests and interpretations with behavioral implications, both of which take place under the permanent scrutiny of constituencies and external observers. It is based on actors recognizing their limits of rationality and, therefore, the need for third parties or specific expertise. This is true for political as well as epistemic authorities. Second, political authorities with rights to enforce remain the exception in global governance, and meta-authorities (constituting a system of rule) exist only in a very rudimentary sense. The global governance system therefore falls short when measured against criteria derived from the constitutionalized system of rule. The global governance system can be described

---

[20] It is in this way stratification between states gets institutionalized as a result of the rise of a global political system. Stratification is conceptualized as interacting with authority but not as replacing it.

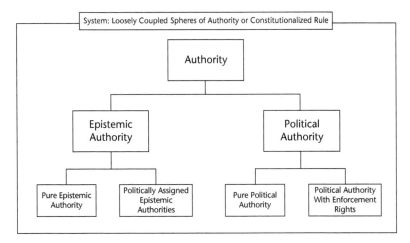

Figure 2.2. Types of authority in political systems

as one of loosely coupled spheres of authorities with a weak separation of powers within these spheres.

Third, it is wrong to say that "in the absence of agents with system-wide authority, formal relations of super- and subordination fail to develop" (Waltz 1979: 88). In contrast, hierarchy may develop within sectorally circumscribed spheres of authority and thus needs to be located between anarchy (no hierarchy at all) and constitutionalized rule (a recognized meta-authority). To the extent that inter- and transnational institutions have authority, institutionalized forms of super- and subordination can develop in a number of different guises: in the relationship between international institutions and states (pockets of hierarchy); in a stratified relationship between states within an institution (e.g. veto rights); in the relationship between private authorities and governments (e.g. rating agencies can create pressures on government via their authority over investors); and the relationship between international institutions and individual actors (direct international authority).

All those forms of authority (as captured in Figure 2.2), including the associated stratification processes and pockets of hierarchy, point to forms of power relationships that cannot be reduced to either coercion or to persuasion. These different types of authority can operate either in a context of loosely coupled spheres of authority or as part of a system of constitutionalized rules with institutional meta-authorities.

3

Legitimation Problems

Political and epistemic authorities in the global governance system often affect the autonomy of addressed governments and non-state actors. Therefore, global governance arrangements with authority need to be legitimated both to governments and to non-state actors. I refer to this as the "authority–legitimation link." This link has both a normative and an empirical meaning. Normatively speaking, all liberal reasoning agrees that limitations of autonomy for individual actors through rules require justification. This normative insight seems to be shared by almost all social actors. In this regard then, the normative view of political philosophers is backed by social practice. To put it in the words of John Lennon, political philosophers may be dreamers, but they are not the only ones. This chapter argues accordingly that the rise of transnational and international authority has changed world politics in empirical terms—it has brought the issue of legitimacy and issues of normativity to the fore.

The authority–legitimation link implies that international institutions without the ability to act in absence of complete consensus of member states have no—or at best very few—legitimation needs. As long as the intergovernmental level was restricted to merely developing a *modus vivendi* of interaction, requiring the consent—and serving the interest—of each individual member state, a two-stage process of legitimation was sufficient. The decisions taken beyond the level of the constituent members were legitimated through the (assumed) legitimacy of their representatives. This has changed with the rise of international and transnational authorities. These authoritative institutions now restrain the freedom of constituent members and therefore need to be justified with reference to common goods and normative principles. In this chapter, the legitimation requirements of, and legitimation strategies in, global governance will be discussed. The thrust of the argument in this chapter is that the legitimacy of the global governance system is structurally precarious. Two legitimation problems can be identified: a technocratic bias in the justification of authority and the lack of impartiality in the exercise of authority.

These legitimation problems trigger a set of causal mechanisms, leading—via increased politicization or counter-institutionalization—to either a decline or a deepening of global governance. I will explore these causal mechanisms theoretically in Chapter 4 and empirically in the second part of the book. The present chapter introduces the distinction between authority and legitimacy, and links the two concepts via the concept of legitimation (section 3.1). On this basis, the impartial pursuit of a shared social purpose is developed as the most important source of empirical legitimacy beliefs. In this view, an international authority must develop an authentic legitimation narrative and display a sense of impartiality to be seen as legitimate (section 3.2). Against this backdrop, the most relevant legitimation narratives are discussed in section 3.3. In section 3.4, it will then be argued that, mainly due to the loose coupling of authorities, most of these legitimation narratives can hardly be utilized for global governance institutions. This leads to a technocratic bias in the justification of inter- and national authority, making them vulnerable in practice to delegitimation efforts. Section 3.5 goes on to identify another systematic legitimation problem of the global governance system that derives from institutionalized inequality and the weak separation of powers: the built-in tendency toward arbitrariness and partiality in the exercise of authority.

3.1 The Authority–Legitimation Link

The close link between public authority and legitimacy is broadly accepted in different pockets of social science. In normative terms, the exercise of authority in general requires justification, which makes, according to Rainer Forst (2011), the right to justification the most fundamental right. Armin von Bogdandy et al. (2010a) put it similarly from a legal perspective: international public authorities have the legal capacity to restrict freedom, which makes a justification of them necessary. In line with this view, Rodney Barker (2001: 24) suggests empirically that claiming legitimacy—i.e. legitimation—is a defining component of any government. Regarding international organizations (IOs), Dominik Zaum (2013: 8) writes that "international organizations need to engage in legitimation, to justify their roles and practices and ground them in their wider social context." In general, the exercise of public authority requires legitimation, whereby legitimation refers to the social process through which legitimacy beliefs are produced—this may be well-reasoned justification as well as blunt manipulation. The rise of authority thus "is normally accompanied by the permanent attempt to arouse and nurse the beliefs in legitimacy" (Weber 2013b: 450, author's translation). This is what I label the "authority–legitimation link."

The distinction between "legitimacy beliefs" and "legitimation processes" is important, because it helps to disentangle authority and legitimacy, while still maintaining their close link via the notion of legitimation processes (see Nullmeier et al. 2012). Such a conceptual separation between authority and legitimacy runs counter, however, to a usage in the social sciences, where an understanding of authority is often defined as "legitimate power." Also in International Relations (IR), many ideas are based on such a close link between legitimacy and authority as to make "legitimate authority" a pleonasm and the two notions virtually indistinguishable (see e.g. Ruggie 2004). The key implication of this view is spelled out bluntly by Hurd (2007: 61): "the phrase 'legitimate authority' is redundant." Similarly, Michael Barnett and Martha Finnemore (1999: 707) see IOs as "autonomous sites of authority" that act independently from the state that created them, and whose influence results from "the legitimacy of the rational–legal authority they embody." Hooghe et al. (2016: 16) also define authority as "the capacity to make legitimate and binding decisions for a collectivity."

This fusionist view ("authority is legitimate power") leads to two counter-intuitive implications. First, if legitimacy and authority are two sides of a coin, then the more authority an institution has, the more legitimate it must be. From a normative point of view (external perspective), this is absurd, because only the unconstrained master would enjoy full legitimacy. But it is also problematic from an empirical perspective which looks at internal percep-tions of authority, since institutions sometimes acquire new institutional competences without necessarily being seen as more legitimate by all affected actors. Second, the fusionist view does not allow for the distinction between authority holders and institutionalized authority. One may consider, for instance, a specific practice of an authority holder (a specific government) as illegitimate, while still recognizing the authority (the government) in principle. The second objection against the fusionist view is based on the conceptual need for the possibility of illegitimate authority.[1]

In contrast to the fusionist view, legitimacy can most generally be described as the "generalized perception or assumption that the *actions* of an entity are desirable, proper, or appropriate within some socially constructed system of norms, values, beliefs, and definitions" (Suchman 1995: 574, emphasis added). The legitimacy of a public authority thus refers to the acceptance of an institution's activities: the exercise of authority as appropriate among its

---

[1] See the contributions by Alter et al. (2016); Peters and Karlsson Schaffer (2013); and Marmor (2011), who argue similarly in defending the separation of authority and legitimacy. See also Daase and Deitelhoff (2015), who argue that the notion of legitimate authority prevents the understanding of resistance to rule.

constituencies (internal legitimacy) and outside observers (external legitimacy; see Tallberg and Zürn 2018, in preparation). The views and beliefs of these audiences (i.e. constituencies and observers) are seen as the outcome of a process in which, on the one hand, authority holders and other supporters (most often deliberately) seek to make a political institution more legitimate by boosting beliefs that authority is exercised appropriately. This process is called legitimation—the permanent attempt to stimulate and nurse the beliefs in legitimacy, in Weber's words. It is in this sense that the exercise of public authority is most often accompanied by legitimation narratives of the authority holders. On the other hand, where actors seek to undermine the legitimacy of a political institution, one can speak of delegitimation. Legitimation and delegitimation processes provide the link between authority and legitimacy.

It follows that legitimacy is related to—but not synonymous with—authority. In Suchmann's definition, legitimacy refers to actions of an entity. Similarly, David Beetham (1991: 3) argues that we call something "rightful or legitimate" if it is "acquired and exercised according to justifiable rules." These two well-known definitions point to the decisive difference between authority and legitimacy. Both authority and legitimacy are based on the willingness to follow, but the process of recognition applies to different levels (Zürn 2012a). The first level refers to the recognition of an authority as desirable in principle in order to achieve certain goals and common goods. The second level of recognition is about the appropriate exercise of authority. Without first-level recognition, there would be no institutionalization of authority, as well as no pooling of authority or delegation to IOs in the first place. Whereas a commonly recognized authority can advance the common good, it certainly does not always do so. The authority may be a necessary condition for achieving a common good, but it is certainly not sufficient. It is only if the authority is being appropriately exercised in line with the social purpose for which it was created. Whereas the first-level recognition of authority refers to the recognition of the social purpose and the *ex ante* acceptance of capacities, the second-level recognition of legitimacy refers to the practice of exercising authority and the *ex post* acceptance of activities. To exemplify, anarchists in the late nineteenth century questioned all the authorities in many states in Europe (they did not think that the state should have authority at all), while most communists were in favor of a strong state, but questioned the actual regime's legitimacy (they questioned the specific exercise of authority). In a nutshell: Legitimacy beliefs involve a judgment about the exercise of an authority. In this sense, the concept of legitimacy is parasitic on the concept of authority. Legitimacy beliefs are formed in an ongoing process of legitimation and delegitimation.

Legitimacy beliefs about and legitimation processes of international and transnational authorities have received little attention for a long time (see

Tallberg and Zürn 2018, in preparation, for an overview).[2] When IR scholars have addressed legitimacy in the context of global governance, the dominant approach to date has been normative. Drawing on political theory, IR scholars have debated the existence of a democratic deficit in global governance, and alternative assessments of the legitimacy of IOs. The focus has been on the normative standards that should be used when evaluating IOs' right to rule—most often democracy—and the extent to which these institutions meet these standards—i.e. to what extent they are worthy of recognition (*Anerkennungswürdigkeit*, in the language of Max Weber). It is this body of literature that led Clark (2005: 12) to speak of a "veritable renaissance of international legitimacy talk."[3]

It is only recently that we have seen contributions that move the focus more on to the empirical side of legitimacy and legitimation of transnational and international authorities. First, students of public opinion have conceptualized public support or trust for IOs as an indicator of their legitimacy, and explored the factors that lead citizens to accept or oppose them (Norris 2000; Hooghe and Marks 2005; Ecker-Ehrhardt and Weßels 2013; Maier et al. 2012). Second, some have argued explicitly that agreed normative criteria such as transparency, accountability, or participation are central to actors' legitimacy beliefs. To the extent that IOs fail to draw on normatively accepted sources of legitimacy, they risk losing societal acceptance and thus political effectiveness (Zürn 2004; Buchanan and Keohane 2006; Bodansky 2013). Third, a growing number of contributions have addressed how IOs are legitimated or delegitimated through communicative practices and strategies aimed at boosting or undermining the acceptance of these organizations. In contrast to the classic IR approaches, these bodies of work usually focus on the legitimacy of IOs in relation to a broader set of actors, including citizens (Bernstein 2011; Brassett and Tsingou 2011; Nullmeier et al. 2010; Zaum 2013).

In sum, the empirical study of global governance legitimacy so far has not attracted the systematic attention it requires. It is however crucial in the context where transnational and international authorities are entitled to make binding interpretations and decisions. In order to be perceived as legitimate, it must be also recognized that these competences are exercised so that they serve the common goods. Here the issue is legitimacy.

---

[2] In IR in general, legitimacy has been used as a term from time to time (Carr 1964; Claude 1966; Franck 1990; Risse et al. 1999), but not anchored in the study of international authority.

[3] A first strand of normative legitimacy research focuses on whether and how the input side of global governance can be democratized. The legitimacy of IOs is, according to this view, based on their ability to meet democratic standards of participation, transparency, and accountability (see Held 1995; Zürn 2000; Buchanan and Keohane 2006; Held and Koenig-Archibugi 2005; Scholte 2011; Steffek 2003; Keohane et al. 2009). Another strand of research has instead explored normative values associated with the output side of global governance, assessing the extent to which IOs produce outcomes that contribute to efficiency, justice, and fairness (see e.g. Pogge 2002b, as well as Buchanan and Keohane 2006).

3.2 Sources of Legitimacy: The Impartial Pursuit of a Shared Social Purpose

Legitimacy is not just another term for a just order or for justice; it is not the social purpose itself. Legitimacy is not a primary or substantial goal, such as democracy, peace, or justice; rather it is an institutional virtue that remains dependent on some shared goals or social purposes that underlie it—the sources of legitimacy (see Forst 2015: ch. 8). The sources of legitimacy in a given authority relationship need not necessarily be worthy of recognition in the normative sense or from any external perspective. They just need to be recognized by the constituencies in an authority relationship—i.e. they refer to internal beliefs in legitimacy.

What then determines legitimacy beliefs in relation to international authorities? Simplifying slightly, there are three broad alternative answers to this question (see Tallberg and Zürn 2018, in preparation). According to the first perspective, legitimacy beliefs are the direct product of objective features of international authorities that audiences care about. Based on rational evaluation of these features, citizens and elites hold international authorities to be legitimate or not. Most existing literature on public opinion toward IOs is based on this assumption (e.g. Gabel 1998; Rohrschneider 2002; Chalmers and Dellmuth 2015). According to the second perspective, perceptions of legitimacy are unrelated to the features of international authorities. Instead, legitimacy beliefs vis-à-vis international authorities are a by-product of trust in national political institutions or other cues that are independent of the quality of decision-making procedures in international authorities and the quality of decisions by them. Recent work on the European Union (EU) and the United Nations (UN) adopts this understanding (Harteveld et al. 2013; Armingeon and Ceka 2014; Dellmuth and Tallberg 2015).

According to a third perspective, legitimacy beliefs are the outcome of a social process where individuals' prior beliefs interact with legitimation and delegitimation efforts. Legitimacy beliefs are then based on information that is derived from interpretative struggles about international authorities. These struggles consist of public strategies of authority defenders to legitimize, and of authority challengers to delegitimize, international authorities. The process leads to judgments which are based on framing, informational shortcuts, and cues. This perspective follows the logic of bounded rationality.

The third perspective is more plausible than the other two. On the one hand, it is certainly untenable to assume that social actors possess the knowledge, time, and capacity to rationally evaluate IO features, independent of how these features are communicated, contested, and justified in public discourse. A broad literature in political psychology and political theory postulates and demonstrates that cuing, framing, and deliberations by elites and media reports influence attitudes (see e.g. Dellmuth and Tallberg 2018, in preparation). While the objective features of IOs set certain parameters, contestation and justification of IOs affect how these features translate into legitimacy beliefs. On the other hand, it seems unreasonable to assume that legitimacy beliefs are completely unrelated to IOs, their procedures, and their policies. While individuals' trust vis-à-vis political institutions in general might matter, this cannot explain variation in legitimacy beliefs across IOs within the same audience. The process of legitimation and delegitimation is thus decisive for the development of legitimacy beliefs.

Such legitimation and delegitimation processes are however bound by the need to refer to a socially constructed system of norms, values, beliefs, and definitions (Suchman 1995). More specifically, legitimation usually involves the claim that the social purpose—which is the reason the authority was institutionalized in the first place—is being pursued with impartiality. The reference to an impartial pursuit of collective norms instead of specific interests represents the necessary ground for any promising legitimation strategy. The grammar of any legitimation effort thus consists of two components: impartiality and a social purpose.

Impartiality includes non-arbitrariness, but goes beyond that in including a sense of minimal fairness according to which like cases are treated alike. Certainly, existing authorities and the purposes and procedures they stand for reflect power relationships and do have distributive effects. Yet the exercise of authority and the application of rules needs to be impartial in order to be seen as legitimate. Faith in legitimacy dissipates immediately if the rulers are perceived as being exclusively self-serving. If the practice of an authority is seen as serving special interests in the concerned society, legitimacy fades away as well. We can use the authoritarian Mubarak regime as an example. The legitimation efforts were more or less successful as long as the leadership was seen as a specific Egyptian or Nasserist way to avoid the perils of backwardly Islamism and Western parochialism. However, once it became evident that the old Nasserist regime had degenerated into an apparatus serving the selfish privileges of a small ruling class, legitimacy beliefs dwindled rapidly. Legitimate authority—at least in modernity—requires, in the first place, perceived impartiality in the application of rules.

Against this background, David Beetham (1991) considers legal equality to be the necessary basis of any legitimate order. In this view, "rule by (transparent) law" is a fundamental condition for legitimate authority, and has made "belief in legality…the most ubiquitous form of legitimacy belief" (Weber 1968: 19, author's translation). While I share the view that, in modernity, there is a common and necessary condition for all forms of legitimacy, I do not think it is grasped appropriately by the notion of legality—rather it is the more abstract and general notion of impartiality in the application of rules. There may be, for instance, authorities that generate the belief in legitimacy by pointing to the incorporation of experts and the need to make decisions without being bound too closely to lengthy legal procedures. The impartiality element of legitimacy beliefs can thus be produced by referring to different procedures on which the exercise is based—legality being one of those, the "objective" procedures of science another. In any case, the belief in an impartial exercise of authority is a decisive determinant for strong legitimacy beliefs (Tyler 1990). Avoiding the impression that authority is exercised partially or even arbitrarily is a necessary condition for legitimacy. While impartiality is necessary, it is not sufficient to generate legitimacy beliefs.

Impartiality must be fused with a *social purpose* consisting of common goals and procedures on how to achieve it. Public authorities must legitimate their activities by producing the belief that they serve a common good in an impartial way without violating dominant beliefs. This view is reflected in Beetham's (1991: 11) elegant formulation: "a given power relationship is not legitimate because people believe in its legitimacy, but because it can be justified in terms of their beliefs." The empirical study of legitimacy therefore requires looking not primarily at the direct acceptance and support for a given institution, but at values broadly shared within a community, as well as at the extent to which an authority serves those values in practice. This allows an external perspective in assessing the practice of an authority and to consider a government as empirically illegitimate even if it enjoys high acceptance rates in the population.

As a source of legitimacy, authorities need to create beliefs that they—in practice—pursue the underlying social purpose in an impartial way. In other words: impartiality plus one or more common goods make up the sources of empirical legitimacy. Legitimation strategies aim at creating the impression that the exercise of authority is grounded in sources like participation and representation, accountability and transparency, fairness of outcomes, rule of law, individual rights, expert knowledge, tradition, strong leaders, wealth, and relative gains that increase the collective self-esteem. This list does not aim to be complete across all regions and periods in world history. In any case, legitimacy beliefs should not be conflated with democratic legitimacy. Empirically speaking, there are many other sources of legitimacy beliefs. Most of them can partially replace each other (cf. Möllers 2012), but are often used in parallel. One way to group sources of legitimacy is the distinction between the quality of decision making (procedure) and the quality of the decisions (performance). According to this distinction, both the achievement of common goods (e.g. social welfare) and the way the decision has been made (e.g. democratic participation) can serve as sources of legitimacy.[4] Both can be used for the construction of legitimation narratives.

3.3 Legitimation Narratives

Sources are the raw material of legitimation processes. Yet the legitimation of public authorities is rarely based on one source of legitimacy alone. In practice, different sources of legitimacy are crafted together in a narrative that binds the authority back to the impartial pursuit of the social purpose. This bundling of different sources of legitimacy leads to *legitimation narratives or strategies*.[5] The sources of legitimacy provide reasons that are embedded and combined in narratives of justification (see also Forst 2015: ch. 3). Legitimation narratives usually do not consist of single claims or references, but rather a combination of different sources. Narratives involve stories that mix reasons and deceptions in order to explain and justify a normative order (see Koschorke 2012).

At the same time, challengers of authority also craft and use such narratives in their attempt to delegitimate authorities. Legitimation and delegitimation narratives are real world accounts directed at the audiences of authorities. They are constructed by authority defenders or challengers in light of both the authority's purpose and the beliefs of the addressed community. They are patterns in the evaluative communication about authorities that vary in terms of the standards invoked for justification or challenges (see Gronau 2015). Narratives require at least "minimal coherence" in the sense that discursive justification, symbolic and photographic representation, and institutional reforms go along well (Gronau 2015: 479). Delegitimation narratives can be expected to be less demanding in terms of coherence, but outright contradictions limit the success as well.

While some "fiction" is part of all narratives, legitimation narratives must also appear somewhat consistent with the social purpose of the authority and its practice. At the same time, one can expect a lot of real-world variance

[4] This, of course, is similar to the distinction between input and output legitimacy introduced by Fritz Scharpf (1970, see also 1999). In order to account for the processes that take place in the black box, Vivien Schmidt has added throughput legitimacy (Schmidt 2013). By freeing the distinction from its system-theoretical language, the distinction between the quality of decisions and the quality of decision-making however avoids sophisticated discussions about what counts as input and what as throughput. See also Tallberg and Zürn (2018, in preparation). See also Halberstam (2009), who considers the three sources of "voice," "rights," and "expertise" as an encompassing typology.

[5] Strictly speaking, narratives refer to the discursive level only. Sometimes, institutional reforms or certain policy measures are used as part of an attempt to justify authorities. In this case, the term "legitimation strategy" seems to be more appropriate. Yet I prefer the term narrative in general, since it leaves open the question whether a certain justification is authentic or merely for strategic reasons.

with respect to this criterion. Legitimation practices can therefore be ordered on the basis of the relationship between the practice of an authority, normatively justifiable sources (external view), and the beliefs of constituencies (internal view).

The ideal case is that constituencies hold beliefs according to which an authority's practice is legitimate for reasons that are compatible with normative theory.[6] The external view of the normative theorist and the internal perspective on the sources of legitimacy thus converge with the observed practice and justification of the authority (External View ~ Internal View ~ Practice). In these cases, the normative concepts have developed (at least some) explanatory power: the power of ideas like autonomy, self-determination, and equality are then equally relevant in the social world as in the world of normative theories.

This is different from the situation in which the authority's practice and justifications meet legitimacy beliefs based on norms and values of a society that are not direct derivatives of modern normative theory, and thus do not converge with external views, but are still broadly shared within a society (External View ≠ Internal View ~ Practice). In this case, legitimacy is about the "justifiability of institutions in terms of reasons embedded in the real social identities" (MacDonald 2012: 57) of the constituency under question. Based on this idea that legitimacy may be less than justice but still an institutional virtue, the views and motivations of the subordinates are taken as a starting point to identify the politically acceptable (Williams 2005).

Finally, the causal strength of the authority–legitimation link shows in that even the practices that are neither in line with the beliefs of the constituency nor morally defensible are often legitimated with narratives. In this case, authority holders and defenders construct a form of legitimation narratives that pretends to be based on moral or ethical sources of legitimacy, but in fact is not. Authority holders may, for this purpose, manipulate constituencies and strategically build on exclusion of outsiders via, for instance, enemy images to produce legitimation (Practice ≠ Internal View ≠ External View).

Whereas the third type of legitimation narrative seems to be most precarious, all narratives of legitimation and delegitimation can fail. The legitimation narrative chosen by authority holders and defenders can be challenged and contested by authority subordinates and observers. The outcome of contested legitimation is open. The effect of producing legitimacy is thus not built into the concept of legitimation narrative. One may distinguish the following legitimation narratives.

---

[6] In order to fill the notion of "defensible in terms of normative theory" with meaning, it must be associated with specific normative reasoning. In the remainder, I take arguments which are developed broadly in the context of liberal normative theory as normatively defensible (see Rawls 1971 and Habermas 1996).

3.3.1 *Participatory Narrative*

This legitimation narrative is based on equal opportunity of participation for all those affected by regulation, or at least of all those to whom the regulations are addressed.[7] Participation can take place directly or indirectly via representatives. Representation in turn can be organized along functional or territorial lines. While the forms of inclusive participation can be multi-faceted, they are a necessary component of democratic decision making (Dahl 1989). The deliberative theory of democracy points to another component of this narrative: public discourse and contestation. It is based on the conviction that the mere aggregation of predefined interests must be accompanied by an open process of deliberation about the right way for a collectivity (Habermas 1996).

The narrative usually also includes accountability and transparency.[8] Complete accountability involves setting the standards for the authority against which it shall be held accountable, monitoring the outcomes, and sanctioning if the authority fails to achieve the goals (cf. Grant and Keohane 2005). Yet even complete accountability should not be confused with democracy. Accountability does not require the participation of all those who are affected by a decision—it only makes the decision makers electorally, legally, or in other ways *ex post* accountable to others. It is a means of control, not of participation. Yet participation, in turn, is ineffective if there is no accountability. Therefore, accountability most often is an ingredient of the participatory narrative.

Different actors can be involved in assuring accountability: internal actors assigned as independent monitoring agencies, all the shareholders (subjects) of an organization, all those affected by the exercise of an authority (stakeholders), or even external actors (Hirschmann 2015). IOs are often directly accountable to the member states and indirectly accountable to non-state actors and societies. In any case, accountability presupposes some minimum level of transparency. Without any transparency, there can be no accountability. Electoral accountability plays an important role in this narrative. Western democracies—as well as the EU, to some extent, with its strong parliament and parliamentary election system—often refer to this narrative as self-legitimation. In these cases, there is some convergence of external and internal views, as well as practice.

3.3.2 *Legal Narrative*

The legal narrative of legitimation is based on the protection of basic rights and the rule of law. Since authorities usually reduce the autonomy of indi-

---

[7] This difference between all those affected and all those addressed points to one of the major divisions within normative democratic theory (see Karlsson Schaffer 2012).

[8] Accountability and transparency are not considered to be a distinct narrative, since they are in one way or another way part and parcel of most narratives.

viduals, it seems—especially from a liberal point of view—decisive that the exercise of authority does not violate individual rights in a disproportionate way, and that institutional provisions prevent such an outcome. Procedures that guarantee decisions that protect and promote individual rights, therefore, can produce beliefs in legitimacy (Hayek 1960). The rule of law is arguably the most important of these procedures.

The redress to the rule of law is, on the nominal level, one of the few universally accepted sources of legitimacy (Tamanaha 2004). There are, however, many different definitions of the rule of law, ranging from very thin ones (often indistinguishable from rule by law) to thick ones (containing a recognition of individual rights). Beyond the most minimalist version, the grammar of all arguments about the rule of law is roughly the following (see, among others, Carothers 2006). The rule of law first of all implies "authority of law and not of people." Therefore, people in position of authority should exercise their power within a constraining framework of public norms that includes limitations on the abuse of public power for private gain. Second, the rule of law requires "legal certainty and predictability." This is the requirement that norms and rules must be clearly defined in advance and accessible to all; it also includes adjudication procedures and the specification of the consequences of norm violations. Third, this concept of the rule of law includes "legal equality"; i.e. the law must be the same for all legal subjects and must not contain arbitrary distinctions or special personal prerogatives for those in a position of social or political power (Chesterman 2008; Hurd 2011).[9]

While the rule of law is not identical to the protection of individual rights, they often go hand in hand, emphasizing the role of courts. Yet, accountability plays a different role in the legal narrative. While accountability is the key mechanism to bind most individuals "in authority" to the protection of individual rights, the accountability of legal bodies is often minimized. In this narrative, courts and judges must be freed from mechanisms of accountability in order to decide autonomously and impartially. This reflects the general idea that it is the independence and autonomy of the legal system that may have a legitimacy-generating effect. In the realm of global governance, defenders of international courts often use this narrative.

3.3.3 *Fairness Narrative*

This narrative of legitimation shifts the focus from procedures to outcomes, and aims at justifying the exercise of authority by fair outcomes. To the extent that an authority is seen as responsible for a fair distribution of resources and benefits, the likelihood of legitimacy of this authority increases.

---

[9] For a detailed discussion, see Reinold and Zürn (2014).

Fairness can be based on needs, merits, or equal distribution (see Tyler et al. 1997), and the weighing of these different understandings of fairness is a major element of any normative theory of distributive justice (Rawls 1971).

The exact determination of what is considered a fair outcome is in this narrative seldom explicated and usually far below the sophistication of most theories in political philosophy. In any case, it refers to some correction of inequality as produced by market, nature, or by accident. The fairness-based legitimation narrative is therefore usually linked to authorities that have the capacity to significantly redistribute opportunities and wealth—i.e. organizations that channel a significant amount of resources available as exemplified by the welfare state. In the global governance system such institutions hardly exist. The fairness narrative therefore is most often associated with opposition and the aim of delegitimating the international economic institutions.

3.3.4 The Technocratic Narrative

This legitimation narrative builds on non-prejudiced expertise and knowledge of the facts. Expertise is normally derived from the concept of science as an independent search for knowledge with no regard for particular interests, and based on a systematic methodology. Connected with this narrative is the hope for successful goal-oriented policies that especially promote the welfare of the community. Authorities derive their support from the quality of output (Scharpf 1991: 621–8) and its epistemic foundations. The idea is that the delegation of decisions and interpretations leads to policies that achieve shared goals most efficiently or effectively. In crisis situations, the technocratic narrative may even be transformed into a narrative of necessity. In this case, the decision-making institutions adopt a rhetoric of a state of exception which requires quick decisions which are without alternative.[10]

The technocratic legitimation is often accompanied with the idea of *ex post* "accountability"—a procedural component of this pattern of legitimation. The strategy is based on the sentiment of trust in science. The technocratic narrative is central in modernity, where it replaces more traditional accounts. As we will see, it is of special importance for the global governance system.

3.3.5 The Traditional Narrative

This narrative of legitimation builds on habituation, internalization, and references to the past. It often uses symbols to reproduce habituation and the dignity of the past, for it is still true that "the status quo has a certain aura of

---

[10] See Kreuder-Sonnen (2016) for an intriguing analysis of emergency policies by IOs.

legitimacy" (Snyder and Diesing 1977: 25). The open justification that accompanies such a narrative usually follows the conservative equation of authority and order, and is best expressed in an utterly modern formulation: never change a running system. It involves two arguments. First, something that has worked for a long time is good. Second, since the whole thing is complex, it is unlikely that single improvements can be produced without producing undesired side-effects that may undermine the system as a whole. This narrative is very much based on sentiments of loss. The ongoing relevance of religion is based on a similar reasoning. Like tradition, religion often points to internalized ethical beliefs short of moral justification.

The traditional narrative has often been used by conservative governments and established elites, as well as by religiously motivated movements against the undermining of the traditional order. As opposed to these "traditional forms" of traditional authority, tradition in the context of global governance does not refer to the traditional rights of a ruling family, but refers to the power of established norms to *"eingelebte Gewohnheit"* (routinized habits) (Weber 1968: 12). Social norms that have a long tradition enjoy a certain level of plausibility and respect just because they have been around for so long.

The power of tradition plays out in two ways. On the one hand, traditions are the best candidates for socialization and internalization (Checkel 2005). This essentially means that long-standing practices of authorities are moved out from the realm of reflexivity. On the other hand, if practices have prevailed for a long time, the appeal of the argument "that it is dangerous to change things" increases. In this sense, it seems fair to say that tradition points to a form of output legitimacy that builds on past successes, while expertise builds on the promise of future success.

Traditional and especially religious narratives may be particularly important in delegitimating international authorities. While a close nexus between religion and politics is rejected in most parts of the Western world, it has recently been revived especially in other regions. In contrast to tradition, religion as a source of legitimacy works not only silently, but it can lead to a loud and dramatic appeal against change that has already taken place but needs to be reversed in the name of a holy figure. Some of the most important international authorities are targets of such revolutionary, religiously motivated movements.

3.3.6 *Relative Gains Narrative*

This legitimation narrative strengthens the feeling of self-esteem of a collectivity through their augmentation compared to others. It builds on gains relative to others. The production and use of an imagined community (Anderson 1983) often takes place in the form of sharp border-drawing between insiders and outsiders (Walker 1992). This narrative usually points to past achievements, often personalizes the success, and emphasizes a down-to-earth mentality thus often pointing to a mass–elite divide. The guarantor of success is most often a single person or a certain party. This legitimation narrative externalizes any procedural considerations as an unnecessary brake on right and timely decisions. While in some cases expertise may play an important role, the narrative most often has an anti-intellectual tone and emphasizes collective self-esteem instead. The relative gains narrative is hard to defend in terms of normative theory.

The rise of economies in Asia fostered attempts to develop a narrative that combines the battle against poverty and the avoidance of overtly arbitrary rule with forms of authoritarianism and little societal openness. Keane (2014) calls this the "new despotism." In the Chinese version of this narrative, it is founded on real achievements, and expertise is given a proper role. In the nationalist–populist version of this narrative—as in Hungary (Orbán), Russia (Putin), and Turkey (Erdoğan)—it has a much more personalized and anti-intellectual touch. In addition to nation states, regional IOs may refer to the relative gains narrative as well. The EU, for instance, is often defended as means to prevent the decline of the European voice in world politics. To the extent that sharp border drawing mobilizes for the common good and distracts attention from a normatively dubious way of exercising authority, the use of it becomes partially manipulative.

3.3.7 Manipulative Narrative

All legitimation narratives contain some decoupling of practice from justification. All narratives idealize the practice of an authority. The notion of a manipulative narrative therefore sits uneasily as another source of authority. One may nevertheless separate a manipulative legitimation narrative aiming primarily at distracting from the purpose of the authority. To the extent that an authority serves aims that are not shared by the affected community and cannot build on impartial procedures, authority holders try systemically to manipulate constituencies by misrepresenting the facts and procedures, and creating false impressions. "Fake news" is an important element of a manipulative (de)legitimation narrative. Consumption, glamour, and leader cult also play important roles in such narratives. They usually come with the systematic manipulation of information of what authorities do, and about the circumstances in which they do it. Early critical theory (especially Marcuse 1991) pointed to such mechanisms of manipulation as part of the capitalist system. Similarly, the current talk about post-factual campaigns emphasizes manipulative aspects of legitimation. Foucault's (1982) emphasis on given knowledge orders and episteme as sources of authority points in a similar direction.

While manipulation may be successful in terms of creating legitimacy beliefs, it does not point to a social purpose, rather, it aims at hiding it. While a certain amount of hiding is common to all real-world narratives, it is especially relative gains-based and traditional narratives that are most often accompanied by manipulative efforts. It is therefore no accident that populist right-wing governments in Eastern Europe target the media before proceeding further in establishing an order that builds on a relative gains-based legitimation narrative. In extreme cases, manipulative narratives can be completely detached from the reality. If, for instance, a leader uses the threat of a coup d'état as a legitimation narrative, but there is in fact no real danger of such a coup, it is a fully manipulative narrative. Arguably, the North Korean government is closest of all political authorities to work almost exclusively with such a manipulative narrative.

To sum up, public authorities can encourage belief in their legitimacy if their practices create the appearance of supporting the common good in an impartial way. Any legitimation narrative is therefore pressed to create this impression. If it fails, it causes opposition and resistance and, in the long term, the decay of authority. Against this backdrop, it is now possible to point to two legitimation problems that are built into the global governance system. These problems are systemic, located at the level of interaction between authorities in the global governance system, and are identified from a constitutionalized perspective (see Chapter 2, section 4). These legitimation problems are derived from the difference between an observed perspective and principles of constitutionalism leading to expectations about empirical legitimation process and legitimacy beliefs.

3.4 Legitimation Problem I: Technocratic Bias

Global governance institutions cannot easily make use of all these legitimation narratives. This causes in effect a legitimation problem. To start with, manipulative narratives are hardly available for global governance institutions. To be sure, IOs—as any authority—aim at presenting the state of affairs in a way that is good for them, but the reflexive nature of inter- and transnational authority relationships runs against manipulative narratives. While there is a tendency to increase the glamour of some IOs by combining humanitarianism with global celebrities (Cooper 2008; Richey and Ponte 2013), this is a long way from being a manipulative narrative.

Second, global governance institutions are, relatively speaking, historically young. Moreover, the societies that participate in global governance institutions have often developed quite different—if not conflicting—ethical traditions. Most importantly, global authorities generally include groups that submit to different world religions (and some local religions as well). The *traditional legitimation narrative* therefore also seems to be not a good choice for public authorities in the context of global governance.

Third, a *relative gains narrative* with significant manipulative elements is also very unlikely to work for IOs. International and transnational authorities can hardly build on border drawing and communal bonds for the very reasons that they appeal mostly to a global community. The use of relative gains or manipulative legitimation narratives by global IOs is thus unlikely. However, it may be expected that regional institutions emphasize the importance of strengthening a region compared to others. There are indications that, in its current circumstances, the EU is moving somewhat toward such a narrative.

Fourth, the employment of the *fairness-based legitimation pattern* often presupposes programs and activities that involve either redistribution or capacity building on the side of the weaker actors. Inter- and transnational institutions are usually regulatory but not (re)distributive agents. Compared to nation states, which channel up to 50 percent of their gross domestic product (GDP), the material basis of global governance institutions is small. While there are some signs for an increasing role of international institutions in distributional matters—in monetary affairs and climate policy, as well as development programs—the major task of international and transnational institutions remains regulation.[11] For these reasons, fairness-based legitimation strategies are currently only of limited use for inter- and transnational authorities. At the same time, their regulations do have distributive effects, which can be used for fairness-based delegitimation strategies by critiques and challengers. The fairness-based narrative therefore is employed most often for the purpose of delegitimation of global governance arrangements.

Most importantly, inter- and transnational authorities can hardly utilize the *participatory narrative* either. Participation by all those affected by a given policy and broad public deliberations depend *de facto* on a setting with hierarchical sites of coordination between different sectoral authorities, since final decisions must be identifiable and assignable. In a national political system, hierarchical coordination takes place via formal procedures on the side of the authorities, for instance, via cabinet rules, supreme courts, or parliaments, and more informally through broad public debates within the constituency. The role of the head of government as the one who is in the position to decide if conflicts between ministries arise is a case in point. Moreover, in many constitutional states, supreme courts often decide on an appropriate valuation if

---

[11] But see the excellent studies in Genschel and Jachtenfuchs (2014), which demonstrate how the EU has entered those holy realms of the nation state. See Kuhn (2015) for a good treatment of the socio-cultural conditions for transnational solidarity in Europe.

fundamental goals conflict; for instance, between freedom and security. In Westminster systems, the parliament plays this role. Moreover, broad public debates are characterized by an exchange of opinions in which different views and positions about the society as a whole are put forward and participants from different sectors contribute (Neidhardt et al. 2004: 11).

Only if big political questions—for instance about the relative value of freedom and security, or whether a society should prioritize growth, or a clean environment—are at stake, larger segments of the population can get involved. Free elections, discursive will formation, party systems favoring those parties representing a broad range of interests, and majority decisions are the mechanisms that have made political participation of broad segments of the public possible in the territorial state. To be effective, these mechanisms depend on big issues. It is for this reason that the coherent and authentic use of the participatory legitimation narrative depends, to a significant extent, upon the presence of a body with meta-authority, i.e. the recognized capacity to resolve conflicts across spheres of authority in the hierarchical mode.[12] Since both parliaments and governments in democratic political systems consist of elected representatives, who in turn are organized in political parties, they are the most typical cases of the participatory legitimation narrative.

Beyond the nation state, the conditions for a successful participatory legitimation narrative are lacking to a large extent. Contrary to national political systems, the global governance system consists of a complex and fluid patchwork of overlapping jurisdictions. Each issue area has developed its own norms and rules, and the membership varies from issue area to issue area. The membership of the Organisation for Economic Co-operation and Development (OECD), for instance, is significantly different from that of the World Trade Organization (WTO). Debates and discourses take place almost exclusively within sectoral publics that do not address the side effects of certain measures for other issue areas. In such sectoral publics, the medium of interaction is often the Internet, specialized press, or personal exchanges or communications at conferences and meetings (Zürn and Neyer 2005: 201). Public debates about big political questions hardly take place, since meta-authorities are weak.

Against this background, the international system has informally produced some substitute institutions that sometimes seem to assume coordination in a hierarchical fashion. To begin with, immediately after the Second World War and after the end of the Cold War, the US government filled the role to

---

[12] Among others, Dryzek (2006) and Macdonald (2012) argue that normatively acceptable participation is possible in non-hierarchical settings. Indeed, deliberation and participation can work very well in sectoral settings. In order to stimulate broad participation beyond the group of people who are not immediately affected, it is however necessary to engage in political struggles about the relative value of conflicting goals.

some extent (Ikenberry 2011a). In this early moment of unipolarity, the President of the United States identified the most urgent issues, set priorities, and even assigned the tackling of the issues to specific institutions. But this period of unipolarity turned out to be limited in time. The United States is certainly still a major actor when it comes to meta-authority, and if there is one "ruler" in the global governance system, it is the US government; but the functions associated with meta-authorities are at best badly fulfilled by the United States. A second candidate for meta-authority in the global governance system is the UN Security Council (UNSC). After the complete failure of the UN General Assembly (UNGA) to take over this role, the UNSC in particular has aspired to it by deciding on all those issues in which the goal of peace and the protection of human rights seem to contradict each other. But it too often finds itself unable to act, given the veto powers assigned to the P5, and is thus unable to play this role.

In recent years, the G7/8/20 therefore seem to have defined themselves most visibly as central coordinators by giving other international institutions a sense of direction, and by taking up those pressing issues which are not sufficiently dealt with by existing international institutions and assigning the task to one of them (Zürn 2012b: 740). These attempts have, however, remained limited. Moreover, they generate resistance on the side of many other actors, because membership of these institutions is not only restricted, but also highly exclusive. The members of these institutions are self-nominated in the role as coordinators and lack authorization to act in this function.

All these three candidates playing rudimentarily the role of a coordinator between different sectors and levels—the US government, the UNSC, and the G 7/8/20—share two features. First, they are completely detached from many of the most affected societies. There are no formal and only limited informal channels available through which societal actors can make these institutions responsive to their demands. Moreover, these institutions were not created for the purpose of coordination in the first place. They are probably the most nascent elements of an emergent order. Global governance, therefore, is troubled by a strange lack of subjects: something happens, but no one has done it (Offe 2008). This prevents the use of a participatory legitimation narrative emphasizing majoritarian decision making and accountability.

On the contrary, inter- and transnational authorities often take the form of non-majoritarian institutions. Non-majoritarian institutions can be defined as governance entities "that (a) possess and exercise some grant of specialized public authority, separate from other institutions and (b) are neither directly elected by the people, nor directly managed by elected officials" (Stone Sweet and Thatcher 2002: 2). In theory, their major task is to limit and control the public powers and to implement the norms set by the legislative.[13] In this conception of democratic rule—in line with the notion of separation of powers in a constitutionalized system of rule—parliaments are the norm setters and, together with the executive, they are considered the most important majoritarian institutions that stand for the foundational component of a political system. Non-majoritarian institutions have, in this design, mainly a limitational function.

Yet in the context of global governance, these non-majoritarian institutions go beyond the limitational function. They set norms and structure the interpretation of reality; they exercise political and epistemic authority. Political authority often emphasizes accountability to member states. Yet, the participatory legitimation narrative can hardly be tapped into. Inter- and transnational institutions, central banks, and constitutional courts, as well as regulatory agencies, display primarily a technocratic and sometimes legal legitimation narrative when justifying their authority. In general, their legitimation narrative consists primarily of notions of effectiveness, wealth, superior knowledge, and sometimes the protection of human rights.

Politically assigned epistemic authorities (PAEAs) emphasize expertise even more often than international political authorities. National and international courts—the institutional expressions of legal epistemic authority—build, in addition, on the liberal pattern of legitimation; i.e. the protection of individual rights and the rule of law. In general, the legitimation of spheres of authority depends on results and their ability to adapt to new circumstances. In this respect, they point to notions of experimentalist governance (Sabel and Zeitlin 2012).

For all these reasons, the association between the global governance system as one with only loosely coupled spheres of authority and technocratic and legal legitimation narratives looks like a logical and smooth development at first sight. In this view, it is only a fully constitutionalized political system of rule that can employ participatory and fairness narratives. By contrast, limited public authorities seem to be less demanding in terms of legitimation than the constitutionalized state (see e.g. Majone 1994; Moravcsik 2006; but see Follesdal and Hix 2006). This development can be broadly summarized as shown in Figure 3.1.

A closer look reveals that the association between the global governance system and technocratic and legal narratives is not smooth. Rather, it points to a contradiction within currently dominant belief systems. On the one hand, democracy with the participatory legitimation narrative at its core is, according to available survey data, accepted worldwide as a desirable political order. In all countries covered by the World Values Survey, the majority of respondents are in favor of democracy. With only two exceptions (Colombia and

---

[13] See the contributions in Preuß (1994), especially those by Stephen Holmes and Jon Elster.

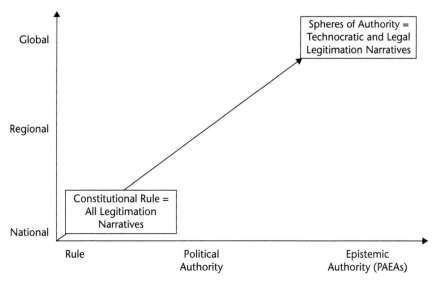

Figure 3.1. Legitimation narratives in short supply

Source: Zürn, M. (2017), "From Constitutional Rule to Loosely Coupled Spheres of Liquid Authority. A Reflexive Approach," *International Theory*, 9/2: 261–85, 279

Russia), this view is taken by more than 80 percent of the population. On the other hand, political institutions that do not draw on genuinely democratic sources of legitimation—inter- and transnational institutions, the EU, but also courts and central banks—are gaining in importance throughout the world. As a result of this development, the effective power of political institutions that justify themselves on participatory and majoritarian grounds is reduced.

This tension adds up to a paradox when we look at survey data showing for a long time a widespread support for this institutional development, especially in Western societies. While still believing that democracy is the superior normative principle, people in parliamentary democracies seemed to like epistemic authorities much more than political institutions that are inherently connected to majoritarian rule in a constitutionalized state; i.e. to parties and parliaments. In recent decades, comparative research on democracy has found a decline in political participation, evidenced in the average OECD country by a steady fall in voter turnout and a marked decrease in party membership since the 1960s (Hay 2007: 21). This is especially critical if developments are accompanied by low confidence in party politicians, the government, and the parliament. In fact, among the multitude of public institutions, political parties in the United States and the EU consistently scored worst on confidence—worse even than big business and the media. Parliaments, too, scored badly, generally ranking fourth-to-last of twelve public institutions.

Compared to parties and parliaments, constitutional courts and central banks enjoyed a very good reputation in most countries. In many Western countries, especially in Germany, the constitutional court still outscores consistently all other national political institutions. More generally, in all twenty-two countries covered by the 2008 European Social Survey, people had greater confidence in the legal system than in the parliament and parties (Norwegian Social Science Data Services 2011). The same holds for Eurobarometer data, according to which, however, the legal system was in turn considerably outscored by the police and the military.[14]

International institutions were also grounded in a remarkable degree of recognition. In the consolidated democracies of the West, the UN enjoyed greater political trust than national parties and parliaments (Hay 2007: 34). The succeeding waves of the World Values Survey Reports also showed that a majority of people in the world has confidence in the UN (Furia 2005). Throughout the world, 49.2 percent assessed the UN positively (*a great deal* or *quite a lot* of confidence); this figure falls only slightly to 48.1 percent, when respondents from EU member states are discarded. The UN had markedly lower scores only in the Middle East (Iran 38.9 percent; Iraq 13.4 percent). The figures for China (66.2 percent) and India (64 percent) were even higher than those for Europe.

This broad support of authorities that do not legitimize themselves on the basis of a participatory narrative may be labeled as "the democratic paradox": while participatory democracy requires a constitutionalized political order—in which especially the coordination of governance and the delegation of authorities is controlled by majoritarian institutions—the people who, in principle, are in favor of democracy for a long time trusted especially non-majoritarian institutions that are often beyond the reach of majoritarian institutions.

To the extent that this paradox becomes open, it creates precarious dynamics in the processes of political legitimation. As a result, the legitimation of reflexive authorities becomes reflexive as well; conflicts over which justification is appropriate for which form of political authority may arise more and more. In most of the twentieth century, the question about legitimacy was one in which the standards of democratic decision making in national political systems were relatively consented and uncontested. The legitimacy question was whether and to what extent these standards were fulfilled. Today, the very standards are contested. In such reflexive legitimation conflicts, it is not only the question "Was the decision legitimate?" that is questioned but

---

[14] The figures on confidence in various professions show a similar picture. In Britain, e.g., doctors, teachers, and scientists head the overall field, judges have a clear lead within professions that play a role in the political system in a broader sense—with 60 percent more positive than negative assessments; followed by policemen (26 percent more). Tailing the overall field are ministers, politicians, and journalists with 51 percent more negative than positive scores (Hay 2007: 35).

also the standards themselves: not only the "what" (What counts as effective basis for legitimation?) gets disputed, but also the "who" (Who decides about this?) and the "how" (How and under which conditions can we answer these questions and institutionalize the answers?) are starting to come under fire as well (Fraser 2009; Keane 2009). It is these questions which feed the rise of a new cleavage that seems to partially complement and partially replace the old cleavage between left and right (see de Wilde et al. 2018, in preparation). Open borders, authorities beyond the nation state and minority rights are challenged by populist groups that are often based on a non-pluralist understanding of the majority (Müller 2016).

Whatever the outcomes of these reflexive legitimation conflicts will be at the end of the day, transnational and international authorities have to face the problem that their legitimation narratives almost necessarily have a technocratic bias. Since participatory, fairness-based, traditional, relative gains, and manipulative legitimation narratives can hardly be used by global governance institutions, they are stuck with technocratic and to some extent legal legitimation narratives. These narratives are however—in line with the notion about reflexive legitimation conflicts—increasingly being challenged: transnational protest movements see these institutions as servants of a global (neo)liberal elite that hides its power with legal expertise and a technocratic knowledge order; right-wing populist parties within national political systems challenge lawyers and technocrats in IOs for being distanced from the people and their feelings (defined as the silent majority); political elites in rising powers criticize global governance institutions as instruments of Western domination. In other words, it is the bias toward these two legitimation narratives that is increasingly politicized and contested.

3.5 Legitimation Problem II: Biased Exercise of Authority

There is another legitimation problem inscribed into the current structures of the global governance system. A successful legitimation narrative must nurture the belief that the authority serves the social purpose and provides for the common good in an impartial way. While the loose coupling of spheres of authority circumscribes the utilizable legitimation narratives, the weak separation of powers undermines non-arbitrariness and impartiality of international institutions. It leads to a biased exercise of authority.

Although international institutions begin by giving all sovereign states a seat at the table, they simultaneously perpetuate inequalities (see Viola et al. 2015). In many international institutions, formal political equality is maintained in the rule-setting stage in that any decision about the content of rules requires the consent of all states. This formal political equality helps smaller states to increase their bargaining power, and thus can be seen as an equalizing force. Yet Randall Stone (2011) has documented how the informal influence of resource inequality can offset the apparent move toward formal political equality already at the negotiation state. Sometimes this happens by moving decisions to informal forums, such as the G-groups, where powerful states hold sway (Vabulas and Snidal 2013), but often it happens through informal processes within formal organizations. The green room negotiations of the WTO, for example, privilege a small set of powerful actors in the process of rule setting.

As long as international institutions are intergovernmental bodies based on consent, their effect on sovereign equality is ambivalent, but often positive overall. Although both procedural and substantive rules are likely to reflect power inequalities in these institutions, the legal equality expressed in the consent principle acts as an equalizing force. Insofar as international institutions exercise authority however, the consent principle is undermined and a centralization of power takes place. If this dynamic is not balanced by a strong separation of power, there are three reasons why this leads to the institutionalization of inequality.

First, the more an IO exercises authority over states and societies, the more powerful states want to see substantial policies in line with their preferences. Powerful states accept the authority of international institutions only if they can be sure that the institutions will enable them to maintain their privileged status. For this reason, they often demand privileges, such as exceptional treatment or special rights. Thus, international institutions capable of exercising authority over members, such as the UNSC, are likely to privilege powerful states regarding both the substantial content and the procedures.

The content of international rules therefore sometimes reflects the power distributions to a level that undermines basic principles of legal equality. For instance, only days after the International Criminal Court (ICC) began functioning, the United States was granted temporary special rights in the form of Resolutions 1422 and 1487 (Deitelhoff 2009), according to which American soldiers who committed crimes when deployed on UN missions could not be indicted. Corresponding exceptions were also offered in the design of the Ottawa Landmine Convention and the Kyoto Protocol. In the latter, the United States negotiated favorable conditions so that questions concerning equal treatment could justifiably be raised. If the United States, which is amongst the top producers of per capita CO_2 emissions and is also among the richest countries in the world, is allocated significantly lower emission reduction obligations than many other countries, this would appear to be an expression of differential rights sanctioned by law. Within a constitutionalized separation of power, supreme courts are likely to quash such a law as being unconstitutional. In short, as international institutions gain authority, powerful states are especially careful that they do not contradict their interests.

At the same time, the most powerful states ask for procedures that ensure their privileged role by weighted voting rights and vetoes. These institutional privileges may become so deeply entrenched over time that political inequality is very hard to change even if the underlying resource distribution has changed. On the UNSC, for example, France retains its veto position even though it has been surpassed as a great power by other states. While the UNSC would never be constituted the same way today, the difficulty of agreeing on a new membership, the interests of existing permanent members in not opening up the membership question, and the possibility that trying to change things might disrupt the existing arrangement have been sufficient reasons to preserve the prevailing arrangement. Given that any attempt to abolish the special position of the veto powers can be thwarted by this very same veto, we have institutionalized inequality. The World Bank and the International Monetary Fund (IMF) provide additional examples of the institutionalization of political inequality. In a system with an established separation of power, there would be pre-defined mechanisms to change such a degree of asymmetric influence on decision making.

Second, the more an IO exercises authority over states and societies, the more it depends on the resources of its most powerful members. While this is a general mechanism, it is especially relevant when it comes to the authority to enforce decisions. This can again be best illustrated with reference to the UNSC. When a UNSC resolution authorizes an intervention in order to maintain international peace, the material resources—financial and military—allocated to the problem is enormous. The IOs do not have these resources at their disposal, but depend in this respect on the most powerful member states.

This dependence of international authorities on national resources leads, in the absence of a separation of power, to the lack of an independent administration. As a result, the implementation of decisions and interpretations by inter- and transnational authorities will tend to be selective and biased in at least two ways: it depends on the willingness of powerful states to act, and it will exhibit a bias against enforcing laws on powerful states and their allies. The UN, for example, continues to depend on the willingness of individual states—such as the United States and its allies—to implement peace enforcement operations decided on by the UNSC. Because powerful states are only interested in intervening in conflicts in exceptional cases, the UN itself can only selectively enforce its laws (Zangl and Zürn 2003). The UN was not in a position to militarily intervene, for example, in the civil war situations in Myanmar, Sudan, Angola, or Liberia, as no powerful state was willing to send its armed forces on a military mission authorized by the UN.[15] Thus, the most powerful states, and above all the United States, effectively decide when fun-

---

[15] See Binder (2009, 2017) for an account of factors driving the selectivity of interventions.

damental norm violations are sanctioned and when they are not, and the UN's peace enforcement remains necessarily selective. It also means that an intervention of the international community in countries like China or the United States is excluded by definition. The rules therefore cannot be applied to significant parts of the world by the international authority in a consistent way. Without sufficient independent capacity to implement and enforce the decisions and interpretations, the impartial exercise of authority is impossible. Again, in the absence of an effective separation of power, the rise of inter- and transnational authority leads to the institutionalization of inequality.

Third, the more an IO exercises authority directly over society, the more the "one-state, one-vote" principle loses normative dignity. This is reflected in the changing ways in which institutions legitimate their authority. Given the double constituency of global governance, there is an increasing need to create a direct link between the international institutions that exercise authority and the societal targets of regulations. In view of the dramatic differences in the size of states—ranging from a few thousand inhabitants in countries such as Liechtenstein to over 1.3 billion in the case of China—the sovereign equality of states does not provide a normatively compelling principle for the representation of societal interests (Luban 2004), especially when international institutions exercise authority directly. The exercise of direct authority strengthens the claim that states with large populations should have more influence than those with smaller populations. In this sense, the delegation of authority to institutions might amplify the political inequality between states for normative reasons. The institutionalization of inequality between states of different sizes however leads only then to normatively acceptable results, if it is accompanied by an effective separation of power.

In sum, the more the consent principle is replaced with international authority, the more political inequality between states becomes institutionalized. Since the separation of powers in global governance is weak at best, serious legitimation problems might arise. The implementation of norms may become selective, the rules themselves sometimes violate legal equality between states, and the executive practice undermines the appearance of impartiality. As far as the idea that "like cases should be treated alike" is the most significant source of legitimacy, the undermining of impartiality poses the most serious legitimation problem.

As Andrew Hurrell (2007: 281) writes: "The problem of unbalanced power is not that unchecked power will lead inevitably to tanks rolling across borders. It is rather that radically unbalanced power will... undermine the procedural rules on which stable and sustained cooperation must inevitably depend." The rise of international authority undermines both sides of the sovereign equality formula: states do not always have final authority, as they are embedded in a global governance system in which they are not equal.

Overall, this chapter's claim is that the authority–legitimation link takes effect in the context of global governance to the extent that international institutions exercise authority. It is the rise of authority that makes legitimation necessary. And it is, in turn, the impartial conduct in the provision of common goods that is likely to make the exercise of authority legitimate. It takes authentic legitimation narratives to nurture this belief in legitimacy. However, a global governance system with only loosely coupled spheres of authority limits the legitimation potential that can be tapped by inter- and transnational authorities. Inter- and transnational authorities are more or less left with legitimation narratives that create a technocratic bias. Even more problematically, the necessary component of all successful legitimation—impartiality—is violated due to institutionalized inequality in a context of weak separation of powers. Therefore, the global governance system has both structural and severe legitimation problems.

4

The Theoretical Model

Causal Mechanisms and Hypotheses

The global governance system contains a set of normative principles that make sovereignty conditional, as well as pockets of reflexive authority beyond the nation state. The technocratic bias in the legitimation narratives and the power bias in the exercise of authority, however, hamper the ability of global governance institutions to nurture the belief in their legitimacy. As a consequence, the exercise of authority all too easily overburdens the legitimacy potentials of inter- and transnational institutions.

At the core of the theory of global governance is thus the authority–legitimation link (ALL), which states that international institutions exercising authority need to nurture the belief in their legitimacy. The authority–legitimation link points to fundamental challenges for the global governance system: with the rise of international authorities that are, at the same time, more intrusive, state consent is undermined and societies are effected directly. Consequently, legitimation problems arise, followed by processes of delegitimation, which then trigger responses by the challenged institutions. The final outcome of these processes can be deepening or fragmentation and decline. *Deepening* refers to institutional changes that target the deficits of the global governance system. It is different from symbolic adjustments in that it leads to a significant change of institutional practice. *Decline*, on the other hand, points to a decrease in the level of international authority. *Fragmentation*, finally, is the outcome if alternative institutions are set up, creating a competition between different international authorities, and the coordination of interface conflicts between these institutions fails. In the long term, fragmentation most often leads to decline.

Accordingly, the theory of global governance consists of a set of specific relationships among (1) the level and type of authority, (2) the legitimation

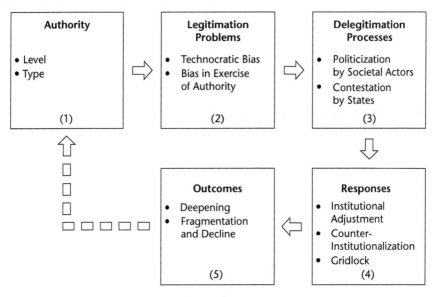

Figure 4.1. The model

problems arising from the deficits of the global governance system, (3) the delegitimation processes triggered by these deficits, (4) the responses to these challenges, and (5) the outcomes of this process. These outcomes affect in a feedback loop the level and type of authority relationships and the legitimation problem (see Figure 4.1).

In developing such behavioral expectations, the central features of the global governance system—as developed in Chapters 1 to 3—are combined with concepts of historical institutionalism. For this purpose, I first briefly introduce some standard historical-institutionalist concepts. In a second step, the notion of reactive sequences is discussed in more detail by distinguishing it from other path-dependent processes. Against this backdrop, it is argued that the authority–legitimation link produces reactive sequences either via the route of societal politicization or via counter-institutionalization by states. These reactive sequences may result in either a decline or a deepening of global governance depending on the responses of authority holders.

4.1 Historical Institutionalism

Historical institutionalism, in general, is an approach to studying the development of political institutions that differs in some respects from rational and sociological institutionalism (see Hall and Taylor 1996). It assumes that all actions take place in institutional environments, and that these environments structure opportunities and, at times, beliefs and desires of actors. Any given institution thus affects future choices, and, in turn, choices affect institutions. In this perspective, which assumes an ongoing interplay between institutions and their environment (cf. Steinmo et al. 1992; Carlsnaes 1992), the sequence and timing of events as well as path dependencies are decisive elements of any explanation (Pierson 1994; Mahoney and Thelen 2010; Thelen 1999).[1] Historical institutionalism offers pertinent concepts such as critical junctures, different types of path dependence, and external shocks for conceptualizing these institutional dynamics in International Relations (IR).[2]

During a *critical juncture*, structural constraints lose importance and "there is a substantially heightened probability that agents' choices will affect the outcome of interest" (Capoccia and Kelemen 2007: 348). According to Soifer (2012), it is the joint presence of permissive conditions (weakened structures) and productive conditions (an agent with purpose and resources) that leads to a critical juncture. If only permissive conditions are in place, we can talk about a missed opportunity; if only productive conditions are in place, we usually talk about visions that have failed in the face of reality. Critical junctures are essentially moments of agency that often serve as starting points or watersheds for an historical-institutionalist story. They are often brought about by developments that are outside of historical-institutionalist reasoning. In this sense, the emergence of critical junctures remains external or contingent to the theory. Yet after certain paths are taken in a critical juncture, these decisions produce their own endogenous dynamics. In Max Weber's metaphor, historical decisions set the trains of history down different tracks; in the language of modern social science, critical junctures connect two punctuated equilibria (Krasner 1988; see also Jupille et al. 2013).

The post-Second World War constellation provides the first critical juncture for the rise of global governance. It was a critical juncture in which at least two options were available to central decision makers: to restore the international balance of power system that had led to two world wars in the twentieth century, or to create a set of effective international institutions that manage economic interdependence and establish collective security. After the fresh historical experience of a complete disaster, the loosening of permissive conditions allowed for the famous window of opportunity and for institutional choice. At the same time, the United States gave up its isolationist principles and took global leadership, thus providing the productive conditions.

---

[1] Classic works in comparative political economy have always emphasized the role of sequences (see especially Gerschenkron 1962; Moore 1966).

[2] For important contributions on the use of historical institutionalism in IR, see Büthe and Mattli (2011); Fioretos (2011, 2017); Hanrieder (2015); Jupille et al. (2013); Rixen et al. (2016).

A second critical juncture came up when the Soviet Union faltered. The blockade between East and West regarding all really global institutions was suddenly gone and it opened new opportunities and permissive conditions. Especially in the first years after the fall of the Berlin Wall, the US government used the opportunity to make crucial decisions for a new, more institutionalized order. On the basis of these decisions and the apparent willingness of Russia to join in, a system of global governance was brought about.

The core concept of historical institutionalism is *path dependence*. Critical junctures may lead to institutional decisions that turn out to be path dependent. While there are different understandings of path dependence, the notion of self-reinforcement—i.e. mechanisms which change opportunities, beliefs, and desires of involved actors in favor of an existing practice—is certainly the prime example of path dependence (David 1985; Arthur 1994; Pierson 2004). Self-reinforcement stands for institutional change in the direction of deepening of an institution, which should not be conflated with stasis (Rixen and Viola 2016: 18). In cases of self-reinforcement, it becomes more and more costly to change the institutional design. It thus provides an explanation for stability that is absent in most IR theories (see Büthe 2002). Self-reinforcement can explain why dysfunctional decisions taken at a critical juncture can stay in place. QWERTY—the inefficient (as we know today) keyboard system that developed with the first typewriters—is the most famous example.

The post-war institutions generated self-reinforcing dynamics, especially the Bretton Woods regimes in the Western world. These institutions—to a large extent as an unintended consequence—changed the power constellation in international economy as well as within the societies in developed capitalist economies in favor of liberal forces. As a result, the liberal international institutions deepened and proved resilient to, for instance, the oil crisis in the 1970s.

All institutions—as self-reinforcing and locked-in as they may be—are occasionally confronted with *external shocks*. External shocks are drastic changes in the environment that challenge the institutional status quo (shock) and were not (co-)produced by the institutions under question (external). Such an externally induced shock again creates opportunities and room for agency: it may cause a new critical juncture.

The end of the East–West confrontation constituted such an external shock for the post-Second World War system that allowed for the rise of the global governance system. The majority of the maldevelopments in the Soviet Union and other so-called "socialist states" were produced internally, quite independently of international institutions. The rise of new (communication) technologies and globalization then put additional pressure on the socialist world that it could not withstand. The attempt by Mikhail Gorbachev to reform socialism and adapt to a new world failed. The socialist camp faltered.

4.2 Reactive Sequences

Path dependence is often defined as "a dynamical process whose evolution is governed by its own history" (see David 2007: 92).[3] Given that institutional properties always—at least marginally—mediate the way in which institutions adapt to external challenges, this broad usage makes path dependence practically a synonym of institutional development. Where institutions merely respond to external challenges that have not been caused by the institutions themselves, the term institutional adaptation seems more appropriate than the concept of path dependence. In these cases, institutional factors intervene between the exogenous trigger and the institutional outcome.[4]

In contrast, path dependence—in a more narrow sense—implies that institutions endogenously generate their own external feedback, which reinforces or undermines their reproduction (Greif and Laitin 2004). Most research on path-dependent institutional change in political science has centered on mechanisms of self-reinforcement. In comparative politics, the historical-institutionalist approach has focused on mechanisms through which policies reshape social and state actors' interests and capacities over long periods of time in ways that stabilize and deepen existing institutions (Pierson 1994). In IR, set-up effects, network effects, and cognitive effects can be identified as the three most important types of mechanisms via which institutions may produce self-reinforcement (see Chapter 5).

The current legitimation problems of the global governance system, however, point to something else: self-undermining processes. These are processes that are (co-)produced by the institution(s) under question that threaten to undermine the conditions necessary to maintain the very same institution. This type of path dependence is hardly developed and elaborated in historical institutionalism in general (but see Jacobs and Weaver 2015) or in theories of international institutions specifically.

As a basic heuristic, the idea of institutional change through reactive sequences, however, is very well-established in the social sciences in general. It underlies famous arguments about structural crises where a social system has been produced by conditions which are "eaten up" over time by this very social system. Marxist theories of imperialism, the Weberian theory of

---

[3] This section draws from Hanrieder and Zürn (2017).

[4] The works of Kathleen Thelen and her co-authors (Streeck and Thelen 2005; Mahoney and Thelen 2010) have been especially seminal in conceptualizing those more fine-grained forms of change. Layering entails the introduction of new rules on top of or alongside existing ones; drift, the changed impact of existing rules due to shifts in the environment; and conversion, the changed enactment of existing rules due to their strategic redeployment; see Mahoney and Thelen (2010: 15–16). In this way, change is conceptualized in a more sophisticated way than in other theories, and thus does not fall "into the trap of an either/or fallacy" (Moschella and Vetterlein 2016).

the economic success of Protestantism, the neoconservative analysis of demand inflation, and plenty of other crisis theories build on this explanatory pattern (Elster 1985). This general logic of reactive sequences is well-suited to study legitimation problems of inter- and transnational authorities.

Reactive sequences can be defined as mechanisms that contain a change in opportunities, beliefs, or desires, eroding support for the institution. Reactive sequences thus consist of processes that are at least partially produced by the institution under question, and that threaten to undermine the conditions necessary to maintain an institution. The institution thus endogenously produces challenges and challengers.[5]

Dynamics of negative feedback to international institutions have probably attracted most attention in the domain of global trade liberalization. Aside from mobilizing winning coalitions—mostly export-oriented industries—global trade institutions such as the General Agreement on Tariffs and Trade (GATT) have generated negative backlash among the losers of liberalization leading to state contestation (Goldstein and Martin 2000; see also Goldstein and Gulotty 2017). They have also been challenged in worldwide anti-globalization protests by civil society groups, where the authority of international organizations (IOs) such as the World Trade Organization (WTO) was broadly contested by societal actors. In general, the increased resistance against "neoliberal institutions"—and its politicization—can be seen as a result of such an undermining reactive sequence (see Zürn et al. 2007: 139).

Nevertheless, reactive sequences need not end up with the decline of an institution. To the extent that the institution in question responds adequately to a challenge, the final outcome of a reactive sequence can be—at the end of the day—a deepening of the institution in question. While the defining feature of a reactive sequence is an immediate negative response triggered by existing institutional features and practices, the final outcomes depend upon actor choices and can lead to either a decline or a deepening of the institution in question.

One can point here to the economic history of the United States as an illustration. The economic and political crisis after Black Tuesday in 1929 was certainly co-produced by the institutional design of the interface between the political and economic systems. Capitalism contained self-undermining dynamics that were not managed sufficiently by the political system. The resulting crisis led to the election of Franklin D. Roosevelt as president, whose administration used the existing room to maneuver to establish a New Deal. As a result, the legitimacy and support of the US political and economic system

---

[5] This is different from Mahoney (2000), for whom self-undermining processes are only one subtype of reactive sequences. He uses the term to extend historical institutionalism from self-reinforcing mechanisms to any kind of mechanism producing change endogenously.

Table 4.1. Types of institutional development (based on Hanrieder and Zürn 2017: 106)

	Self-reinforcement	Reactive sequences	Institutional adaptation
Path dependence criterion: Is the demand for change (co-) produced by the institution in question?	Yes	Yes	No
Status quo bias: Is the process of change mediated by the existing institution?	Yes	Yes	Yes
What is the immediate outcome?	• Stabilization (positive feedback)	• De-stabilization (negative feedback)	• Outcome is closer to the status quo than it would be without the institution
Via which causal mechanisms?	• Set-up effects • Network effects • Cognitive effects	• State contestation • Societal Contestation	• Reinterpretation of institutional forms • Accumulation of institutional forms
Which mid-term outcome?	• Deepening	• Fragmentation and decline • Deepening	• Institutional change

reached new heights. A reactive sequence of this sort contains, in the first place, a self-undermining dynamic, yet it is a viable possibility to resolve the subsequent crisis.[6]

Table 4.1 summarizes the types of institutional development indicating the emphasis on path-dependent processes that are—as opposed to mechanisms of institutional adaptation—endogenously produced. Within the group of path-dependent processes, self-reinforcement dynamics are furthermore distinguished from reactive sequences by the immediate outcome, which is stabilization of the institution in the former case and destabilization of the institution in the latter.

4.3 The Authority–Legitimation Link

With the elaborations about the features of the global governance system and the concept of reactive sequences, the building blocks of the theory of global governance are now complete. The features and institutional shortcomings of the global governance system that emerged in the 1990s trigger two types of reactive sequences: contestation by societal actors mainly in the form of politicization and contestation by state actors mainly in the form of

---

[6] To the contrary, self-reinforcing processes do not push for an immediate response or choice. For this reason, self-undermining processes plus a response are called reactive sequences.

counter-institutionalization. Both are an expression of the legitimation problems of the global governance system.

4.3.1 *State Contestation*

State contestation in global governance points to the distributional consequences of international institutions and to the fact that they are power-laden. Against this backdrop, two sequences can be distinguished dependent on the institutional design:

Institutionalized inequality: International institutions are created and shaped by powerful actors with a certain social purpose that also pre-determines distributional questions. In addition, they often stratify chances for influence through the allocation of governance positions such as voting rights or seats in governing bodies. Moreover, the dependence on state resources in the implementation of these decisions again favors powerful states. In other words, international authorities often—but not always—institutionalize inequality (see Chapter 3). If the powerful founders (established powers or incumbent states) have institutionalized inequality from the beginning, and if there is no separation of powers to control this inequality, a shift in the underlying power constellation leads to contestation from the rising powers.

The shift in the power distribution can be produced endogenously. To the extent that the powerful states shaped and used the institution benevolently (instead of exploitatively), it may lead to outcomes from which also the weaker states benefit. Over time, then, the relative power distribution can change even in favor of the weaker members. The increased power base of weaker states may lead, as the next step, to demands for changes in the substantial and procedural rules. These states then challenge institutionalized inequality and ask for change. The contestation of voting rights in the International Monetary Fund (IMF), membership rules in G7/G8, or the failure of nuclear disarmament in the context of the Non-Proliferation Treaty are cases in point.

The authority holders may respond to these delegitimation practices by either incorporating the new actors and their demands or by ignoring and resisting them. If the demands are not met, the weaker but rising states may use their increased power base against the existing institutions, produce gridlocks, and aim at the establishment of alternative institutions. The latter practice may be labelled counter-multilateralism or counter-institutionalization (see also Morse and Keohane 2014). Counter-institutionalization describes situations and strategies in and through which international institutions are challenged via the use of other international institutions. These interactions between delegitimation practices and responses can lead either to a decline or a deepening of global governance.

Sovereign equality: In the cases where powerful actors have not used their dominance to institutionalize inequality, transformative dynamics may result from the clash between internal institutional power and power within a given sphere of authority. This mechanism seems most often to be taking place when those states, having determined the rules of an institution in the first place, do not control its procedures.

Powerful states often give smaller ones a voice for accepting the institutionalization of their rules. If interests or circumstances change, these powerful actors can no longer change the institutional features so easily. The weaker actors (such as developing states) then often use and protect their institutional privileges against demands for change from the more powerful states. This pathway leads to a constellation where the initial key supporters of an institution face an entrenched status quo coalition, and thus can no longer project their power in the given issue area within the institution. These key players are often the most powerful states that shaped an institution in the beginning, but lost control over time because of institutional rules that, relatively speaking, empower weaker states.

The powerful states thus begin to delegitimate the existing institution with the goal of redistributing institutional power. These states often have the capacities and opportunities to opt for competing institutions more easily than other actors in the international system or most of the actors in a domestic setting. The absence of meta-authorities in the global governance system thus allows powerful, but dissatisfied actors to shop between existing institutions or to create new ones that better match their interests (Alter and Meunier 2009; Morse and Keohane 2014; Raustiala and Victor 2004). Counter-institutionalization by powerful states is a frequent strategy in this constellation when the majority of the weaker states resist institutional adaption. This pathway is common in many United Nations (UN) organizations, where the "one-state, one-vote" principle facilitates decisions and interpretations that the major donors and contributors disagree with. Hence, otherwise powerful members such as the United States or states from the European Union (EU) face a coalition of institutional winners—materially weak but formally empowered, ensuring that the institution is not easily adaptable to great power demands. Where the powerful states cannot circumvent these structures through informal means (Kleine 2013; Prantl 2005; Stone 2011), they may react by withholding support. Even if they do not altogether give up their membership,[7] the incumbents can delay, reduce, or freeze their budgetary contributions while simultaneously increasing their support for other institutions. They turn to inter- and transnational institutions that assume

---

[7] Full-fledged exits are rare in international institutions but it happened, e.g., when the United States and the United Kingdom withdrew from UNESCO in the 1980s.

partially complementary but also conflicting governance tasks, and thereby decrease the relevance of the original institution. In other words, they engage in counter-institutionalization. A more competitive institutional environment and thus a weakened position of the original institution will often be the by-product of such developments. Hence, it is likely to lead to a fragmentation or a decline of global governance.

Yet counter-institutionalization is not necessarily the endpoint of an institution's power mismatch trajectory. Growing competition from the outside will put pressure upon the original institution, which now has to "adjust" to a more competitive environment. Even though it may not fully adopt the policy and organizational models that competitors are practicing, the original institution may add some new elements as a reaction. This is why the outcome of state contestation is rarely all-out institutional change or an institution's death, but often a growing complexity through "layering"—i.e. the adding of new organizational elements onto a rigid but increasingly irrelevant historical core (see Streeck and Thelen 2005).

Both mechanisms of state contestation are of great relevance to the development of the global governance system. They play out differently, depending on the degree to which inequality is institutionalized. On the one hand, the outcome of the sequence in which new powers arise and challenge the institutionalized privileges of incumbent states depends on the availability of institutional alternatives for rising powers and the functional necessity to include rising powers in the first place. When incumbents, on the other hand, feel inhibited by the formal rules that place them in minority, the possibility of alternative institutions is most often easily available. Whether this form of state contestation ends in institutional adjustment or in decline seems, therefore, to depend upon authority holders: whether they adapt informal rules so that the dominant powers can get through their programs to some extent even if they are—formally speaking—in the minority.

4.3.2 Societal Contestation

Reactive sequences also involve non-state actors. In order to achieve a sufficient level of societal legitimacy, authority holders and defenders need to intensify their legitimation efforts toward their non-state constituencies to the extent that their intrusiveness escalates. At the same time, a growing intrusiveness will increase the activities of societal actors toward the authority. This mechanism plays out most often as societal politicization. If international institutions exercise intrusive authority over states and societies, the growing demand for legitimation leads to politicization that can, in turn, produce distinct reactions by authority holders.

On the one hand, core decision makers in IOs can respond to politicization by going on as usual and adhering to their legitimation narrative. In this case, authority holders dare to be the ongoing target of transnational protests and are in danger of losing legitimacy. One may call this "business as usual strategy." The UN Security Council (UNSC) up to now is one example.

Similarly, authority holders can also change their institutional practices and legitimation narrative symbolically. In this case, authority holders respond to delegitimation with attempts at re-legitimation. Many of the economic international institutions that were the target of protests against neoliberalism and the hidden rule of multinational companies responded, for instance, by increasing transparency (Woods and Narlikar 2001). In general, the increased access of transnational actors to IOs can partially be read as a strategy of IOs to increase legitimacy (Tallberg et al. 2013). However, the success of these symbolic re-legitimation strategies has been quite limited and it usually leads to decay. The outcome of this status quo-oriented response is usually fragmentation or decline. The Doha Round of the WTO is a case in point. Due to growing domestic and transnational resistance, the negotiators are stuck in gridlock, and international trade policy has fragmented into regional trade and investment agreements.

Alternatively, authority holders may also engage in more substantial revisions in order to respond to politicization and delegitimation. Analysts have interpreted some World Bank reforms—for instance, the Extractive Industries Review Process (Weidner 2013)—as substantial response to politicization. In a similar vein, some of the institutional responses to allegations about human rights violations by international authorities can be interpreted as substantial adaptation (see Chapter 8). In these cases, substantial reforms tackling the deficiencies of the global governance system take effect, leading to a deepening of the global governance system.

In sum, contestation may lead to a deepening of global governance; in other cases, when institutional adjustment is symbolic at best, they spur institutional fragmentation and decline.

4.3.3 *Four Causal Mechanisms*

The theory of global governance is based on a meta-theoretical position that can be labeled "scientific realism" (see Introduction). Given that unobservables are considered as real forces in the world, this background not only justifies extensive conceptual discussions, but it also leads to a research strategy that complements a variable-based form of causal reasoning with one that focuses on causal mechanisms and pathways. Mechanisms and pathways include a broad set of conceivable causes such as reasons, norms, and discourses.

When social scientists in the positivist tradition use the term "explanation," they usually think about "independent variables" causing "dependent variables." In this book, another—and more encompassing—form of causal reasoning based on causal mechanisms is utilized. Causal mechanisms refer to regular processes that link an initial condition with an outcome via a number of steps in between. Methodological individualists are mainly interested in mirco-mechanisms involving individuals that causally connect two related macro-outcomes, according to the logic of Coleman's bathtub or boat (see Coleman 1990). Others use the concept to refer more generally to recurrent processes that comprise a thick sequence or chain of events, thus reducing the distance between an independent and a dependent variable so that each step becomes intuitively compelling (e.g. Bennett and Checkel 2015; Mahoney 2012). In this view, "x initiates the sequence a, b, c, which yields y" (see Pierson 2004: 87).

"Causal mechanisms" as used here combines the two understandings. My understanding of causal mechanisms includes both a sequences of events (composite mechanisms) that puts relationships between social facts in a broader social context and micro-processes that link two macro-phenomena (linking mechanisms). *Composite mechanisms* refer to recurrent processes that comprise a thick sequence or a chain of events, thus reducing the distance between independent and dependent variables. By carving out a sequence instead of a bivariate relationship between variables, the explanation is contextualized and localized. *Linking mechanisms* refer to micro-processes via which two chain links are connected. In the social world, most of these linking mechanisms refer to social choices based on desires, beliefs, and opportunities.

Given the complexity and dynamism of the global governance system, grasping different versions of reactive sequences through which global governance evolves is both important and challenging. In this vein, two avenues are suggested in the form of a reactive sequence: state contestation or societal contestation. Each of these reactive sequences can lead to either the decline or the deepening of global governance. In combining delegitimation practices and outcomes, it is now possible to single out four causal mechanisms that consist of different sequences (see Table 4.2).

Table 4.2. Four causal mechanisms

Delegitimation \ Outcome	Decline	Deepening
Societal Contestation	1	2
State Contestation	3	4

The four causal mechanisms that are decisive for the theory of global governance are elaborated on in more detail in Part II of this text. All of them are specifications of the ALL. The first causal mechanism derived from it states that a rise of international authority leads to the rise of politicization if political opportunity structures are existent. The rise of politicization often involves a broadening of legitimation narratives. Whether this temporary change in legitimation narratives leads in the end to the decline or deepening of global governance depends on whether the adjustment is substantial or symbolic. Most often it is symbolic. *Undermining via Politicization* (CMALL 1) thus points to the following sequence: CMALL 1 = rise of authority + political opportunity structures → societal contestation → temporary broadening of legitimation narratives → decline. The causal mechanism Undermining via Politicization will be discussed in Chapter 6. Note that each of the four phenomena on the interactive level is connected via social choices. The major method used in this chapter is semi-automated content analysis, which is a form of quantitative tracing of causal mechanisms.

In Chapter 8, we will look at cases in which disapproval by societal challengers of international authority has led to a deepening of global governance—CMALL 2. In these cases of *Reinforcement via Politicization*, the rise of authority includes direct authority over individuals that may lead again to societal disapproval and politicization. If the challengers can form a strong coalition, authority holders respond by substantial institutional reforms (CMALL 2 = rise of authority + capacity to violate individual rights → societal contestation → coalition → deepening). Later in the same chapter, the scope conditions of successful politicization will be studied. The method used is comparative process tracing in ten cases. It amounts to a method that will be called "comparative qualitative process tracing" (see Zürn and Heupel 2017).

The other two causal mechanisms are triggered by mismatches between procedural rules of international institutions and power distribution between states. It can also come in two versions. International institutions with institutionalized inequality will produce contestation by disadvantaged states if their power rises in the shadow of these institutions. In this case, the incumbents may either respond by rule adaptation or the rising powers counter-institutionalize. In most cases, some form of adaptation can be observed. We can label this mechanism *Counter-Institutionalization by Rising Powers* (CMALL 3 = authority + institutionalized inequality → change in power constellation → demands to institutional reforms and threats to counter-institutionalize by rising powers → institutional reform and deepening).

International authority with a "one-state, one-vote" rule can lead to state contestation if powerful states experience a loss of control. This type of state contestation often leads to fragmentation and decline. It can be labeled *Counter-Institutionalization by Incumbents* (CMALL 4 = authority + "one-state, one-vote" → institutional power mismatch → counter-institutionalization by incumbents → fragmentation and/or decline). These two mechanisms are explored in Chapter 7. The major method used there is the qualitative case study that allows for a structured and focused comparison (George and Bennett 2005: ch. 3).

4.3.4 And Six Propositions

Causal mechanisms consist of a sequence of events that are connected in the form of a chain. Each of the connections points to social choices in between and therefore to probabilistic relationships. Testing causal mechanisms therefore can be especially hard. If the *causal mechanisms* consist of four components and three links—as is the case in the four CMALLs—the correlation between the trigger and outcome gets lost in transmission. Even if each of the single links has 80 percent likelihood, the overall likelihood that a specified trigger produces a certain outcome falls to 50 percent ($0.8^3 = 0.512$). Yet this formulation makes clear that we should not build up an artificially strict separation between variable research and *causal mechanism* research. It is possible to derive propositions from the theory of global governance looking at specific relationships among (1) the level and type of authority, (2) the legitimation problems arising from the rise of international authority, (3) the delegitimation practices triggered by these legitimation problems, (4) the institutional responses to these challenges, and (5) the outcomes as well as their effect on the authority pattern in the global governance system. It is therefore possible to formulate a set of hypotheses, which will be elaborated on indirectly in subsequent chapters. They seek to explain why the conflicts about global governance grow, why the institutional deficits of the global governance system may endogenously undermine global governance, and under which scope conditions a decline or a deepening is likely:

(1) A high degree of authority can be expected to lead to politicization.

(2) Especially when the level of political authority rises, it is to be expected that the technocratic legitimation narrative is challenged. It is then considered as insufficient legitimation that hides interests and ideology.

(3) International institutions that have institutionalized inequality will be challenged especially by those states that have increased their power base and ask for equal (state) participation via counter-institutionalization.

(4) The success of counter-institutionalization by rising powers depends on outside options for challengers.

(5) Incumbent states that do not control the procedures of a given institution will attempt to counter-institutionalize.

(6) The deepening of global governance is likely when the authority holders are vulnerable and if the authority challengers have strong coalition partners.

The theoretical framework developed in the previous chapters entails more than just six hypotheses. However, the listed hypotheses will be explored in the remainder of the book, as they constitute the core of a theory of global governance. The theory holds that most of the backlashes to global governance in the last decade can be explained by endogenous dynamics of the global governance system. It is wrong to equate growing tensions and conflicts with support for a realist theory and the rise of smooth and silent management of interdependence as support for a global governance perspective. On the contrary, the institutional deficits of the global governance system that emerged in the 1990s have produced tensions, contestation, and resistance. Nevertheless, all these contestations take place in a given institutional framework and are embedded in a set of normative principles.

Part II
The Contestation of Global Governance

Part I has set forth a theory of global governance. It is based on the notion of a global governance system consisting of normative principles, authority patterns, and legitimation struggles. It utilizes the authority–legitimation link (ALL) and the notion of reactive sequences in order to come up with testable propositions, mainly in the form of four composite causal mechanisms. In Part II of the book, these four causal mechanisms will be explored with different empirical strategies. I will distinguish between contestation by societal actors that may lead to a decline (Chapter 6) or deepening (Chapter 8) of global governance and contestation by state actors that can lead to either decline or deepening as well (Chapter 7). Each of the chapters uses different methods to bolster the propositions. Chapter 6, among other things, utilizes semi-automated content analysis. The method of structured, focused comparison is used in Chapter 7. Chapter 8 builds on the strategy of comparative process tracing.

Substantially, the following claims are proposed: The rise of political and epistemic authority beyond the nation state increases the likelihood of its politicization. Growing resistance can be expected against international institutions to the extent that international institutions exercise authority in a way that overburdens the existing stocks of legitimacy. The legitimacy of international authorities thus becomes contested, leading to struggles of legitimation and delegitimation. These struggles can lead to either a decline or a deepening of global governance arrangements. It depends on the capacity of authority holders to adapt substantially to the new demands and on the capacity of authority challengers to build coalitions questioning the status quo.

Before examining some conjectures of the theory, Chapter 5 provides a sketch of the rise of the global governance system. On the basis of data drawn from the International Authority Database (IAD), it can be shown that there are two decisive historical moments. The first critical juncture takes place around 1949, when the postwar institutions were created that then allowed for the deepening of cooperation between states. The second critical juncture occurred in the early 1990s. It is only after the breakdown of the Soviet Union that a new, extremely steep, and still ongoing rise of international authority can be observed. This second surge indicates the rise of the global governance system.

5

The Rise of the Global Governance System: A Historical-Institutionalist Account

When International Relations (IR) scholars want to understand change, they most often focus on what Robert Gilpin (1981) labeled routine "changes within a given system" or systemic changes, i.e. changes in institutional arrangements. On the contrary, a system change is something more fundamental; it points to a change in the constitutive actors and principles. In the 1990s at the latest, there was such a shift from a more or less cooperative system of states based on Westphalian sovereignty and intergovernmentalism to a global governance system. The global governance system is different in the sense that it has a double constituency: Both states and societal actors have rights and obligations. Moreover, it consists of normative principles and institutionalized authority patterns, as well as legitimation narratives, and is embedded in world society. How can we explain this shift to a global governance system? What has driven this development?

The current chapter aims at explaining how the system emerged. It does so by providing a thick description of these developments. It is not a rigid test of such an account. It does therefore dispense with the comparison to alternative explanations or accounts based on power shifts in class relations and economic interests, ideational changes, or the distribution of power among states. To the extent possible, it rather incorporates these perspectives. Prior to that, data about the development of international authority will be provided, showing that the later 1940s and the early 1990s were the decisive points in time for the rise of the global governance system.

5.1 Empirical Patterns of International Authority

What does the pattern of international authorities look like? Is reflexive authority really on the rise in the global governance system? The goal here is to show that a rise in international public authority can be observed over time, accelerating especially in the 1990s. For this purpose, the highly aggregated data of the International Authority Database (IAD) will be used. This database captures the degree of authority exercised by IOs according to their institutional design. This operationalization is chosen since any authority relationship usually includes an element of perpetuation. Institutionalization, in turn, is the most important form of perpetuation in world politics.

This brings us in the midst of a rich literature that has focused on the independence (e.g. Abbott and Snidal 1998), centralization (Koremenos et al. 2001), and legalization (Abbott et al. 2000) of international institutions as well as delegation of competences to these institutions (Nielson and Tierney 2003; Pollack 2003). Within this theoretical milieu, scholars have recently begun data collection efforts to investigate different features of regional organizations (see Haftel and Thompson 2006; Goertz and Powers 2014) or international organizations (IOs) in general (Green and Colgan 2013; see also Green 2014; Tallberg et al. 2013). Most importantly, Hooghe et al. (2017) have collected data on the authority of seventy-four IOs over the period 1950–2010. Their project distinguishes between the pooling of authority to an IO body, in which member states directly participate, and the delegation of authority to independent IO bodies.

In line with these efforts, a Berlin group at the WZB Berlin Social Science Center has developed a database about authority of IOs. This database is based on the concept of reflexive authority, and it uses the following operational definition: International and/or transnational institutions have authority when the direct and indirect addressees recognize, in principle or in practice, that an institution can make competent judgments and decisions that come with the ambition to be binding at least for some members of the global governance system. Based on the theoretical concept of reflexive authority, the operational definition consists of recognition on the side of authority addressees and competence on the side of authority holders, both on the level of the institutional design. The data is retrieved from a careful analysis of legal documents such as IO founding treaties, their amendments, and procedural protocols starting with 1948. Competence is measured as the product of autonomy of the institution *times* the scope, whereby scope refers to the number of issues regulated by the IO and autonomy points to the sum of delegation and pooling. Recognition is measured in terms of the level of obligation and bindingness for the members.

In the IAD,[1] we aggregate these measures as:

$$authority = \sqrt{scope \; x \; bindingness \; x \; (pooling + delegation)}$$

---

[1] The IAD is a common effort of a number of scholars (formerly) located at the WZB. The group consists of Martin Binder (now University of Reading), Xaver Keller (now Gesellschaft für

This means that authority is the function of the depth of recognition of the interpretations and decisions by an institution that has delegated or pooled competences with a given breadth or scope of the mandate.

We collected data on the political and epistemic authority of a sample of thirty-four IOs (and more than 230 IO bodies) across seven policy functions derived from the policy cycle.[2] These are (1) agenda setting, (2) rule making, (3) monitoring, (4) norm interpretation, (5) enforcement of decisions, (6) evaluation, and (7) knowledge generation.[3] These functions focus on different activities of IOs reflecting the notion that authority is exercised when making decisions or interpretations. We used founding treaties and all the changes made to them over time to assess formal authority. In doing so, we have developed a coding instrument with which we collect—for each of our seven policy functions—information according to a three-step logic. First, does the IO have the right to authorize any of these functions? Second, if so, who carries out the function (IO body, member state, other actor, including non-state actors)? Third, how is the function carried out and how "authoritative" is it? The possible authority values range from 0 to the (theoretically possible) value of 10.25.[4]

To start with, IOs differ in terms of authority across time and across cases. According to our measurement, it is—not surprisingly—the European Union (EU), the United Nations (UN, including the Security Council (UNSC)) and the International Monetary Fund (IMF) that are the most authoritative ones. Yet even beyond this top three list, quite consequential IOs populate the global governance system, among which are the World Bank, the World Trade Organization (WTO), but also regional organizations, such as the African Union (AU) (see Figure 5.1).

More to the point of the historical development of international authority, we can state that the overall growth of authority by international institutions is indeed an ongoing process in which it is possible to identify two

Internationale Zusammenarbeit (GIZ)), Autumn Lockwood Payton (now Alfred University), Alexandros Tokhi, and Michael Zürn. The data from this project are derived from an encompassing coding of the IOs' key statutory documents. For further details, see Zürn et al. (2015).

[2] We draw on similar selection decisions as Tallberg et al. (2013) and Hooghe et al. (2017), and arrive at a joint sample, which allows the participating scholars to pool their respective analyses and thereby produce a more complete understanding of international authority in a later stage.

[3] These functions draw from the public administration literature (see e.g. Anderson 1975; Jenkins 1978; May and Wildavsky 1978). Several studies have adapted similar functions for the study of international politics and institutions, including, for instance, Bradley and Kelley (2008); Abbott and Snidal (2009); Avant et al. (2010).

[4] This value is possible when applying the following formula with the theoretically possible maximum values: $Authority_{it} = \sqrt[2]{scope_{it} \times \Sigma(bindingness_{ijt} \times autonomy_{ijt})}$, where i is IO, j policy function, and t year. The resulting maximum total authority score is: $\sqrt[2]{5 \times 21} = 10.246$.

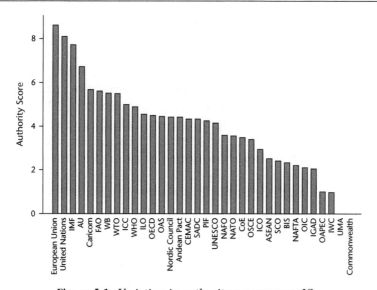

Figure 5.1. Variation in authority scores across IOs

Source: International Authority Database (IAD), Zürn et al. 2015, unpublished[5]

growth phases: a growth period running from the end of the Second World War to 1970, and a second one, from 1990 until today. Clearly, 1945 and 1990 point to two critical junctures (see Figure 5.2).

How can we account for this pattern over time? I submit a primarily *historical-institutionalist account* of system change. From this perspective, the rise of the global governance system was produced in the first place by an interactive sequence of both effects of post-Second World War institutions and responses to these effects. The story thus starts with the post-Second World War settlement, for it carried the seeds of the transformation. This development obtained an additional, externally induced thrust with the fall of the Iron Curtain between the East and the West finally allowing the global governance system to take place.

This account uses the historical-institutionalist concepts introduced in Chapter 4: critical junctures, self-reinforcing path dependences, reactive sequences, and external shocks. Together, they created a global governance system in the 1990s. They led to a post-anarchic international system that involves authority beyond the states. In this conception, world society has produced a political system of its own consisting of normative principles, reflexive authorities, and specific legitimation narratives. In this way, a global governance system emerged that is different from other systems in the history of world politics since 1648.

---

[5] The ranking is based on all time high values for each IO.

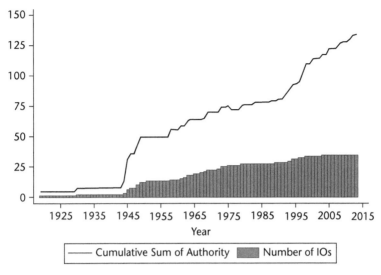

Figure 5.2. IOs: Variation in authority over time

Source: IAD Zürn et al. 2015, unpublished

The remainder of this chapter will develop such a historical-institutionalist account for the rise of global governance. The chapter will end with a general "reactive sequence model" of the development that led from the post-Second World War order to the global governance system in the 1990s and its growing contestation from 2001 on.[6]

5.2 The End of the Second World War as a Critical Juncture

During the final years of the Second World War, the leaders of the alliance against the fascist axis began to plan about the post-war world. The meeting of experts from the United States, the Soviet Union, China, and the United Kingdom in Dumbarton Oaks from August to October 1944 is best known in this respect. The outcome of the meetings in the picturesque mansion was already a fairly precise plan of the UN, including a strategy about how to win the support of the rest of the world, in spite of the privileged position of the major powers in the UNSC. At about the same time, the plan for the economic Bretton Woods institutions evolved as well. These plans together mark the beginning of the establishment and consolidation of a liberal

---

[6] Important elements of such an account are provided by Ikenberry (2011a) and Hale et al. (2013). However, they do not systematically apply a historical-institutionalist framework, nor do they theorize reactive sequences. Most importantly, according to their account, the counter-reactions leading to gridlock are targeted at policies, and not at authorities.

economic order with open borders to avoid repetition of a world economic chaos as in the years after Black Tuesday in 1929. The United States gave up its isolationist stand (Ambrose 1983), and instead aimed at an institutionalized world order under its leadership. It was seen as a means both to meeting the interests of an economy that was at that time by far the most productive, and exporting the political ideas standing behind American exceptionalism (Kolko and Kolko 1972). Further steps in this process were the UN Charter in 1945, the Marshall Plan in 1948, and the North Atlantic Treaty in 1949.

While the United Kingdom accepted its role as junior partner, Stalin and the Soviet Union had their own ideas. The seizure of Eastern Europe and its integration into a "socialist empire" caused a *de facto* split between the East and the West. As a result of these developments, the United States ended up with two separate tiers of the international system: a Western tier, which accepted US leadership; and a global tier dominated by the East–West relations and the conflicts between the two superpowers. Within the Western world, it became possible to manage the economic interdependence of the developed industrialized countries in a beneficial way in the context of the Bretton Woods institutions. In the global context, the situation was different. Although the Charter of the UN established a complete ban on the use of force between states, it remained relatively weak because of the blockade between the Western and Eastern blocs. The system competition between the liberal West and the socialist East commenced in a largely unregulated form.

5.2.1 *Embedded Liberalism*

Prior to the Second World War, a few international regimes existed for the coordination of trans-border traffic and communication. Most of the relevant international organizations (IOs) like the International Postal Union, agreements about the interface management of different railway systems, and commissions for trans-border shipping, were created in the second half of the nineteenth century (Rittberger et al. 2013). These regimes were relatively easy to agree upon since they resolved coordination problems with limited distributional conflicts. As issue areas with incentives for free-riding and with long-term distributional implications—such as trade regulations, currencies, and financial markets—are more difficult to regulate on the international level, they remained largely unregulated for a long time.

This changed after the Second World War. The international trade regime and the regime for the regulation of currency and financial affairs were crucial to the management of economic interdependence. These institutions were supposed to prevent a repetition of the disastrous spiral of protectionism that began after Black Tuesday in 1929 and caused the world economic crisis (Kindleberger 1986). In the absence of such institutions, the particular short-term interests of national governments could easily lead to a race of protectionism and devaluations of currencies (Keohane 1984).

The idea of coordinating trade and currency policies in order to reduce tariffs and to avoid devaluation races led to an American and British cooperation in setting up the trinity of the General Agreement on Tariffs and Trade (GATT), the International Monetary Fund (IMF), and the World Bank. Harry Dexter White (for the United States) and John Maynard Keynes (for the United Kingdom) were the architects of this setting. The international trade regime came into being on the basis of the GATT in 1947. It asked states to abolish any quota for the trade with industrial goods and to reduce tariffs. Most importantly, it established the "most-favored-nation principle" so that any advantage, favor, privilege, or immunity granted by any contracting party to products of another party had to be accorded to all other contracting parties. The IMF was founded already in 1944. It was supposed to support a liberal international economy by a regime of free convertibility of currencies anchored in fixed exchange rates with the US dollar, which in turn was bound by gold reserves to guarantee its value. In addition, the World Bank was established in order to accelerate development projects and processes in the less developed parts of the world.

Based on the lessons learned from the interwar period, it needed American leadership plus an increased willingness of the European states to follow the lead in order to establish institutions that reduced transaction costs and thus fostered cooperation (Keohane 1984). Although these institutions served state interests and functioned in the mode of executive multilateralism without significant societal participation, they were rooted in a social purpose: the global extrapolation of the democratic welfare state that required a certain international environment to flourish (Katzenstein 1985).

The social purpose on which these international institutions were based is aptly expressed by the term "embedded liberalism." Embedded liberalism is understood as a basic focus on free trade and open borders, which is, however, concretely embedded in national political systems that can cushion the shocks and inequalities triggered by the global market (see Ruggie 1983). The international institutions created on the basis of the principle of embedded liberalism facilitated relatively unlimited trade between all industrialized states, simultaneously allowing for significant differences in the political and societal developments of the nation states (see Hall and Soskice 2001). The concept of embedded liberalism thus refers to a specific combination of liberalized international markets and nation state market interventions.

The international institutions of embedded liberalism facilitated the development of democratic welfare states, some of which—for instance Sweden— have more than 50 percent of gross domestic product (GDP) at their disposal.

Other countries like Switzerland remained, with roughly 30 percent, at much lower levels (Esping-Andersen 1990). It is this variance that points to the two decisive elements and meanings of embeddedness: It allowed for the possibility to cushion failure in liberal world market competition (welfare embeddedness) as well as allowing for a free choice of the national welfare systems (the liberal international regimes were embedded in a system of democratic states).

From the perspective of the theory of IR, the achievements of this order are historical in scale. Democracy, international institutions, and interdependence were mutually reinforcing in this arrangement, which resulted in stable peace among the democratic welfare states (Russett and Oneal 2001). These security effects of embedded liberalism account for a large part of its success. Against the background of the perceived threat from the Soviet Union, it was possible for the first time to establish a transatlantic and, in part, also transpacific security community (Deutsch et al. 1957) within the world of the Organisation for Economic Co-operation and Development, the so-called "OECD world." The historic compromise thus served the interests of the political elites in international stability and a unified West against the "Soviet threat," the interests of export industries in open markets, and the interests of labor in conditions that allow for the development of the welfare state. It was a constellation that brought about the age of social democracy (Scharpf 1987).

5.2.2 Prohibition on the Use of Force

Prior to the nineteenth century, the territorial integrity of a state depended mainly on its own defense and capacity, which made war the dominant form of conflict management between states in the seventeenth and eighteenth centuries (see e.g. Holsti 1991). The attempts to establish a successful management of interdependence in the area of security constantly failed for a long period of time. It was only after the Napoleonic Wars that the prohibition on force and the principle of non-intervention in internal matters gradually attained certain effectiveness. The establishment and gradual strengthening of the prohibition on the use of force in intergovernmental affairs has since featured in the history of international politics. The development can be demonstrated quantitatively through the content analysis of official announcements. Apart from setbacks immediately before and during the two world wars, it is possible to observe a comparatively progressive strengthening of this norm (cf. Kegley and Wittkopf 1989: 471). Combined with its counterpart principle of non-intervention in the domestic affairs of a state, it represented the foundation of the Westphalian system. The most important stages in this development were the Congress of Vienna in 1815, the establishment of the League of Nations, the Kellogg–Briand Pact in 1928, and the founda-tion of the United Nations (UN).

In 1945, the Charter of the UN for the first time established the complete prohibition on the use of force among states. Only two circumstances could justify the use of force: individual or collective self-defense in the case of an attack, and a resolution of the UNSC authorizing the use of force for the purpose of securing international peace. Although the norm about the pro-hibition on the use of force in intergovernmental affairs developed further, due to the East–West divide, the mechanisms for the implementation of sanctions through UNSC resolutions remained largely blocked. Instead, two military blocs—the North Atlantic Community and the Warsaw Pact—emerged and institutionalized hierarchies within both sides of the divide.

In spite of this blockade, the UN system developed some management capacities in the shadow of the Cold War. The general design of the UN system and the norms enshrined in the Charter allowed for some institutional innovations, especially when both superpowers had an interest in avoiding the escalation of conflicts in other parts of the world. Most importantly, the peacekeeping forces in support of truces and peace treaties established a practice that underlined the ambition of the UN system to be responsible for international peace. The UN also involved a number of special bodies and special organizations to handle issues like health, environment, and especially development assistance, thus paving the way for a broadening of international regulation including new issue areas.

Because of the veto rights of the two superpowers, the East–West rivalry was little affected by the UN. The post-war settlement with the Iron Curtain running in the middle of Europe was never formally agreed upon, but the result of adaptive behavior on both sides reflected the power constellation rather directly. As soon as the Soviet Union had their own nuclear weapons at their disposal, a dangerous nuclear stalemate prevailed, leading to a num-ber of crises that brought the world to the brink of a nuclear war. The Korean War (1950–53), the Berlin Crisis (1961), the Cuban Missile Crisis (1962), and later the Yom Kippur War (1973) stressed that a nuclear war can happen unin-tentionally as result of a crisis that runs out of control.

In this situation, the goal was to identify strategies and instruments that helped to avoid escalation and allowed for minimal cooperation in order to avoid the worst outcome: nuclear war (see especially Schelling 1960; also Snyder and Diesing 1977). Against this backdrop, a rethinking of nuclear deterrence eventuated. The credibility gap of the doctrine of mutually assured destruction (MAD) was detected. Why would the United States risk its exist-ence with a nuclear first strike, if the United Soviet Socialist Republic (USSR) had taken West Berlin? The answer to this question is the goal of dominance in each step of the escalation ladder, and thus the new doctrine of flexible response (Stromseth 1988; Daalder 1991). This change in strategy helped pave the way for further cooperation and some *détente* between the blocs.

With the benefit of hindsight, it can be stated that the post-war order was a matter of institutional choice taken in a situation of a critical juncture and embedded in the social purpose provided by US leadership, as well as the emerging system competition between the East and the West. The US leadership realized that the constellation was permissive and provided the productive conditions where possible (Ikenberry 2009). With the end of the war in sight, the members of the victorious alliance moved into a situation of enormous institutional leeway. The old system was shattered. A need for a new order was broadly felt, and the members of the alliance with the United States at the top were seen as the only appropriate actors to create one. As often is the case in critical junctures, the decision makers themselves mainly perceived the situation as a crisis with a feeling that actions had to be taken urgently and that they were being strongly circumscribed by other actors. In crises, a gap often arises between the "objective" easing of structural constraints and the subjective perception of urgency on the side of the decision makers. The growing gap between the Stalin-led Soviet Union and the other members of the alliance against Nazi Germany in particular was seen as a major impediment.

In parallel, the internal Western order of embedded liberalism developed relatively smoothly. Taken together, we can see from 1945 until 1950 a first rise of authority which is also reflected in a similar rise of the number of IOs (see Figure 5.2). The emerging order was however an intergovernmental one. Whereas some of the IOs founded in this period are nowadays the most authoritative one (see Figure 5.1), overall, the international institutions were ascribed relatively little authority of their own. Moreover, they contained, to a large extent, "simple international rules" that were in the beginning not very intrusive, targeted at states only, and were relatively easy to assess with respect to their effects. The rise of international authority therefore grew in parallel with the rise of the number of IOs in this period.

5.3 The Self-Reinforcement of Post-Second World War Institutions

The Bretton Woods institutions were remarkably successful for a long time. They supported stable growth in the Western industrial states for almost thirty years. They promoted the integration of the capitalist economies and, as a result, increased economic power of their leading members and strengthened the role of export-oriented branches of industry in domestic politics. They contributed particularly to the prevention of a spiral of protectionism and devaluation during economic recessions. In the meantime, the UN system remained relatively weak in managing security issues. It remained dependent on bilateral agreements of the superpowers that—especially after the Cuban Missile Crisis in 1962—developed slowly in a nascent form. The establishment of a red telephone symbolized the willingness to establish crisis management institutions in order to avoid misperceptions and unwanted escalation.

The international trade regime, especially, deepened over time. In essence, the early GATT reduced tariffs on manufactured goods, and these reductions increased the importance of non-tariff barriers over time. The Tokyo Round of trade negotiations (1973–79) began then to deal with non-tariff barriers such as anti-dumping, government subsidies, government procurement, and licensing procedures. With the Uruguay Round (1984–94), those non-tariffs barriers were reduced as well. The regime developed mechanisms of self-reinforcement by endogenously increasing the returns, thus creating path dependence. Historical institutionalism has identified a long list of potential endogenous sources of self-reinforcement. They can be grouped into three categories as set-up effects, interaction effects, and cognitive effects (see Zürn 2016a: 201–11).

From the very moment when an institution is set up, it establishes some mechanisms that lead to additional support and protection of the institution. The constitutive members of an institution sink the costs caused by its very creation (Williamson 1975). In addition, there are veto points to be overcome when trying to change an institution (Tsebelis 2002), as well as the usual collective action problems in order to change a given status quo (Olson 1971). Moreover, where an institution comes with an organization and administration (which, in the political sphere, they most often do), it creates vested interests. The set-up effects are thus those that materialize from day one on. In his seminal *After Hegemony*, Robert Keohane (1984) essentially puts forward a set-up costs argument in showing that international institutions may remain even after the scope conditions that made them possible are gone. The lowered transaction costs can keep an ongoing cooperation effective, in spite of changed circumstances which would make a reiteration of the agreement impossible. While set-up costs do not explain the deepening of the economic institutions, they do explain why they could live on despite serious economic crises and changed scope conditions in 1970s and 1980s. Whilst the UN could not fulfil their promises for a long time, its set-up provided an organizational frame and the ambition to be responsible for war, peace, and development, which continued to exist even in times of crisis.

In addition to resilience based on set-up costs, a process of deepening and self-reinforcement via interactive mechanisms took place. Interaction effects can come in the form of network effects (e.g. if a given software is used by many, it becomes more attractive for others to use it too), institutional embedding (i.e. mutual backing of enmeshed institutions), and power reinforcement (i.e. strengthening of those who benefit from and support an institution). In the case of the post-Second World War liberal institutions, it was power reinforcement that was most important. They strengthened their supporters relative to their opponents. Especially in the early decades, when the openness toward advanced industrial goods went together with ongoing protection of agricultural and some simple industrial goods, the economies with a strong productivity and a comparative advantage in producing goods that involve high technology benefitted most. Major beneficiaries in the early decades of these institutions were thus not only the United States and Great Britain, but also Japan, Germany, France, and Canada. This institutional effect increased the international influence of their governments and allowed to drive the further development of GATT with additional rounds of trade liberalization (Ruggie 1994; Lake 2009; see Hale et al. 2013: 3).

What is more, on the level of domestic politics, a deepening of existing institutions followed. This is demonstrated in Helen Milner's (1988) work about the domestic strengthening of export-oriented industries within the most powerful industrialized countries. As trade was sectorally reallocated on the basis of comparative advantage, exporters expanded, and multinational corporations arose to capture the economies of scale. As a result of this redeployment in favor of comparatively advantaged sectors, opponents of free trade within countries grew weaker, and proponents of economic openness grew stronger (see also Lake 2009: 31). The first decades after the Second World War thus saw—as an interaction effect—the consolidation of the dominance of export-oriented firms over firms with a focus on the domestic market in almost all industrialized countries. It helped to establish the hegemony of internationally minded capital (Cox 1987).

Finally, cognitive reinforcement of the liberal regimes took place through processes like learning (one learns that the institution works), adaptive expectation (one gets used to it and wants to avoid a new need for adaptation), and local bookkeeping (one sees the benefits of something without asking whether there are even better alternatives). These cognitive mechanisms may have been less important in the case of the post-Second World War order, but they certainly played a role.

Similar processes of self-reinforcing institutionalized cooperation took place in the superpower relations. The early moves toward rapprochement between the superpowers in the area of crisis management continued in the second half of the 1960s. With an ongoing Vietnam War and clear signs of economic problems on both sides, both superpowers felt that an unlimited competition between the two was not only extremely dangerous, but also too expensive. A number of arms control treaties—most importantly the

Nuclear Non-proliferation Treaty of 1968—but also institutionalized cooperation in other areas—such as trade and environment—were significant outcomes of *détente*. As climax of this development, the Helsinki Declaration of 1975 not only pointed to the principle of sovereignty and the territorial integrity of states, but also asked for "respect for human rights and fundamental freedoms, including the freedom of thought, conscience, religion or belief," and the "fulfillment in good faith of obligations under international law." With this agreement, the East–West relations became finally institutionalized as well.

From the 1960s on, one can see a stabilization and partial deepening of an international order that was based on sovereignty but included the possibility of institutionalized cooperation in absence of a centralized world state. The IAD shows for this period between 1950 and the late 1970s a modest rise of international authority which was partially driven by an increasing number of IOs and partially by a deepening of international institutions (see Figure 5.2). This stabilization and partial deepening resulted largely from the self-reinforcing dynamics and path dependencies produced by set-up costs, interaction effects, and cognitive processes. In this sense, the institutional developments in this period need to be seen as path-dependent from the earlier decisions taken in the critical juncture. This self-reinforcing dynamics even worked in the context of East–West relations, where international regimes—i.e. East–West regimes—then emerged (Rittberger 1990; Haftendorn et al. 1999).

5.4 Reactive Sequences and Transnational Norm Entrepreneurs

The first signs of resistance to embedded liberalism came from the leaders of the newly independent states of the Global South. They essentially demanded more protection for their infant industries and redistribution within the given system. This culminated in demands for a New International Economic Order (Bhagwati 1977; Cox 1979). The term was derived from the Declaration for the Establishment of a New International Economic Order, adopted by the UN General Assembly in 1974, and it referred to a wide range of trade, financial, commodity, and debt-related issues. The actual changes deriving from this debate remained limited. Other developments were more consequential.

In some ways, the Bretton Woods institutions were, so to speak, too successful. Embedded liberalism triggered a continuous dynamic of deepening liberalization and accelerated technological development, the interaction of which prompted a push for globalization (Beisheim et al. 1999; Held et al. 1999). As an effect of intensified cross-border transactions, national policies alone were, in some areas, increasingly unable to achieve their desired outcomes from the late 1970s on. The effectiveness of state policies was challenged in the policy fields in which the spatial scope of national regulations no longer extended to the real boundaries of the societal transactions (e.g. increased environmental externalities) and national measures would decrease the competitiveness of the production (e.g. decreased willingness of global producers to finance national welfare regimes) (Zürn 1998). The choices available for effective national market intervention and social protection programs were thus restricted by the rapid increase in direct investment and the highly sensitive financial markets in particular.[7] Both of these developments were in line with the growing relevance of transnational finance capital, a relative decline of national export industries, and the rise of a transnational class (van der Pijl 1998).

Moreover, the deepening of the liberal order comprised a continuous strengthening of international regimes that asked states to open borders in order to allow the free exchange of goods, capital, labor, culture, and the like, but it remained weak regarding measures aimed at changing or correcting market outcomes on the international level (Streeck 1995). As Fritz Scharpf (1999) would put it, negative integration prevailed over positive integration. In addition to the structural pressure of globalization, this skewed distribution in the content of international regimes put an institutional pressure on states to weaken their mechanisms of social protection. Thus, the paradox of post-war liberalism lies in the fact that it attacked its own institutional cushioning mechanisms. It undermined its own basis of success and produced losers in the industrialized countries in which the welfare state and societal support for weaker individuals was strongly entrenched. At the same time, globally active companies invested increasingly in all parts of the world, utilizing cheap labor costs in poor countries. While the self-reinforcing dynamics of liberalization went on and moved

---

[7] One should add that the diminishing of the welfare state and especially the notion of a race to the bottom remains empirically contested. Many studies observed a continuation of welfare spending without significant changes—especially since welfare state functions can also work as risk insurance in the face of increased economic openness (Garrett 1998; Rieger and Leibfried 1997; Rodrik 1997) and allows for economically efficient interventions (Krugman 1994; Barro 1996). Therefore, different varieties of capitalism may choose different strategies of adaptation and, in this, even lead to a further divergence of regulation (Hall and Soskice 2001). However, many of these studies emphasizing the stability of the welfare states looked at a relatively short time period after the new thrust of globalization set in. More recent studies show that state welfare expenditures have indeed diminished to some extent (Busemeyer 2009; Elkins et al. 2006; Höpner and Schäfer 2007; but see also Bergh and Karlsson 2010; Dreher et al. 2008). It has also been convincingly argued that looking at actual expenditure levels is a bad indicator. The more relevant indicator would be individual entitlements for social benefits. While, for instance, the level of unemployment expenditure did grow, the amount of money received by the individual beneficiaries dropped in almost all G7 countries (Pierson 1996; Anderson and Pontusson 2001). Overall, whereas an unmediated race to the bottom certainly does not take place, it seems a fair assessment that the relative costs of maintaining the welfare state at a constant level have increased over time.

embedded liberalism toward neoliberalism, a reactive sequence began to produce counterforces.

Therefore, it can be expected that—besides struggles against the retrenchment of the welfare state at home—demands arise for common international policies to intervene into markets. Since the 1980s, one can positively observe such demands to change the (neoliberal) one-sidedness of international institutions. International regulation thus entered new issue areas outside the economic and the security realm. Human rights regulations and international environmental agreements are only the most visible cases in point.

Since the end of the 1970s, a number of important human rights conventions were adopted, such as the Convention on the Elimination of All Forms of Discrimination against Women (1979), the Convention against Torture and Other Cruel, Inhuman or Degrading Treatment or Punishment (1984), and the Convention on the Rights of Children (1989). In addition, numerous regional agreements strengthened human rights norms on the level beyond the nation state. The UN World Conference on Human Rights in Vienna (1993) declared the protection of human rights a prime task for the UN. Numerically, one can easily see a significant rise of human rights declarations and conventions from the early 1980s on (Beisheim et al. 1999: 343).

The number of new international environmental agreements also grew after the 1972 Stockholm Conference, which is seen by many as the starting point of international environmental politics (Zürn 2002: 96). In particular, the success of the Vienna Convention (1985) to protect the ozone layer and the subsequent protocols (above all, the Montreal Protocol) heralded a period in which the widespread expectation was for international environmental politics to be the field of the future (see e.g. Haas et al. 1993; Breitmeier et al. 2006). International regimes in the area of social and redistributive policies to strengthen the national welfare state however remained the exception. The International Labour Organization (ILO) stayed a relatively weak player in the concert of IOs (Senti 2002).

The politics of those market-braking agreements and conventions was different from earlier market-making international agreements. Very often, non-state actors were agenda setters and governments in a reactive position. Environmental non-governmental organizations (NGOs) emerged around the world and demanded regulation to contain the externalities of growth in a liberal world order. Greenpeace, World Wildlife Fund (WWF), and Oxfam are only the best known ones. In the field of human rights, NGOs like Amnesty International or Human Rights Watch recorded and monitored human rights violations around the world and put human rights more visibly on the international agenda. In 1993, 700 NGOs with 8,000 individuals participated at the UN World Conference on Human Rights. International institutions, in general, opened up to non-state actors (Tallberg et al. 2013).

This is noteworthy not least because embedded liberalism was created by means of a special method of international decision making, which can be described by using the term "executive multilateralism" (Zürn 2004). This term is intended to convey a decision-making mode in which government representatives coordinate their policies internationally at a remove from parliament and the public. On the one hand, therefore, this executive multilateralism refers to a system of decision making that is open to all of the states involved, incorporates a generalized behavioral principle, creates expectations of a diffuse reciprocity, and is seen as indivisible (Ruggie 1992). On the other hand—and this aspect has been ignored for a long time—post-war multilateralism was strongly government-centered and hostile to the public. The rules of embedded liberalism were negotiated internationally and implemented nationally without comprehensive participation of the legislatures or the systematic involvement of national or transnational societal actors. It largely hung over the known channels of influence of the democratic welfare state. Of course, it also had a domestic policy dimension, which was however dominated by economic interest groups and remained largely outside the visibility of national publics.[8] With the development of new market-braking regimes, executive multilateralism had reached its limits.

The extension of international regimes to new issue areas and a changed politics of regime making can be seen as part of a reactive sequence. With the deepening of the post-war regimes, liberalization became one-sided and began to undermine its own shock absorbers. This process was accentuated by weakened labor unions reflecting the decline of industrial production in relation to the rise of service industries. At the same time, however, the awareness of global interdependencies increased as a result of more and more open borders. As a reaction to this, progressive movements transnationalized and entered the realm of world politics, now demanding market-braking regulations that complement liberalization by referring to global norms. The success of such norm entrepreneurs (Liese 2006) depended, to some extent, on the diffusion of norms (Keck and Sikkink 1998) and on processes of persuasion and arguing on the side of often non-state actors (Risse 2000; Deitelhoff and Müller 2005), as well as the rhetorical traps into which state leaders often fall, especially when the decoupling between rhetoric and behavior is strong (Risse et al. 1999; Schimmelfennig 2003).

The evaluation of the outcomes of these efforts remains disputed. International environmental regimes and global human rights norms are seen by many as ineffective and weak. Others, however, point to the counterfactual

---

[8] See also Keohane and Nye (2000: 1–41), who refer to a club model of international politics in this context. For a general analysis of the effects of excluding the public from policy making, see Culpepper's (2011) work on "quiet politics."

and argue that the situation would be quite different without these international norms. In any case, the new regulations changed the quality of international rules to a certain extent. They were more intrusive and they often referred to societies as the final addressees of the regulations. However, these new international institutions were not yet seen as authority holders. Most of the new regulations came in the form of (sometimes non-binding) international conventions and transnational agreements without establishing a lot of additional authority beyond the national state.

These developments are reflected in Figure 5.2. On the one hand, we see that the number of IOs has stagnated in the 1980s. The unconditional support for new international venues of governance has waned. On the other hand, we see an ongoing—yet slowed down—rise in the authority of already existing IOs. It is mainly responses to growing criticism, rather than new initiatives to strengthen international cooperation in general, that are typical in the 1980s.

5.5 The Fall of the Wall and the Rise of the Global Governance System

The dissolution of the socialist camp can be seen as another step in the path-dependent story described so far in this chapter. With *détente* between East and West, and especially with the Helsinki Declaration of 1975, individual rights entered the realm of the Soviet bloc, which strengthened opposition in the long run. Gorbachev's *perestroika* partially responded to opposition groups asking for more freedom and partially to globalization and the pressure that it put on the intransigent Soviet economy. Its failure brought down the Soviet Union.

Yet it seems a bit overdrawn to see the decline of the Soviet Union as primarily an effect of the post-Second World War institutional order. The fall of the Soviet empire therefore is modeled here as an external force that created a new critical juncture by releasing the dynamics of functional differentiation in world politics and making the final step toward a system of global governance possible.

In any case, the end of the Cold War changed world politics fundamentally. The divide between two communities of states split Europe in the middle and blocked the UNSC. It structured world politics by separating two spheres, with only one of them entailing dynamics of globalization and global governance. The dissolving of this structure created new opportunities and permissive conditions that were taken up especially by the governments of the United States and, within Europe, mainly Germany, France, and the EU. At this critical juncture, the leaders of the so-called Western world took some decisions that paved the way for the emergence of a global governance system.

The shift was most dramatic within Europe. In order to embed German reunification in European integration, the Kohl government gave in to French pressure and accepted a currency union. Besides this deepening of the EU, its enlargement is most remarkable. It took a while until the EU as a whole realized the opportunities associated with enlargement. The collapse of communism came quickly and was not anticipated. Moreover, the EU struggled to deal with the sudden reunification of Germany while keeping its monetary union project on track. In the end, however, enlargement took effect.

Immediately after the end of the Cold War, a rush toward the EU started. For most Eastern European states, EU membership was seen as a guarantee for economic wealth and independence from Russia. In 1993, responding to the demand, the EU developed the Copenhagen criteria according to which a country must accept human rights, be a democracy, operate a free market, and be willing to adopt the entire body of EU law (*acquis communitaire*) before it can become a member of the EU. In this way, the EU exerted an enormous pressure for liberal reforms in those countries. It can be seen as the most successful case of external intervention into domestic affairs in recent history (see e.g. Kelley 2004b, 2004a). Within little more than a decade, a large number of formerly socialist states in Eastern Europe were integrated into the EU, and partially also into the North Atlantic Treaty Organization (NATO)—in spite of many critical voices within the West and in Russia (Schimmelfennig 2005).

In the end, eight Central and Eastern European countries (the Czech Republic, Estonia, Hungary, Latvia, Lithuania, Poland, Slovakia, and Slovenia), plus two Mediterranean countries (Malta and Cyprus) were able to join the EU on May 1, 2004. This was the largest single enlargement in terms of people and number of countries. Following this, Romania and Bulgaria, which were deemed as not ready to join in 2004, acceded nevertheless on January 1, 2007. In 2013, Croatia followed. At that time, European integration clearly served as a stepping stone and not as a stumbling block for global integration. The EU extension toward the East was seen by most as an attempt to accelerate the integration of Eastern Europe into an open global system, even if this move has arguably undermined reforms in Russia in the long term.

On the global level, a number of global conferences (see Brozus 2002) with significant participation by non-state actors led to a wave of new international agreements in the 1990s. Three of them are probably most remarkable, for they highlight the normative principles of the emerging global governance system.

First, the 1992 Uruguay Round on trade led to the establishment of the World Trade Organization (WTO) in 1995. Not only did the new agreement have significant impact on trade—so that the trade regime now targeted subsidies, property rights, product regulation, and many other non-tariff trade barriers (Kahler 1995)—but also the WTO included a dispute settlement process that took away the veto power from the states. It is only in the case of a unanimous decision by the member states that a decision by the Dispute Settlement Body (DSB) or the Appellate Body can be rejected, indicating a significant rise in the delegation of authority to international bodies (see Zangl 2006). Currently, 160 states are members of the WTO.

Second, the Kyoto Protocol (1997) to the UN Framework Convention on Climate Change (UNFCCC) set binding obligations on industrialized countries to reduce emissions of greenhouse gases (GHGs). At that time, it was seen as an extension of the success of the ozone regime to a much more encompassing challenge for the future of humankind. It "recognizes that developed countries are principally responsible for the current high levels of GHG emissions in the atmosphere as a result of more than 150 years of industrial activity, and places a heavier burden on developed nations under the principle of 'common but differentiated responsibilities.'"[9] Over 190 states are parties to the protocol and many developed countries have agreed to legally binding reductions of their GHG emissions in two commitment periods. However, the United States, as one of the major emitters, did not ratify the protocol. Although it is clear that the commitments do not suffice to combat climate change effectively, it was seen by many in the 1990s as the first step in an ongoing process to set up an effective and strong international regime against global warming. The whole negotiation process entailed a global common good narrative, including the willingness of the European states to deliver in advance.

Third, the International Criminal Court (ICC) is based on the Rome Treaty, which was adopted in July 1998 against the vote of the United States (Deitelhoff 2006). It has the jurisdiction to prosecute individuals for the international crimes of genocide, crimes against humanity, and war crimes. To a significant extent, the ICC followed the model set by the International Criminal Tribunal for the former Yugoslavia (ICTY; see Bothe and Marauhn 2000). The ICC is intended to complement existing national judicial systems and it may therefore only exercise its jurisdiction when certain conditions are met. Nevertheless, it established a relationship between international institutions and individuals, thus pointing to rights for individuals and non-state actors. The ICC began functioning on July 1, 2002, the date that the Rome Statute entered into force. Currently, there are 123 states that are party to the Rome Statute and therefore members of the ICC.[10]

On top of all that, the UNSC began to play a much more active role in world politics. The changed role of the Council was first demonstrated after Iraq

---

[9] UNFCCC, Kyoto Protocol <http://unfccc.int/kyoto_protocol/items/2830.php> last accessed November 9, 2016.

[10] ICC, Rome Statute of the International Criminal Court <https://www.icc-cpi.int/resource-library/Documents/RomeStatuteEng.pdf> last accessed November 14, 2016.

invaded Kuwait in 1989. President George H. W. Bush was able to carefully forge a coalition of states that allowed the Council to brand Iraq as an aggressor and to authorize an intervention coalition that drove Iraq out of Kuwait. The hopes associated with this move were very well-expressed by Bush (1991) himself: "Until now, the world we've known has been a world divided—a world of barbed wire and concrete blocks, of conflict and Cold War. Now, we can see a new world coming onto view. A world in which there is the very real prospect of a new world order." The success of this action appeared to indicate that the final step had been taken in the establishment of the prohibition of the use of force and the notion of collective security if it is violated.

It did not stop there. In the following years, the UNSC identified humanitarian disasters and civil wars as a threat to international peace and intervened with military means in some of those instances (Chesterman 2004). Somalia, Haiti, Bosnia, and Afghanistan are well-known examples. The UNSC thus established a regime of peace enforcement that intended to externally enforce domestic peace (Zangl and Zürn 2003). In the case of Kosovo, the Western states attempted to get another authorization of the Council to enforce peace in a civil war. Since Russia's traditional ally, Serbia, was the target of such an intervention, it was signaled clearly that the draft of a resolution will not get through the Council. Eventually, the NATO intervened in this war without the Council's authorization. This was interpreted by some as an anticipation of a norm of responsibility to protect (R2P). While the validity and application of this norm remains contested even today (see e.g. Reinold 2012), it also points to individual and societal rights, to the common good, and an unprecedented degree of authority and intrusiveness of international institutions.

5.6 Public Authority in the Global Governance System

The described historical developments are reflected in the IAD. Figure 5.2 shows an enormous rise of international authority from the 1990s on. The cumulative value of international authority has almost doubled in the last twenty-five years, while the number of IOs remained relatively stable. Against this backdrop, we can speak of a system change: The global governance system emerged from the 1990s on.

This global governance system consists of loosely coupled spheres of both political and epistemic authority. In order to get a more detailed and specific picture of the components of the system and the relative relevance of epistemic and political authority, the overall development of IO authority can be disaggregated according to policy stages as coded in the IAD. International public authority plays out at different phases of the policy cycle (see Figure 5.3).

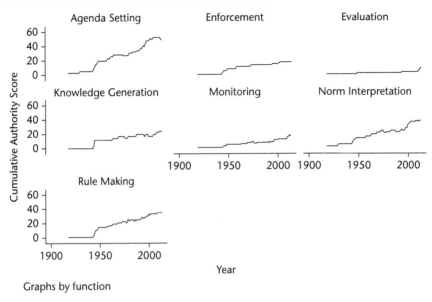

Figure 5.3. Authority variation in policy stages over time

Source: IAD Zürn et al. 2015, unpublished

5.6.1 *The Development of Political Authority*

Political authority refers to the capacity of IOs to make decisions that come with the ambition to be complied with. Political authority can come as requests, but also in a deeper form of authority including the right to enforce decisions. The policy stage, which is most closely associated with international political authority, is *the negotiation or decision phase (rule making)*. According to Figure 5.3, rule-making authority has grown significantly over time, and it now has the third highest authority value of all functions. In this policy stage, we can observe a significant share of majoritarian decision making in international institutions. Majority decisions and the exercise of dominance by strong countries enhance the capacity of international institutions to act by avoiding vetoes by single states and overcoming blockades. Today, roughly 50 percent of all IOs and two-thirds of all those with the participation of at least one great power have the possibility to decide by majority (see Blake and Payton 2008). A closer look at international environmental regimes supports the general finding: 58 percent of all cases include the formal possibility of majority voting. At the same time, this possibility is used much less often—only in 20 percent of the cases (Breitmeier et al. 2006: ch. 4).

Yet, even if majoritarian decision making is—in practice—employed far less often than it is formally available, it exerts pressure on veto players and increases their readiness to seek compromise. The formal possibility of international institutions to set rules by majority in connection with a *de facto* preference of states for consensual decision making represents an attempt to balance the contradictory aims of maintaining international institutions' ability to act and fostering states' readiness to implement measures decided upon.

Majoritarian decision making thus increases the ability of international institutions to set rules, by canceling the vetoes of individual states and overcoming blockades. Some of the most important and significant IOs contain the possibility of majority votes—the UNSC, the World Bank, and the IMF are well-known examples. As these examples show, majority voting in important IOs often goes hand in hand with a weighing of votes. Powerful states obviously want IOs to be effective and demand overcoming consensual decision making, since they do not want to be stopped by small states with a small population. At the same time, they do not want to be exploited by the majority of the smaller states and therefore often demand weighted voting so that most often a coalition of the strong states easily holds the majority.

The *enforcement of decisions (enforcement)* is the other stage in the policy cycle, which is at the core of political authority. According to our measure, we can observe an increase even in enforcement capacities on the international level (see Figure 5.3). This indicates an amplified readiness to levy material sanctions against violators of international norms.

In addition to IOs, transnational institutions also exercise political authority to some extent. In these cases, private actors exercise authority partially with the ability to bind parties that have not agreed to the rules or interpretations. Besides the often mentioned *lex mercatoria*, the *lex sportiva*—i.e. a set of transnational rules agreed upon by the national sport organizations—expanded and took greater hold in recent decades. The *lex informatica* is another case where private actors play a significant role in setting and enforcing public rules (Bartley 2007; Schuppert 2012). Such a governance without government, in part, was encouraged by states being happy to reduce their workload; in part, it is a response to the failure of intergovernmental politics to produce appropriate regulation; and, in part, it is a result of the strategy of especially business actors to prevent public regulation by setting their own standards. The level of political authority exercised by private actors remains, however, limited.

5.6.2 The Development of Epistemic Authority

Epistemic authority is based on expert knowledge and impartiality. The interpretations of an epistemic authority are taken into account because they appear to be both knowledgeable and nonpartisan. Epistemic authority is especially akin to the notion of reflexive authority and to the global governance system. It points to the special role of knowledge in global governance.

The remarkable rise of *politically assigned epistemic authorities* (PAEAs) within IOs is reflected in Figure 5.3. Those stages in the policy cycle that are most closely associated with epistemic authority have grown in relevance within public IOs. It is especially in the policy stages of norms adjudication, agenda setting, and knowledge generation where we can see strong growth.

First, the need for *monitoring* is in general greater if international norms no longer just apply to the borders between countries but, instead, begin to regulate activities within the boundaries of sovereign territories. Self-reporting and some mutual observation by the states party to an agreement are often not sufficient to guarantee compliance. Thus, the need for independent actors who process and make information on treaty compliance available is growing. Such information could be provided by autonomous organizations established as part of a treaty regime's safeguards. Two prominent examples of such organizations are the IMF (for the global financial system) and the International Atomic Energy Agency (for the Nuclear Nonproliferation Treaty) (Dai 2007: 50–3). In addition to such bodies, the role of international secretariats in regulatory monitoring has increased notably in recent years (see Siebenhüner and Biermann 2009).

Even more important in this regard (but not reflected in Figure 5.3) is, however, the growing significance of NGOs, mostly as pure epistemic authorities. Especially transnational civil society organizations (CSOs) collaborate with actors who have been negatively impacted by rule violations. Together, they have undertaken informal, independent regulatory monitoring (see Hirschmann 2015). For example, the monitoring of internationally standardized human rights has long been transferred informally to human rights organizations like Human Rights Watch.

Regarding disputed cases of *norm interpretation*, a significant increase in international judicial bodies can be noted as well (see Alter 2014). Of all policy stages, norm interpretation has the second highest aggregate score (see Figure 5.3). To the extent that the quantity of international obligations has grown, so, too, have the number of collisions between international and national regulations, as well as the number of conflicts between different international regulations. The establishment of court-like proceedings is one possibility for dealing with such interface conflicts. Moreover, some of these courts that have the express task of protecting individual rights respectively accept complaints by or against individuals. The European Court of Human Rights (ECtHR) and the ICC are the best know examples (von Bogdandy and Venzke 2014).

Finally, states compete with non-state organizations in the fields of *agenda setting*, *knowledge generation*, and *policy evaluation*. The set of organizations that evaluate the effectiveness of existing regulations and place new problem areas on the international agenda has widened in accordance with the extent to which the addressees of international regulation have become societal actors. Indeed, agenda setting has the highest authority score of all policy stages. Again, international secretariats and transnational NGOs are the actors who have increasingly taken up these governance functions. On the one hand, PAEAs—often affiliated with the secretariats of IOs—have gained in importance. On the other hand, those NGOs with pure epistemic authority that identify international problems and call for international regulations have also clearly taken on greater significance. The role of Transparency International in the development of the Anti-Bribery Convention (see Metzges 2006) is just one example. In any case, the normative pressure resulting from the epistemic authority of such knowledge bodies and agenda-setting actors weakens the ability of individual governments to oppose international norm development processes (see Meyer 2005).

Institutionalized epistemic authority comes mostly in the shape of PAEAs. If organizational bodies receive the mandate to authoritatively interpret facts and norms from political authorities, then it means that an act of delegation of competences and the related institutionalization has taken place. PAEAs are those transnational or international institutions that do not make binding decisions, but have the competence to make, often very consequential, interpretations. In the context of global governance, the International Panel on Climate Change (IPCC) or the role of OECD in education policy (i.e. Programme for International Student Assessment (PISA)) are two examples. Judging on the basis of IAD, it is this type of authority that seems to have grown especially strongly in the global governance system. All of the polity functions typically performed by PAEAs have strong growth rates from the 1990s on.

Moreover, the rise of so-called self-regulations in which NGOs—especially businesses and CSOs—developed governance arrangements to address specific problems have grown strongly as well (for an overview of transnational governance, see Hale and Held 2011). In these cases, private actors exercise public authority, partially furnished with the ability to bind parties that have not agreed to the rules or interpretations. Moreover, certification systems for consumers—such as the Forest Stewardship Council or Rugmark—were widely expanded, and the number of sectoral codes of conduct multiplied in the 1990s (see Kolk and van Tulder 2005; Scherer et al. 2006).

Public private partnerships, such as Internet Corporation for Assigned Names and Numbers (ICANN), which regulates the allocation of Internet addresses, and the Roll Back Malaria Initiative, for instance, can also be seen as an indication for a trend toward an increased relevance of private actors in global governance arrangements that set in especially after 1989 (Beisheim et al. 2008; Beisheim and Liese 2014). Overall, these regulations are significant and they grew in the 1990s (see Abbott and Snidal 2009). Together, they underline the trend toward sectoral spheres of authority that are only loosely coupled.

Against this background, it seems fair to state that a growth of political authority and an especially steep rise of PAEAs took place in the 1990s. This happened as the result of the interplay of institutional dynamics set up with the establishment of the post-Second World War order and the breakdown of the Soviet empire.

5.7 Releasing Functional Differentiation

The rise of different components of global governance can be seen as a result of both the reduced level of ideological differences in the international society and a push toward world society and functional differentiation beyond national borders. Whereas the dissolution of the blockade in the UNSC is a direct result of the change in the Soviet Union, the growing sense of responsibility for all human beings and the rise of self-regulatory arrangements on the global level indicate a movement toward world society. In this perspective, global governance constitutes a political system as part of a broader social process in which functional differentiation has gone global.

Classical differentiation theorists have analyzed national societies. In their view, modernity is distinguished from pre-modern societies in that segmentary differentiation between families, clans, and local communities *and* stratificatory differentiation marked by hierarchies of class, casts, or race is superseded by functional differentiation as the "dominant organizing principle." Functional differentiation points to function systems, such as economy, art, and politics, which pursue specific tasks for society as a whole and follow their own logic. In the economic system, the production of wealth is the task, which is driven by the logic of profit.

By conceptualizing modernity as a shift from the primacy of segmentary to a primacy of functional differentiation, early differentiation theorists implicitly pointed to the inherent limits of the territorial organization of societies (Durkheim 2012; Parsons 1967). If social organization follows primarily a functional logic, spatial limitations are secondary. They may temporarily hinder the full development of the functional logic, but, in the long run, they need to give in to the needs of different function systems.

In this perspective, the Westphalian system always was an unstable construction. Its decline was inscribed in the very principles on which it was based. The anarchical international system was built on two organizing principles: first, a segmentary differentiation among territorial units; and second, the competition between these territorially defined units. The latter organizing principle, however, undermined the first one in the long run. It created a permanent pressure to modernize in order to survive in a competitive system. Without societal modernization in terms of a continuing specialization of tasks and the division of labor leading to a productive economy, states risked falling behind in the competition. To put it differently, the anarchic international system did actually entail an evolutionary mechanism as envisioned by Waltz (1979). The decisive criterion for long-term success, however, was not military strength—as Waltz wants it—but economic productivity and success. While a militarily strong state like the Soviet Union did not survive, a militarily weak but economically successful state like Sweden is still part of the system. The side effect of this productivity competition between states was increased interdependence due to growing needs of different function systems to move beyond national borders. In this way, the competition between states undermined the autonomy of the national political systems in the long run.

Contrary to other function systems, the political system has the ambition to regulate all the other systems. Whereas outstanding differentiation theorists are—to say the least—skeptical about this ambition and the "steering capacity" (Mayntz et al. 1988) of the political system (see Luhmann 1984; Stichweh 2013), both its monopoly on the legitimate use of force (Weber) and its publicness (Habermas) make it arguably special. To the extent that conflicts in the realm of segmentary differentiation between states can be securitized, national political systems indeed seem to be able to exert control over other function systems (Buzan et al. 1998). Therefore, in most of the twentieth century, national political systems still controlled the dynamics of other function systems to a significant extent. Other function systems like economy and science could reach beyond national borders only to the extent that the political system tolerated it. By inserting the political logic into all aspects of society, totalitarian political systems even aimed, in the twentieth century, at controlling other function systems and keeping them fully in the cage of the national society. As a response, liberal political systems also established mechanisms to curb function systems. Within the context of segmentary competition between the superpowers, political systems brought sports to work against their own logic and to boycott the Olympic Games, disciplined economic East–West transactions by prohibiting the export of dual use goods, and, with Berlin, financed a whole city by ignoring all other standards of distributing financial resources. With the freeing of functional differentiation, these politically imposed restrictions lost grip.[11]

---

[11] In Luhmann's concept, world society had already developed in the eighteenth and nineteenth centuries when the political system evolved differently to other function systems on an international scale and when communication across the globe became possible.

With the end of the Cold War, the power of functional differentiation developed to its full potential, since the disciplinary effect of the segmentary competition between states lessened. As a result, the relationship between different function systems changed. The global drive of function systems like economy, law, art, sport, and science could now fully prevail and the national political systems had no good reason (or the means) to limit this development. To the extent that function systems globalize and produce outcomes that are counterproductive or affect other function systems negatively, there is rather a growing need for re-regulation on the global level.[12] This need is partially met by governments, partially by self-regulation, and is partially left unsatisfied.

The case of the international financial system may serve as an example.[13] Its development in the 1980s and especially 1990s is often cited when the notion of a decoupling of a function system from society as a whole is activated. In this case, the inner logic of the system drives it away from the function it has to fulfil for the society as a whole. Indeed, the global financial system—after being unleashed by the liberalization programs of Thatcher and Reagan (see Helleiner 1994)—could prevent any serious outside intervention into its own system by referring to some weak forms of self-regulation, mainly in the context of the Basel Accords. It was only after the recent global financial crisis that the call for political regulation grew louder. The subsequent efforts of political leaders around the world, however, were only partially successful (Mayntz 2014).

In sum, globalization has changed the relationship between different function systems, favoring the ones that easily reach beyond national borders, especially the economic one. Whereas the fall of the Soviet Union accelerated the internal dynamic toward more global governance, the freeing of functional differentiation also determined the shape of the global governance system: In the absence of possibilities to discipline other function systems, the global governance system was essentially one of loosely coupled spheres of authority. Political actors used the critical juncture to make decisions in favor of a global governance system—however, it was one that was full of shortcomings and lacking an overall vision.

---

[12] For Ulrich Beck (1996: 54–5), the problem goes even deeper. In his view, the combination of functional differentiation with instrumental rationality produces uncertainties such as nuclear disasters and climate change that entail risks of self-endangerment for the whole system. He thus predicts these side effects of functional differentiation to become the driving force of social history in a reflexive modernity.

[13] None of the best-known differentiation theorists (Emile Durkheim, Max Weber, Talcott Parsons, Niklas Luhmann, and Jeffrey Alexander are probably the five most important ones) considered the financial system as a function system of its own. They all saw it as part of the economic system. It is only recently that there has been talk of a financial system. This points to the problem of properly distinguishing different function systems in a world that is full of division, which has plagued differentiation theory for a long time (see, however, Luhmann 1984).

To be sure, the dominance of political considerations can return. The possibility that national political systems or the global system might strike back cannot be excluded, and it becomes more likely as the costs of uncurbed function systems become obvious and the problems associated with them become politicized or even securitized. As we have seen in the response to transnational terrorism and the economic crisis since 2008, the state can—at least partially—seize back control over areas it had previously conceded to the operation of other function systems. Moreover, 2016 could come to be seen as a tipping point in which right-wing populist movements re-established the relevance of national borders.

5.8 Conclusion

The historical-institutionalist account of the rise of the global governance system has been presented in the form of a thick description instead of a falsifiable set of hypotheses and an empirical test. This account can, however, be summarized in the form of a model—understood as a schematic statement of a theoretical argument—that depicts causal relationships. This model at hand embeds the more specific theory of contested global governance—which focuses on the last steps in the model only—in a broader perspective on world politics. Such an account emphasizes endogenous institutional dynamics while accepting the importance of external forces. The argument is summarized in Figure 5.4.

In this account, the global governance system developed in the 1990s as a result of a path-dependent sequence that started with the choice of embedded liberalism in the 1940s. The post-Second World War constellation provided a critical juncture that led to institutionalized embedded liberalism and collective security under American leadership. Afterwards, "self-reinforcing mechanisms" strengthened this institutional design. Yet the strengthening of liberal international institutions undermined the concept of embedded liberalism by weakening its shock absorbers. As a consequence, the resistance against neoliberalism pushed states to accept not only market-making but also market-braking international institutions. Global governance institutions thus received more authority and became more intrusive, irrevocably challenging Westphalian sovereignty. This whole dynamic was accelerated by an external push when the Soviet empire faltered and functional differentiation could develop its full potential. Together, these developments created a new critical juncture. As John Ikenberry (2011a: 7) puts it: "The rise of American unipolarity and the erosion of norms of state sovereignty—along with the deep shifts in the global system—have eroded the foundations of the old order and thrown the basic terms of order and world politics into dispute."

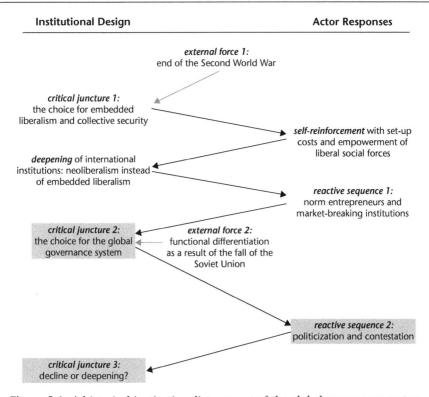

Figure 5.4. A historical-institutionalist account of the global governance system

As a result of the decisions taken in this situation, a global governance system emerged. It consists of loosely coupled spheres of both political and epistemic authority. Overall, the authority of IOs has increased remarkably. As a consequence, this global governance system co-produces new reactive sequences. It contains serious deficits undermining its acceptance and sustainability leading to resistance and demands for change. These demands for change come in the form of societal and state contestation. These new reactive sequences do not, however, end with contestation. There is the possibility of global governance authorities to respond to these challenges by responding to the demands and improve the legitimacy of the international authorities. In some instances, this has worked and led to a deepening of global governance; while in other instances, the outcomes are better described as a decline of global governance arrangements (see Hale et al. 2013). The obvious question that arises here is about the scope conditions for these different directions and the causal mechanisms at work.

In the following chapters, the causal mechanisms and hypotheses derived from the features of the global governance system discussed in Chapter 4 will be elaborated. In doing so, the final two boxes in Figure 5.4 will come into focus: "reactive sequence 2" pointing to societal and state contestation of international authority, and "critical juncture 3" within which it will be decided whether the global governance system deepens or declines. These two boxes are the core dependent variables of the theory of global governance as presented here. Moving beyond the thick description in this chapter, the behavioral implications derived from the theory will be scrutinized in Chapters 6 to 8.

6

The Politicization of Authority beyond the Nation State

International institutions are politicized by numerous so-called anti-neoliberal globalization groups such as Association for the Taxation of Financial Transactions and Citizens' Action (ATTAC) or Occupy, acting on the transnational level, as well as by resisters at the national level who seek to prevent the undermining of national sovereignty, for instance, via referenda on European integration or the prevention of intrusive trade agreements. All of the European right-wing populist parties from the Front National, to the German AFD (Alternative for Germany), to the British UKIP (United Kingdom Independence Party), to name just a few, are united in their demands for political renationalization. Only part of the current politicization of international institutions, however, comes in the form of resistance against global governance institutions. Many transnational non-state actors publicly address international institutions in a positive way, for instance, by calling for drastic intensification of climate policy measures at the international level (see Hadden 2015). Similarly, there have been numerous demands for much stronger interventions by the International Monetary Fund (IMF) and multilateral development banks as a response to the financial crisis after 2007. Moreover, various non-state groups—both civil society organizations (CSOs) and interest groups—seek permanent access to international institutions in order to facilitate their influence on internal agendas and policy formulation, as well as to hold these institutions accountable in the phases of policy implementation. Public resistance to international institutions and their more intensive utilization are both expressions of the process that is referred to as "politicization." Politicization thus is a two-sided process consisting of both demands for more international authority (re-legitimation) and challenges to existing authorities (delegitimation).

Politicization of international institutions is a relatively new process. Whereas the politicization of episodes of foreign policy has a long history, the politicization of international institutions has a comparatively short one. The public debates preceding each of the two world wars, the Vietnam War, and the German Ostpolitik are all instances in which *foreign policy* strategy and decisions gravitated to the center of political debate. World politics, therefore, has been at the center of political debates for a long time. The politicization of *international institutions*, on the other hand, is a relatively new phenomenon. Although historians have pointed out that the League of Nations already faced the "glare of publicity and pressure of mobilized publics" (Pedersen 2007: 110) and that this had a decisive impact on internal negotiations and external operations, such politicization was driven by only a few individuals and voluntary organizations seeking to push specific issues on the League's agenda. Similarly, the anti-apartheid and Third World movements in the 1970s can be considered predecessors to current developments; but then again, the broad politicization of international institutional policies and procedures with electoral effects was largely lacking at that time. In contrast, the politicization of international institutions points to a process through which widening arrays of actors—such as individual citizens, non-governmental organizations (NGOs), parties, lobby groups, and governmental bodies—are (re)oriented toward international institutions.

In this chapter, therefore, I argue that the notion of international cooperation as a purely executive, legal, or technocratic matter misses some decisive features of world politics today. International institutions are seen not only by political, but also by societal actors as political institutions exercising public authority requiring legitimacy. Against this background, two broad claims are put forward. According to the first, the politicization of international institutions can be ascribed to the patterns of authority described in Chapter 5. The more political authority international institutions exercise, the more attention they attract, the more actors participate in debates, and the more polarization in opinions takes place. The second broad claim is that, when it comes to its effects, politicization is a double-edged sword. On the one hand, it leads to a broadening of legitimation efforts including participatory and fairness-based narratives. Often, such a broadening of legitimation narratives is accompanied by substantial reforms, leading to the deepening of global governance. On the other hand, politicization may also lead to a significant legitimacy gap that can undermine the authorities as a whole. If politicization is responded to with friendly or unfriendly neglect, it may lead to gridlock and the decline of international authority.

These two broad claims follow from the first specification of the authority–legitimation link (ALL). Undermining via Politicization (CMALL 1) is the first causal mechanism derived from the model and empirically scrutinized in this chapter. I proceed in five steps: First, the meaning of the concept of politicization is discussed (section 6.1) before the causal mechanism through which authority may lead to politicization is explored (section 6.2). The section ends with a set of hypotheses, which are then used to explain the politicization of the European Union (EU) (section 6.3) and of international institutions (section 6.4). Finally, it is shown how such politicization may lead to a temporary broadening of legitimation narratives by defenders of international economic institutions, although resonance and institutional reforms seem to remain the exception (section 6.5).

6.1 What is Politicization?

Politicization, in general terms, means the demand for, or the act of, transporting an issue or an institution into the field or sphere of politics—making previously unpolitical matters political (see Zürn 2013: 13–16). The logical structure of politicization thus can be understood as follows: "an actor (x) wants to move something (y) to the position (b)." Clarifying these three components of the core meaning of politicization is necessary in order to come up with an operational definition. The degree of difficulty in clarifying varies. The most fundamental question is to define the sphere of the political, and thus to decide where something needs to be moved to before we can speak of politicization. The objects and subjects of politicization are then comparatively easy to identify.[1]

To start with, the whole notion of moving something into the field of politics presupposes functional differentiation (Alexander 1990). Before it can be moved from one to the other, there has to be a differentiation of spheres or function systems in the first place. So how then can the sphere of politics—the political, so to speak—be separated from other function systems? By drawing on two long-standing traditions of political thought, we can distinguish at least two major meanings of the political. The political can be defined either by the ability to make collectively binding decisions (Max Weber, Carl Schmitt, David Easton, and Niklas Luhmann are some of the heroes of this line), or by public debates about the right course in developing the collective will and in handling collective problems (Aristotle, Alexis de Tocqueville, Jürgen Habermas, and John Ruggie are proponents of this tradition).

Colin Hay (2007: 79) provides a link between the two different conceptions by characterizing the political sphere as the "realm of choice"—or, more precisely, the "realm of public choice"—to which issues and institutions are being moved most often from the realm of nature and of necessity. A debate is therefore only then political if it presupposes the *possibility* of

---

[1] Parts of this section draw on Zürn (2016b).

making a collectively binding decision or interpretations that change the status quo. Not only private issues can be drawn into the political sphere, but also issues and institutions that were formerly located in economic, legal, administrative, or technocratic realms or function systems.

Politicization can then be defined as moving something into the realm of public choice, thus presupposing the possibility of making collectively binding decisions on that matter. Full-scale politicization consists of three components: (a) the growing *salience* of an issue, involving (b) a *polarization of opinion* about this issue, and (c) an *expansion of actors and audiences* engaged (see e.g. de Wilde and Zürn 2012; de Wilde et al. 2016b; Hutter and Grande 2014; Hutter et al. 2016; Rauh 2016; Zürn 2014). Edgar Grande and Swen Hutter (2016: 31) put these three components in a concise formula: "politicization = salience x (actor expansion + polarization)."

Moreover, politicization can take place on three different levels: individual awareness on the micro-level, organizational mobilization on the meso-level, and public debates on the macro-level (see Ecker-Ehrhardt and Zürn 2013). *Awareness* points to a greater interest in an issue or a recognition that political institutions can make decisions as shown in survey data or experiments. This is the micro-component, which can be observed by looking at individuals. *Social mobilization* refers to an increase over time in the amount of resources spent influencing decision making in political institutions. This element points to social protest, to parties, and interest groups as core components of politicization, and is located on the meso-level. *Public debates* refer to conflicting views of the common good and opposing demands put to political institutions. These macro observations usually take place on the level of mass media.

What is moved into the political sphere? In his account of political society, the late Michael Thomas Greven (1999: 78) stated very explicitly that "[i]n principle, everything can become an object of political communication, i.e. can become politicized. This contingency can be hence redressed only by political decisions" (author's translation). To put it differently, besides decisions, non-decisions too can be politicized (see Bachrach and Baratz 1962). Politicization can be based on perceived gaps in international regulation (on non-decisions) and they can be based on perceived legitimation deficits of existing regulations (on decisions) (see Habermas 2007: 430).

Moreover, not only (non-)decisions, but also decision-making procedures and the institutions carrying out decisions or interpreting authoritatively, can be the objects of politicization. If not only a decision but the entire decision-making entity is at stake, then the normative framework of the institutional order (polity) is subject to politicization. If the process of decision making is under question, we may speak of the politicization of politics; and if simple decisions or non-decisions are at stake, we may speak of the politicization of policies.

Finally, who moves it? The subjects or *agents* of politicization are in essence all of the individuals or groups who participate in the political process, such as politicians, experts, and representatives of interest groups, or those who are in a position to organize political protests. At times, celebrities, too, may be agents of politicization—e.g. celebrities can introduce certain matters into the political space or bring about political intervention. While this chapter focuses on non-state actors, activities of governmental bodies can contribute to the politicization of international institutions as well. For instance, the often hypocritical blaming of EU institutions within the member states, for instance by ministers, can also contribute to the politicization of the EU—as a side-effect of party competition in the domestic realm (Gerhards et al. 2009).

The meaning of politicization is transporting an issue or an institution into the political sphere by individual or collective actors. The operational definition reads as follows:

> (Non-)decisions, decision-making processes, or the institutions that make decisions are politicized if the awareness (of individuals), social mobilization (of social groups), and public debates (in the mass media) indicate that they are seen as being in the realm of public choice. If something is politicized, one should see increasing salience of the matter, a broader participation, and increased contestation about it.[2]

Based on this definition, a multi-dimensional space of indicators for politicization can be set up (see Table 6.1). Each of the cells in the 3x3 matrix can

Table 6.1. Indicators of politicization (based on Zürn 2016b)

	Salience	Contestation (Polarization)	Expansion of Actors
Micro (Beliefs)	Importance relative to other issues, decision-making processes, or institutions	Different beliefs about the issues, decision-making processes, or institutions	Individuals with different traits see the issues, decision-making processes, or institutions as important
Meso (Mobilization)	Importance relative to other targets of mobilization	Mobilized actors/groups stand for different positions	Many different types of actors/groups mobilize
Macro (Public Debates)	Often mentioned in media (relative to other matters)	Polarization of statements/claims in media	Expansion of contributors to the debate

[2] This is also very much in line with the definition presented by Barry Buzan, Ole Waever, and Jaap de Wilde (1998: 29): "Politicization means to make an issue appear to be open, a matter of choice, something that is decided upon and that therefore entails responsibility, in contrast to issues that either could not be different (laws of nature) or should not be put under political control (e.g. a free economy, the private sphere, and matters of expert decision)." Similarly, Iris Young (2004: 377) defines politicization as "activities in which people organize collectively to regulate or transform some aspects of their shared social conditions, along with communicative activities in which they try to persuade one another to join such collective actions or decide what directions they wish to take."

point to both resistance against political institutions and their utilization for preferred policy goals.

When moving to measuring politicization, it is obviously hard to provide data that fills all the nine cells and is able to distinguish between the different types of politicization. For practical reasons, any study about politicization needs to focus on some aspects while neglecting others. The decision depends, however, not only on the taste of the analyst, but also on the goal of the study.

6.2 Why is there Politicization? What are its Effects?

Why does the rise of international authority lead to the politicization of international institutions? Why are some international institutions more politicized than others? And why can we expect that this process is especially accentuated in those inter- and transnational institutions that display the most grave legitimation deficits in global governance?

The causal model of a theory of global governance can be utilized to answer these questions. Accordingly, the ALL plays out in different versions. In order to understand the dynamics of politicization, I start with exploring Undermining via Politicization (CMALL 1). This causal mechanism posits, in the first place, that a rise of international authority leads—*ceteris paribus*—to the rise of politicization if the rise of authority overburdens existing legitimation narratives. Second, the theory also allows us to formulate expectations about the effects of politicization (see Figure 6.1).

CMALL 1 represents a reactive sequence. Choice is therefore built into the model and none of the three steps identified in the model is deterministic. The mechanism can be stopped at each of the three arrows. Each of the steps points to probabilistic relationships that can be formulated as hypotheses. CMALL 1 will be elaborated by evaluating the evidence regarding six hypotheses. Hypotheses 1 to 3 elaborate the first arrow in CMALL 1, hypothesis 4 the second, and hypotheses 5 and 6 the final one.

To start with, authority is—according to the operational definition provided in Chapter 5—the function of the depth of recognition of the interpretations and decisions by an institution that has delegated or pooled competences with a given breadth or scope of the mandate. If an inter- or

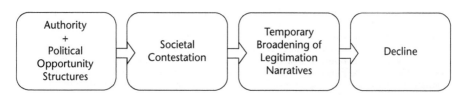

Figure 6.1. CMALL 1: Undermining via politicization

transnational authority exercises more authority than before, it covers more issues, has moved voting rules in the direction of majoritarian voting, delegated tasks to the international organization (IO), or increased bindingness. As a result, it makes more and more relevant and intrusive decisions and interpretations. If this occurs, we can expect more awareness, mobilization, and debates about the content of these decisions and interpretations. The more authority, the more politicization is the simple formula. More conflicts about policies can thus be expected. Since decisions usually have a higher level of bindingness or "coerciveness" than interpretations, we can moreover expect that the output of institutions with political authority will become more politicized than that of institutions with epistemic authority. Finally, the more legitimation deficits an institution has, the more politicization we can expect of it. We should therefore expect, for instance, that the United Nations Security Council (UNSC)—an IO with significant authority and significant institutional deficits—has produced most legitimation conflicts after the expansion of the peace enforcement efforts without the participation of all the affected parties.

- H 1: The more authority an inter- or transnational institution exercises, the more politicization by non-state actors can be observed ("authority transfer thesis").
- H 2: Political authorities display higher levels of politicization than epistemic authorities.
- H 3: The more governance deficits an inter- or transnational institution displays in terms of the technocratic and the power bias, the more politicization by both state and non-state actors can be observed.

These three hypotheses about the sources of politicization can be derived from a theory of global governance. However, this should not conceal that, for a complete explanation of the level of politicization, other variables have to be taken into account as well. The translation of authority into politicization above all requires the mobilization of resources (McCarthy and Zald 1977) and adequate political opportunity structures (Kitschelt 1986). In this sense, the authority of inter- and transnational institutions depends on the presence of conditioning or intervening variables like referenda, crises, social groups with resources, and mobilizing ideologies (de Wilde and Zürn 2012; Schmidtke 2016; Grande and Hutter 2016; Hutter and Grande 2014). These resources and opportunities can be located on the national and the transnational level.

Politicization also has consequences. With the rise of politicization, a broadening of legitimation narratives can be expected for two reasons. On the one hand, the challengers of technocratic authority blame authority holders for not taking into account other criteria of legitimacy, which, for instance, are emphasized by the participatory or fairness narrative. In this way, they bring themes and standards to the public debate about the authority that go beyond the mostly dominant technocratic narrative. If the degree and the type of political authority overburdens the existing stocks of legitimacy, authority holders consider, on the other hand, new legitimation practices that respond to the challenges.

- H 4: An increased degree of politicization leads to a broadening of narratives that are referred to in the legitimation process.

Whether this change in legitimation narratives leads in the end to the decline or deepening of global governance, however, depends on whether the adaptation is substantial or symbolic. If it remains symbolic and the legitimation narrative in the long run moves back to being mainly technocratic, then we can expect an ongoing authority–legitimation gap, which may lead to deadlock and the decline of global governance. Substantial responses, in contrast, indicate a deepening of global governance.

- H 5: The broadening of legitimation narratives is a necessary but not sufficient condition for substantial responses to delegitimation efforts that lead to the deepening of global governance.
- H 6: If authority holders do not—or only symbolically—respond to delegitimation efforts, deadlock and the decline of global governance can be expected.

These claims and mechanisms run counter to relevant strands of theorizing about inter- and transnational relations. First of all, major theories of International Relations (IR) and international institutions question the idea that international institutions possess authority in their own right (Waltz 1979; Keohane 1984). They see the international system as anarchical. Second, international relations are widely seen as a social realm dominated by executives and technocrats, even when power and authority are exercised. Henry Kissinger (1957) sees the withdrawal of foreign policy and international negotiations from public debate as a defining and desirable element of international relations. In this line of thinking, Andrew Moravcsik (2006), while accepting that the EU exercises authority in some areas, maintains that this takes place only in policy fields that are not of interest for the people and therefore do not require (democratic) legitimation. In general, international institutions, even when they exercise authority, are most often still seen as sites of executive, legal, and technocratic governance protected from public and societal pressures. The politicization of international institutions is not foreseen in these interpretations of world politics.

These claims and hypotheses also complement those analyses that see a process of renationalization directed against European and international institutions. These studies point to the changing conflict structure in populations

144

affected by European and international integration that is said to enhance the risk of right-wing populism (Kriesi et al. 2012; Hooghe et al. 2002; Hooghe and Marks 2009; Kitschelt 1997; Burgoon 2009; Scheve and Slaughter 2004; Mayda and Rodrik 2005). The winners and losers of globalization, it is argued, can increasingly define themselves, creating a mobilization potential on which national political elites can draw when need be. Since party political competition for socio-economic alternatives is lacking, these conflicts take place more and more on a cultural dimension marked by identity considerations (Hooghe and Marks 2004). Thus, where political conflict about authorities beyond the nation state becomes manifest, populist and national positions are expected to gain in strength, greatly limiting the scope of international negotiations and considerably hampering global governance.

The use of the concept of politicization modifies these renationalization views. While the struggle about the soundness of international authorities contains at least two sides, the politicization of international institutions indicates not only a rise of opponents to global governance, but also polarization in attitudes about global governance including the strengthening of pro-global governance forces. Similarly, politicization does not automatically equate with growing resistance to the EU as a political system but is just as much about demands toward changed policies at the supranational level. Politicization can thus lead to both decline and deepening. The politicization of international authority may indicate a hollowing out of national democracies; it can at the same time be seen as a necessary (but certainly not sufficient) condition for the democratization of authorities beyond the nation state (Zürn 2014b).

In the remainder of this chapter, the plausibility of the six hypotheses derived from the causal model are probed. I start out with the causes of politicization (sections 6.3 and 6.4). In section 6.5, I move to the effects of politicization. These explorations are based on secondary literature, a qualitative investigation, and semi-automated content analysis.

6.3 The Politicization of the European Union

No other institution beyond the nation state has so many mechanisms to overcome national vetoes and no other is so intrusive into national societies than the EU. In this sense, the EU seems to be an easy case to test the authority transfer hypothesis, but also a good starting point to trace the part of CMALL 1 that connects the rise of authority with politicization.

The process of European integration was, for a long time, mainly an elite-driven project. After the founding period, when the fathers of European integration were moved primarily by foreign policy considerations (Milward

1992), the Treaties of Rome brought economic interests to the fore, which were then driving negotiations among national executives, transnational industrial interests, and supranational civil servants (Moravcsik 1998). However, decision-making processes and the content of decisions remained, for a considerable amount of time, relatively hidden to the broader public. There is no question that there has been talk of a democratic deficit in the EU for decades, and the response by the authority holders to these allegations was not least the creation and strengthening of the European Parliament and many other—often mainly symbolic—acts to show the nearness of the Brussels institutions to the people. In spite of these efforts, Brussels remained a remote place from the perspective of most Europeans. After the Single European Act, the project of liberalizing European economies was often ascribed to the individual national governments; at the same time, most people associated the EU above all with a rampant bureaucracy.

Especially since the beginning of the 1990s, the increasing scope and depth of supranational EU policy created a counter-movement to the remote decision making dominated by executive and technocratic bodies only. The range and intensity of societal demands toward the supranational level have greatly increased over time, and the European integration process has attracted considerable media coverage, polarized public opinion, and even provoked open protests at several stages. In effect, this politicization puts an end to the "permissive consensus" that had formed the social basis for elitist and non-transparent decision making (Hooghe and Marks 2009). It challenges the traditional yardsticks for assessing the EU. Instead of focusing on economically efficient outputs as the key criterion for positive assessment, the EU is now seen as a political institution that exercises authority, and is therefore subject to the need to justify public authority with a more elaborate set of sources of legitimacy. The EU and its decisions have been moved from the realm of technocratic necessity to the realm of public choice.

I want to show two things: that EU politicization grew roughly in parallel with the rise of authority of European institutions, and that it followed a path that is in line with the theory of contested global governance. I begin with a brief review of the literature before findings from our own research are presented.

6.3.1 *State of the Art*

The concept of politicization was (at least implicitly) first introduced to European integration before the 1990s. Early neo-functionalist theories hypothesized already that—as an instance of "spillover"—the growing saliency of European issues would be one of the unintended consequences of the integration process (Haas 1958: 11–19; Schmitter 1969). The concept of politicization was then rediscovered in the 2000s, when scholars of multi-level governance used it to make sense of the series of contentious EU treaty referenda, which indicated that the population's "permissive consensus" on European integration could no longer be taken for granted (see Hooghe and Marks 2009; Zürn 2006). While the early neo-functionalist reading of politicization was mainly interested in politicization as a means to foster the European integration process, the more recent usages emphasize the challenge of politicization for the integration project.

The politicization of the EU in the latter meaning became a vibrant research field (see the contributions to de Wilde et al. 2016b). There are three convergent findings. To begin with, one can state that there is a remarkably high level of agreement in the relevant literature regarding the development of politicization. Until the early 1990s, the term "permissive consensus" had been used to describe the attitude of European societies toward the institutions of the EU. Rarely has a formula coming out of the social sciences been less contested. Quite remarkably, the verdict about the end of permissive consensus seems to be similarly consensual (see Schmitter 2009: 211–12).

Second, when it comes to explaining politicization, the authority transfer hypothesis receives significant support. Paul Statham (2010: 295), for instance, summarizes the results of a study about the making of a European public sphere as follows: "We find that the more decision-making power shifts to the European level for a policy field, or over time, the more attention for and criticism of the [EU] rise" (see also Koopmans and Statham 2010).

Some more recent contributions test the authority transfer hypothesis by looking at variations in being affected by EU authority. Henning Schmidtke (2016) picks countries that are differently affected by EU authority. He demonstrates the power of an "explanatory framework which views authority transfer as the driving force of politicization and country-specific economic and socio-cultural contest as two potentially conditioning variables which shape the strength and direction of the authority transfer effect on the national level" (Schmidtke 2016: 67). Compatible with this finding, Edgar Grande and Swen Hutter (2016: 40) demonstrate that, on average, membership debates cause more politicization in the mass media than major treaties and enlargement debates. The process of countries entering the EU and accepting the whole *acquis communautaire* without exercising any voice clearly involves the highest level of transfer of authority from the perspective of the single country; extending the authority of the EU comes second; sharing the authority with even more members comes third.[3]

---

[3] The general support for the authority transfer thesis notwithstanding, there are case studies that point to pockets of EU authority with little politicization. Herschinger et al. (2013) show that, in the issue area of internal security, transgovernmental institutions with significant levels of authority are barely politicized. Similarly, there is little politicization of the European Investment Bank in spite of significant authority (Hilgers 2014). In both cases, the institutional form seems to serve as a protective shield.

Third, in spite of the general trend, there are significant variations across time and space. Attempts to explain national variation often focus on the sources of mobilization and the political opportunity structure (e.g. Leupold 2016; Hoeglinger 2016; Grande and Hutter 2016). These studies highlight the role of resource mobilization and especially political opportunity structures. They are compatible with the authority transfer thesis. By positing a driving force that explains the commonality of politicization across countries as a second image reversed explanation (Gourevitch 1978), there is no denial that specific "mobilizing potentials" and "opportunity structures" must be existent before politicization can be observed.

6.3.2 Quantitative Assessment of EU Politicization

In order to bolster these findings and to show a parallel rise of EU authority and EU politicization, I utilize an index that brings together indicators for the visibility of the EU in the media, the polarization of public opinion on EU membership, and mobilization on EU issues in the public spheres of the six founding members of the EU between 1990 and 2011.[4] The indicator, developed by Christian Rauh (2016), aggregates the three components of the politicization concept, allowing us to draw cross-temporal conclusions on the extent of politicization before and during the Eurozone crisis. To start with, for the measurement of the visibility of the EU, a text-mining analysis approach has been utilized. Trading off some analytical depth for the benefits of the required large-scale comparison, a (semi-)automated analysis of articles referring to the EU in *L'Echo* (BE), *Frankfurter Allgemeine Zeitung* (DE), *Le Monde* (FR), *Corriere della Sera* (IT), and *NRC Handelsblad* (NL) has been carried out. Visibility is operationalized as the average share of all articles mentioning the EU (varying between 1.6 percent and 8.2 percent). The polarization of public opinion on the EU is captured on the micro-level by the variance and kurtosis of the distribution of individual attitudes to EU membership in the corresponding waves of the Eurobarometer.[5] The extension of actors is proxied by looking at public mobilization by an extension of Uba and Uggla's (2011) count data on "Euro protests," covering all events such as demonstrations and rallies at which the EU and its actors were either the source or the addressee of the demands expressed (see also Imig and Tarrow 2001). The values of the individual

---

[4] This section draws from Rauh and Zürn (2014).

[5] Both elements are needed to avoid distortions through isolated extreme positions. Greater variance could, e.g., be produced by only a few but extreme positions. However, if greater variance is accompanied by a low kurtosis of distribution, this indicates that polarization is increasing in breadth, and is therefore more relevant for the general level of polarization. See also Down and Wilson (2008: 32).

indicators were z-standardized over the period under study and aggregated into an index of average monthly values.[6]

These data summarized in Figure 6.2 show a robust politicization trend over time, but also strong fluctuations in the short term. Events that caused particularly marked peaks of politicization are the ratification of the Maastricht Treaty from 1992 and 1993, the enlargement of 2004, and the failure of the Constitutional Treaty in 2005.

What is more, the comparative perspective of the index highlights that the financial and currency crises produced the highest level of societal politicization of the EU between 2009 and 2011. After the "reflection period"—mainly imposed by Angela Merkel and Nicolas Sarkozy—and the subsequent adoption of the Lisbon Treaty, which happened largely out of the public eye, the politicization indicator rose markedly between summer 2008 and autumn 2009. This reflects the increased visibility of the treaty ratification process, which came to public attention with the lost referendum in Ireland and the constitutional complaints in Germany; but it also mirrors the increasingly

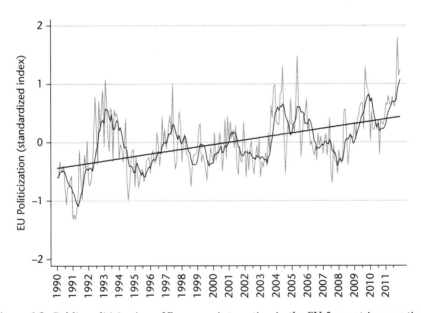

Figure 6.2. Public politicization of European integration in the EU-5 countries over time

Source: Rauh, C., and Zürn, M. (2014), "Zur Politisierung der EU in der Krise," in M. Heidenreich (ed.), *Krise der europäischen Vergesellschaftung?* (Wiesbaden: Springer Fachmedien Wiesbaden), 121–45[7]

---

[6] For a detailed treatment and discussion of the politicization index, see Rauh (2016).
[7] The figure plots the mean of z-standardized indicators for public visibility, polarization, and mobilization on EU topics. The grey line shows the monthly values, and the black one the six month moving average. In addition, a simple ordinary least squares (OLS) time trend is provided.

Europeanized discussion on government rescue measures for failed banks and the reorganization of financial markets in the light of the worldwide liquidity squeeze. This manifests itself not only in growing media attention on the macro-level, but also—and above all—in the growing polarization of public opinion on the micro-level, as well as in active mobilization on EU issues on the meso-level. Examples of such mobilization were a French strike for greater job security parallel to a meeting of European heads of state and government in March 2009, and the demonstration organized by the German Trade Union Federation (DGB) for a European social pact a month later, which attracted almost 100,000 participants. These events stress that politicization does not automatically equate with growing resistance to the EU as a political system, but is just as much about demands toward changed policies at the supranational level.

During spring 2010, the politicization levels in the EU-6 countries declined briefly. In the course of the year, however, the financial crisis developed more and more into a crisis of the European currency. The piecemeal revelation of the Greek budget deficit and the downgrading of Portugal's credit rating in March 2010 spurred fears that other Euro countries would be affected as well. Political discussions on appropriate political responses and further institutional reforms intensified in the course of the year.

In parallel to the increased media attention, the number of public demonstrations on EU issues rose in the second half of the year. Once again, growing political demands addressed to the supranational level were manifested particularly in protests organized by trade unions. On 29 September 2010, more than 50,000 people demonstrated in Brussels against the austerity policy as the sole possible supranational reaction to the crisis, accompanied by concerted action in almost all European capitals.

For the following year, 2011, the index shows a further increase in EU politicization. This accompanied the ongoing debates about the re-regulation of the financial markets, especially about a European rating agency, a transaction tax, and the capitalization level of financial institutions and the institutional architecture of the monetary union. The politicization index reached its highest peak during the summit marathon in October 2011, shortly before the adoption of the fiscal pact two months later. It should be noted that all three components of politicization—visibility, polarization, and expansion of actors—rose again over this period.

Of course, an assessment of the long-term effects of the financial and economic crisis on the societal politicization of the EU remains provisional at this stage. However, both short-term patterns during the crisis and the long-term comparison to earlier discursive opportunities such as the Maastricht ratification or the debate on the Constitution stress that the extent of EU politicization among the public in the EU-6 countries has reached unprecedented dimensions. It seems fair to conclude that in accordance with H 1, the rise of authority is accompanied by the growth of politicization over time. In line with H 2, the comparatively high level of politicization of the EU seems also to be due to the fact that a significant extent of political authority is involved.

6.3.3 Qualitative Interpretation

The developments during the financial and economic crisis in the EU provide a textbook example for the two sides of politicization. It involves complaints about the lack of the right policies on the one hand, and complaints about the overstretch of supranational institutions—given their limited legitimacy—on the other. They are connected by a sequence of events that is typical for the politicization of international institutions. In the first place, the process is triggered by regulatory deficiencies at the European and international levels. Second, the consequence has been an increase in the authority of institutions beyond the nation state, thus preparing the ground for further politicization. Third, this has been particularly marked as the crisis that made the importance of European policies for broad sections of society far more apparent than they were in the past. Lastly, the crisis therefore creates a situation of political contestation that provides a risk as well as a window of opportunity for altering the course of political and societal integration of Europe.

In the first step, and pursuant to the Treaty of Maastricht, the Economic and Monetary Union centralized monetary policy at the European level in 1991. Monetary policy is completely in the hands of European institutions, headed by the European Central Bank (ECB), which is independent of both member states and other EU-level actors (Article 130 of the Treaty on the Functioning of the European Union (TFEU)). The Governing Council of the ECB, in which national central banks are represented, takes decisions by majority voting. At the same time, the scope of action is constitutionally limited by the "no-bailout" clause, which excludes any liability of the union and other member states for the debts of a member state (Article 125 TFEU). Moreover, European institutions were given only very limited supervisory powers over the budgetary policy of member states to perpetuate the debt limits laid down on accession (Article 126 TFEU). This overall architecture was the outcome of a largely intergovernmental negotiation process (Moravcsik 1998: 379–471), which created an unprecedented degree of political authority beyond the nation state. However, the compromise combining centralized monetary policy and decentralized fiscal policy proved deficient. This institutional design caused the debt crisis as countries with low growth in

151

productivity could not devalue their currencies, while it also prevented common solutions such as a fiscal equalization scheme.

It is thus no surprise that the crisis, in the second step, very soon provoked demands to eliminate the regulatory deficiencies by shifting further authority to European institutions. These demands have been met to a considerable degree following a functionalist understanding of European integration (Schimmelfennig 2012: 502–4). The best example is the so-called "Six-Pack," a series of legislative initiatives presented by the European Commission to tighten the Stability and Growth Pact one year after the Greek deficit became known. The European Parliament and the Council adopted these measures in the autumn of 2011, making national budgets subject to supranational control even during the planning phase. Furthermore, the procedure for decisions on sanctions has been reversed: sanctions no longer depend on the active consent of member states, but can at best be prevented by a qualified majority. The fiscal pact adopted in the autumn of 2011 has a similar aim. Over and beyond the actual Maastricht criteria, it imposes an almost balanced budget on member states, requires national debt brakes with constitutional status, and makes these fiscal policy measures subject to sanctioning by the European Court of Justice (ECJ). Moreover, the European Stability Mechanism (ESM), which can meanwhile buy government bonds and recapitalize banks, is also not based on national veto rights, but allows individual member states to be outvoted by a qualified majority. European institutions have been strengthened at the level of decision-making powers.

These measures in connection with the crisis make, in a third step, supranational authority tangible for broad sections of society and provide a political opportunity structure par excellence. This is of course particularly the case for the societies of "debtor countries." For them, the prescribed austerity policies mean drastic reductions in individual well-being—reductions that can quite clearly be attributed to decisions taken at the supranational level. Nothing demonstrates this with greater symbolic force than the troika of "liquidator" inspectors from the IMF, the ECB, and the European Commission. The cuts in pensions and wages were drastic. The growing poverty was palpable in Athens and could not be overlooked even in the otherwise so noble Madrid. But in the "donor" states, too, individual and collective welfare is massively affected by current supranational decisions, and the public pays great attention accordingly, especially when the possibility of financial transfers are discussed.

Finally, the political authority of European institutions has been called into question on grounds of insufficient legitimation. The increase in direct exercise of political authority by European institutions strongly contrasts with only mediated and only fragmentary representation of all the societal interests affected (Scharpf 2009). The Commission's rights to control national budgets and the expansion of the powers of the ECB mentioned above are cases in point. Deficient legitimacy can also result from the (self-)empowerment of national executives at the cost of elected representatives in national parliaments or in the European Parliament. Summit diplomacy—which has repeatedly played a major role during the crisis—with recurrent pictures of black limousines outside the Justus Lipsius building, negotiations behind closed doors, and the early morning announcement of results to which "there is no alternative" are unlikely to signal an inclusive and representative decision-making procedure. Where Europe intervenes profoundly in the well-being of broad sections of society and is hence controversial among the public, a purely output-oriented legitimation operating only on the basis of practical constraints and expertise can no longer suffice to sustain public consent.

This look at the process with which politicization unfolds provides further support for the authority transfer hypothesis. Most fundamentally, the more authority the EU exercises over the course of time, the more politicization can be observed. We definitely see more than just growing resistance against the EU: both additional demands for more European regulation and the general questioning of EU authorities and their legitimacy can be observed. Moreover, and in line with H 2, the more obviously the EU exercises political authority instead of "only" epistemic authority, the better the chances for politicization. Finally, in support of H 3, in cases of high levels of authority, legitimation deficits become more obvious. However, the concrete level and type of politicization of international authority in different national contexts depends on intervening resource mobilization capacities and political opportunity structures.

6.4 The Politicization of Other International Institutions

Isn't the politicization of the EU a special case, driven by its extraordinarily high level of authority? Do we really see a politicization of international institutions, or is the degree of inter- and transnational authority still below the threshold at which politicization sets in? Are international institutions with relatively higher degrees of authority more politicized than others? Are international institutions with political authority more politicized than those who exercise mainly epistemic authority? Do severe legitimation deficits translate into further politicization? In answering these questions, I start with a brief review of the literature on the theme, and then provide a qualitative analysis of different international institutions.

6.4.1 *State of the Art*

In general, research on the politicization of inter- and transnational institutions is less developed than that on the politicization of the EU. When it comes to quantitative measurements in terms of salience, act expansion, and contestation in the public media—which dominates the field of EU politicization research—only two efforts stand out, both dealing with international tax policy (Rixen and Zangl 2013; Schmidtke 2014). Both of them conclude that the authority transfer hypothesis explains the outcomes better than alternative hypotheses. Some case studies come to similar conclusions (Binder 2013; Viola 2013).

There is however a tradition of rich research about transnational protest that is cognate to the concept of politicization. This work—originated by scholars like Donatella della Porta, Dieter Rucht, and Sidney Tarrow—has shown that there are many indications for an ongoing transnationalization of social protest (della Porta and Tarrow 2005; della Porta 2007; della Porta and Caiana 2009; Gronau et al. 2009; Pianta and Zola 2005; Rucht 2013; Tarrow 2001, 2005). Similarly, a more recent strand sees the rise of "new transnationalism"—i.e. "the outpouring of contention across borders in the past decade" (Tarrow 2005: 7)—as a consequence of internationalism. Internationalism, in turn, stands for "a dense, triangular structure of relations among states, nonstate actors, and international institutions" (Tarrow 2005: 27). Moreover, della Porta and Tarrow (2012) see transnational movements that target international institutions as the latest and most important move in the transnationalization of social protest. Indeed, della Porta (2011) uses the concept of politicization to grasp these developments (see also Steffek and Hahn 2010 and Steffek et al. 2007).[8]

Moreover, in a path-breaking effort, Frank Nullmeier and colleagues (Nullmeier et al. 2010) analyzed legitimacy claims of affected actors and compared some nation states with some IOs as targets of legitimacy demands. They show that the EU, G8, and the United Nations (UN) are meanwhile regular targets of legitimation debates—in intensity not far from national political systems—and that the concrete level and intensity of these debates are strongly influenced by the perception of the capacities of these institutions.

Overall, existing research on the politicization of inter- and transnational institutions is either directly supportive of—or at least compatible with—the hypotheses formulated in section 6.2. While the authority transfer hypothesis already works with lower levels of authority, it needs to surpass a certain minimal level. Most international institutions did not possess this minimum level before 1989, and still today many institutions have only marginal levels of authority that do not suffice for politicization.

---

[8] But see Jaeger (2007), who sees the rise of global civil society as a partially depoliticizing force.

6.4.2 Qualitative Exploration

In this section, the focus will be on different governance functions.[9] Building on the reported findings, it will be argued that the observed pattern is compatible with the authority transfer hypothesis (H 1), that epistemic authority is less strongly politicized than political authority (H 2), and that the degree of institutional deficits is relevant in this process (H 3).

Rule-making: International institutions that set rules via majority decisions exercise political authority. Majority voting plays a significant part in global governance and increases the probability that individual states will implement measures, even when doing so runs counter to those states' initial will or intent.

Where the authority of international institutions rests on majoritarian decision making, the transparency and fairness of the decision-making process become of prime concern to societal actors and minority states. Information disclosure has been a priority of transnational advocacy addressing the World Bank. Receiving states, NGOs, and parts of the Global Justice Movement (della Porta and Tarrow 2005) justify their demands not only by alluding to the enormous impact of the World Bank's projects and policies on local communities, but also by drawing attention to voting power inequalities between members and pointing to the Bank's substantial leverage over loan recipients (Nelson 2009). Past and current criticism of international authority goes well beyond issues of lacking transparency, however, it repeatedly insists upon fairness in terms of equal inclusion in the negotiation process of those affected by the decisions of such an authority. The lack of representativeness on the UNSC, which is further intensified by the veto power of the permanent members, is particularly blatant and has been condemned by societal actors and governments (Binder 2013). The exclusion of entire regions from the crucial processes of preliminary and parallel negotiations in the WTO's Green Room has also triggered frequent calls for more representative decision-making procedures (cf. O'Brian et al. 2000; Krajewski 2002).

Monitoring: Monitoring and verification are increasingly carried out by agencies that are not directly under the control of states. In general, the need for monitoring is greater if international norms no longer apply just to the borders between countries but, instead, begin to regulate activities within the boundaries of sovereign territories. Whenever such behind-the-border issues (Kahler 1995) are at stake, mutual observation by the states that are party to an agreement is often not sufficient to guarantee compliance. Thus the need for independent actors who process and make available information on treaty compliance is growing steadily. Such information is provided by the

---

[9] This section draws from Zürn et al. (2012a).

international secretariats of treaty systems (Biermann and Siebenhüner 2009) and autonomous organizations, such as the World Health Organization (WHO) or the International Atomic Energy Agency (IAEA), to name just two prominent examples (Dai 2007: 50–3). These are cases of politically assigned epistemic authority (PAEA). NGOs may also function, more or less informally, as monitoring agencies. Amnesty International and Human Rights Watch, for instance, are important actors for monitoring compliance with human rights standards. In general, Jonas Tallberg and colleagues have shown that, since the 1980s, the access of NGOs to international policy processes has increased significantly (Tallberg et al. 2013).

But has this trend in increased monitoring led to the politicization of such agencies? Monitoring and verification often involve PAEAs. It can therefore be expected that such institutions will be less politicized than rule-making institutions. While remarkable instances of politicization suggest that the authority to monitor and verify international rule implementation is considered as significant, the overall level of politicization has indeed remained limited. The IAEA, for instance, is widely acknowledged for its expertise in monitoring the peaceful use of nuclear energy, not least in accordance with the Nuclear Non-Proliferation Treaty. The Nobel Prize Committee honored this organization in 2005, confirming societal expectations that the IAEA could "prevent nuclear energy from being used for military purposes" and could "ensure that nuclear energy for peaceful purposes is used in the safest possible way" (The Nobel Peace Prize 2005). However, despite its sterling reputation, the IAEA has been criticized repeatedly. In 2006, after worldwide public attention was drawn to several reports on the health impacts and environmental consequences of the Chernobyl accident in 1986, a campaign led by Greenpeace and several anti-nuclear NGOs attacked the IAEA for "whitewashing the impacts of the most serious nuclear accident in human history" (Greenpeace International 2006), and called for more effective monitoring. In the aftermath of the earthquake and the tsunami that struck Japan in March 2011, culminating in the disastrous Fukushima nuclear accident, the IAEA has once again come under fire for downplaying the effects of that catastrophe.

Western publics in general recognize some UN agencies and actors, like the UN Secretary General, the UN Office of the High Commissioner of Human Rights (OHCHR), or the World Food Programme, as among the most credible sources of information on humanitarian crises. This recognition has been highly influential on how Western publics make up their minds over complex issues such as the Darfur conflict (Ecker-Ehrhardt 2010). At the same time, these agencies have been criticized repeatedly for alerting the world to some crises (e.g. Somalia or Kosovo), but failing to do so with others (e.g. Rwanda or Myanmar). Similarly, the UN Commission on Human Rights (UNCHR) and its successor, the UN Human Rights Council (UNHRC), have been regularly criticized for applying double standards and addressing human rights violations selectively—e.g. focusing on Israel but ignoring the Palestinians (cf. Terlingen 2007) or catering to great power interests by refraining from addressing human rights abuse by Russia, China, or the United States. Such instances of public criticism of international authority are necessarily selective, but they support the basic claim of a theory of contested governance; namely, that the exercise of authority leads to its politicization. At the same time, these epistemic authorities are less politicized than the more political ones, and the targets of criticism are rather specific outcomes than institutional deficits.

Norm interpretation: Regarding norm interpretation, the significant increase in the number of international judicial or quasi-judicial bodies, with currently around 100 of them active (see Chapter 5), is most important. If we look at fully developed international courts only, there are now at least twenty-four permanent international courts (ICs). Eighty percent of operational ICs have a broad compulsory jurisdiction, and 84 percent authorize non-state actors—supranational commissions, prosecutors, and/or private actors—to initiate litigation. These ICs have collectively issued over 37,000 binding rulings in individual contentious cases, 91 percent of which were issued since the fall of the Berlin Wall (Alter 2014: 4).

In line with the general authority transfer thesis, it can be shown that societal actors politicize these judicial authorities and activities as well, and that the level of politicization lies in between that of political authorities and that of purely epistemic authorities. Even though civil society has been one of the driving forces behind the institutionalization of the ICC, and even though the legal authority of the Court has been generally well-received, the ICC has met with stern criticism vis-à-vis a number of its investigations—among them Uganda, the Central African Republic, and Namibia (e.g. Baines 2007; Glasius 2008)—whereby the Court was accused of being selective by focusing on "the losers' side" of civil war. Civil war victims have also criticized the Court harshly, maintaining that their expectations of receiving justice were disappointed by the ICC's focus on higher ranking individuals accused of war crimes, by its lack of outreach, and by the protracted pace of investigation (e.g. Clarke 2007). In effect, some of the African states plan to retreat from the ICC. Ad hoc tribunals like the International Criminal Tribunal for the Former Yugoslavia (ICTY) and the International Criminal Tribunal for Rwanda (ICTR) have been similarly criticized (see e.g. Spoerri and Freyberg-Inan 2008).

The same holds for the WTO Dispute Settlement Body (DSB). Civil society actors have greatly exploited the opportunity to attend selected panel meetings or to file *amicus curiae* briefs with that body; that is a strong sign of public awareness and mobilization (e.g. Eckersley 2007). In the meantime, however, evidence suggests that civil society actors' inclinations to take part in WTO DSB proceedings have subsided. This is because civil society access to the DSB proved to be less effective than these actors had initially anticipated, for having their own expertise heard during proceedings, especially toward later stages of the process involving the WTO's Appellate Body (e.g. van den Bossche 2008). In sum, it can again be observed that increased authority in rule interpretation also comes with increased politicization in terms of substantial public aware- ness and contestation on normative grounds. At the same time, courts as major instances of PAEAs are less politicized than political authorities.

Enforcement of decisions: Only a few international institutions have the capacity to enforce their own decisions, thus exercising the strongest form of political authority. Nevertheless, we can observe that the practice of levying material sanctions against violators has increased. For example, *jus cogens* has expanded and, according to some interpretations, now includes *inter alia* the prohibition of crimes against humanity, genocide, and apartheid. In the same vein, the UNSC's use of coercive measures under Chapter 7 has increased from below 4 percent before 1989 to roughly 40 percent afterwards (Johansson 2009). Moreover, the World Bank (and also the IMF) has increasingly employed conditional loans—i.e. loans that are tied to the recipient state's fulfilling certain conditions, like carrying out specific economic or political reforms (Mosley et al. 1995). In these cases of enforcement authority, high levels of politicization with a strong emphasis on institutional deficits can be expected.

There is indeed considerable evidence that the acquisition of enforcement authority by international institutions has led to a very high level of politi- cization. Regarding the UNSC's willingness to legitimize the use of force, societal actors have repeatedly campaigned against UN non-action in cases like Myanmar or Darfur as instances of inappropriate selectivity (Binder 2013). The same holds for the conditionality built into the World Bank's or the IMF's structural adjustment programs, which have served as focal points for NGO campaigns and global justice activism ever since (Park 2010). It is again in these cases of high levels of authority that the institutional deficits of the global governance system are directly addressed. The UNSC and the Bretton Woods Conference are often criticized for institutionalized inequality, for the lack of representativeness, and for the lack of a separation of powers.

Another form of enforcement takes place when international authorities implement their policies directly (Abbott and Snidal 1998: 12–13). Transitional administrations that were set up after the end of the Cold War in Eastern Slavonia, Kosovo, or East Timor, for example, represent such a type of author- ity. In these cases, the UN took on far-reaching executive, legislative, and judicial powers (Caplan 2004). Again, high levels of politicization with a strong emphasis on legitimation problems can be expected.

Societal actors indeed have repeatedly contested implementing authorities, stressing legitimacy concerns. Consider, for instance, the Sudanese refugees' three-month-long protests at the UN High Commissioner for Refugees' (UNHCR) Cairo office in late 2005 (Moulin and Nyers 2007). Refugees not only demanded aid and official recognition of their status as refugees according to the Geneva Convention, they also insisted upon inclusion in the UNHCR decisions affecting them.

In much the same way, transitional administrations have been contested by subjected citizenries forced to accede to post-conflict rule by international actors. Prime examples in the literature include Timorese frustration with UN Transitional Administration in East Timor (UNTAET), which was accused of failing to involve and integrate the local population sufficiently in the reconstruction of government structures. Similarly, local communities and international advocates alike contested UN Mission in Kosovo (UNMIK), pointing to questions of inclusion and accountability (e.g. Chesterman 2004; Ford and Oppenheim 2008).

Summing up this qualitative exploration, we can state that the authority hypothesis (H 1) is corroborated: higher levels of authority lead to higher levels of politicization. The challenges put forward against international institutions with high levels of authority are targeted not only at their policies but also at their legitimation and the question whether the authority is exercised appropriately. Especially institutions like the UNSC, the IMF, and the World Bank are criticized for non-transparency, technocratic narrow-mindedness, and a power bias (H 3). It also seems to be true that different types of authority lead to different ways and levels of politicization: the exercise of authority is more strongly politicized than the exercise of epistemic authority, even if it is politically delegated epistemic authority (H 2).

6.5 Effects of Politicization

In order to probe the final steps of the causal mechanism—according to which high levels of authority and politicization lead to an extension of legitimation narratives (H 4), and thus to a situation in which authority holders have to make critical decisions (H 5 and H 6)—I again look first at some recent contributions, and then add a study of our own, focusing on these issues.

6.5.1 State of the Art

In general, research on politicization has focused so far mainly on causes, and much less on consequences. Yet the politicization of international institutions may affect both the level of national politics and the international level in different ways (see Zürn 2014). Regarding the effect on national political systems, it seems most important to disentangle the intricate relationship between the politicization of international institutions on the one hand and the rise of new cleavages within national party systems between integrationists and demarcationists on the other (Grande and Hutter 2016; Grande and Kriesi 2013; Kriesi et al. 2012). The growing gap between elites and "masses" is to a significant extent driven by different evaluations of international institutions (see Hooghe 2003; Teney and Helbling 2014; de Wilde et al. 2016b).

On the level beyond the nation state, politicization may affect the content of decisions (policies) as well as the decision-making process (politics). There are only few studies on the effects of politicization on policies so far. Lora Viola (2013) argues that politicization was critical for policy change in the WHO. An empirical investigation by Christian Rauh (2016) about the effect of politicization on EU policies deserves special mention in this context. It shows very convincingly that consumer protection policies of the EU Commission become more consumer-friendly when the politicization index displays higher values.

Moving to effects on politics beyond the state, it must be stated first that politicization empowers certain non-state actors—those working on the basis of the liberal script and who are comfortable on the international floor—over others. In this way, politicization increases the pro-Western bias of many international institutions (Ecker-Ehrhardt and Zürn 2013). At the same time, the Western CSOs are those who ask most fervently for participation and fairness. Without politicization, an extension of legitimation narratives is therefore unlikely.

At the same time, it seems that politicization or the fear of politicization has an effect on the legitimation practices on international and transnational authorities. Rocabert et al. (2017, in preparation), for instance, demonstrate that high levels of political authority increase the likelihood of the creation of international parliamentary institutions (IPIs). In other words, IOs that are considered as strong and intrusive are those that develop legitimation strategies that draw on sources of legitimacy that go beyond the technocratic narrative. Along the same lines, Dingwerth et al. (2018, in preparation) examine the use of democratic rhetoric as a discursive legitimation practice of IOs and show that it has risen over the observation period, with an especially steep growth rate in the 1990s. Nowadays, many organizations move beyond the technocratic narrative and make some use of participatory and liberal language when describing who they are and what they do. Most importantly, media visibility and protests against IOs are positively associated with the use of a democratic rhetoric. Politicization seems to lead to an extension of legitimation narratives.

These studies lend some support to the hypothesis that more strongly politicized IOs with a high level of authority tend to develop legitimation strategies that reach beyond the technocratic narratives (H 4). At the same time, it seems that the reference to participatory and legal narratives does not necessarily go along with substantial changes.

6.5.2 A Quantitative Analysis

When and how do legitimation narratives of IOs change?[10] CMALL 1 predicts a change in IO legitimation narratives as a function of the increasing IO authority and the societal politicization it produces. In order to examine this claim, we trace the temporal logic of this argument for the three core institutions of global economic governance: the IMF, the World Bank, and the WTO.[11] It will be shown that the technocratic legitimation narrative—which, for a long time, was used almost exclusively—was complemented by a fairness and a participatory narrative when protests and politicization reached peak levels.[12] These new narratives, however, lost relevance again when politicization protests moved beyond their peak.

To see whether the alternative narratives driving such protests have also permeated elite-level discourses in response, we utilize a text-mining analysis approach. In order to allow for a large-scale comparison, we resort to the (semi-)automated analyses of a large number of texts.[13] To this end, a processing pipeline that parses, cleans, and annotates the full texts of newspaper reports provided by various online databases—such as LexisNexis, ProQuest, or Wiso, to name a few—has been written (Rauh and Bödeker 2013). This rather flexible solution removes the need for limited sampling points and enables the analysis of the effects of politicization in the complete corpus of all IO-related articles that a newspaper has published and digitalized during the period of interest.

But which media outlets matter for our purposes? We look at media sources that provide a rather segregated forum for elite discourse, have an international outreach, are less biased by specific national concerns, and are thus actually recognized by global decision-making elites. Therefore, our data collection strategy focuses on renowned quality newspapers with international

---

[10] This section draws from Rauh and Zürn (2015).
[11] While the initial analysis aims to trace the whole mechanism—and therefore includes the North American Free Trade Agreement (NAFTA) in order to increase variance in authority—the focus in this section is on the question of whether politicization has led to an extension of legitimation narratives, and how sustainable the change was. In this analysis, the focus is on the temporal change of IOs that were politicized strongly in a certain period.
[12] The narratives are described in Chapter 3. We translated these narratives in a legitimation dictionary that guided the analysis (see Rauh and Zürn 2017, Appendix 1, in preparation).
[13] For an introduction to the method, see Grimmer and Stewart (2013) as well as Rauh and Bödeker (2013).

audiences and a significant share of global business news. All of these papers should be published in English to serve as transnational media for elite communication. We selected three leading international business newspapers between 1992 and 2012. Such journals provide us with rather sensitive discourses on global economic governance that is likely to be noticed and be addressed by supranational decision makers. On the basis of these concerns, our final newspaper sample contains the *Financial Times* (London, UK, roughly 426,000 daily copies in 2012), *The New York Times* (New York City, United States, 1,086,798 copies), and *The Straits Times* (Singapore, 365,800 copies). As control sources, we utilized *The Guardian* and *The Washington Post* as national news, in order to see how discourses developed in national contexts that are directed toward a broader public.

To begin with, the technocratic legitimation is, within the elite-level discourse, clearly dominant in all three IOs under question. While alternative narratives—as captured by references to fair distribution and to more equal representation—can be traced, they play mostly a marginal role at best. While the ratio between the narratives is not even across the three IOs, it is remarkably similar. Legitimation narratives referring to fairness play a slightly bigger role in the cases of the World Bank and the IMF than in the WTO, where issues of participation seem to be slightly more important than in the other two (see Figure 6.3). A look at our control sources, *The Guardian* and *The*

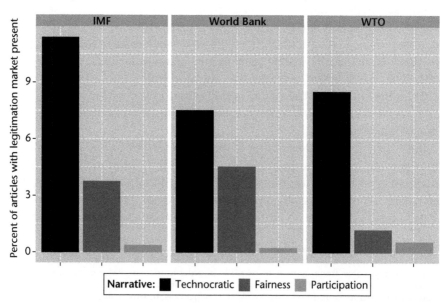

Figure 6.3. Overall presence of technocratic, fairness-based, and participation narratives

Source: Rauh, C., and Zürn, M. (2015), "Legitimation Dynamics in Global Governance: Civil Society Evaluations of the IMF, the World Bank, and the WTO in the International Business Press," *Paper presented at Legitimacy and Legitimation in Global Governance Workshop, April 16–17, Stockholm.*

Washington Post, displays a strongly (*The Guardian*) or moderately (*The Washington Post*) divergent pattern (see Figure 6.7). On average, the fairness-based narrative is dominant in the case of the World Bank, and more or less on a par with the technocratic narrative in the cases of the WTO and the IMF.

In order to test our hypotheses, we need to move beyond static case comparisons and take a temporal perspective. The most important question in that respect is about the timing of politicization. The data by and large confirms the view that the Battle of Seattle in 1999 marks the birth of a strong and visible anti-globalization movement (see Figure 6.4) directed at global economic governance institutions. This politicization wave leveled out until 2005 in the case of the IMF and the World Bank. The WTO experienced—probably due to the conflicts over the Doha round—a second, but weaker episode of politicization that levelled out until 2010. Whereas the politicization went down to low values again after these intense periods, the platform thereof is nowadays a bit higher than before the Battle of Seattle.

Against this backdrop, it is now possible to tackle the questions about the effects of politicization. First, did politicization produce an extension of legitimation narratives via the presence of CSOs in elite discourses? The theoretical expectation is that the technocratic legitimation narrative was especially strong before politicization took place. Indeed, before the rise of politicization, the economic governance IOs were legitimated within elite

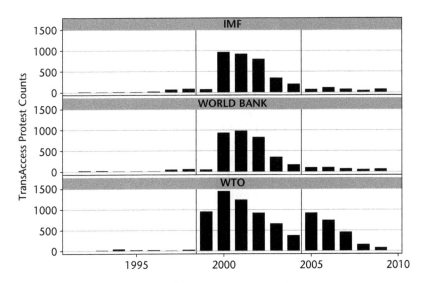

Figure 6.4. IO Politicization over time (by protest counts)

Source: Rauh, C., and Zürn, M. (2015), "Legitimation Dynamics in Global Governance: Civil Society Evaluations of the IMF, the World Bank, and the WTO in the International Business Press," *Paper presented at Legitimacy and Legitimation in Global Governance Workshop, April 16–17, Stockholm.*

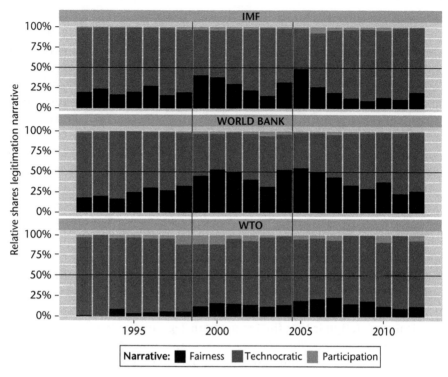

Figure 6.5. Relative yearly share of legitimation narratives

Source: Rauh, C., and Zürn, M. (2015), "Legitimation Dynamics in Global Governance: Civil Society Evaluations of the IMF, the World Bank, and the WTO in the International Business Press," *Paper presented at Legitimacy and Legitimation in Global Governance Workshop, April 16–17, Stockholm.*

papers almost exclusively with a narrative that emphasizes apolitical procedures, efficient decision making, and impartial expertise and performance
criteria—such as stable and open markets, economic growth, and liberalization. In other words, the dominant legitimation narrative of the authority
holders and their defenders has for a long time been a technocratic one.
Whereas the technocratic narrative completely dominated legitimation practices in the WTO before the protests, the IMF and the World Bank were at
least partially justified with reference to other narratives already before 2000.

With the rise of politicization, alternative narratives entered the debate
essentially only from 1999 on (see Figure 6.5). The fairness narrative focusing on issues such as poverty alleviation, fair distribution of wealth, and, to
some extent, environmental and human rights concerns then entered the
elite-level discourse in international newspapers, especially about the World
Bank and the IMF. In the case of the World Bank, the share was around 50
percent; in the case of the IMF, it came close to this number. In elite-level

discourses about the WTO, the fairness narrative gained some relevance after 1999, remaining yet on a much lower level. At the same time, the participatory narrative focusing on an equal representation of different interests in terms of both state and CSO participation played a larger role in the WTO, although the overall number of the participatory narrative stayed clearly below the fairness narrative in this period. It is fair to state that the combined share of the participatory and especially fairness-based narrative went up after 1999—which is again completely in line with expectations.

With this, the second part of the first question can be tackled: Is this rise due to an increased presence of CSOs in elite discourses? In an aggregate perspective, the presence of public interest CSOs in our corpus of elite-level newspapers is rather low. In total, across the whole corpus of 87,011 newspaper articles, public interest CSOs are to be found only 1,207 times in the immediate IO context.[14] As expected, CSO access to this elite-level segment of the public sphere is thus on average relatively small. Moreover, it is heavily skewed in favor of CSOs of Western origin. It remains limited to well-endowed and transnationally organized groups. More than half of all public interest CSO occurrences can be attributed to the top five organizations. Particularly, Oxfam—a confederation of seventeen national organizations mobilizing on poverty and social injustice—dominates the picture, followed by Transparency International, Greenpeace, Christian Aid, and the World Wildlife Fund (WWF) (see Table 6.2).

These CSOs are much more present in the analyzed elite papers during peaks of politicization. This again meets the theoretical expectations. At the same time, there are some deviations that need to be mentioned. First of all, the overall CSO participation in this discursive sphere remains relatively small and reaches a maximum of 4 percent. Given the absolute dominance of executive actors in all media content analysis, especially regarding international

Table 6.2. Top 10 occurring public interest CSOs in the corpus

CSO	Occurrences	% of CSO occurrences
Oxfam	319	26.43
Transparency International	109	9.03
Greenpeace	72	5.97
Christian Aid	63	5.22
World Wildlife Fund for Nature	59	4.89
Human Rights Watch	36	2.98
Global Witness	29	2.40
World Development Movement	29	2.40
Amnesty International	28	2.32
People's Development Initiatives	27	2.24

Source: Rauh and Zürn 2015

---

[14] Compare this to US governmental actors, who appear in total 2,583 times in the immediate IO context.

institutions and the high level of segregation of the newspapers under consideration, the numbers indicate nevertheless a significant change and the rising visibility of CSOs in episodes of politicization. Politicization does of course not work like an on/off switch. In the case of the IMF and the World Bank, CSOs seem to have already been present, to some extent, before the politicization phase started in 1999. Moreover, politicization did not have an immediate effect but probably a delayed one: presence of public interest groups seems to have increased slowly and it peaked between 2003 and 2006. Overall, the presence of CSOs in elite newspapers grew in line with our hypothesized causal mechanism after the first politicization peak.

We can now move to the second question: Did the CSOs and the alternative narratives stay after the level of politicization declined again in elite discourses? Here, the answer is mainly negative. First, the number of CSOs and alternative narratives went down again after the period of high politicization (see Figure 6.6), whereby the numbers of alternatives developed almost fully in parallel with politicization, while CSOs stayed a bit longer and even showed a new peak in 2005 and 2006. Second, we see some variation along the three IOs. Regarding the World Bank, the rise of politicization and the presence of alternative narratives seem to go hand in hand in elite discourses. With the decline of protests, the alternative narratives declined again, yet remaining

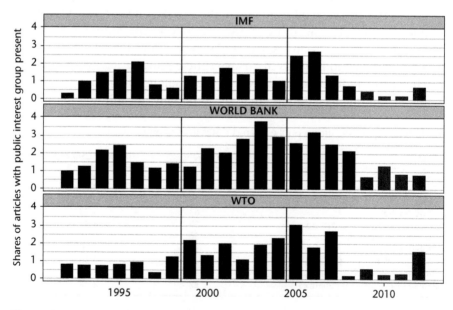

Figure 6.6. Presence of CSOs in the corpus

Source: Rauh, C., and Zürn, M. (2015), "Legitimation Dynamics in Global Governance: Civil Society Evaluations of the IMF, the World Bank, and the WTO in the International Business Press," *Paper presented at Legitimacy and Legitimation in Global Governance Workshop, April 16–17, Stockholm.*

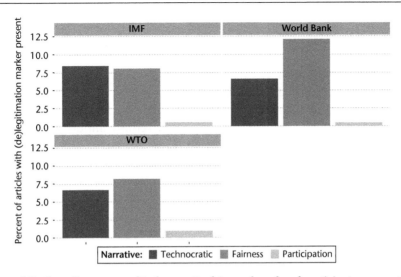

Figure 6.7. Overall presence of technocratic, fairness-based and participatory narratives (*The Guardian/Washington Post*)

Source: Rauh, C., and Zürn, M. (2015), "Legitimation Dynamics in Global Governance: Civil Society Evaluations of the IMF, the World Bank, and the WTO in the International Business Press," *Paper presented at Legitimacy and Legitimation in Global Governance Workshop, April 16–17, Stockholm.*

still on a higher level than before. The IMF also followed this path, with a minor presence of the participatory narrative—that was not present at all before 1999—remaining. In the case of the WTO, the decline of alternative narratives in elite discourse is not as steep as in the other two cases.

The picture is quite different for newspapers addressing a national public (*The Guardian* and *The Washington Post*) (see Figure 6.7). The criticism toward the global economic institution did not go away. It remained—although at a lower level. While, at the peak of politicization, the fairness-based narrative is dominant in all three IOs (most clearly in the World Bank), it stayed dominant in the case of the World Bank and moved to around a third in the two other organizations. The participatory narrative is weak in all IOs—even in *The Guardian*.

The results of this analysis can be summarized easily by taking up its two guiding questions. Does politicization lead to the entry of new legitimation narratives? And do those new legitimation narratives stay in elite discourses even if politicization recedes? While the answer to the first question is positive, the answer to the latter is negative.

6.6 Conclusion

The hypotheses about societal politicization derived from a theory of contested global governance are, to a large extent, corroborated by the evidence provided in this chapter. Most importantly, the more authority an inter- or transnational institution exercises, the more politicization by non-state actors can be observed. This core statement of the theory about the causes of politicization—the authority transfer hypothesis—holds especially if we look at political—as opposed to epistemic—authority and if the institutions stick to institutional features that produce legitimation deficits. Moving to the effects of politicization, we can state with a certain amount of confidence that an increased level of politicization leads to a broadening of narratives that are referred to in the legitimation process. However, this temporary change in legitimation narratives does not necessarily lead to substantial reforms. In the cases analyzed in this chapter, such changes occurred only to a very limited extent.

Whether an extension of legitimacy narratives will lead to a deepening of global governance seems to be contingent. It appears to depend on whether the adaptation of the authority holders is substantial or symbolic. If it remains symbolic and the legitimation narrative in the long run moves back to be mainly technocratic, then we can expect an ongoing authority–legitimacy gap, which may lead to a deadlock and the decline of global governance. In contrast, substantial responses may indicate a deepening of global governance.

The next two chapters will take up this contingency by looking at variations. In this respect, even the three international economic institutions analyzed in this chapter vary to some extent. The authority holders and defenders of the WTO changed the technocratic legitimation narrative only marginally, arguably less so than the World Bank and the IMF. In the case of the WTO, it is hard to identify any institutional or policy changes in the last fifteen years. Consensus decisions by the ministerial meetings, a decisive role of "green room meetings"[15] during the negotiations, and a very strong dispute settlement body are the unchanged basic features. As a result, the Doha round deadlocked and failed with what will probably be far-reaching consequences for the WTO as a whole (see Chapter 7). There are many indications that the world trade system is becoming increasingly regionalized and its governance is moving away from the WTO to often bilateral trade and investment treaties, which are, however, themselves very much politicized in the Western world—the Transatlantic Trade and Investment Partnership (TTIP), of course, above all.

In the case of the IMF, politicization produced a visible change in the legitimation narratives in elite discourse, but the alternative narratives waned in the most recent years. There was no—or at best little—response to the demand of CSOs. However, the IMF experienced an institutional reform that adjusted the quota and the voting rights, giving countries like China, India, and Brazil more weight. In the financial crisis, it even gained additional authority.

---

[15] The members of the club behind the green doors changed however (see Chapter 7).

The World Bank has been most open for alternative legitimation narratives—especially since the late 1990s. In this case, alternative legitimation remained, to some extent, even after the politicization peak was over. At the same time, a number of policy reforms and some institutional reforms (see Chapter 8) took place. It seems that the impact of politicization was highest in this case. Regarding the World Bank, politicization has led to a more stable extension of legitimation narratives, to more or less substantial reforms, and to a deepening of global governance.

7

Counter-Institutionalization in the Global Governance System

The politicization of international institutions is not the only way in which global governance is contested. In recent decades, harsh criticism and complaints about injustice put forward by representatives of countries from the Global South have also become much more audible. These calls are accompanied by a determination to make change happen this time. Earlier calls for a "new international economic order" and a "new information and communication order" were very high on the agenda in the 1970s (Steffek 2013). The discernible institutional changes remained very limited, however. In contrast, some of the current demands for changes are put forward with force and have already triggered some institutional changes.

It is the combination of two developments that has produced the current wave of contestation of international institutions by states. First, the authority of international institutions has risen, thus increasing the demand for legitimation. Second, the distribution and nature of international power has been shifting rapidly. The economic dynamic in countries outside the G7 group of established powers has shifted the power away from the traditional custodians and beneficiaries of the global governance system. Emerging and developing countries from the Global South are taking on a much greater role in the global economy, and they increasingly seek to translate market power into influence in international institutions. Established authority holders therefore need to take demands for change more seriously. For many observers, these developments point to a fundamental change toward a new international system. The challenges have provoked numerous debates and questions. What do rising powers want? Are they revisionist, satisfied, or somewhere in between? Do rising powers constitute a bloc across issue areas, squarely confronting established powers? How do authority holders and established powers respond to the challenge? Why do they deliberately weaken some international institutions but not others? Given the emphasis on sovereignty by rising powers and lack of commitment by established powers, is the authority of international institutions destined to wane in the coming years?

In this chapter, these questions are approached from the perspective of a theory of global governance. In section 7.1, the two causal mechanisms (derived from the authority–legitimation link) of state contestation introduced in Chapter 4—one being more likely to end in decline, the other in a deepening of global governance—will be discussed in more detail (CMALL 3 = Counter-Institutionalization by Rising Powers and CMALL 4 = Counter-Institutionalization by Incumbents). Section 7.2 provides a discussion of the concepts of rising and established powers in the global governance system. In section 7.3, I present the design of research about "Contested World Orders" (see Stephen and Zürn 2018a, in preparation) and report the results of the comparative case studies in order to show that the challenge by rising powers to the global governance system is limited. The most relevant strategy in the dispute is counter-institutionalization—and not attempts to overhaul the global governance system as a whole. I then present evidence in support of CMALL 3 in section 7.4 to show that it is especially institutionalized inequality that is targeted by rising powers. Depending on the response of established powers, this may lead to fragmentation of the global governance system, but is more likely to lead to substantial adaption and reform of existing international institutions. Finally, in section 7.5, it is argued that counter-institutionalization is not only employed by rising powers. In the face of new challenges, established powers themselves are instrumental in undermining the institutions that they have founded if they lose control over them. While counter-institutionalization by rising powers sometimes leads to institutional reform and even deepening of global governance arrangements, counter-institutionalization by established powers more often leads to decline.

7.1 Rising and Established Powers in the Global Governance System

In the global governance system, differences in state power often translate into international authorities that are close to the substantial interests of powerful states. At the same time, the need to include less powerful states and the principle of sovereign equality often translates into procedural rules that give the less powerful at least some voice. Thus, international institutions enshrine both a *de facto* inequality in their operations and a commitment to legal and political equality. In the long term, the benefits to the less powerful states increase to the extent that the established rules no longer fit the (changed) interests of the more powerful states.

However, this long-term equalizing force of international institutions is undercut, if the rise of international authority is accompanied by institutionalized inequality as in the cases of the United Nations Security Council (UNSC) or the International Monetary Fund (IMF). Institutionalized inequality is a key of the theory of global governance, which emphasizes the embeddedness of distributional conflicts in a global governance system as well as the stratification that comes with it. Yet if the power distribution changes in the global governance system in favor of formerly weak powers, three possible responses are conceivable: ongoing subservience, demands for change within the system, and attempts to overthrow the system.[1] Ongoing subservience means acquiescing in given forms of institutionalization in spite of some dissatisfaction. This is what conceptions of traditional authority would expect. In contrast, exit is what International Relations (IR) scholars usually expect. If a state is unhappy with the working of an institution in an anarchical system and is able to go other ways, from this perspective, exit or non-cooperative moves are the logical choices. In the global governance system, however, both of these responses are rare. Given the normative principles of the global governance system, dissatisfaction should rather translate into voice than into subservience (loyalty) or exit. The recognition of a common good implies that full exit is hardly a choice, and reflexive authority makes full obedience unlikely.

While states are—to a significant extent—the driver behind the rise of international authority in a global governance system, they deal with it in a reflexive manner. They often see international authority as a means to influence developments outside of their territory that affect their own national constituency and, at the same time, aim at minimizing the effects on their own autonomy. As a consequence, states simultaneously recognize and challenge inter- and transnational authority. The powerful Western states contest, to some extent, the very same international institutions that they have created and formed the moment they produce decisions they dislike. The World Health Organization (WHO) may be the archetype of this process. Nevertheless, the response is not to exit. Instead, states choose voice, and voice includes both critical communication and demands for change. In institutional terms, voice means, above all, to form new institutions closer to the current interests in order to influence or replace the old international institution: This may be labeled "counter-institutionalization." Counter-institutionalization refers to practices through which international institutions are weakened or challenged via the use of other international institutions with similar

---

[1] The triad of deference, challenge of the system, and change within the system is a special case of Hirschman's (1970) more general typology of exit, voice, and loyalty.

tasks.[2] Whereas exit from cooperative schemes is the principal response of dissatisfied states in an international system, this role is taken by counter-institutionalization in a global governance system.

Counter-institutionalization can take two different forms. Dissatisfied states can engage in *regime shifting* or *forum shopping* in order to "relocate rulemaking processes to international venues whose mandates and priorities favor their concerns and interests" (Helfer 2009: 39). Even if the incumbent states do not exit, they can minimize their contributions while simultaneously increasing their support for other institutions with a similar mandate. They can turn to international or bilateral institutions that assume partially complementary but also conflicting governance tasks, and thereby decrease the relevance of the original institution. A more competitive institutional environment—and thus a weakened position of the original institution—will often be the by-product of such developments. Alternatively, dissatisfied states can engage in *competitive regime creation*. This strategy goes beyond regime shifting. By establishing a new institution alongside an existing one in the same issue area, dissatisfied actors challenge the governance authority of the existing institution (Schneider and Urpelainen 2013; Urpelainen and Van de Graaf 2015). While regime shifting utilizes fragmentation, competitive regime creation fosters it.

With these concepts, the institutional dynamics in the global governance system can be understood as reactive sequences. First of all, rising powers do not have an interest in undermining global governance as such, but target primarily those specific institutions in which established powers have crafted institutionalized inequality and secondarily those in which costs—at least from their perspective—are distributed unfairly. This is to say, rising powers do not aim at a fundamental change of or exit from the global governance system; rather, they want to change the specific institutions. They do not challenge the authority as such, but the specific exercise of authority. Rising powers are therefore expected to counter-institutionalize. The perceived alternative to the status quo is not exit from the global governance system, but changing it to one that is more beneficial to the rising powers. A global cleavage cutting across different issue areas between the established and the rising powers can therefore not be expected. Conflict constellations should instead be embedded in and structured by the design of specific international authorities.

Second, if incumbent states are privileged in the decision-making process of an authority (institutionalized equality), a shift in the power constellation

---

[2] Morse and Keohane (2014) use the term "contested multilateralism." Yet the contestation of multilateralism can take place in many forms by many actors, including protest, resistance, and exit. The term "counter-institutionalization" highlights in contrast that international institutions (minilateral or multilateral) are utilized by states to change disliked international institutions.

leads to contestation and delegitimation by the rising powers (counter-institutionalization by rising powers). Institutions like the Non-Proliferation Treaty regime, the World Bank, the IMF, the UNSC, and the G7/8 meetings are cases in point. International authorities with strongly institutionalized inequality are the major targets of counter-institutionalization by rising powers. Rising powers put forward demands for reform and threaten to counter-institutionalize. Yet the rhetoric of counter-institutionalization by rising powers is not necessarily the endpoint of an institution's power mismatch trajectory. The original institution may "adapt" to the new environment that it may have co-produced in the first place. The authority holders may give in to the demands and initiative reforms that alleviate institutional inequality. The outcome of such a sequence is rarely all-out institutional change, but often growing complexity through "layering"—the adding of new organizational elements onto a rigid but increasingly irrelevant historical core (see Streeck and Thelen 2005). The reactive sequence labeled "Counter-Institutionalization by Rising Powers" (CMALL 3) is summarized in Figure 7.1.

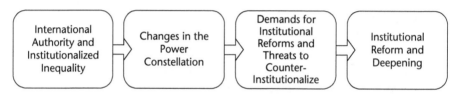

Figure 7.1. Counter-institutionalization by rising powers (CMALL 3)

Third, the prevalence of the "one-state, one-vote" principle leads to counter-institutionalization by incumbent states if they experience a loss of control. The WHO, UN Educational, Scientific and Cultural Organization (UNESCO), and some of the new trade and investment treaties undermining the World Trade Organization (WTO), as well as the UN Human Rights Council (UNHRC) are cases in point. The causal mechanism, counter-institutionalization by incumbents, therefore often unfolds from a constellation where the key supporters of an institution face an entrenched institutional status quo coalition and thus cannot project their power within the institution any more. These key players are often the most powerful states that shaped an institution in the beginning, but lost control over time because of institutional rules that, relatively speaking, empower weaker states. Powerful states often give less powerful ones a voice for accepting the institutionalization of their rules. If interests or circumstances change, these powerful actors can no longer easily change the institutional features. The weaker actors (such as developing states) then use and protect their institutional privileges against claims for change, causing a reversed power mismatch. This situation results in counter-institutionalization by incumbents, which

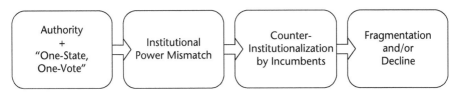

Figure 7.2. Counter-institutionalization by incumbents (CMALL 4)

often leads to a decline or at least fragmentation of global governance (see Figure 7.2).

In the remainder of this chapter, I explore these three propositions on the basis of a comparative analysis of rising power practices in different institutionalized issue areas carried out in the context of a project about "Contested World Orders."[3]

7.2 The Faces of State Power

Counter-institutionalization challenges to the global governance system derive from the changed role of international institutions in world politics, and from the change in the distribution of power between states.[4] The combined gross domestic product (GDP) of six of the largest non-OECD (Organisation for Economic Co-operation and Development) countries in the world—Brazil, Russia, India, Indonesia, China, and South Africa (BRIICS)—represented in 1995 around a third of that of the G7. By 2013, this had risen to nearly three-quarters (OECD 2008). In addition, expectations about the future have fueled perceptions of importance: The OECD expects this growth trend to continue, so that by 2030 the BRIICS will represent nearly one-and-a-half times the economic output of the G7.[5] In 2008, the US National Intelligence Council (2008) surveyed these trends and concluded that "with the rapid rise of other countries, the 'unipolar moment' is over and Pax Americana— the era of American ascendancy in international politics that began in 1945— is fast winding down." In January 2013, the OECD (2013) published a new

---

[3] In this project financed by the Leibniz Association the WZB Berlin Social Science Center, Peace Research Institute Frankfurt (PRIF), and German Institute of Global Area Studies (GIGA) served as partners. For the complete set-up and results see Stephen and Zürn (2018a, in preparation). Other contributors to this project are Pascal Abb, Martin Binder, Melanie Conti-Zimmer, Sophie Eisentraut, Annegret Flohr, Anja Jetschke, Malte Lellmann, Autumn Lockwood-Payton, Harald Müller, Dirk Peters, Miriam Prys-Hansen, Milan Röseler, Alex Tokhi, and Klaus Dieter Wolf.

[4] Sections 7.2 and 7.3 draw from Stephen and Zürn (2018b, in preparation) and Stephen and Zürn (2014).

[5] Calculated for the year 1995 from the IMF World Development Indicators; for the years 2013 and 2030, from the OECD. For overviews about the power shift see *inter alia* Gray and Murphy (2013); Kahler (2013); Kappel (2011); OECD (2010); Young (2010).

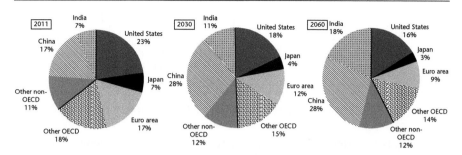

Figure 7.3. Percentage of global GDP in 2005 purchasing power parities (PPPs). Global GDP is taken as sum of GDP for 34 OECD and 8 non-OECD countries

Source: OECD 2013

paper on the long-term trends in world economy, highlighting the importance that is attached to these developments. While this study points to a decline in growth of the rising economies in the next decades, it still visualizes the transformation strikingly. According to these calculations, India, for instance, will have a share of 18 percent of the global GDP in 2060, i.e. double the value of the Euro area (see Figure 7.3).

But do these economic changes really point to a new power distribution in world politics? Power is a multivalent concept that cannot be reduced to the possession of material resources, although resources may be an important background condition for most forms of power (see Barnett and Duvall 2005). However, sticking with the economic realm as the hitherto most tractable sign of international power shift, there are at least three separate mechanisms by which an increased share of the world's economic activity translates into an increased influence on international institutions. These three mechanisms closely reflect the well-known three faces of power (Lukes 2005; see also Bachrach and Baratz 1962 for two faces).

First, economic expansion increases the sources upon which a state can draw in its dealings with other states. Economic resources can be converted into instruments of relational power, such as bureaucratic capacity, epistemic resources, and the ability to furnish material (dis)incentives and side payments. They can also ultimately be converted into military capabilities, as often underlined by realist theories. Similarly, having a large economy also conveys bargaining power through the leverage of access to large internal markets, which are particularly relevant in economic policy fields such as trade (Krasner 1976). This bargaining power and influence is reinforced to the extent that economic size is associated with a central position in world networks, fostering rising states' "network power" (Hafner-Burton et al. 2009). In other words, economic resources increase coercive power.

Second, a country's share of the world economy is significant from a systemic point of view. Countries with particularly large shares of the world economy have a functional importance to the global economy that makes them "systemically significant." This systemic significance applies to the size of markets, to the banking system, but also to non-economic developments such as harmful emissions in climate change. The threshold for systemic significance has moreover been lowered as a result of economic globalization, as it increases spillover dynamics and thus the need for states to coordinate and collaborate in their decisions in order to govern effectively. Consequently, new powers have achieved a significant level of structural power.

A third indication of the emergence of new centers of power lies in the less tangible realm of status and recognition (Galtung 1964; Paul et al. 2014). Not only have rising powers articulated aspirations to change how global politics are run, but they have increasingly been accorded recognition of their new status by established powers and other participants in global governance. President Obama's public recognition that India is "not simply emerging; India has emerged"[6] is typical of this. External recognition is complemented by the increased self-identification of some states as rising powers, which can be seen in the proliferation of new coalitions and networks of rising powers (Flemes 2013), such as IBSA Dialogue Forum (India, Brazil, South Africa; since 2003), BRICS (association of Brazil, Russia, India, China, South Africa; since 2008/9), and BASIC bloc (Brazil, South Africa, India, China; since 2009). The biggest emerging economies are forming clubs that are joined by other states from the Global South, and they bring new beliefs and ideas to the table of international institutions. To the extent that these new beliefs and ideas prove to be attractive to others, they begin to exercise soft power (Nye 1990).[7]

These three faces of power can play out in different contexts. While power transition theorists conceive power mainly as resources that can be utilized in all contexts and consider therefore the so-called "overall power structure" as most important, others cast doubt on the fungibility of power across issue areas. In contrast to power transition theorists and different forms of realism (Waltz 1979; Tammen et al. 2000), social theorists such as David Baldwin (1979: 193) have argued that "the notion of a single overall international power structure unrelated to any particular issue-area is based on a concept of power that is virtually meaningless." Given the limited fungibility of

---

[6] Barack Obama, "Remarks by the President to the Joint Session of the Indian Parliament in New Delhi, India," The White House, 8 November 2010. Available at <http://www.whitehouse.gov/the-press-office/2010/11/08/remarks-president-joint-session-indian-parliament-new-delhi-india>.
[7] Soft power is, of course, quite a broad category that includes both power via persuasion and power via authority (see Chapter 2).

power, especially institutionalists often point to "issue area structure" as the relevant context for assessing power relationships (Keohane and Nye 2001). For this reason, the nature and extent of contemporary power shifts, and the question of which countries qualify as "rising powers," are issues that need to be taken up in a manner sensitive to institutional and issue area contexts (Lesage and Van de Graaf 2015).

What are rising powers then? In current debates, rising powers are states with growing power in all three dimensions. Compared to earlier periods, they have more resources available, affect the structure of the system more fundamentally, and have more soft power. Three conditions must be given: First, rising powers have a sufficiently stable and institutionalized control over their territory and are therefore in the position to ask for more sovereignty; second, they control markets which overstep a certain threshold in terms of market size;[8] and third, their economies have grown strongly on average over the last decades (> 4 percent) and, moreover, are expected to do so in the future as well.

Applying this definition strictly, the term "rising powers" may be limited to countries like China, India, and possibly Brazil (the latter with clearly lower growth rates than the other two). Most other countries in the Global South fail already with respect to the threshold criteria in market size (GDP = population * GDP per capita) or the growth criteria. If one lowers these requirements a bit, countries like Indonesia, Mexico, South Africa, and Turkey may be seen as rising powers as well. We contrast rising powers with established powers. Established powers are those which are top ranked in terms of technology and resources per capita. They have privileged positions in decision-making procedures in international institutions. In the economic realm in particular, the representatives of the United States, United Kingdom, Japan, Germany, Canada, and France have been considered as the solely decisive authority holders for a long time.

The concept of established powers is operationalized by G7 membership, and thus includes Italy. Rising powers are often equated with the BRIC (Brazil, Russia, India, China), BRICS (adding South Africa), or BRIICS (adding Indonesia). For practical purposes, this operationalization is used in this chapter as well. Yet it is obvious that Russia hardly fits into the category of a rising power. It is neither a rising power nor a really established power. While China, to some extent, belongs by now in both categories, Russia lacks the economic dynamic to be considered a rising power and the economic resources to be considered an established power. BRICS focus on international institutions as venues by which to shape global governance according to their own

---

[8] At the minimum, one can (somewhat arbitrarily) set it at a population of at least 80 million people and a GDP of at least 10,000 US dollars per capita.

preferences and values. In this sense, they act as challengers of the current global governance system, while the established states are the incumbents or authority holders.

7.3 Are We Witnessing System Change?

Against this backdrop, the first set of questions aims at identifying the intensity of the challenge. Do rising powers, in a close coalition, aim at a system change and to overthrow the order; or are they demanding only an adaptation of the institutions to the new power distribution, i.e. a systemic change? Are there demands for a system change, or are BRICS reassured by changes within the system? Changes within a system are minor and regular, system change is fundamental, and systemic change refers to changes in the governance of the system and lies in between the two (see Gilpin 1981).

Different theoretical perspectives give different answers to these questions. Realists interpret the demands of rising powers as demands for system change. Based on power transition theory (PTT) (Gilpin 1981; Modelski 1987), it is argued that this conflict is fundamental, dangerous, and war prone. According to PPT, the rising powers will act in a close coalition in order to fundamentally change the international order in their favor. Rising powers are thus seen as revisionist powers. Even hegemonic wars become conceivable (Gilpin 1988; Organski and Kugler 1981). This theory leads to the expectation that rising powers confront the established powers via coalition building, creating a clear cleavage between status quo powers and revisionist powers that cuts across different issue areas and resembles the East–West cleavage after the Second World War.

Liberals mainly see demands for changes within the system including some more far-reaching changes in substantial rules of international authorities. In this view, rising powers aim at joining the global governance system (Ikenberry 2011a) or already are major stake- and shareholders (Kahler 2013). At the same time, the current global governance system is seen as capable of adapting to the challenge and of incorporating rising powers (Schweller 2011; Gu et al. 2008). This perspective leads to the expectation that the rising powers' positions are essentially favorable to global governance institutions and do not contest them, but work within them in order to serve for their policy preference in a routine mode. Moreover, the content of their demands should vary mainly with their political systems. Liberal democratic rising powers are expected to be closer to the liberal democracies of the established powers than authoritarian states.

According to the theory of contested global governance, a systemic change in Gilpin's terms is to be expected. Rising powers act within the institutional structures of the global governance system and demand changes in policies as well as in institutional design. In contrast to the realist perspective, it expects few attempts to overthrow the system as a whole. In contrast to the liberal perspective, it expects to see significant distributional struggles within the system, leading sometimes to institutional reform and sometimes to institutional decline—depending upon rising powers' preferences and the institutional status quo (for similar arguments, see Hurrell 2007; Morse and Keohane 2014; Zangl et al. 2016).

In order to test for these expectations, we study systematically revealed preferences of rising powers regarding international institutions and how they compare to incumbents. We ask about the positions of rising powers on the degree of liberalism inscribed into inter- and transnational rules, about the extent to which those inter- and transnational institutions should exercise authority, and which distributional changes are asked for.

While international institutions have been increasingly affected by the rise of new powers, their impact on global governance will be a product not only of their increased power but also of their preferences and beliefs. Preferences are properties of actors that differentiate between the desirability of alternatives; indirectly, these preferences give an indication of broader descriptive (ontological) and normative (ethical) beliefs (Frieden 1999; Legro 2005; Zürn 1997a).

In order to assess rising power preferences, we distinguish three dimensions. We begin with the *content of policies* and ask to what extent the actor advocates or opposes the institutionalization of liberal policies and principles. The degree of liberalism is most apt to capture the decisive differences in preferred policy content systematically and across cases. Liberalism is associated with both economic openness (the lack of political barriers to the unhindered exchange of capital, goods, and labor) and political individualism (human rights). International institutions are liberal to the extent that they promote individual rights and the reduction of political barriers to the cross-national exchange of material goods (capital and commodities), labor power (services and migration), and ideas (cultural goods and knowledge). In contrast, more interventionist demands and claims ask for political interventions in order to reduce the unwelcome effects of free exchange—be it inequality, environmental degradation, or the erosion of national cultures and habits—either on the national or the international level (Corbey 1995; Scharpf 1996b; Zürn 1997b).

Moving to *politics*, we ask, second, to what extent the rising powers thrive at a better distribution of status in the decision-making process of these international institutions. It is the issue of whether the politics of a given IO allow for fair participation of all the affected states and an even-handed implementation. Finally we ask, on the *polity level*, about the extent of support for or opposition to the transfer of public authority. In this regard, we want to know, on the one hand, whether international rules are called for or are opposed. On the other hand, we aim at understanding the preferred institutional form. Here, we distinguish mere intergovernmental cooperation from international authority.

On the basis of this conceptualization, a set of international institutions that vary regarding their authority, the extent of liberal content, and their stratification of status were studied closely: the WTO-based trade regime, the IMF, the Non-Proliferation Treaty regime, the climate regime, the UNHRC, and the WHO. As for international institutions that work across different issue areas, we focus on the G8/20 and the General Assembly. This structured, focused comparison of cases studies (George and Bennett 2005) yields three findings that are of special importance here.

First, on a general level, it can be stated that the global governance system and international authority as such are hardly challenged by rising powers. The case studies show that an established and ritualized confrontation between BRICS and established powers that cuts across different issues does not exist. We see neither a generalized rejection of international institutions nor a systematic, cross-cutting preference of rising powers to have less international authority and less regulation. To the contrary, the conflict lines vary from issue area to issue area and are either along the lines of conflicts about institutionalized inequality in the decision-making process or on the content of policies. In most cases, the most contested issue is the distribution of decision-making positions within a given institution. In all the cases of institutionalized inequality, those who have privileged positions stand against those who challenge international authority. In the case of the UNSC, for instance, the P5, including China and Russia, defend their vetoes and are very hesitant in giving the same privilege to others. The same is true for the Non-Proliferation Treaty regime (Müller and Tokhi 2018, in preparation). The challengers consist of those powers that do not have privileged institutional positions. The same pattern applies to cases like the G-summits (Peters 2018, in preparation), the IMF (Tokhi 2018, in preparation), and the Quad (Canada, European Union (EU), Japan, the United States) within the WTO (see Zangl et al. 2016). In all these cases, a change in the membership of "executive bodies" is demanded. When these demands are met, contestation declines. In all the cases of institutionalized inequality, it is the issue area-specific distribution of distributional privileges that structures the conflict lines, not the Western established powers versus BRICS.

Second, a confrontation between established powers from the West and rising powers is more likely in the context of institutions following the "one-state, one-vote" principle. In these cases, however, it is *only* the content of the regulation (policy) that is at stake. If it comes to economic regulation, rising powers often demand more regulation of the markets. In the case of international trade, this dispute follows roughly along the line between incumbents and challengers (Stephen 2018, in preparation). However, the most outspoken proponents of "embedded liberalism" that takes into account developmental concerns are India and Brazil. Given their democratic constitution and, compared to China, relatively limited economic and military power, they are—from the perspective of PTT—rather unlikely candidates for a leadership role in a coalition directed against the established powers.

It is also important to note that the defining element of this coalition is more regulation, not less international authority. All BRICS have a preference for something that may be labeled "embedded liberalism." They all ask for a version of liberalism that is more regulated and less neoliberal. This often leads to demands for more national discretion, but in some cases to demands for more international regulation as in the case of the IMF's role in financial markets.

It is this common antipathy to neoliberalism that also provides the symbolic cohesion for the voting patterns in the General Assembly, which pit to some extent the BRICS states against the G7 states (see Binder and Lockwood Payton 2018, in preparation). Looking at the substantial arguments made there and the ongoing importance of the Palestinian issue, it is again Brazil and India that seem to play the role of leaders in this coalition. Their leadership role certainly does not derive from material power distribution, but from their longstanding positions as speakers of the Non-Aligned Movement (NAM). To the extent that there is a systemic conflict line about the current world order, it seems to be still one that exists among the developing world and the richest countries of the world. If a contentious issue calls up such a confrontation, the ideational commonalities of the NAM suffice to create a coalition against the coalition of the G7.

In line with these findings, BRICS also do not contest the authority of institutions run by private actors as long as they do not openly challenge sovereignty (see Coni-Zimmer et al. 2018, in preparation). The maxim of protecting national discretion is therefore not only guiding emerging powers' position toward international institutions, but also informs their assessment of political authority exercised by private actors in transnational institutions.

Altogether, the BRICS seem to act as conservative globalizers (Kahler 2013). They are rather restorative than revolutionary in that they try to re-establish the institutional setting before the neoliberal turn, including the dominant role of states in this system. Yet they lack a coherent and shared alternative vision of global ordering that in effect would bundle positions across different issue areas. Only such a revolutionary vision could create an overall conflict line that overcomes the specific institutional as well as policy interests in given institutions and cuts across different issue areas. The tendency of turning the clock back to nation state-centered embedded liberalism, which allows for enough national discretion, does not provide sufficient ideological fodder for such a conflict line.

Third, there is little variation between different rising powers based on their domestic structure. Regime type accounts—to some extent—for the variation regarding human rights-related policies as in the cases of the UNSC and UNHRC. In these issue areas, democratic rising powers such as Brazil, India, and South Africa behave slightly differently than authoritarian rising powers (Binder and Eisentraut 2018, in preparation; Jetschke and Abb 2018, in preparation). Yet, in most other issue areas, the predictive power of domestic structure is very limited.

Overall, these findings contradict both the realist PTT and liberal expectations. To begin with, it is hardly compatible with the PTT, when rising powers accept existing international authorities in principle, are on the side of the status quo, and defend it against established powers that see a need for change. This is a full reversal of the expectations derived from PTT. Moreover, we could hardly identify a confrontation between BRICS as challengers on the one hand and the G7 states as established powers on the other, with China and the United States at the center of the two groups. Closest to this pattern expected by PTT in our set of studies is certainly the voting behavior in the General Assembly (see Binder and Lockwood Payton 2018, in preparation). The aggregated voting of states points to a significant convergence of rising power preferences that coincides with their institutionalization as BRICS in the current decade. In fact, as this dispersion score reveals, the BRICS now vote almost as cohesively as the G7 members. This finding creates a puzzle at first sight. While we cannot observe such a confrontation in specific issue-area institutions, it suddenly pops up at the level of the issue-overarching General Assembly. In this sense, the summation of many small conflicts with differing conflict coalitions seems to add up to a full-grown systemic conflict line. Yet such a *deus ex machina* explanation is not plausible. The observations rather point to the mainly symbolic meaning of voting in the General Assembly.

The findings also question liberal expectations and John Ikenberry's (2011a) arguments about the quality, adaptiveness, and resilience of a liberal world order. First, it is often the most "liberal" (as we define it) proposals and aspects of institutions that the rising powers *do* contest—e.g. Singapore issues at WTO, capital mobility at IMF, responsibility to protect (R2P) as means of human rights protection, very intrusive institutions and strong human rights protection mechanism, and so forth. If liberal world orders are integrative, why then do rising powers challenge most robustly the most liberal proposals for change? There is also little evidence that rising powers feel they had a say over or had access to America's leadership and behavior, and the "opportunities for access and participation" (Ikenberry 2010: 514). Moreover, the domestic structure of rising powers seems to account little for differences between preferences of rising powers.[9]

In contrast, the findings are compatible with the behavioral implications of a theory of global governance. It is first of all primarily the institutional structure and distributional biases of the governance system that create conflict lines. In this sense, it is an endogenous institutional dynamic that produces these conflicts. Decisions taken regarding the institutional set-up to meet the demands and protect the interests of established powers are less accepted and are increasingly challenged with the growing strength of rising powers. The emerging struggles may come with a principled rhetoric, but they are fed by distributional and institutional interests. While there is some cohesion of the BRICS against a strong neoliberal order, there is none when it comes to institutional positions. When so-called rising powers find themselves on the side of those who are privileged by institutional rules, such as China in the UNSC, there is little critique of the status quo. To the extent that we see some solidarity of privileged rising powers with the Global South as a whole, this seems to be driven by the NAM identity and the regional context. The more symbolic the struggles and the less consequential the debates, the higher the likelihood that emerging powers support the Global South perspective. In these cases, Brazil and India—and not China—are the speakers.

Second, the findings can be interpreted as evidence that speaks against an attempt for a system change. State contestation is not directed against institutionalization, and not against the global governance system as a whole; contestation is mainly directed against the politics of institutionalized equality and the policies of neoliberalism. To put it differently, rising powers ask for more than just routine changes within the given system, but they do not aim at overhauling the system—they do envisage a system change.

As part of the struggle over the institutional design and regulatory content, established and rising powers aim at a systemic change and use counter-institutionalization. The current crisis of the global governance system is due to a struggle over the substance and content of global governance. It is not an attempt to re-install a Westphalian system with unconditional sovereignty by rising powers. Yet counter-institutionalization can lead to changes that may eventually lead to a system change as well. In terms of the theory of global governance, we see two causal mechanisms at work; both of them can lead to a deepening or a decline of the global governance system.

---

[9] Russia is the exception. While the Russian government often derives their preferences from the role in the international institution, they sometimes behave like a revisionist power. This "Russia is special" finding is compatible with all the perspectives. Looking at the international distribution of power, Russia qualifies neither as a rising nor as an established power. In a more historical perspective, Russia is better classified as a declining power with interests that often diverge from the established powers, but also with institutional privileges that alienate them from the rising powers.

7.4 Counter-Institutionalization by Rising Powers

The starting point of the first state contestation mechanism—counter-institutionalization by rising powers (CMALL 3)—is international institutions that not only reflect the social purpose of the most powerful states, but also involve institutionalized inequality. The likelihood that the most powerful and important states ask for a privileged role in the decision-making process increases along with the level of authority exercised by the institution. It does not come as a surprise, therefore, that those post-Second World War IOs with the highest level of authority—such as the UNSC, the IMF, the World Bank, and the institutions around the Non-Proliferation Treaty—came with decision-making rules that privileged the most powerful states. While the G-summits remain in the governmental mode, it is still a case of institutionalized inequality because of highly selective membership rules.

In spite of institutionalized inequality, the redistribution of power in favor of weaker states can be the long-term outcome of international regulation (Ikenberry 2001; Stone 2011; Hanrieder and Zürn 2017). To the extent that the international authority has a common good orientation, it can help rising powers more than established powers, even if the latter dominate the institutions. A power shift can also arise from, or be amplified through, an actor's later accumulation of power in the issue area due to developments external to the international institution under question. In both cases, however, some or all of the incumbent states have lost power in the issue area, but are still not willing to adapt the institution to the new power constellations and demands. This form of power mismatch leads to contestation by rising powers.

International institutions with institutionalized inequality that exercise significant authority are easy targets of criticism. It hardly comes as a surprise then that these IOs are blamed for being exclusive and for representing the interests of the Western world only. While some of these delegitimating criticisms have been put forward by societal actors as well, BRICS and other representatives of the Global South are the most vociferous proponents of this criticism. The most authoritative IO besides the EU—the UNSC—has been the target of harsh criticism from, among others, the three non-permanent BRICS members. South Africa, Brazil, and India have pushed for reform of the UNSC and advocated a narrow, but rule of law-based interpretation of R2P (Jetschke and Abb 2018, in preparation). South Africa turned out to be the most vocal proponent of reforms, "including the option of veto abolition and the right of regional groupings to pre-select new members from their ranks" (Jetschke and Abb 2018, in preparation: 18). The mentioned rising powers ask for a broadening of the UNSC and more controlled use of the veto.

Similarly, the IMF was not only heavily criticized for its unfair distribution of voting rights, but also for uneven implementation practices (Tokhi 2018, in preparation). The call for more even-handedness in surveillance had been one of the long-standing demands from developing countries in the IMF (see Zangl et al. 2016). The institutions around the Non-Proliferation Treaty, especially the International Atomic Energy Agency (IAEA), also have been targeted as US puppet institutions, permanently changing the criteria for surveillance and condemnation and neglecting the other side of the coin: nuclear disarmament (Müller and Tokhi 2018, in preparation). In the case of the World Bank, China opted for counter-institutionalization with the establishment of the New Development Bank (NDB) and the Asia Infrastructure Investment Bank (AIIB). According to Faude and Stephen (2016: 19), "[t]his constitutes a reaction to insufficient reform of voting shares within the World Bank to accommodate the rise of new powers as well as to the dissatisfaction of many developing countries with the conditionality that Western donors attach to their assistance and with the amount of their assistance." Finally, the G7/8 meetings have always been considered as a rich man's club that lacks legitimacy to make decisions for the global community. In essence, the criticism of China, Brazil, India, and South Africa has been very similar in this respect. The strategy chosen differed, however: While Brazil, India, and especially South Africa had an eye on more participation in the meetings, China in particular considered G7 as a Western club and BRICS as the appropriate institutional response—a form of counter-institutionalization (Peters 2018, in preparation).

Counter-institutionalization by rising powers (CMALL 3) can lead to gridlock and some fragmentation, but it can also lead to institutional change. In fact, institutional adaptations occur as the outcome of this causal mechanism more often than in CMALL 4 (see the next section). The share of cases with substantial institutional adaptation responding to the new power constellation is significant. To begin with, the IMF has adapted in two ways. The voting rights have changed so that they are now closer to the changed power distribution. While the ratification of this adaption has taken some time, it began to be implemented early in 2016. Even more remarkable is that the surveillance practice of the IMF is now more even-handed than before the financial crisis in 2007 (Tokhi 2018, in preparation; Zangl et al. 2016). Most visibly, the G7 seems to be downgraded by now to a preparatory meeting for G20 summits. As Dirk Peters (2018, in preparation: 6) explains:

> In reaction to the Asian financial crisis, the G8 finance ministers, moreover, created a new format in 1999 that was intended to foster coordination of financial policies in a wider circle of "systematically relevant" countries—the G20 (Kirton 2013). The G20 included the G8 members, Australia, and a number of advanced developing states, including all BRICS. They met on the level of finance ministers on a yearly basis until 2007. From 2008 on, the frequency of meetings was increased due to

the fallout from the subprime crisis. Moreover, the G20 now also began to meet on the level of state leaders. At the G20 summit in Pittsburgh in 2009, G20 leaders declared that they "designated the G20 to be the premier forum for our international economic cooperation."[10] While G7/8 summits continued after that date, the G20 summits were intended to be seen as the major forum for economic coordination from then on and this was understood by some at the time to imply that the G20 would eclipse the G8 as a forum for international economic cooperation.

Yet, contestation by rising powers can also lead to gridlock and fragmentation. As a response to ignorance of their demands by the authority holders of the World Bank, China established new development banks more or less under their own control. In this case, however, one may ask whether these new institutions are really there to change existing ones (competitive) or whether they are seen instead as necessary and harmless additions that provide credits for developing projects in Asia with fewer strings attached than the highly legalized World Bank projects (complementary).

No institutional adaptation occurred also in the cases of the Non-Proliferation Treaty and the UNSC. Due to a lack of opportunities to counter-institutionalize in this specific issue area, rising powers have begun to block these institutions. As a result, observers identify, for instance, a decline in IAEA authority and a decline of the non-proliferation regime (Müller and Tokhi 2018, in preparation). Similarly, the voting behavior of Russia and China in cases of humanitarian interventions has weakened the UNSC. While they opted to abstain from the Libya resolution (1973), they vetoed similar resolutions on Syria. In these cases, some of the rising powers have had a privileged position from day one on and used it to undermine the institution when their demands are not met. Whether contestation by rising powers ends in institutional adaptation or in fragmentation depends on the degree of prior privileges of rising powers and the availability of counter-institutionalizing strategies (see also Zangl et al. 2016; Faude and Stephen 2016).

7.5 Counter-Institutionalization by Established Powers

The post-Second World War order has been built by the United States with the support of their Western allies and with limitations stemming from the Soviet Union. The norms and rules of those institutions reflect Western and especially American ideas and interests. Similarly, the global governance arrangements developed in the 1990s during the unipolar moment reflected US visions of world order (Krauthammer 1991). Why should the United States or other powerful incumbents now act against this order?

---

[10] "G20 Leaders Statement: The Pittsburgh Summit," September 24–5, 2009, Pittsburgh, <http://www.g20.utoronto.ca/2009/2009communique0925.html> last accessed January 10, 2015.

Counter-institutionalization by incumbents (CMALL 4) provides an answer to this question. In this case, the founders of an institution accepted the "one-state, one-vote" principle on the procedural side, partially because the institution under question was not considered as especially powerful, and partially because the incumbents felt so strong that they did not care about the formal procedures and instead wanted to gain support and legitimacy. With external changes and learning in the issue area taking place, the incumbents then often ask for new policies. However, this change is blocked by the majority of less powerful member states utilizing the "one-state, one-vote" principle. In case informal methods of influencing the outcome fail, incumbents often increase pressure by threatening to exit or by adding a new institution that works in parallel to the existing ones. Additionally, they redistribute resources from the old to the new institution. The outcome of this form of counter-institutionalization is most often either decline via deadlock or a combination of institutional adaptation and decline.

Counter-institutionalization by incumbents is especially likely when the international institution in question has acquired authority over time. In this case, the entrenched rules not only affect the distribution of costs and gains, they also intrude into domestic affairs. Powerful states in this situation are especially eager to challenge disliked substantial outcomes and sovereign equality in procedures. Counter-institutionalization by established states is therefore a typical strategy in the global governance system. It reflects the circumstance that even opposition to international institutions does not usually make the exit from the global governance system likely.[11] Opposition in the global governance system typically leads to voice via counter-institutionalization.

In an article titled "Contested Multilateralism," Julia Morse and Robert Keohane (2014) show how a Western coalition of powerful states has moved the issue of property rights away from the World Intellectual Property Organization (WIPO) to the WTO. They furthermore show how the United States and allies moved issues out of the context of UN Convention on the Law of the Sea (UNCLOS) to an informal Proliferation Security Initiative (PSI) network, and how Germany and partners moved an initiative to strengthen a renewable energy initiative out of the International Energy Agency (IEA) to the International Renewable Energy Association (IRENA). The pattern of these cases is obvious. Western states with sufficient resources have, in coalition with non-state actors, a strong interest in initiating certain international actions and programs. Yet they are confronted with a strong—and to some

---

[11] One may consider US resistance against the International Criminal Court (ICC) a counter-example. However, note that this attempt to get rid of an institution took place immediately after its formation. Over time, US policy has become more moderate and can increasingly be defined by the concepts of counter-institutionalization and deference.

extent authoritative—IO that is responsible for the issue area, but not responsive to these demands.

Within UN organizations, for instance, the "one-state, one-vote" principle often facilitates organizational decisions with which the major donors and contributors disagree. Hence, otherwise powerful members such as the United States or states from the EU face a coalition of institutional winners—materially weak but formally empowered states, ensuring that the institution is not easily adaptable to great power demands. Where the incumbents cannot circumvent sticky structures through informal means, they turn to international or bilateral institutions that assume partially complementary but also conflicting governance tasks, and thereby decrease the relevance of the original institution (Hanrieder 2014). They engage in counter-institutionalization. Out of our set of cases, the WTO during the Doha round, the institutional change from the UN Commission on Human Rights (UNCHR) to the UNHRC, and the developments in global health governance fall into this category.[12]

To start with, the WTO is an IO that exercises a significant amount of authority in international trade governance. The WTO was created in 1995 as a result of the Uruguay round. The rules are legally binding, the monitoring process is partially delegated to the secretariat, and the WTO's dispute settlement procedure leads to decisions and interpretations that are almost automatically adopted. The WTO is ranked as one of the IOs with the highest authority score in the WZB International Authority Database (IAD rank eight; see Chapter 5). At the same time, the conference of the parties is still decisive in setting the rules. In spite of informal mechanisms privileging powerful states during the negotiation process, it decides on the basis of consensus and the "one-state, one-vote" principle (Steinberg 2002; Narlikar 2005).

Already by 1999, a critical mass of members were convinced that there was something to gain from a new negotiation round, which led to the launch of the Doha Development Agenda in 2001 (Hurrell and Narlikar 2006). While the developing world wanted to revisit the Special and Differential Treatment (SDT), the established powers wanted to focus on the "Singapore issues", i.e. trade and investment, competition policy, transparency in government

---

[12] The case of climate governance, to some extent, follows a similar path. The Conferences of Parties that finally accepted the Paris Agreement were based on consensus. Whereas the rising powers defended the status by emphasizing the common but differentiated responsibility and by asking established powers to comply with their commitments, (some of) the established powers aimed at change by bringing in some of the rising powers with rapidly growing economies, which are by now major emitters (see Prys-Hansen et al. 2018, in preparation; Faude and Stephen 2016). Yet, the institutional starting point is different. Global climate governance has been fragmented from the beginning. It was the empirical case that brought David Victor (2004) to introduce the concept of regime complexity in the first place (see also Keohane and Victor 2011; Raustiala and Victor 2004 on plant genetic resources). Given this starting point, the Paris Agreement indicated institutional adaptation rather than further fragmentation.

procurement, and trade facilitation.[13] The established powers thus insisted on further liberalization and authorization of the WTO without being willing to give up their special treatment in agricultural issues. Implementing all of the Singapore agenda would have meant a significant rise of authority for WTO to limit national interventions into the global market.

The respective constellation of interests was not new for international trade politics. However, it was new that, with Brazil and India, the developing world had recognized leaders and that they formed a coalition that put forward their positions with verve and self-confidence. While the established powers pushed for further liberalization, the countries of the Global South, with primarily India and Brazil as speakers, resisted this push. At a minimum, they asked for compensation regarding issues of their major concern—i.e. agriculture and special treatment. In this sense, it was a distributional conflict on substantial issues with a considerable normative undertone regarding the value of economic liberalization. As a result, the Doha round has now stretched on for over fifteen years, the outcomes tend toward nil, and the process was already correctly described as a "decade long stalemate" (Cho 2010) more than five years ago.[14]

This gridlock subsequently translated into fragmentation. Partially in response to this gridlock, the major economies are turning increasingly toward "bi-regional" agreements that are often labeled as trade and investment treaties, indicating that they often include agreements on the Singapore issues. As Matthew Stephen (2018, in preparation) has shown, 144 new regional trade agreements have been concluded since the Doha round began; the rise of regional trade agreements began in the early 1990s, accelerating after 2000. The best known agreements are the Trans-Pacific Partnership, the Transatlantic Trade and Investment Partnership (TTIP)—both involving the United States—and the Association of Southeast Asian Nations' (ASEAN) Regional Comprehensive Partnership Agreement, involving both China and India.

While the ratification of many of these new agreements may fail in some of the established powers due to their high levels of societal politicization, the outcome is in quite stark contrast to the institutional adaptations to alleviate institutionalized inequality. The established powers seem less willing to compromise with rising power demands and, in response to them, counter-institutionalize.

---

[13] See Stephen (2018, in preparation) for a detailed account of the positions taken during the Doha negotiations.

[14] To the contrary, the procedural conflict about the informal privileges for established powers in the decision-making process led to institutional adaptation (see Zangl et al. 2016). The membership of the Quad—the informal group negotiating concrete matters behind closed doors—was changed. Japan and Canada as representatives for established powers were replaced by Brazil and India. This within-case variation is thus fully in line with the differences between the two causal mechanisms discussed in this chapter.

Another case in point is the development in global health governance (see Hanrieder and Zürn 2017). The WHO was founded "as the directing and coordinating authority on international health work" (Article 2(a)). It has exercised a significant amount of authority by covering a broad scope of operations including preparations for international negotiations, delivery of technical support, technical coordination for specific health issues, and providing expertise in the area of infectious health issues (Hein 2016). The WHO is, according to our authority database, similarly authoritative as the WTO (IAD rank ten, see Chapter 5), but it is also based on consensus-based decision making in the conference of the parties. As in the WTO, the attempts of established power to push through change failed at a certain point, leading to counter-institutionalization and fragmentation.

In the early post-Second World War decades, health governance was practically centered on one focal institution—the WHO, with later UN Children's Emergency Fund (UNICEF) as a subordinated IO. At the end of the 1970s, however, several sponsors of global health work grew dissatisfied with the WHO's universalistic ambitions. The Primary Health Care (PHC) paradigm that prevailed from the early 1970s became a particular target of criticism. At a 1979 meeting at the Rockefeller Foundation's Bellagio Center, a counter-concept of Selective Primary Health Care (SPHC) was hence put forward (Cueto 2004). The rationale underlying SPHC was that, rather than waiting until health systems were strong enough to comprehensively take care of people's health needs, targeted high-impact interventions should be the dominant strategy. Such interventions could be disease-specific vaccination or treatment campaigns, or specific measures to improve nutrition or maternal and child health. Yet the reform failed due to the resistance of the majority of WHO members.

As a consequence, major donor states such as the United States, and donor agencies such as the World Bank, increasingly turned to agencies outside of the WHO for implementing health assistance. This turn was a direct consequence of the power mismatch inside the WHO, where key funders could control neither organizational policies nor the selection of organizational leaders. This mismatch became more striking still as Director-General Halfdan Mahler was succeeded by the Japanese Hiroshi Nakajima in 1988, who won the Director-General nomination against the candidate sponsored by the United States (Chorev 2012: 156). The Japanese government had secured the support of developing countries for their candidate, who, throughout his two tenures (1988–98), faced serious allegations of fraud, nepotism, and poor leadership by most WHO main donor countries (Viola 2013).

An example of a counter-institutionalizing response by established powers was, for instance, the creation of new entities such as the Joint UN Programme on HIV/AIDS (UNAIDS). As a consequence, the WHO was considered to be an agency in "crisis" by the mid-1990s (Godlee 1994). The WHO was, however, neither shut down nor transformed altogether (see Hanrieder 2015: ch. 5). Rather, with the arrival of Director-General Gro Harlem Brundtland in 1998, the WHO accelerated a process of layering donor-driven programs on top of its core structures and policies. It incorporated programs that are broadly in line with the "Selective Primary Health Care" (SPHC) philosophy by co-initiating and hosting numerous public–private partnerships for health, such as the Global Fund to Fight AIDS, Tuberculosis, and Malaria. These partnerships are based on separate funding and donor agreements, and thus contribute to a process of organizational fragmentation where corporate policies and budgets cannot be enacted due to the separate governance of the organizational layers. Hence, even though the WHO has officially remained an advocate of "Primary Health Care" (PHC) and universal health coverage, this approach has been marginalized in an organization that is mostly run on extra-budgetary donations that are earmarked for isolated projects. In this case, counter-institutionalization by incumbents proved to be successful, also changing the targeted institution. The agreement on the Global Strategy and Plan of Action on Public Health, Innovation and Intellectual Property (GSPA) underlines this development as well (Hein 2016). In this sense, the WHO is a case of a blend of institutional adaptation and fragmentation as outcome of the causal mechanism, "counter-institutionalization by incumbents."

In sum, the causal mechanism "counter-institutionalization by established powers" unfolds from a constellation where the incumbents of an institution face an entrenched institutional status quo coalition and thus can no longer project their power within the institution. These key players are often the most powerful states that co-shaped an institution in the beginning but lost control over time because of institutional rules that, relatively speaking, empower weaker states. If interests or circumstances change, these powerful actors can no longer change the institutional features easily. The weaker actors (such as developing states) then use and protect their institutional privileges against claims for change. This resistance to change becomes much more forceful with the arrival of rising powers. This often leads to a deadlock. Counter-institutionalization by incumbents is most likely when the IO under question has authority, but has not established special rights for the more powerful states. In this causal mechanism, counter-institutionalization typically leads to fragmentation and decline.

7.6 Conclusion

States increasingly contest international institutions by the strategy that can best be labeled "counter-institutionalization." Counter-institutionalization is a strategy to change the global governance system instead of moving out of it. It uses international institutions against international institutions. It goes beyond routine changes within the system, but falls short of system change: It is a case of systemic change. In order to change existing institutions, alternative ones are utilized, new institutions are created, coalitions are formalized, and existing institutions are contested.

Counter-institutionalization comes in two forms. Counter-institutionalization by incumbent states means, above all, regime shifting and competitive regime creation. Incumbent states build and use parallel governance forums, especially when the dominant institution exercises authority on the basis of the "one-state, one-vote" principle. In that way, Western states insist on institutionalized inequality. They ask for a global governance system that gives them a privileged role and allows for double standards. The costs of this strategy are significant. On the one hand, fragmentation in the global governance system is increasing over time. As a result, the reduction of transaction costs—a major reason to develop international institutions in the first place (Keohane 1984)—is to some extend reversed. A complex institutional landscape, with many parallel opportunities to achieve results, is useful for the Western states in distributional terms (Benvenisti and Downs 2007). It is detrimental to the collective costs of achieving a working global governance system (Drezner 2013; Faude and Parizek 2018, in preparation). Even more fundamentally, the insistence on institutionalized inequality between states exacerbates the legitimation problems of global governance (see Chapter 3). While it is defensible that large nations with a large share of the world's population have a greater say in world politics, it undermines legitimacy and any legitimation efforts when institutionalized inequality—in combination with a lacking separation of powers—is used to treat like cases differently.

To some extent, rising powers also use the strategy of counter-institutionalization. They aim at changing existing, Western-biased institutions. They do not want to be just included, as the liberal order theory suggests, rather they want to re-shape the global governance system. Nevertheless, the "distance" between rising power states' preferences and beliefs and the content of given international institutions is often less dramatic than expected by PTT. Rising powers do not aim to overhaul the existing international institutions; rather, they want to reform them from the inside. In essence, counter-institutionalization by rising powers aims at voice—not at exit or loyalty. At the same time, there is an ongoing suspicion that stronger international institutions are instruments of Western dominance and help to promulgate an unequal distribution of benefits. This tension leads to ambiguous responses, unified by the struggle against institutionalized inequality.

Taken altogether, substantial institutional adaptation in order to integrate rising powers and their societies into the global governance system is a possibility. However, it has so far mostly happened when the new powers are needed to resolve urgent problems, i.e. when they possess "systemic significance." If this condition is not met, established powers often sidestep demands from the rising powers by regime shifting and competitive regime creation. While this helps established powers to succeed in distributional terms— partially alleviating politicization pressure from the home front—it weakens the global governance system as a whole. It questions both efficiency and legitimacy of the system—the former by increasing transaction costs, and the latter by producing outputs that violate the basic principles of legitimacy: non-arbitrariness and legal equality.

8

The Deepening of Global Governance

The contestation of inter- and transnational institutions does not necessarily lead to the decline of the global governance system. If key decision makers respond appropriately, international authorities can come out stronger than before. This is, however, a highly contingent process. What can be observed therefore is a parallelism of decline and deepening of global governance arrangements.

On the one hand, Joost Pauwelyn, Ramses A. Wessel, and Jan Wouters (2014: 734), using multilateral treaties as indicators, show a sharp decline in new bilateral and multilateral treaties signed in the last decade and deposited with the United Nations (UN). Most importantly, multilateral treaties went down to 406 in the 1990s and to 262 in the 2000s. On a more detailed level of ratification of international treaties, a similar pattern can be observed: The steep rise of ratifications of multilateral treaties in the 1990s and early 2000s has stopped, and there has been a significant decline in ratifications of new treaties (Dai and Tokhi 2015).

On the other hand, new global governance institutions are still being established and a deepening is observed within some of the existing ones. Moreover, the current crisis does not necessarily affect the institutions that are already in place in a negative way. While the growth of international authority has slowed down from 2010 on, it still keeps growing (see Chapter 3). The decline in growth rates of international authority seems to be much less accentuated than in the case of new international treaties. Moreover, it seems that some of the already existing authorities respond to the current crisis by addressing the shortcomings of the global governance system, resulting in a deepening of global governance. Existing institutions respond to legitimation problems and implement institutional reforms by, for instance, extending participation to non-state actors (Tallberg et al. 2013) or by establishing international parliamentary institutions (Rocabert et al. 2017, in preparation). Regarding both of these indicators for reform, the growth started in the early 1990s and has continued without interruption even after 2010.

Taken together, one can state that the global governance system is in trouble and further growth has slowed down significantly; decline and, to some extent, deadlock is taking place. At the same time, existing international institutions respond to contestation, and at least some of these changes include substantial institutional reforms. Accordingly, it has been shown in Chapter 7 that state contestation can—in particular circumstances—lead to institutional change.

Against this backdrop, this chapter attempts to systematically demonstrate the possibility of substantial reform in the face of societal pressure. Its goal is to examine the conditions under which the authority–legitimation link (ALL) can deepen global governance in reactive sequences involving non-state actors and how this can play out in different pathways. The argument will be exemplified in the field of human rights protection. In section 8.1, I discuss one more causal mechanism derived from the ALL, reinforcement via politicization (CMALL 2), and derive expectations to be tested from it. In section 8.2, the substantial field of the exemplary study is introduced—human rights provision in international organizations (IOs). I then go on to present the findings of a collaborative project in section 8.3, and scope conditions in section 8.4. In the conclusion to this chapter, I condense the findings and emphasize the role of scope conditions of different reactive sequences.

8.1 Improved Legitimacy via Societal Pressures

International institutions have authority over states when the addressees recognize—in principle or in practice—that an institution can make competent judgments and decisions that request deference even if they run against their interests. IOs may also exercise authority over individuals to the extent that they directly regulate their behavior (see also Bodansky 2013; von Bogdandy et al. 2010b). In this case, states lose their role as intermediary between their citizens and the international level. For instance, sanctions imposed by the United Nations Security Council (UNSC), originally intended to influence the behavior of states, now often address individuals such as terror suspects, warlords, or autocrats, and their protégés (Drezner 2011). In peace missions, likewise, direct authority relations arise between IOs and individuals, especially when such organizations assume government functions in transitional administrations. Furthermore, projects sponsored by the World Bank and the International Monetary Fund (IMF), although formally implemented by recipient countries, have to respect strict requirements with serious repercussions for individuals, and thus come close to direct authority over individuals. In these cases, the autonomy of individuals—instead of collective actors—is affected. In some cases, this more or less direct link between IOs and individuals even leads to allegations that human rights are violated. Such cases will be analyzed in the remainder of this chapter.

If the exercise of authority affects human rights, the technocratic legitimation narrative does not suffice. The addition of a legal narrative seems to be the obvious choice in responding to such delegitimation claims. This pattern of justification is based on legal accountability, the protection of basic rights, and the promotion of legal equality. Central decision makers of an IO therefore need to overcome the hurdles that often prevent a legal legitimation narrative. The protection and promotion of individual rights can then have a legitimacy-generating effect.

Altogether CMALL 2 is defined as follows: The first arrow in Figure 8.1 states that the rise of direct international authority and the capacity for violating human rights lead to social grievances and the demand for the protection of rights. Those who complain will seek coalition partners (arrow 2) and if they find them and can significantly increase the pressure, authority holders adopt institutional provisions intended both to prevent human rights violations and, in case of violations, hold themselves accountable for such violations (third arrow). This causal mechanism can be labeled "reinforcement via politicization."

Again, CMALL 2 is a causal mechanism that denotes a reactive sequence. While the powerful states and supranational bodies within them may be the drivers of authoritative IOs, actors other than key executives of the international authority and of the core member states ask for legalization. Institutional change thus results from an interaction between key IO actors, including the executives of the most powerful states, and "non-core" actors, such as smaller member states, members of domestic parliaments, courts, or civil society organizations (CSOs).[1]

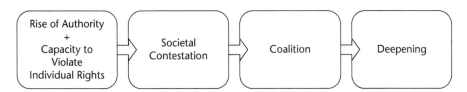

Figure 8.1. Reinforcement via politicization (CMALL 2)[2]

---

[1] In this sense, this exploration of the rise of human rights protection can be seen as part of the more general mechanism of "contentious politics" between authority holders and the people affected (see Tilly and Tarrow 2007; Tarrow 2015).

[2] See Zürn and Heupel (2017), where a similar mechanism is labeled "authority–legitimation mechanism" (ALM).

Given that CMALL 2 represents a reactive sequence, choice is again built into the causal mechanism. Each of the three steps is probabilistic, i.e. each step requires specific conditions to occur. Even when we observe a general association between rising authority and new institutional provisions, the specific causes for IO provisions to protect human rights depend on specific circumstances. Moreover, CMALL 2 encompasses different pathways from international authority to human rights protection provisions, i.e. different types in which the causal mechanism plays out. This means that equifinality—namely, the possibility that a given outcome can come about in many different ways—has to be taken into account.

CMALL 2 will be tested employing the method of qualitative process tracing, which is a method designed to probe causal mechanisms (Checkel 2006: 363; Bennett and Checkel 2015; George and Bennett 2005: 206–7). Process tracing involves the use of evidence from *within a case* to make causal inferences. It is therefore necessary to look at within-case developments and to select cases in which both the starting point (international authority) and the end point (human rights protection provisions) of the causal mechanism are given.[3] Accordingly, the selection of cases follows a different logic than conventional comparative research.[4] Usually, process tracing is employed in single case study research. There is however no need for this limitation, which very often weakens the generalizability of findings. In fact, exploring and examining causal mechanisms via process tracing makes it advisable to go beyond the one case that has often been the basis of the theoretical intuition in the first place. CMALL 2 has therefore been tested in ten case studies in a design that may be labeled "comparative qualitative process tracing" (Heupel and Zürn 2017a).[5]

8.2 Human Rights Provisions in International Organizations

In states like the Congo and Kosovo, peacekeepers have been accused of sexually abusing the women they were supposed to protect.[6] In addition to misconduct on the part of the UN personnel during peacekeeping activities,

---

[3] These are conditions also mentioned by Schimmelfennig (2015) for deductive—i.e. in his view, efficient—process tracing.

[4] The objection from the point of comparative research that selecting on the starting and the end point makes the theory irrefutable does not hold. Testing a mechanism means to check the extent to which the steps in between occur as specified in the theory. As will be shown, there is one case in which the hypothesized steps in between are not in place.

[5] The project "International Organization and the Protection of Individual Rights" has been financed by the German Research Association (DFG). Besides Monika Heupel, Gisela Hirschmann and Theresa Reinold also made valuable contributions (see their chapters in Heupel and Zürn 2017a). The remainder of this chapter builds on this work (see Heupel and Zürn 2017b and Zürn and Heupel 2017).

[6] Sections 8.2–8.4 draw from Zürn and Heupel (2017) and Heupel and Zürn (2017b).

a number of UN policies have arguably violated human rights as well (Verdirame 2011). In fact, comprehensive trade sanctions that hurt innocent people in targeted countries and the blacklisting of individuals without due process have violated human rights. In addition, other IOs besides the UN have also been accused of violating human rights. North Atlantic Treaty Organization (NATO) personnel have been charged with sexual exploitation and of illegal detention of prisoners. The European Union (EU) has also been criticized for its blacklisting practices. Furthermore, the international financial institutions in particular have received bad press for infringing upon subsistence rights and aggravating poverty.

Today, IOs do not only formulate normative standards based on individual rights and the rule of law, but they are also capable of violating these standards themselves. To the extent that IOs increasingly exercise public authority, take decisions and implement them independently, or at least lay down strict conditions for their implementation, violations of human rights that then occur are no longer attributable to states alone, but also to the IOs themselves. In other words, the rise of international authority has led to the possibility that human rights violations may be associated with an IO. As a result, IOs have been confronted with a rising number of allegations that they have violated human rights.

Authority holders have responded to these predicaments. In recent years, we have seen a debate that has pointed to the applicability of rule of law prescriptions to IOs. This is nicely illustrated by comparing a statement by the president of the UNSC in 2006 with one made in 2010. In a meeting of the Council held in 2006, the president stated that the "Security Council attaches vital importance to promoting the peace and the rule of law, including respect for human rights, as an indisputable element of lasting peace."[7] Four years later, the respective opening of the paragraph reads as follows: "The Security Council expresses its commitment to ensure that all UN efforts to restore peace and security themselves respect and promote the rule of law." This indicates a remarkable shift from promoting the rule of law and human rights to promoting *and* respecting the rule of law and human rights. Subsequently, in 2012, the Declaration of the High-level Meeting of the General Assembly on the Rule of Law at the National and International Levels recognized that "the rule of law applies to all states equally, and to international organizations, including the [UN] and its principal organs."[8] In the words of one international lawyer, "[t]oday, there is arguably no international body that questions the relevance of human rights norms to its activities" (von Bogdandy 2013: 298, author's translation).

---

[7] See UN Doc. S/PRST/2006/28.
[8] UN Doc. A/67/L.1 (September 19, 2012), adopted as UN Doc. A/RES/67/1 (September 24, 2012).

More concretely, some IOs have attached provisions for the protection of individual rights to specific policies. They have established prevention provisions to ensure that they do not violate human rights in the first place, and they have provided avenues for complaint for those affected. These provisions are not always consistently implemented, but their very introduction is already a noteworthy development. For instance, a number of provisions have been developed by the UN in an effort to guarantee that human rights are protected within the framework of peacekeeping missions. Between 2003 and 2009, the UN established procedures to prevent peacekeepers and other actors involved in UN missions from sexually exploiting women and children. In doing so, the UN has forbidden every form of sexual exploitation in the context of peacekeeping in express codes of conduct (UN Secretary General 2003). In addition, compulsory training modules were created for peacekeepers to enhance their awareness of the new regulatory regime. Finally, bodies to receive complaints from victims were established both in the UN Secretariat and in individual missions. The UN has also set itself rules of behavior toward prisoners in peacekeeping operations. In the late 1990s, the UN Secretary-General published a bulletin stating that prisoners were to be treated in accordance with the Geneva Conventions and customary international law (UN Secretary General 1999). In parallel, an ombudsperson and later the Human Rights Advisory Panel were established in the mission in Kosovo.

Evidently, UN peacekeeping is not an exception. In addition, the African Union (AU), the EU, the Food and Agricultural Organization of the UN (FAO), the International Criminal Court (ICC), the UN Development Programme (UNDP), the UN Refugee Agency (UNHCR), and the World Bank have all attached broad provisions for the protection of human rights, including both prevention and complaint mechanisms, to their policies. Furthermore, the Council of Europe, the International Labour Organization (ILO), the IMF, NATO, the Organisation for Economic Co-operation and Development (OECD), the Organization for Security and Co-operation in Europe (OSCE), the Southern African Development Community (SADC), the World Health Organization (WHO), and the UN Educational, Scientific and Cultural Organization (UNESCO) have all now established at least either prevention measures or complaints procedures in an effort to avoid human rights violations. As a representative of a small IO put it during an informal conversation with this author, there are some devices that a small IO needs to have by now, in the area of human rights protection, before it is accepted as a member of the family. Therefore, it seems justified to talk about a trend towards an institutionalized standard of human rights protection that "applies to all States equally, and to [IOs], including the [UN] and its principal organs," in the words of the former Secretary-General Ban Ki-moon.[9] The institutional response to the allegations of human rights violations has, in effect, led to a deepening of global governance in these cases.

In order to account for these institutional dynamics in terms of the causal mechanism "reinforcement via politicization" (CMALL 2), cases of international authorities that are accused of violating human rights in the exercise of their authority and whose policies directly or indirectly affect individuals have to be singled out. In the collaborative research project "International Organizations and the Protection of Individual Rights," we chose the UN, the EU, NATO, the World Bank, and the IMF, thus focusing on highly authoritative IOs. Regarding the introduction of provisions for the protection of human rights as the end point of CMALL 2, IO reactions to charges of human rights violations in ten case studies were examined. Four cases cover UN and EU sanctions policy (see Heupel 2017a, 2017b, 2017d, 2017e), another four cover UN and NATO peacekeeping (see Hirschmann 2017b, 2017a, 2017d, 2017c), and two cases cover World Bank and IMF lending (see Heupel 2017c and Reinold 2017).

Table 8.1 provides a summary of the cases covered in the analysis.[10] The main consideration guiding the case selection (beyond the presence of the mechanism's starting and end points) has been to guarantee the generalizability of the findings—hence different IOs, different policy instruments, and provisions for the protection of different types of rights.

Table 8.1. Overview of cases

Policy	IO	Human Rights Violation
Sanctions	UN	Subsistence rights
	UN	Due process rights
	EU	Subsistence rights
	EU	Due process rights
Peacekeeping	UN	Bodily integrity rights and right not to be subjected to inhuman or degrading treatment
	UN	Due process rights
	NATO	Bodily integrity rights and right not to be enslaved
	NATO	Due process rights
Lending	World Bank	Subsistence and cultural rights
	IMF	Subsistence rights

Source: Zürn and Heupel 2017

---

[9] UN Doc. A/67/L.1 § 2 (September 19, 2012), adopted as UN Doc. A/RES/67/1 (September 24, 2012).
[10] Section 8.4 provides more information on the cases.

8.3 The Findings

The central result of the analysis is that the causal mechanism, reinforcement via politicization, works in nine out of the ten cases studied. The UN and the EU both introduced provisions for the protection of due process rights in their sanctions policies to regain legitimacy. The introduction of provisions for the protection of subsistence rights in UN sanctions policy was also a response to external pressure and delegitimation efforts. Both the UN and NATO designed provisions for the protection of human rights for its peacekeeping missions to counter efforts of delegitimation. Similarly, the World Bank and the IMF established protection provisions in response to allegations that their policies violated human rights. All these nine cases involved charges against an IO that it had violated human rights. This led to normative disapproval, especially by CSOs, who engaged additional actors that were neither central government nor IO decision makers (middle powers, parliaments, courts, other IOs, the media, etc.), managing to exercise such an influence that the central decision makers in the IO opted for the adoption of provisions for the protection of human rights.

In only one case—comprehensive EU sanctions infringing upon the subsistence rights of innocent individuals—central decision makers anticipated the possibility of human rights violations and the ensuing disapproval, and acted in an anticipatory mode that is not directly captured by CMALL 2. Arguably, however, the EU foresaw the possibility of hardship through comprehensive trade sanctions and the ensuing criticism only against the background of similar experiences of the UN. In this way, the anticipatory action in this case can be seen as parasitic to reinforcement via politicization. It was foreseen and EU decision makers launched respective reforms in an anticipatory way.

These results corroborate the postulated causal mechanism. Accordingly, to the extent that IOs establish direct authority relationships with individuals, human rights violations become possible. If authoritative IOs infringe upon human rights, concerned actors seek opportunities to delegitimate the IO and demand introduction of provisions for the protection of human rights. Assaults on their legitimacy endanger the authority of IOs. If the opportunities to exercise pressure on the IOs suffice, the latter introduce provisions for the protection of human rights in order to regain legitimacy.

The quality of the human rights provisions, however, varies remarkably. We distinguish therefore between comprehensive provisions for protecting human rights in IOs, which most often include both prevention and complaint provisions, and more limited provisions, which most of the time contain only prevention provisions. Prevention provisions—i.e. provisions by means of which the IO aims to avoid human rights violations in the first

Table 8.2. Quality of human rights protection provisions

Comprehensive provisions	Limited provisions
• EU Sanctions: Due process rights • UN Peacekeeping: Bodily integrity rights and the right not to be subjected to inhuman or degrading treatment • World Bank: Subsistence and cultural rights • UN Sanctions: Due process rights • UN Peacekeeping: Due process rights	• NATO Peacekeeping: Bodily integrity rights and the right not to be enslaved • UN Sanctions: Subsistence rights • EU Sanctions: Subsistence rights • IMF Lending: Subsistence rights • NATO Peacekeeping: Due process rights

Source: Heupel and Hirschmann 2017

place—include, among others, standard setting, monitoring, and training. Complaint provisions serve to enable aggrieved individuals to hold to account and sanction the IO.

We utilized a coding scheme consisting of five indicators for prevention provisions and five indicators for complaint procedures to assess the quality of human rights provisions (Heupel and Hirschmann 2017). The result is a bifurcated distribution of cases that allows us to distinguish between limited provisions for human rights protection (five cases) and comprehensive ones (also five cases) in binary terms (Table 8.2).

These differences in the quality of the human rights protection provisions raise questions concerning the explanation of this variance. Under which conditions are comprehensive provisions possible? Are there some typical switches in CMALL 2 accounting for these differences?

8.4 Scope Conditions

There is no uniform way in which reinforcement via politicization unfolds. Rather, the mechanism proceeds via three distinct equifinal pathways that we labeled *legislative institution building*, *judicial institution building*, and *like-minded institution building*, depending on the dominant coalition partner of CSOs in the process. In addition, a fourth causal pathway that is closely related to CMALL 2, namely *anticipatory institution building*, is identified. Whereas the general finding reported in the section above (CMALL 2 is present in nine out of ten cases) comes close to fulfilling the requirements for a test of hypotheses, the identification of the four pathways and their scope condition is a purely inductive exercise, suggesting hypotheses to be tested in future research. It is in effect an exercise in hypotheses-generation.

In presenting the findings, the relevant questions about the unfolding of CMALL 2 are tackled in order. As an initial issue, it has to be judged whether international authorities were associated with human rights violations or if the authority holders were able to act preventively. In case human rights

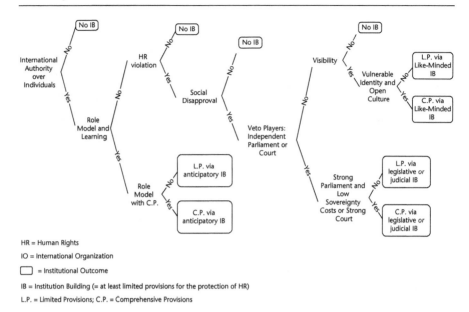

HR = Human Rights

IO = International Organization

☐ = Institutional Outcome

IB = Institution Building (= at least limited provisions for the protection of HR)

L.P. = Limited Provisions; C.P. = Comprehensive Provisions

Figure 8.2. The CMALL 2 tree

Source: Heupel, M., and Zürn, M. (2017), "The Rise of Human Rights Protection in International Organizations. Results and Theoretical Implications," in M. Heupel and M. Zürn (eds.), *International Organisations and Human Rights. Explaining Limitations of International Authority* (Cambridge University Press), 297–331

violations are associated with IOs, three subsequent questions structure the process model. First, to identify the respective pathway, which coalition partners were available? Second, what are the conducive scope conditions for the pathway? Third, which conditions are necessary so that the pathway leads to comprehensive—instead of only limited—human rights provisions?

These questions can be translated into a selection tree (Figure 8.2). This visualization is useful as an aid in grasping the interplay of variables and pathways within the general causal mechanism "reinforcement via politicization." The major findings of the case studies are presented along the tree from the left to the right and the four pathways are introduced along the way.

8.4.1 *Provisions without Violations*

In all but one case, CMALL 2 proved to be present. In this one case, institution building preceded allegations of human rights violations. This means that there is the possibility of choice at the point where possible human rights violations are anticipated—even before charges are put forward. This is where the first pathway to the institutionalization of human rights provisions comes in.

In the case of comprehensive EU sanctions, no charges of human rights violations before the establishment of provisions for the protection of human rights could be found. Instead, a pathway was observed that we label *anticipatory institution building*. Anticipatory institution building refers to a process in which the IO introduces human rights protection provisions in the absence of immediate external pressure for institutional change. In this case, central decision makers within the IO observe the negative feedback received by a peer IO and draw lessons for their own policies. Anticipatory institution building of this kind is different from mimicry or simple emulation (see e.g. Meyer and Rowan 1977), since the institutional choice is based on an evaluation of the effects of a given measure. This is different from imitating something merely because it is considered to be part of a script with prescriptive force, without evaluating its effects. It therefore resembles a case of cognitive learning (Hirschmann 2015)—be it in a purely instrumental or a more complex, normative sense (Haas 1990; Haas and Haas 1995).

The protection of subsistence rights in EU sanctions policy is a case of anticipatory institution building (Heupel 2017b). The EU itself did not violate subsistence rights in its sanctions policy and was thus not confronted with direct charges of human rights violations. At the same time, however, some EU member states observed that UN sanctions did violate subsistence rights and that the UN was confronted with harsh criticism that threatened to tarnish its reputation (Hazelzet 2001: 48; Eriksson 2009: 11). Moreover, representatives of EU member states and EU officials participated in meetings in which proposals were developed as to how the negative humanitarian consequences of sanctions could be avoided (Wallensteen et al. 2003: 141). The proposals were primarily devised for the UN, but they were also relevant for EU sanctions policy. Eventually, the EU preventively created provisions for the protection of subsistence rights in its sanctions policy in order to make sure that, unlike the UN, it would be able to prevent rights violations in the first place and not be targeted by a delegitimation campaign.

What scope conditions are conducive to the pathway anticipatory institution building? Institutions learn from each other if the experience one organization has undergone can serve as an example for another institution. Accordingly, a reference organization with a good reputation may develop a set of procedures that can serve as a model for other organizations to develop procedures of its own. This applies to one of the cases—the protection of subsistence rights in EU sanctions policy, in which the EU benefitted from the example of the UN.

What are the success conditions of the pathway anticipatory institution building? IOs seem to orient themselves to a reference organization not only when it comes to a decision on whether human rights safeguards are to be introduced at all, but also when it comes to deciding on the quality of these provisions.

The EU has learned from the experience of the UN that IOs come under pressure when their sanctions policies violate subsistence rights. At the same time, however, the EU could draw the inference that the pressure on the UN subsided, even though it only established limited rather than comprehensive protection provisions.

8.4.2 *Provisions via Internal Veto Players*

In all the cases in which IOs violated human rights, social disapproval and pressure caused a change of practice. Human rights violations thus always generated delegitimation strategies from at least some actors. However, the amount of pressure produced by disapproval varies significantly depending on the availability of coalition partners. The next junction in the selection tree is created by the presence or absence of institutional veto players (Tsebelis 2002) that can be utilized for the purposes of those who press the IO to introduce provisions for the protection of human rights. Two such institutional entry points are decisive in our context: independent parliaments and courts within powerful members. Each of the two entry points leads to a different pathway.

The pathway *legislative institution building* presupposes that the parliaments in democratic member states of IOs play a central role in prompting the rise of human rights protection. Parliaments are often portrayed as actors that restrict governments' ability to conclude international agreements. In the case of legislative institution building, however, parliaments provide for the contrary effect (see also Hasenclever 2001). Normally, the protection of human rights is not a foreign policy priority of the executive. Without domestic dynamics, states have little incentive to invest political capital to force through human rights issues. In the United States, for instance, it was often initiatives by Congress that strengthened the role of human rights considerations in US foreign policy (Forsythe 1988). A parliament tries to achieve human rights safeguards in IOs either by passing laws that bind the executive or by refusing to ratify a treaty or allocating budgetary means unless its demands are met. In the former, the parliament impacts on the executive's foreign policy by conducting investigations, agenda setting, and shaping the domestic discourse (Scott 1997).

The introduction of social and environmental standards and the creation of the Inspection Panel in the World Bank proceeded via the pathway legislative institution building (see Heupel 2017c). Non-governmental organizations (NGOs) mobilized members of US Congress by decrying the negative social and ecological consequences of selected projects, especially a major road building project in the Brazilian Amazon and a dam project in India. As a result, Congress linked the release of funding to the Bank to the improvement of the Bank's underdeveloped social and environmental standards and the creation of a complaints mechanism. The US Executive Director at the World Bank worked hard to win over other member states and Bank management to garner support for the respective reforms. Many borrowing countries and Bank management and staff that had previously opposed such reforms finally withdrew their resistance against provisions (Wade 1997; Udall 1998; Park 2010).

Legislative institution building can also be identified in the case of NATO introducing safeguards against human trafficking in the context of peace operations (see Hirschmann 2017a). Reports of misconduct by US troops deployed in missions as diverse as those in Korea and the Balkans prompted US Congress to initiate investigations. Thereupon, the US President issued a directive propagating a "zero tolerance policy" with regard to human trafficking in the context of military operations (White House 2002). Against this background, the US Ambassador to NATO, together with his Norwegian counterpart, initiated similar rules for NATO. The two ambassadors succeeded in persuading the other member states of the necessity of the Zero Tolerance Policy on Combating Human Trafficking without applying material pressure.

What are the scope conditions that are conducive to the pathway legislative institution building? Our two cases indicate that the pathway is chosen if a parliament is available that possesses substantial autonomy vis-à-vis the executive. This applies particularly to presidential systems in which the parliament possesses independence from the head of government and a comparatively strong position in foreign policy. The US Congress, which is given far-reaching prerogatives in the field of foreign policy by the US Constitution, is a particularly powerful parliament. Congress is empowered to enact legislations relating to foreign policy decisions, authorize financial contributions to IOs and, in the case of the Senate, ratify bi- and multilateral treaties, and confirm the appointment of senior American personnel to IOs. Moreover, Congress can flex its muscles beyond these formal competences by putting topics on the agenda and influencing public opinion. Parliaments in parliamentary systems, by contrast, are in a far weaker position to influence the foreign policy preferences of governments. Hence, in our two cases of legislative institution building, the US Congress played a significant role in facilitating the introduction of human rights safeguards in the World Bank and NATO by prompting the US government to adopt their cause.

In addition, the pathway seems to be facilitated by the existence of similar human rights protection provisions at the domestic level. In both cases, domestic US legislation on social and environmental standards for development lending and on the prohibition of sexual exploitation by US military personnel could thus serve as an inspiration for similar reforms in the

World Bank and NATO (e.g. Operations Evaluation Department 2001: 3; White House 2002).

What are the conditions that allow this pathway to lead to comprehensive provisions? In order to be successful at the end of this pathway, a parliament not only needs to be internally strong but also able to affect the foreign policy of a powerful state. There is a significant difference if the parliament utilized for the purpose of establishing human rights provisions sits in Washington, DC, or in Valletta (Malta). Powerful states have an especially strong influence on IO policies.

Yet the state in question must not only be influential, but be so influential that it can formulate additional rules without fearing that they may backfire. On the basis of our cases, it seems that the activities of an autonomous parliament only lead to comprehensive provisions if the executive that is targeted by the parliament has to suffer no—or only small—sovereignty costs. This is in line with the assumption that states try to keep their sovereignty costs as small as possible when they delegate competences to IOs and promote their legalization (Abbott and Snidal 2000; Hawkins et al. 2006b). The introduction of provisions for the protection of human rights entails sovereignty costs for a state if the provisions have binding implications for it or its citizens. Protection provisions that only apply to the IO bureaucracy or other IO member states, by contrast, entail no sovereignty costs for that state. In the World Bank, therefore, the United States championed ambitious standards that only restrict the leeway of the Bank's bureaucracy and of borrowing states; they do not affect the United States or its citizens. In the case of NATO, the United States espoused only limited protection provisions as these also regulated the behavior of American soldiers on NATO missions.

After allegations of human rights violations, groups that disapprove the practice may be able to put (members of) an independent parliament on their side. This triggers legislative institution building. The pathway seems to be especially successful if the independent parliament sits in an internationally powerful state and if the sovereignty costs for the state in which the parliament resides are limited. Then we may expect comprehensive provisions for the protection of human rights.

Judicial institution building is another pathway that builds on strong veto-player institutions within members of the IO. It refers to a pathway in which the decisive input for the institutionalization of human rights protection provisions comes from higher courts. In this pathway, judges take the side of the complaining parties at the expense of the autonomy of the legislature and executive (see e.g. Stone Sweet 2000). An uncontroversial form of judicial institution building is gap filling, which is often unavoidable as rules—or their scope of application—are often not specified. A more controversial form is judicial activism, which involves judges deliberately transforming the law by using the monopoly of interpreting the constitution (Hirschl 2004; Wessel 2006).

The EU's efforts to guarantee the due process rights of individuals and groups targeted with sanctions followed the pathway judicial institution building (see Heupel 2017a). Terror suspects who considered that their right to due process had been violated soon started to file lawsuits before national courts and before the European Court of Justice (ECJ). A 2006 judgment of the Court of First Instance in the case of *Organisation des Modjahedines du Peuple d'Iran* (OMPI) finally prompted significant reforms to the EU's provisions. In this case, the ECJ decided that the procedure according to which the EU selected parties for sanctions lists violated the claimants' right to due process and, based on this assessment, revoked the EU sanctions against OMPI (Court of First Instance 2006). The Council of the EU feared that this judgment would set a precedent and modified its listing and delisting procedures (Guild 2008: 189). Since then, the wave of lawsuits especially before the ECJ has not come to a halt and more and more plaintiffs have won their cases against the EU. Most due process reforms that the EU has instituted to date with regard to its sanctions policy have been a reaction to ECJ judgments (Eriksson 2009: 22).

In the UN as well, provisions for the protection of due process rights of sanctioned parties have been improved over time following the same pathway (see Heupel 2017d). Affected individuals turned to national courts and especially to the ECJ. The ECJ was to assess whether the implementation of UN sanctions by the EU was reconcilable with the EU's legal principles. In the late 2000s, the development of UN provisions has clearly been driven by the jurisdiction of the ECJ. In 2008, in its famous *Kadi* case, the ECJ proscribed the implementation of UN sanctions against Yassin Abdullah Kadi in the EU, arguing that the sanctions violated fundamental rights as guaranteed in the EU (European Court of Justice 2008). The UNSC was afraid that this judgment would not only obstruct the implementation of its sanctions in the EU, but might also motivate similar judgments by other courts in the future. The Council therefore improved its listing and delisting provisions to take account of the demands of the ECJ (see Heupel 2017a).

The choice of the pathway judicial institution building depends, in the first place, on what type of right is violated. In the case of courts chosen by litigants, independence is given and therefore does not vary across cases—as opposed to parliaments. Yet another condition seems to be especially important for this pathway in accounting for variation. In the two cases in question, a civil right—namely, the right to due process—was violated. This suggests that the pathway, "judicial institution building," is activated if the right that is allegedly infringed is generally considered to be justiciable—i.e. perceived to be enforceable before a court of law. While there is a consensus among law scholars that civil and political rights are enforceable, there is disagreement as to whether this applies to social, economic, and cultural rights as well (Nolan et al. 2007). This distinction is also evident in the legal practice of national and international courts. Individuals whose civil or political rights are violated can, therefore, more easily find a court that accepts their claims. The perceived justiciability thus provides the legal opportunity structure for the pathway.

The two case studies on the evolution of due process safeguards in UN and EU sanctions policy suggest that *judicial institution building leads to comprehensive human rights safeguards if the IO is confronted with the judgments of a strong court.* First, this can be the case if the state or the community of states in which the court is located is a central actor in the IO. This applies to the UN case study in which the ECJ issued judgments on the implementation of UN sanctions in the EU. Second, this can be even more the case if the court that is used by private litigants to improve human rights safeguards in an IO has jurisdiction over the IO. This applies to the EU case study in which the ECJ issued judgments on EU sanctions policy.

In recent years, more and more international courts which may be accessed by private litigants have been created. These courts assess the legality of administrative actions of IOs as well as their conformity with basic constitutional principles (Alter 2014). Strategic litigation is, therefore, an increasingly promising means of enforcing human rights protection provisions in IOs. In light of the history of the ECJ, it is not surprising that its decisions are a particularly powerful driver of institutional change. Over the years, the ECJ has systematically expanded its competences in order to strengthen the rights of individuals; initially against states and, more recently, also against IOs. The court did not shy away from asserting the establishment of individual rights protection against the interests of powerful EU member states either (Mattli and Slaughter 1998; Tallberg 2000). In any case, the ECJ enjoys a high reputation, which makes non-compliance with its decisions more difficult than, for instance, disregard of demands of civil society actors.

Actors that disapprove human rights violations can trigger the pathway judicial institution building, if the violation concerns a justiciable right that courts are willing to assume. This pathway seems to be especially successful if the court rules over internationally powerful actors. In that case, we can expect comprehensive provisions for the protection of human rights.

8.4.3 *Provisions via External Pressure*

If the actors who want to introduce provisions for the protection of human rights do not find domestic veto players to act as entry points, they still can aim for a political campaign that puts direct and public pressure on the IO. This then leads to the causal pathway of like-minded institution building.

Like-minded institution building characterizes a pathway in which protection provisions are established in IOs in reaction to the input of norm entrepreneurs who condemn IOs' behavior and suggest reform proposals. The term "like-minded" here refers to a coalition of CSOs and states with a common agenda (Warleigh 2001: 629; Cooper 2002). The term is used in such a way that it encompasses all kinds of actors who are neither central decision makers within the IO nor executives from powerful member states. "Like-minded" actors usually do not possess substantial institutional power resources, but nevertheless find ways to shape IOs' agenda (Cooper 2002). They are often organized in transnational advocacy networks, they conduct campaigns to alert the public about IOs' harmful behavior, and thus try to exercise material and moral leverage to influence IOs (Keck and Sikkink 1999: 97). Like-minded institution building relies on the presumption that change is induced by external pressure that the like-minded actors can exert by appealing to the transnational and different national publics. Therefore, framing (Tversky and Kahneman 1981) and persuasion (Risse and Sikkink 1999) play an important role. They often highlight the discrepancy between IOs' behavior and existing norms and provide arguments for why IOs should comply with human rights norms.

In five of the ten cases, human rights protection provisions emerged in IOs via like-minded institution building. Three out of four peacekeeping cases fall into this category, among them the cases on the evolution of UN provisions for the protection of the detainees' right to due process and provisions against sexual abuse by peacekeepers (Hirschmann 2017d, 2017c). The UN faced criticism already in the early 1990s by NGOs that denounced human rights violations in the handling of detainees in its peace missions (e.g. Amnesty International 1994). At the same time, the International Committee of the Red Cross drew up standards for the handling of detainees and tried to persuade the UN of their relevance. Years later, the Council of Europe and the UN Ombudsperson in Kosovo publicly condemned UN detention practices in Kosovo, increasing the pressure to implement the proposals (UNMIK Ombudsperson 2000; Council of Europe 2002). Furthermore, since the early 2000s, the UN was also confronted with media and NGO reports decrying cases of sexual exploitation by peacekeepers in UN missions (e.g. Save the Children UK 2002). Once public pressure had risen to the extent that it threatened to undermine the legitimacy of UN peacekeeping generally, the UN Secretariat started to develop reform proposals (UN General Assembly 2005; Hirschmann 2017d: 13–18). When devising respective guidelines, the Secretariat cooperated closely with NGOs before they were eventually adopted by the intergovernmental UN bodies.

In NATO, provisions for the protection of due process rights of detainees equally emerged via the same pathway (see Hirschmann 2017b). NATO came under considerable pressure when NGOs and other IOs deemed its detention practices as incompatible with international humanitarian law (OSCE 2002; Amnesty International 2004). During NATO's intervention in Afghanistan, pressure on it increased when NGOs began to denounce the detention practices of troop-contributing countries (Amnesty International 2007). As a consequence, NATO introduced limited human rights protection provisions to safeguard the due process rights of detainees.

In two further cases, namely the case on the protection of subsistence rights in UN sanctions policy and the IMF case, coalitions of like-minded actors prompted IOs to introduce at least limited safeguards to protect the livelihood of affected population groups when IO policies are implemented (see Heupel 2017b; Reinold 2017). In the UN sanctions case study, the widespread suffering of civilians as result of the UN's broad economic sanctions against Iraq in the 1990s motivated numerous NGOs, as well as UN bodies themselves, to brand UN sanctions practice a scandal (e.g. Mueller and Mueller 1999). Moreover, NGOs and physicians supplied humanitarian goods to Iraq in contravention of UN sanctions. Like-minded actors developed policy recommendations. Particularly influential in this regard were the so-called Interlaken, Bonn–Berlin, and Stockholm Processes, which were organized jointly by the respective governments as well as academic institutions, insofar as they served to relay policy recommendations to representatives of UNSC members (e.g. Watson Institute 2001). Eventually, the UNSC created a working group that was briefed by external experts (UN Security Council 2005) and was ready to consider limited reforms.

Similarly, the IMF's structural adjustment lending triggered massive protests. CSOs such as Oxfam International as well as academics and parts of IMF's management attended to the issue and developed, in cooperation with the World Bank, the instrument of Poverty and Social Impact Assessment (PSIA) (IMF 1998: 53; World Bank 2010: 43). The IMF's Independent Evaluation Office also dealt with the issue and published reports that identified malpractice and devised policy recommendations (IMF 2003: 8). Ultimately, the IMF, albeit reluctantly, agreed to limited provisions to mitigate the poverty-related consequences of its lending practices.

The pathway, like-minded institution building, depends on a political opportunity structure in which societal actors can make the rights violations visible. Research on social movements tells us that campaigns are more likely to be organized if human beings can be portrayed as innocent victims who are physically harmed and if a short causal chain between offender and victim can be constructed (Keck and Sikkink 1998: 27). It seems also plausible that widespread rights violations facilitate mobilization.

Our cases show that like-minded institution building could be activated if at least one of the two features of visibility was fulfilled. The case in which the UN introduced safeguards against sexual exploitation in peacekeeping displays two features that make it a suitable basis for a campaign. It is very easy to evoke empathy with victims of sexual exploitation. Additionally, since blue helmets are perceived as UN peacekeepers rather than nationals of troop-contributing countries, it is possible to construct a short causal chain between the UN and the victims of human rights violations. In the UN and NATO cases in which provisions for the protection of the due process rights of detainees emerged, it was more challenging to create empathy with the victims who were detained as potential threats to society. Given that the IOs themselves administered the detentions, however, it was possible to mark them out publicly as being responsible for the rights violations. In the cases that dealt with the emergence of provisions for the protection of subsistence rights in relation to broad UN trade embargoes and IMF structural adjustment programs, it was more difficult to construct a short causal chain, because local actors were able to manipulate the impact of sanctions and the recipients of IMF credits were themselves responsible for implementing the programs. Nonetheless, it was possible to portray the victims as innocent civilians who suffered physical harm and show that rights violations were widespread.

Like-minded institution building leads only to comprehensive protection provisions if the IO—due to its social purpose—is vulnerable to campaigns and has an organizational culture that is conducive to learning (see Barnett and Finnemore 2004). An IO with an identity in which the purpose to protect human rights is firmly embedded can more easily be persuaded to bind itself to human rights standards; it is also easier to entrap an IO that publicly commits itself to the protection of human rights in its own assertions (see Schimmelfennig 2003). Moreover, a flat and open organizational culture enables learning and, in that way, facilitates the introduction of comprehensive protection provisions. In short, mobilization is successful if the IO in question is vulnerable and open.

The cases studied suggest that IOs introduce comprehensive provisions via like-minded institution building only if both criteria are fulfilled. But this does not happen very often—in this instance, only in the two peacekeeping cases in which the UN established human rights safeguards. Because of the strong human rights component in the UN's mandate, the Secretariat was vulnerable to a campaign and, at the same time, it had a comparably open organizational culture. In the other cases, at most one criterion was met. The UNSC is, due to its strong public avowal to the protection of human rights, vulnerable to human rights campaigns, but it does not possess an organizational culture conducive to learning. NATO and the IMF are, due to their military and economic/financial mandates, hardly vulnerable to human rights campaigns; besides, the conditions for learning are present only to a limited extent, because both organizations have a comparatively hierarchical and closed organizational culture.

Like-minded institution building is the last option left if there are no internal veto players available. The process gets triggered if the alleged human rights violations can be made visible and if it resonates with media attention. This process is only successful if the addressed IO is vulnerable to the allegations and if it possesses an open culture conducive to learning.

In sum, CMALL 2 can play out via different pathways (Table 8.3). The selection of a pathway depends on a set of conditions that structure the choices. First, if there is a role model that an IO with the capacity to learn can learn from, anticipatory institution building can take place. Second, if veto players within member states can be utilized, then legislative or judicial institution building is chosen. If none of the conditions is met, like-minded institution building becomes more likely, provided that the rights violations can be made visible. Judicial institution building has the best success rate (two cases of comprehensive protection provisions out of a total of two cases (2/2)), followed by legislative institution building (1/2), and like-minded institution building (2/5).

8.5 Conclusions

Powerful IOs increasingly introduce provisions for the protection of human rights. This trend started after the end of the Cold War, building on isolated developments in the 1970s and 1980s, and grew from 2000 onwards despite the general conditions for the institutionalization of human rights being rather detrimental due to September 11 attacks and the rise of new powers emphasizing state sovereignty. But what will the future hold? Will the trend last, or even intensify? Will more IOs establish human rights protection provisions? Will the quality of existing provisions improve over time? Or will there be a backlash in the sense that IOs stop introducing new provisions and weaken existing ones?

There is good reason to believe that the trend will last and that the norm of human rights responsibility of IOs will continue to spread. First, states have not ceased delegating competences. While there may be a decline in pace, the rise of international authority seems to continue. Some of these IOs have the ability to violate the human rights of individuals who are affected by their intrusive policies. IOs are delegitimated if they violate human rights, and have incentives to introduce human rights protection provisions to (re)establish their legitimacy.

Table 8.3. Reinforcement via politicization: pathways, cases, scope, and success conditions

Pathways	Cases	Scope Conditions	Success Conditions
Legislative institution building	• World Bank Lending: Subsistence and cultural rights • NATO Peacekeeping: Bodily integrity rights and right not to be enslaved	• Independent Parliament: Parliament with sufficient autonomy from the executive *and* • Domestic script (facilitative)	• Strong Parliament: Parliament in dominant member state *and* • Low sovereignty costs: For state whose parliament advocates reforms
Judicial institution building	• EU Sanctions: Due process rights • UN Sanctions: Due process rights	• Justiciability: Rights violation in principle enforceable before a court	• Strong court: Court with jurisdiction over IO or the implementation in important member states that are democratic constitutional states
Like-minded institution building	• UN Peacekeeping: Bodily integrity rights and right not to be subjected to inhuman or degrading treatment • UN Peacekeeping: Due process rights • UN Sanctions: Subsistence rights • IMF Lending: Subsistence rights • NATO Peacekeeping: Due process rights	• Visibility: Campaign on rights violation feasible	• Vulnerable IO identity: vulnerable: due to strong commitment to human rights *and* • Open organizational culture: Conducive to learning
Anticipatory institution building	• EU Sanctions: Subsistence rights	• Role model: Reference organization affected *and* • Open organizational culture: Conducive to learning	• Role model: Reference organization with comprehensive provisions

Source: Zürn and Heupel 2017

Yet the causal relevance of the causal mechanism, reinforcement via politicization, may decline to the extent that a script for legitimate IOs becomes dominant. The presence of such a script implies that actors take their duty to comply with the script for granted and cease to challenge their prescriptive force (Meyer et al. 1997). Had human rights provisions actually become part of an IO script, IOs would now view the introduction of human rights protection as appropriate action and take respective steps even in the absence of direct pressure. Therefore, IOs should increasingly commit to human rights protection not because they are compelled to do so, but because they deem this the *natural* thing to do. Indeed, norm diffusion has already taken place to a certain extent. Out of the twenty most visible IOs,[11] only a few have failed to launch any provisions for the protection of human rights: the Association

[11] Google Scholar counts (retrieved May 9, 2012) were used as a measure of importance. Thanks to Rebecca Majewski and Friederike Reinhold for this research.

of Southeast Asian Nations (ASEAN), the International Atomic Energy Agency (IAEA), the North American Free Trade Agreement (NAFTA), the Shanghai Cooperation Organization (SCO), and the WTO.

It therefore seems fair to say that a deepening of global governance institutions is possible in spite or because of their contestation. It may lead to counter-institutionalization, fragmentation, or decline. However, it may also lead to re-legitimation efforts and, in case of success, a deepening of global governance. To put it differently, reactive sequences are defined by self-undermining processes in the first place; at the end of the whole sequence, the deepening of the institution under question is still a possibility—depending on whether multiple scope conditions are met.

The findings of this part of the book, taken together, suggest that institutional adaptation in favor of alleviating the deficits of the global governance system is most likely to be triggered under two constellations. One is that the delegitimation of existing international authorities by non-state actors leads to a deepening of the institution if there are strong coalition partners; the other is that the addressed institution can be attacked for being openly inconsistent.

Part III
The Future of Global Governance

In Part I of this book, I sketched the contours of the global governance system, which consists of three layers: the underlying normative principles, the authority and legitimation relationships in the system, and the interplay of international institutions. In this account, the global governance system displays fundamental institutional deficits, which lead to severe legitimation problems. This theory has been utilized to develop empirical expectations about politics in the global system. In Part II, I went on to probe these hypotheses and causal mechanisms, showing that the institutional deficits are responsible for the politicization and counter-institutionalization of global governance arrangements. In this sense, gridlock, the tendency toward fragmentation, and possibly the decline of the global governance system as well are endogenously produced. However, delegitimation practices do not necessarily lead to decline. Under specific circumstances, the deficits are likely to be tackled and, consequently, global governance will be deepened.

In this Part III of the book, I move to more slippery ground. I will speculate about the future of global governance as well as the next steps in global governance research. In Chapter 9, I evaluate different normative models of the global order in terms of their empirical likelihood. In the concluding Chapter 10, I summarize the theoretical argument and empirical findings of the book. This leads to reflections about the development of the discipline of International Relations (IR), including the suggestion that a global politics paradigm is on the rise that may supersede the cooperation under anarchy paradigm, which itself followed the war and peace paradigm with which the discipline started.

9

Are there Realistic Models of Global Governance with Cosmopolitan Intent? An Empirical Assessment

The global governance system that emerged in the 1990s has two major institutional deficits. On the one hand, it consists of a set of spheres of authority that are only loosely coupled and lack sufficient coordination. As a result, all these regulatory regimes, which are specific to particular issue areas, develop according to their own logic without sufficient reference to other problems elsewhere. Each of these issue area-specific institutions is dominated by technocrats, administrators, and particular national executives. This technocratic bias limits the set of legitimation narratives that can be plausibly referred to. On the other hand, the global governance system does not possess an appropriate separation of powers. As a result, it is very difficult to make the authority holders—the executives of the most powerful states and the international administrators—subject to checks and balances. This leads not only to extremely unequal access to decision making, it also undermines an even implementation of norms and rules so that like cases are not treated alike. The global governance system thus has a serious power bias. Its technocratic bias and the power bias together generate severe legitimation problems. Against this backdrop, the questions asked in this chapter leave the relatively safe territory of the past and the contemporary. Instead, I dare to look into the future: Which global order would be able to overcome the institutional deficits of the current global governance system? And is a systemic leap toward such a better global governance system empirically conceivable or even possible at all?

In answer to the first question, I will identify four models of global order with cosmopolitan intent: an intergovernmental model of democratic states, a model of cosmopolitan pluralism, a minimal world state, and cosmopolitan democracy. Each of these comprises a practical project that consists of normative

219

ideas and judgments about empirical developments. All these models further-more suggest an institutional architecture that would overcome the deficits of the global governance system identified in this book. In this sense, the four models can be seen as proposals for making the global governance system better and more sustainable.

As for the second question, each of the four normative models comes with the ambition to be non-utopian or realistic in the sense that there is nothing in the world which makes their *functioning* an impossibility. Yet, showing that something is possible is not the same as demonstrating that it is likely. With respect to the four models of global order, the question, therefore, is whether, and to what extent, these models build on empirical assumptions about the socio-cultural and socio-economic conditions of the world that are likely to be present in the future. In order to grasp this likelihood, the notions "contributory trends" or "door-opening dynamics" are introduced. To para-phrase Bill Clinton, even if the headlines for global governance do not bode well at all, the trendlines may be in favor of one or the other model of global order. A model of global order is akin to contributory trends if its feasibility increases over time if current trends continue. Yet contributory trends alone may not suffice; they may also require a window of opportunity to take effect. In this view, ruptures that lead to a critical juncture are needed before new institutional models can prevail. Critical junctures are moments of deci-sion. They are characterized by the joint presence of permissive conditions (loosening of structural constraints) and productive conditions (i.e. agents with purpose and resources).

What might such a critical juncture in 2025 look like? Donald Trump won the presidential election in the US in 2016 and has steered the country for years toward closed borders and unilateralism. In Europe as well, right-wing populist parties came in power, most importantly in France and Germany. Marine Le Pen took advantage of the disillusion following the Macron experiment and won the presidential elections in France in 2021. A few months earlier, large parts of the Christian Democratic / Social Union (CDU/CSU) in Germany feared further disastrous losses at the polls and the victory of a leftist coalition, so they got rid of Angela Merkel and put forward a conser-vative candidate who dared to go into coalition with the right-wing populist party, Alternative for Germany (AfD). As a result, the European Union (EU) unraveled and degenerated to not much more than a free trade zone. The reversal of political liberalization in China went further. In Russia President Vladimir Putin remained in power maintaining a coalition of autocrats with Recep Tayyip Erdoğan in Turkey as his most important partner. To deflect attention from economic problems, each of these autocrats has over the years carried on a number of territorial conflicts with neighbors.

From 2022 on, as a result of these policies and developments, one crisis after another broke out. The financial market collapsed completely. In response many countries closed their borders even more firmly to capital, people, and goods. Overall production has fallen by 10 percent per annum now for three years in a row. Almost everywhere unemployment rates are above 25 percent. The gridlock in climate policy has led to environmental disasters that, directly or indirectly, have killed tens of thousands of people in California and Southern China. Shortly before this, significant parts of Europe were under water after weeks of thunderstorms. Governments have no resources left to support the victims, many of whom have become homeless. Territorial conflicts have led to limited wars and placed an enormous burden on the economies of the autocratic countries, but none of these conflicts has been resolved. Debt levels in the autocratic systems have been going through the roof. Yet it was in just such a situation, in 2024 and 2025, that liberals with an internationalist and ecological orientation celebrated a comeback and won elections in most of the democratic states, most notably in the United States. In parallel, the opposition in countries like China, Russia, and Turkey have also been pressing for liberalization and the old autocrats have had to leave power.

What would happen in such a situation? Would it mean that the global governance system would be revived, but in a new version overcoming the deficits of the post-1990s system? If so, which of the four models of global order would succeed? While critical junctures provide the space for big decisions, they cannot run counter to social conditions. While critical junctures certainly increase the power of decision makers to overcome institutional inertia, socio-cultural and socio-economic conditions still set limits. So how much support for a cosmopolitan order exists in world society? And which model would be suitable given the conditions in world society and its beliefs?

In this chapter I aim to answer these questions by investigating the empirical viability and plausibility of four models of global order with cosmopolitan intent. I start by discussing the relationship between normative and empirical propositions in models of global order. In section 9.2, I present four models of global order with cosmopolitan intent, identifying the normative ideas and empirical premises built into each. Finally, in section 9.3, I embark on an empirical assessment of the feasibility of various normative theories by introducing the concept of contributory trends or door-opening dynamics. These trends may empower a model of global order in a critical juncture. In this way, the notion of contributory trends serves as a bridge between empirical observations and prescriptive ideas about global order and allows for a comparative assessment of the four models.

9.1 About a Difficult Relationship

One can distinguish three types of normative theorizing about global order at different levels of abstraction. First, the elaboration of general moral principles valid at the global level and their relationship with local principles are at the core of the most abstract level. At issue at the second level is the institutional order that best allows such abstract principles to be realized in a concrete global context. Whether we need a "world state" or a "society of well-ordered states" is one of the central questions here. Finally, a third type of normative theorizing deals with the normative assessment of specific choice problems. Can the military intervention in Afghanistan, for instance, be defended in terms of improving global justice?[1]

Whereas normative theorizing about world politics always includes empirical assumptions, the tangle of normative and empirical propositions thickens as we descend the scale of abstraction. Even the most general moral principles are not elaborated in an empirical vacuum. They are based on cognitive premises that point to the possibility of compliance with the principles. Every normative theory of justice or freedom is, therefore, at least implicitly based on causal premises about how life in society works.[2] When it comes to the question of a good institutional order—at the second level of abstraction— empirical propositions play an even greater role, since *ought* implies, at least to some extent, *can*. Prescriptions of institutional order thus need to strike a balance between utopia and realism. If, finally, one tackles the problems of applying normative theory to concrete cases in order to make the morally right decision—e.g. whether or not to intervene with force in an ongoing conflict—the role of empirical assessments becomes, at this third level, even more important.

In this chapter, the second level of abstraction is addressed. It focuses on the political design of inter- and transnational affairs, and examines a subset of prominent proposals for the design of a globalized world: the intergovernmental model of democratic states, cosmopolitan pluralism, the minimal world state, and cosmopolitan democracy. These institutional proposals must operate within a triangle of moral principles, empirical conditions (such as individuals' beliefs, as well as real political processes), and ideas of good institutional design. The three interact with one another (see Figure 9.1). Moral principles are, to some extent, influenced by empirical and institutional matters.

---

[1] The three levels of abstraction correspond to the three understandings of the distinction between ideal and non-ideal theory as laid out by Valentini (2012).

[2] In a current debate in political theory, the importance of concrete social practices is especially stressed. See, among others, Sangiovanni (2008: 138); James (2005); Ronzoni (2009); and Follesdal (2012).

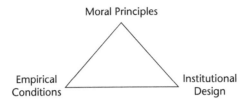

Figure 9.1. Three dimensions of a normative model of global order

Empirical conditions, such as the beliefs of individuals, are influenced by moral considerations as well as their ideas about good institutional order. Institutional design must be informed by moral principles and empirical conditions and handle the tension between them. Any institutional design deriving directly from moral principles and ignoring societal beliefs is not worth a lot. At the same time, the empirical status quo enjoys no normatively privileged position.

Models of a good global order that focus on institutional design and take into account empirical conditions and moral principles constitute a *political project* and, as such, reach beyond philosophical theory. They can realize their potential only if they fulfill a double function, both enabling strong criticism of the institutional status quo and pointing the way constructively toward another order. These models hence represent "thinking and acting realistically without losing the utopian impulse" (Habermas 2010: 53). They aim in other words at a "realistic utopia" (Rawls 1999: 20).[3] Or in the more poetic words of Ralph Emerson Waldo: "The health of the eye seems to demand a horizon. We are never tired so long as we can see far enough."

9.2 Four Models of Global Institutional Order with Cosmopolitan Intent

In the remainder, I focus on those models of global order which have a cosmopolitan impetus and aim at overcoming the institutional deficits of the current global governance system.[4] Literally, cosmopolitanism stands for a political orientation ("politan") with global reach ("cosmos"). It is no surprise, therefore, that this strand of thinking has, without doubt, produced the most important ideas about the construction of a *global* political order, hence the focus here on models of global order with cosmopolitan intent.

---

[3] The dangers of such an enterprise are, on the one hand, to "swing from realism to the affirmative," or an understanding of "human rights in the sense of minimal compromise formulae" (Forst 2010), and, on the other, to design empty utopias.

[4] The remainder of this chapter is based on Zürn (2016c).

In its moral theory branch, cosmopolitanism can be defined by individualism (human beings are the ultimate units of concern), generality (all human beings are of concern), and universality (all human beings are of equal concern) (Pogge 1994: 89; Held 2005: 12–13).[5] In addition, it is not only the pure universalists, but also those "contextualists" who assign the global context a significant meaning, who often categorize themselves as cosmopolitans. While contextualists argue, in principle and contrary to universalists, that there are no undifferentiated, universal obligations, and that justice is therefore context-dependent, some of them see the global as the most relevant context (see e.g. Held 1995) or identify different grounds of justice, and therefore introduce differentiated obligations to different people, still seeing at least some global obligations (see e.g. Forst 1994; M. Risse 2012).

Cosmopolitanism not only has a moral branch, however, it also contains institutional conceptions (Beitz 1994). Whereas a moral conception of cosmopolitanism seeks to develop general obligations, institutional cosmopolitanism addresses the issue of the appropriate institutional design of a political order. Moral cosmopolitanism leads—only in conjunction with certain empirical propositions and premises—to a theory of good institutional order, and thus possibly to an institutional cosmopolitanism. At the same time, a moral cosmopolite may very well proffer institutional recommendations that can scarcely be considered expressions of institutional cosmopolitanism.

Given this broad understanding of cosmopolitanism, one may ask about its boundaries and its counterpart. Simon Caney uses the term "communitarians" (Caney 2005: 15–16; Brown 1992) to describe the exponents of the counterpart, and argues that there are a number of strands of this theory family: political realism, the notion of a community of states, nationalism, and some communitarian and contextualist normative theories. All these cases of communitarian theorizing are based on assumptions about the ontological value of communities, nations, states, or civilizations, and show similarities in their basic arguments. As a result, cosmopolitans and communitarians usually take different sides on contentious issues such as openness of national borders, level of political authority, the concerned reference group, and types of justification (Zürn and de Wilde 2016). Many communitarians would cast doubt on the need to judge the global system as such in normative terms, while cosmopolitans aim at exactly this: a normatively defensible global governance system. The question, therefore, is what models of global order have been developed that see a global governance system in place and want to overcome its institutional deficits.

---

[5] "Moral cosmopolitanism" can be based on various normative groundings. There is, e.g., a utilitarian version (Singer 1979), a contract-theoretical one (Beitz 1979), one based on basic rights (Pogge 1994), and a discursive one (Habermas 1985).

The proliferating literature on global political theory offers many proposals and arguments. Bringing very different theoreticians and approaches together to create four models necessarily involves some simplifying reconstructions, which cannot do full justice to the details of the individual conceptions. Nevertheless, I consider it possible to narrow down the variety in the literature and to posit four models of a global political order with cosmopolitan intent. The organizing criterion in this taxonomy is the role that international organizations (IOs) play in these models in relation to the national authorities, for this is the core issue in any model of global order: In the intergovernmental model of democratic states, IOs are the instruments of states; in cosmopolitan pluralism, they are on a par with state authorities; in the minimal world state, they are partially supranational; and in cosmopolitan democracy, supranationality is encompassing.

a) The intergovernmental model of democratic states: There are doubtless proponents of an intergovernmental model of well-ordered states who do not argue in terms of moral cosmopolitanism; rather, they give communities an independent moral value, and clearly prioritize local obligations over global ones (MacIntyre 1988). However, there are also advocates of an intergovernmental model of democratic states with cosmopolitan intent. Well-known representatives of this position include Thomas Christiano, Robert Dahl, Ingeborg Maus, Andrew Moravcsik, and Fritz Scharpf. This group also includes theorists such as John Rawls and Thomas Nagel who advocate an intergovernmental order of democratic states on the basis of contextualism, while still seeing significant global obligations. In the light of arguments about the "contexts" of justice or empirical beliefs about feasibility, the model is proposed as the best possible set of institutions to further the moral principles of cosmopolitanism. If, in view of empirical conditions, the values or standards of cosmopolitanism can best be realized through an international system of sovereign states based on consent, this institutional order is appropriate on instrumental grounds.[6]

The proponents of the intergovernmental model of democratic states see the organization of politics through the sovereignty of territorial states as the keystone of a global political order. Autonomous governance beyond the state is limited by the consent principle. Such an account of governance "can be grounded in cosmopolitan principles to the extent that the process of consent results from fair negotiations among states that represent the persons in their societies as equal citizens" (Christiano 2012: 70). In this view, an association of democratic states (or at least of "decent societies") offers the best possibility of realizing such values as liberty, self-determination, equality, and solidarity.

---

[6] Dahl (2005) gives six systematic reasons why institutionalizing the principles of a democratic constitutional state at the international level is improbable.

225

The nation state can and should make use of norm-guided cooperation between states and international institutions to facilitate the attainment of goals. Even the transfer of certain powers to agencies beyond the nation state is conceivable as long as it is consented to by all member states and exit remains a viable option. The competence-competence, however, needs to remain firmly in the hands of nation states since such international institutions do not attain democratic legitimacy (BVerfG 2009). Nation states must retain the possibility of retrieving any powers they have transferred in order to protect their constitution. IOs thus need to serve the member states; they cannot dominate them (Maus 2007). Although international institutions can regulate and civilize relations among states, they should not exercise direct rule over individuals. Moreover, international institutions should not intervene in the business of distributive politics. Substantive solidarity and the corresponding social policy can be realized only within the state (Scharpf 1996a; Nagel 2005).

International arrangements must always cope with a two-phase process of legitimation and implementation: Only national representatives legitimated by national societies can make fundamental decisions in international institutions, and such decisions have to be implemented by the various national governments (Scharpf 2009). This preserves the sovereignty of nation states despite international institutions. At the same time, international institutions can contribute to keeping the peace between states (Russett and Oneal 2001); safeguarding democracy, deliberation, and human rights in democratic states (Keohane et al. 2009); and ensuring the efficiency of cross-border economic transactions (Keohane 1984).

b) Cosmopolitan pluralism: This model brings together the most diverse group of authors. Representatives are to be found in legal theory (e.g. Nico Krisch, Mattias Kumm), in the sociology of second modernity (Ulrich Beck), among proponents of multi-level governance without a constitutional anchor (e.g. Liesbet Hooghe and Gary Marks, Allen Buchanan and Robert Keohane), stakeholder democracy (Eva Erman, Terry Macdonald), discursive democracy (e.g. John Dryzek, Rainer Forst), complex world governance (Andreas Føllesdal, Jürgen Neyer), and post-imperial theory (James Tully).

Although proponents of these positions usually state their cosmopolitan intent expressly, and quite clearly negate the normative dominance of the nation state, they often hesitate to formulate full models of a global institutional order. They stress the importance of multiple perspectives, discursive processes, and good reasons often without elaborating on an institutional order. John Dryzek (2008: 470) describes his notion of discursive democratization "as a process rather than a model, which can be applied to all levels in complex multi-level governance, from the local to the global." Or to put it in the words of Rainer Forst (2011: 262), "minimal justice calls for a *basic structure of justification*, maximal justice for a *fully justified basic structure.*" It is the former which is spelled out much more clearly by these philosophers than the latter, for they consider laying out the latter to be the job of real social actors once the basic structure of justification has been provided. In the remainder of this section, the focus is on those proponents who go beyond procedural reasoning and dare to formulate ideas about an institutional design.

The point of departure for all considerations is the observation that the national level is losing its role as the epicenter of statehood. The various components of statehood are being distributed, depending on their function, among various levels in a post-national constellation (Leibfried and Zürn 2005; Genschel and Zangl 2008). Thus, no level is identified as acting as a constitutional anchor for a political order. This entails seeing international institutions as independent orders that are not under the direct control of nation states, but are also not superior to them in a monistic global order: "Law has become postnational—the national sphere remains important, but it is no longer the paradigmatic anchor of the whole order" (Krisch 2010: 8). Given the lack of grounding in society, global constitutionalism writ large is seen as having potentially disastrous consequences. John Dryzek (2006: 64) puts it nicely: "In some circumstances, the peace is disturbed only by philosophers who believe a constitutional solution is required."

The model of cosmopolitan pluralism is built on the affectedness principle (all those affected by political decisions should have a say in them), not on the membership principle (all members of a community targeted by the regulation should have a say). Terry Macdonald is especially clear on this point: "On the stakeholder model, therefore, the demos defined as the group empowered to participate in any given political decision-making process will not necessarily or always be equivalent to the demos defined differently as the population sharing a common scheme of political institutions, and political identities associated with these" (MacDonald 2012: 48).

In spite of this accepted level of fragmentation, the normativity of the political order is not abandoned: "[Legal] Pluralism eschews the hope to build one common, overarching framework that would integrate post-national governance, distribute powers and provide means of solving disputes between the various layers according to rules ultimately set by each layer for itself" (Krisch 2010: 67). It is grounded in coordination between levels and spheres with the aid of *practical reasoning* on the basis of a cosmopolitan morality; i.e. the trilogy of democracy, rule of law, and human rights—which is why Mattias Kumm (2009) calls his model *cosmopolitan constitutionalism*.

Pluralism and cosmopolitan constitutionalism are concepts of legal theory. Political scientists have put forward similar proposals that fall under labels such as accountable global governance (cf. Buchanan and Keohane 2006; Follesdal 1998), complex world governance (Neyer 2013), or multi-level governance (Hooghe and Marks 2001). All these contributions argue for the need to determine the appropriate level or sphere of governance in a flexible, issue-specific way (instead of fixing it), and point, therefore, to the need to democratize all levels and spheres, depending on the extent to which they exercise authority. International norms and standards accordingly transcend national arrangements where national regulation has strong externalities, or a state drastically fails in its responsibility toward its society. National political systems, in turn, can rely above all on the democratic force of their decisions in the event of a conflict of law. In cases of conflict, discursive processes, or legal reasoning taking into account the subsidiarity principle are the mechanisms to decide. Precise institutional proposals for conflict resolution are rare, however. Dryzek et al. (2011) propose, for example, a "deliberative global citizens' parliament," albeit without defining its exact functions.

Cosmopolitan pluralists claim that peace could be made possible, human rights guaranteed, and collective problems tackled democratically in such a global order. However, these studies seldom explicitly address the issue of the distribution and redistribution of material goods. By the logic of the arguments advanced, however, it would have to take place largely in the national framework, rather than through an explicit "redistribution" across state borders.

c) *Minimal world state*: This position finds its best-known proponents among German-speaking political philosophers, including Jürgen Habermas, Otfried Höffe, and Rainer Schmalz-Bruns, but there are also some Anglo-Saxon authors who argue for it on contractualist or deliberative grounds, like Charles Beitz, Robert Goodin, or Mathias Risse. These authors most often favor a state at the global level. However, differently grounded systems of justice and belief systems impose limitations. Since socio-cultural and socio-economic conditions do not suffice for establishing a democratic constitutional state at the global level, second-best solutions are sought which do not renounce the politically constituted democratic polity but do loosen the "existing close conceptual bracketing of democracy and the nation-state" (Schmalz-Bruns 2007: 272) sufficiently to make a world state feasible.

The most important move in this thinking is to distinguish between basic human rights as truly universal rights and other political values that depend more strongly on political and cultural settings. In distinguishing different grounds of justice (Risse 2012), it becomes possible to identify core functions of a state that would have to be moved to the global level (Goodin 2010). What is sought is not a global unitary state but a graduated global minimal state in keeping with the principle of federalism (Höffe 1999: 10). From this perspective, state sovereignty must be made conditional on compliance with fundamental rights (cf. also Beitz 2009). Only in this manner can the two fundamental democratic principles, namely the possibility for a global society to influence itself and the ability to resolve conflicts of norms in the light of fundamental rights, come to bear. The prevalence of civil and political human rights in this model requires at least some supremacy at the global level. The proponents of this position are well aware of the dangers of abuse and the strong legitimation needed by such a "global state." The global enforcement mechanism is therefore to be hedged by supplementing the United Nations Security Council (UNSC) and the General Assembly with a parliamentary assembly, permitting democratic control of central government (Habermas 2007: 450–1).

But the role of international institutions would not be limited to protecting fundamental rights. Wherever cross-border problems arose, international institutions with limited functions would come to bear. The legitimation of such sectoral international regimes would be achieved through sectoral publics, collaboration with non-governmental organizations (NGOs), and a deliberative orientation among participating actors.

The issue of the global distribution of goods is often given little attention in this school of thought. Implicitly, however, Thomas Nagel's political conception of justice appears to be followed and be built into the notion of different grounds of justice: It posits a universal obligation with respect to negative civil rights and liberties, as well as some minimum economic and social rights in the form of development assistance (Nagel 2005: 124); and it lends decisive importance to political boundaries on issues of positive rights and the redistribution of goods.

d) Cosmopolitan democracy: Well-known proponents of cosmopolitan democracy include Daniele Archibugi, Simon Caney, David Held, Rafaele Marchetti, and Thomas Pogge. While the distinction between the intergovernmental order of democratic states, cosmopolitan pluralism, and the minimal world state is essentially about the relationship between different levels of authority, the distinction between the minimal world state and cosmopolitan democracy is mainly about the scope of the global authority, and thus refers to another dimension of difference. In both accounts, international institutions should exercise some supremacy at the very least.

Two main differences in scope justify postulating two separate models. For one thing, in the cosmopolitan democracy model not only are strong international institutions limited to the enforcement of fundamental rights, but the need for primary democratic legitimation extends to all international institutions that regulate cross-border problems. Since the principle of democratic congruence between decision makers and those affected has to be consistently applied, all international institutions that exercise authority have to be democratized. A global parliamentary assembly is intended not only to secure basic rights throughout the world, but also to regulate global problems such as climate change, financial markets, and weapons of mass destruction (see especially Held 1995; Caney 2005). At the same time, the leading proponents of a cosmopolitan democracy stress that the nation state should continue to play a central role and in this context they speak of a "vertical diffusion of sovereignty" (Pogge 2002a: 154–7; Archibugi 2004). Nonetheless, wherever there are far-reaching cross-border effects and where people would be excluded in the event of decentralized decision making (Pogge 2002a: 155), international institutions should exercise supremacy: "Conflicts

Table 9.1. Four institutional models of global order

	Intergovern- mental Model of Democratic States	Cosmopolitan Pluralism	Minimal World State	Cosmopolitan Democracy
Protagonists (examples)	Dahl Moravcsik Rawls Scharpf Christiano	Buchanan/ Keohane Dryzek Krisch Kumm	Beitz Habermas Goodin Höffe M. Risse	Archibugi Caney Held Marchetti Pogge
Basic norms	Prohibition of the use of force; principles of non-intervention, cooperation, and democratic organization of states	Human rights; rule of law; due process; practical reasoning	Human rights; democratic legitimation of the monopoly of force; discursive justification of regulation	Democratic legitimation of all regulation; justice; fundamental rights
Statehood	Territorial states concentrate all the functions of statehood	Statehood unravels in different legal orders; the monopoly of force remains on the nation state level; sovereignty is bound by basic norms	Legitimate monopoly of force moves to the global level; sectoral international regimes; democratic states remain, especially with respect to redistributive policies	Emergence of a rudimentary world state; nation states are part of larger political order
Role envisaged for international institutions	International institutions are agents under the control of the democratically legitimated states; delegated but reversible autonomy	Multi-level governance without primacy for one level (pluralism); in all denationalized fields, international institutions can attain authority	Primacy of international institutions for safeguarding fundamental rights; international institutions can attain autonomous authority varying with the problem at issue	Far-reaching supremacy at the international level for all cross-border problems (monism); states are subordinate entities acting autonomously only with respect to purely national problems

concerning the issue of competence arising as a result of the different levels of governance, must be resolved within a domain of global constitutionalism, and referred to jurisdictional bodies, which in turn must act upon the basis of an explicit constitutional mandate, as Kelsen (1944) had already advocated" (Archibugi 2004: 452; see also Marchetti 2012).

A second difference is that at least some proponents of cosmopolitan democracy place greater weight on distributive justice. Since the extremely inequitable distribution of wealth is blamed at least partially on the existing system of international institutions, a good global order will have to address far-reaching redistribution between national institutions if global justice is to be established (see especially Pogge 2002b). To the extent that redistribution beyond national boundaries is considered normatively essential, democratic majority decisions are needed to achieve it. To this end, greater political centralization is needed to enable the establishment of global economic justice (Pogge 2002a: 149). Otherwise similar notions apply to those underlying the minimal world state. Key functions of statehood and wide areas of competence-competence shift to the global level, so that the rudiments of a genuine global state take shape. International institutions accordingly assume the main responsibility for peace, democracy, and distributive justice in a globalized world.

Table 9.1 summarizes the four models of global order by asking for (i) the fundamental norms underlying each of the models, (ii) its concept of statehood, and (iii) the role and capacities envisioned for international institutions.

9.3 Empirical Presumptions of the Four Models

In what follows, the concern is not to assess the moral viability of these four models of a global institutional order, but to show what empirical credibility they have. But how do we distinguish a realistic from a non-realistic utopia? As a minimum, a realistic utopia must argue that any claims of impossibility are inaccurate, at least in the long run. For instance, many would argue that any cosmopolitan model of global order is more or less doomed to failure. According to this view, cosmopolitan models represent only one—mainly Western—world view that is increasingly contested in the Global South (see Fanon 1961; Said 1978; Amin 1988; Chakrabarty 2000). Moreover, recent years have seen growing contestations of cosmopolitanism within the West that have undermined the willingness of democratic governments to contribute to a global order. Whether these developments make a cosmopolitan order per se impossible, I consider to be an empirical question.

Using claims-making data,[7] it can be shown that cosmopolitan positions regarding the permeability of borders and the allocation of authority dominate political fora as diverse as the United States, Germany, Poland, Turkey, Mexico, the European Parliament, and the General Assembly. For all the five issue areas that we coded (trade, regional integration, human rights, climate change, and migration), cosmopolitan positions are more frequent than their communitarian counterparts in all the seven fora. Table 9.2 shows an index aggregated for all claims (N = 11810) in all issue areas, showing that cosmopolitan claims outnumber communitarians claims. At 0.1475, the mean of this index running from −1 to + 1 is clearly on the cosmopolitan side.[8] Only three types of actor of the twenty-four listed in Table 9.2 tend to speak out in favor of communitarian positions: farmers, trade unions, and right-wing populists. Eight types of speaker make cosmopolitan claims with an average > +0.5: actors in global arenas, government executives, judicial actors, civil society groups, socialist, green, social-democratic, and liberal parties. All the others are in favor of cosmopolitanism as well, but to a lesser extent.

Moreover, and quite unexpectedly to those who consider cosmopolitanism as a merely Western project, in some issue areas countries like Turkey and Mexico (before 2013) took a stronger stance toward open borders and regional cooperation than Germany and the United States. These differences are surprising at first sight. They show, however, that the positions taken are influenced by the existing level of integration and by the direction of refugee flows. On the one hand, the number of voices critical of *further* integration seems to go up when the degree of integration oversteps a certain threshold. Societies that are much less bound by supranational law than European ones seem to be much more positive about more integration. Similarly, the comprehensive support for open refugee and immigration policies in Mexican and Turkish society is determined to some extent by the fact that for a long time

---

[7] In a project on the political sociology of cosmopolitanism and communitarianism, we used—among other methods—the method of representative claims analysis. Coding was structured by a detailed codebook and involved twenty-six variables (see de Wilde et al. 2014): a) Year, b) Source, c) Claimant Type, d) Claimant Scope, e) Claimant Function, f) Claimant Nationality, g) Claimant Party, h) Action, i) Addressee Type, j) Addressee Scope, k) Addressee Function, l) Addressee Nationality, m) Addressee Party, n) Addressee Evaluation, o) Issue, p) Problem Scope, q) Position, r) Intervention, s) Object Function, t) Object Scope, u) Object evaluation, v) Justification, w) Conflict Frame, x) Claimant Name, y) Addressee Name, and z) Origin. In short, we measure WHERE, WHEN, WHO, HOW, directed at WHOM, claims WHAT, for/against WHOSE interests, and WHY. We draw on digital newspaper archives to conduct a stratified sampling using key word searches. In the period 2007–11, for which digital archives for a range of newspapers from all countries were available, we sampled key word strings, with minor grammatical adaptations if the specific language required them. Only articles with at least two of the key words present in the search string were selected for coding.

[8] At this level of aggregation, mean positions on each of the five issues were calculated where each claim demanding integration, open borders, or international cooperation was coded as +1, each claim demanding or enacting the opposite was coded as -1, and claims drawing attention to the issue without specifying a policy preference were coded as 0.

Table 9.2. Distribution of cosmopolitan claims

		Position	
	Mean		Count
Actor Scope	Global	.67	534
	Regional	.49	2940
	National	.43	8336
Actor Type	Executive	.52	4482
	Legislative	.38	2908
	Bureaucracy and Executive	.34	511
	Agencies	.52	176
	Judiciary	.46	491
	Business	.20	50
	Trade Union	.17	65
	Farmers	.39	826
	Media/Journalist	.62	883
	Civil Society	.37	393
	Citizens/People	.44	809
	Experts	.57	216
	Other		0
	None		
Actor Party	None	.46	4973
	Socialist	.52	422
	Green	.57	309
	Social democrat	.58	1517
	Liberal	.59	502
	Conservative	.36	2323
	Far right	.31	293
	Other party	.53	1471
Total		.46	11,810

these two countries have had no immigration. It therefore seems that cosmopolitan positions are especially strong in settings dominated by national politics, while actors in more integrated countries increasingly point to the difficulties and limits of economic openness and regional integration.

Mathias Koenig-Archibugi (2011, 2012) went much further in rejecting propositions about the impossibility of a cosmopolitan world order. Following a rigorous research design, he asks about the necessary conditions for democracy (ethnic and cultural homogeneity, limited size, economic development, statehood, etc.) and finds that—apart from the presence of a polity or a governance system—there is no necessary condition in the strict meaning of the term. Democratic procedures have sometimes even prevailed in very large and heterogeneous environments with low average income and enormous social as well as material inequalities. He convincingly rejects all the impossibility claims regarding global democracy. This is an important step toward models of global order with a cosmopolitan intent being taken more seriously.

Yet rejecting impossibility claims does not tell us a lot about likelihood. Not everything that is theoretically possible is actually likely. In spite of the rejection of the impossibility of democracy beyond the nation state, and in spite of the importance of cosmopolitan positions in public spheres, we need to look at empirical developments that allow for differentiation between the different cosmopolitan models of global order in order to come to a comparative assessment. We need to look at more demanding criteria for assessing potential feasibility and ask if feasibility increases over time when current trends continue. The question then is whether contributory trends or door-opening dynamics are in place.

Contributory trends however cannot be expected to be translated into a new model of global order without strong pressures for change that are perceived by many major actors simultaneously. This is where the notion of a critical juncture comes in as the second condition for the realization of a new model of global order. The critical juncture of 2025 sketched above is treated here as a counterfactual constant for all four models. In order to assess their relative empirical likelihood, I focus on the question which of the models is supported best by the contributory trends.

What empirical aspects have to be taken into account to allow judgments about the potential feasibility of different models to be made? What are the empirical conditions most relevant for translating normative principles into a normatively defensible and feasible institutional design? Following a study by the late Bernhard Peters on the role of empirical social knowledge in normative theories, three types of empirical restriction, or condition, affecting institutional orders can be distinguished: individual attitudes, the cultural/organizational context, and the institutional/structural context (Peters 2000). These three conditions will provide the criteria against which the potential feasibility of the four models is discussed in the remainder of this chapter. To repeat, the goal is not to find out whether these empirical conditions are met, but whether we can see developments that point in the direction of their being met. In this sense, we are searching for contributory developments in three areas: the role of international institutions at the macro-level, social mobilization at the meso-level, and individual attitudes at the individual level.

Relevance of international institutions (macro-level): The key question here is whether international institutions exercise political authority or if they are tightly controlled agents of their member states, and which trends we can observe regarding this question. From the standpoint of the intergovernmental model of democratic states, international institutions are agents of national governments whose purpose is to simplify intergovernmental cooperation. The legitimacy of international institutions, in this connection, depends on their being understood as tools for facilitating negotiations between states for the purpose of achieving Pareto improvements. They are accordingly kept on a tight leash and their activities are subject to—and will remain subject to—strict control by member states (Moravcsik 2008: 334).

From the point of view of cosmopolitan pluralism, in contrast, international institutions increasingly exercise authority that undermines the intergovernmental consensus principle and, to some extent, even permits direct access to societal actors, *de facto* limiting the scope for national democracies to take action. From the point of view of the minimal world state and cosmopolitan democracy, we should even see evidence of the development of a global supremacy, or even of a rudimentary global state.

Practices of political will formation (meso-level): The key question here is whether the minimum communicative and organizational prerequisites for collective will formation exist or can develop at levels beyond the nation state. Proponents of the intergovernmental model of democratic states, in particular, have their doubts. Robert Dahl (2005: 200), for instance, blames the size of international political units for preventing those affected by regulation from "express[ing] their informed consent." The representatives of cosmopolitan pluralism and minimal world state, in contrast, point to a growing willingness among societal groups to develop independent expectations and strategies toward international institutions, and also to the growing importance of international affairs in public debate. Particular reference is made to the activities of transnational NGOs and the international universes of discourse to which they give rise (Dryzek 2008: 482). Although proponents of cosmopolitan democracy admit that there is hardly any trend toward parliamentarization and party formation at the international level, they insist that transnational campaigns substantially influence political decision making and that international public spheres with action potential are coming into being (Archibugi 2004: 457).

Individual attitudes (micro-level): Do individuals automatically assign political responsibility to their national governments, or is there evidence that they increasingly acknowledge political authorities beyond the nation state? Are there any signs of post-national identities? And do these resources of identity and solidarity suffice to legitimize international institutions with coercive authority (minimal world state) and transnational transfers of wealth (cosmopolitan democracy)? For proponents of the intergovernmental model of democratic states, citizens focus on the state as the primary form of political organization (Dahl 2005: 198–201). Even with regard to the European Union (EU), it is noted that "EU policy-making is limited to around 10–20 percent of national decision-making, largely in matters of low salience to voters, while the national polities retain control over most other, generally more salient issues" (Moravcsik 2008: 333). The undiminished entrenchment of political identities in nationally defined societies is also emphasized. Proponents of a minimal world state and cosmopolitan democracy, by contrast, point out that citizens are gradually internalizing cosmopolitan principles, and that there is broad recognition of international interdependencies and the resulting "communities of fate" (Held 2003). The representatives of cosmopolitan

235

democracy also point to the growing potential for cross-border solidarity, shown, for example, by generous donations in the event of humanitarian disasters.

The list of conceivable empirical conditions for the translation of moral principles into an institutional design is very long. The typology provided by Bernhard Peters (2000) catches some of the most relevant ones from the perspective of a theory of preconditions for a normative order. For various reasons, however, others are not included. First of all, the current positions and interests of major powers in world politics are not taken into account, since the focus is on those conditions which are necessary for a given order to function. To put it differently, my interest in this chapter is not to look at the conditions under which a transformation to a new order is likely to happen automatically, but to focus on the conditions that need to be in place so that the new institutional order is sustainable if a critical juncture allows for a transformation.

Second, one of the more controversial questions is whether the mere existence of cross-border transactions and contexts of justice can be considered as an empirical background condition that tells us something about the feasibility of institutional models. For many cosmopolitically inspired authors, globalization and the associated externalities of national political decisions usually provide the necessary context for a theory of global justice (Beitz 1999; Vernon 2010). Rainer Forst goes even further. For him, the necessary context is already supplied by the existence of global injustice. He speaks of a "context of force and domination" (Forst 2001: 166) that can exist in a pre-globalized world as well. There is, indeed, no possibility of denying the *empirical* existence of historically institutionalized practices that contradict all intuitions of justice. Moreover, the negative externalities of purely national policies have increased, leading to "overlapping communities of fate" (Held 2003: 469). For instance, American climate policy has doubtlessly had an existential impact on many Pacific Islanders. From a normative point of view, therefore, their lack of participation in the decision making is deficient. This is, however, the very reason why existing injustice and expanding externalities cannot be taken into account as contributory developments. If such inequities and externalities are postulated as "objective," they point to a functional or normative necessity or to a "context of justice." But their mere existence does not constitute a contributory empirical condition. Injustice does not automatically create institutions to overcome it. If, however, we can empirically identify a growing global consensus in the eyes of the beholder that global interdependencies are increasing and global political institutions are therefore necessary, this should indeed be seen as a contributory development. This is to say that we want to look at those factors which are external to the normative analysis—precisely as suggested by Bernhard Peters' criteria. We need to look at supportive conditions from an internal perspective. The empirical assumptions built into the four models are summarized in Table 9.3.

Table 9.3. Empirical presumptions of the four models of global order

	Intergovern-mental Model of Democratic States	Cosmopolitan Pluralism	Minimal World State	Cosmopolitan Democracy
Relevance of international institutions	International institutions are agents under the control of the democratically legitimated states; delegated but reversible autonomy	Multi-level governance without primacy for one level (pluralism); some international institutions exercise authority	Signs of the development of a *jus cogens* in the field of human rights and peacekeeping; some international institutions exercise authority	Development of vertical diffusion of sovereignty and the beginnings of constitution-alization at the global level
Practices of political will formation	Focus of societal actors on the nation state	Orientation of societal actors toward various institutions	Orientation of societal actors toward various institutions; greater global orientation in fundamental rights issues	Increasing orientation of societal groups toward the global sphere
Individual attitudes	Individual cognitions remain limited to the national context; the public good is associated with the national level; no transnational solidarity	Some individual cognitions reach beyond the national context; public good orientation beyond the national society is possible; disposition for solidarity seldom goes beyond the national context	Some individual cognitions reach beyond the national context; greater global orientation on fundamental rights issues; public good orientation beyond national society is possible; disposition for solidarity seldom goes beyond the national context	Increasing cognitive orientation toward the global sphere; public good is associated with the global level; transnational solidarity develops

9.4 Contributory Trends: Who is Right in which Respect?

Against the backdrop described above, I discuss some empirical trends in three categories: "relevance of international institutions," "practices of political will formation," and "individual attitudes." With respect to the first two categories, I can refer back to material used in earlier chapters. For "individual attitudes," some additional empirical material is presented.

9.4.1 *Relevance of International Institutions*

What role do international institutions play today? Does the empirical analysis of international institutions indicate the potential for an autonomous political sphere (cosmopolitan pluralism) or even a (partly) dominant political sphere (minimal world state and cosmopolitan democracy), or does the nation state retain its dominance (intergovernmental model of democratic states)? What trends are apparent?

As discussed in Chapter 1, international institutions and their supporters *justify* their actions as the pursuit of the *common good* of a community that reaches beyond national borders. International arrangements thus no longer merely coordinate the search for a *modus vivendi*. At least rhetorically, they often actively pursue normative goals in handling the common affairs of the international community of states and world society. Against this justificatory background, international institutions must have the possibility of exercising global authority and many international institutions indeed exercise authority. States are steadily delegating power directly to IOs and partially to transnational institutions. The international human rights regimes, the establishment of the International Criminal Court (ICC), and the active role played by the UNSC since 1990 show that this process is also taking place in "high politics" fields such as security and human rights.

Is this a trend that can be expected to continue in the future? To start with, the normative need for stronger international authorities as a response to a growing interconnectedness between people and problems will, in principle, remain in place. Even if globalization indicators show some signs of less dramatic growth rates, the externalities of ever more powerful technologies connecting people globally will increase further. Yet, the current rise of political movements asking for less permeable borders questions whether this need will be translated into demand. At the same time, minimal world state and cosmopolitan democracy theorists in particular point to self-reinforcing mechanisms as contributory trends. Institutions, according to this view, determine individual attitudes, and changing attitudes, in turn, allow for stronger institutions: The right institutional design produces, to some extent, its own empirical assumptions (see e.g. Zürn 2000). While a dynamic of this kind was certainly part of the story of state and nation building in Europe in the eighteenth and nineteenth centuries (see Anderson 1983; Gellner 1983; Breuilly 1994), the responses to the rise of the global governance system analyzed in earlier chapters show that this is anything but an automatic process. Protagonists of an intergovernmental order of democratic states thus point, at least implicitly, to a counter-dynamic. If international institutions become too strong, in terms of the preparedness of the people to accept them, one would expect a national backlash against those institutions. The decline in support for the EU that set in essentially after the signing of Maastricht Treaty and reached a height during the Eurozone crisis can be seen as a case in point (Scharpf 2011). Taken together, it seems fair to say that while authority beyond the nation state has reached a level where the endogenously produced resistance is significantly slowing down the speed of its growth, it may not be expected to decrease significantly.

How do the four models fare given these developments in the recent decades? To start with, the ongoing trend whereby international institutions acquire increased authority decreases the probability of the institutionaliza-tion of the intergovernmental model. International institutions today are already more than mere forums for Pareto-optimizing negotiations between states. This poses an empirical problem for the intergovernmental model of democratic states. Even if the authority of some international institutions will decline in the future because of legitimation problems, the degree of inter- and transnational authority in the global governance system is clearly above the level envisaged by intergovernmental models.

However, the empirical developments analyzed in this book also point to the structural limits of the development of a global order. The issue of direct redistributive policies is more or less excluded from the sphere of international authority. The "responsibility to protect" norm certainly covers willingness to help deprived people regardless of national borders. But the normative reasoning for these interventions seems rather to follow the logic of emer-gency aid and thus is not evidence of the institutionalization of basic social rights at the international level. This poses an empirical problem for the cosmo-politan democracy model.

What is more, all international regulation is largely implemented at the national level. In both the European multi-level system and the global gov-ernance system, decisions made at higher levels are mostly put into effect by a decentralized political machinery. This shows that nation states are not really willing to relinquish material foundations such as their fiscal monop-oly and their monopoly on the use of force. Political reality has so far pre-vented calls for international taxes to combat poverty or to set up a permanent United Nations (UN) task force from making any headway.

These are serious limitations to the emancipatory dynamic of international authority. Since all relevant resources are tied to the national level, the big-gest and most powerful nation states can escape intervention by international regulation. The undermining of the consensus principle is thus halved. These structural limits highlight utopian elements in both the minimal world state conception and the cosmopolitan democracy model that lack contributory developments. The development dynamics of international institutions hence appear to be best captured by cosmopolitan pluralism, which notes that the independent authority of international institutions is growing without the latter gaining supremacy.

9.4.2 Practices in Political Will Formation

Even if international institutions with authority are developing, this is insuf-ficient for the more demanding models of global order, if that development is not accompanied by denationalized forms of political will formation. The ques-tion, therefore, is whether societal groups develop independent expectations and strategies with respect to international institutions—as assumed by cosmopolitan pluralism and the proponents of the minimal world state—and whether processes of parliamentarization and party formation are in evidence at the international level as developments contributing to cosmopolitan democracy.

As shown in Chapter 6, there is clearly a trend toward the politicization of international affairs. National publics, parliaments, and transnational civil society are no longer willing to simply accept the outcomes of major international negotiations as urgently necessary successes for international cooperation. Transnational protest movements target IOs and treaties. At the same time, many transnational NGOs and social movements are calling for stronger inter- and transnational organizations to satisfy the need for regulation.

Can politicization be expected to continue in the future? According to the authority hypothesis, we can expect politicization to continue as long as international institutions keep exercising significant authority on the basis of insufficient legitimation narratives. To be sure, political opportunity structures need to be in place to enable politicization to happen, but there is little doubt that these opportunity structures will be there from time to time: Crises, elections, and referenda cannot be avoided. The minimal world state vision as well as cosmopolitan democracy even aim at creating these opportunity structures systematically in order to improve legitimacy. To the extent that political competition becomes part of international institutions—as already partially introduced in the EU with the elections to the European Parliament and with an increased role for the Parliament in choosing the President of the Commission—opportunity structures for politicization become institutionalized.

What does this tell us about the four models of global order? To start with, the politicization of international affairs and the denationalization of political will formation, despite their built-in selectivity, are quite the opposite of a contributory development for the intergovernmental model. They undermine the idea that states are the only legitimate representatives of territorially aggregated interests at the international level. Politicization points to an increasing trend to organize interests along sectoral lines in non-state movements and organizations. The politicization of international institutions thus provides some support for the model of cosmopolitan democracy, which argues precisely in favor of self-reinforcing processes of institution building and transnational will formation as indicated by the authority thesis. However, the politicization of international institutions also points to signs of a backlash. Resistance against international integration is growing as well. Moreover, there is no sign that party-like groupings are developing at the international level or that any such groupings are able to aggregate and bundle societal interests across issues in coherent ideological positions, or have the power to even out representational imbalances. Altogether, cosmopolitan democracy is not supported by the contributory trends in this category.

In contrast, the politicization of international institutions does provide evidence in favor of the cosmopolitan pluralism and minimal world state models. It allows cosmopolitan pluralism to function better, since it opens up a means for all authorities to be responsive to all the people and prevents it from degenerating fully to a technocratic and detached web of governing institutions inaccessible to the majority of people. At the same time, it points to the legitimation problems that such a world of overlapping sectoral and territorial, public and private governing institutions necessarily produces: a technocratic bias and a power bias (see Chapter 3). The minimal world state model faces similar problems. While it addresses the coordination problem to some extent by introducing some stratification between different authorities, it fails to solve the problem of how successful legitimation of the centralized component can be achieved. But at least it offers some options for channeling politicization into institutionalized forms of participation. In sum, politicization provides some support for a minimal world state and for cosmopolitan pluralism.

9.4.3 Individual Attitudes (Micro-level)

The question remains whether these developments are also covered at the level of individual attitudes. Do we have here an elite process not backed by attitudes among the population at large, as the intergovernmental model of democratic states suggests? Or is there evidence of a widespread recognition of far-reaching interdependencies that normatively and functionally necessitate cross-border arrangements and will-formation processes? Does the identity potential suffice to legitimize coercive international institutions (minimal world state) and develop cross-border solidarity (cosmopolitan democracy)?

I turn to survey data to answer these questions. Such attitudinal data are notoriously fraught with validity problems. They depend very strongly on exactly how questions are put. They cannot simply be transferred into action potential, and are generally subject to the so-called sunshine effect; i.e. people make themselves out to be more generous than they really are. Furthermore, good attitudinal data are usually available only for countries within the Organisation for Economic Co-operation and Development (OECD). Nevertheless, there is little alternative to the analysis of such survey data when addressing the issue of individual attitudes to a global institutional order.

Proponents of the intergovernmental model often cite Eurobarometer survey data to substantiate the continuing dominance of nation state patterns of thinking, even in the case of Europe. For instance, they point first to the declining support for membership of the EU, which fell from peak values of 72 percent in the early 1990s to 53 percent in autumn 2006, returning to the level prevailing before the euphoria about the Maastricht Treaty and a new Europe without walls (Eurobarometer 2007). With the Eurozone crisis, support fell even further. One question asks about people's image of the EU: The value for a positive image went down from 52 percent in 2007 to 34 percent in 2016 (Eurobarometer 2016b). Second, Eurobarometer data are cited as evidence for the continuing dominance of national identities. On average, some 38 percent of respondents stated that national identity is decisive for them; 52 percent said their identity was primarily national and secondarily European; and only 3 percent claimed an exclusively European identity (Eurobarometer 2015a). These surveys indeed show that the uncritical affirmation of European politics has been lost. The politicization of international affairs naturally involves growing opposition, pointing to the continuing importance of the national level in politics. In fact, the strength of national identities makes the development of coercive institutions above the level of the nation state improbable.

Yet the data also show that the absolute majority of respondents claim a double identity, which, at least in Europe, indicates recognition in principle of political authorities beyond the nation state. For many Europeans, national and European identities go together. According to Eurobarometer polls, a majority of Europeans express at least some identification with Europe. In 2016, 66 percent of the respondents described themselves as European citizens (Eurobarometer 2016a). An equal number of respondents felt some attachment to Europe (59 percent; Eurobarometer 2015b).

This interpretation is supported by a data set on the population in Germany, which contains corresponding questions in a differentiated form. It shows that a considerable percentage of the population assigns key importance to international institutions for a growing proportion of problems. Fifty-five percent of the German population takes the view that the adverse consequences of globalization can be best handled by international institutions. Solutions to the biggest problems of our time, such as climate change, the financial crisis, the proliferation of weapons of mass destruction, or the fight against terrorism, are hence expected from international institutions and not from the nation state—only 11 percent of the population believes the nation state to have the competence to solve these problems (Ecker-Ehrhardt and Weßels 2013).

Regarding these issues, the German population considers all the IOs under study (the EU, World Bank, International Monetary Fund (IMF), World Trade Organization (WTO), G8, and the UN) also to be factually more influential than the federal government. Between 46 and 53 percent of respondents attribute considerable influence to IOs even on developments within Germany, although first place in this respect is conceded to the federal government and the EU (Ecker-Ehrhardt and Weßels 2013). In other words, not only does the population believe the solution of globalization-induced problems by international institutions to be desirable, but it also credits these institutions with substantial influence in practical politics.

The importance given to them should not be confused with an uncritical affirmation of international institutions, for as their influence grows, so too does criticism of their non-transparency, exclusivity, and selectiveness, and thus the propensity to protest actively against them. By these criteria, international institutions and the EU are judged even worse—by an average of 7 percent—than the national political system (Ecker-Ehrhardt and Weßels 2013: 46).

Of course, such an assessment of international institutions in Germany and in Europe is no indication of global acceptance. Although relevant survey data from countries outside Europe are based on very general questions about international institutions and affairs, there is nonetheless some evidence that, as far as attitudes toward international institutions are concerned, Europe does not constitute an exception (Norris 2009). For instance, according to data from Pew Research Center (2013), 53.1 percent of people worldwide take a positive view of the UN (*very favorable* or *somewhat favorable*; thirty-nine nations were included). The figure falls only slightly to 51.4 percent if EU member states are discounted. Similarly, data from World Value Survey (WVS Wave 6 2010–14)[9] shows that 47.3 percent assess the UN positively (*a great deal* or *quite a lot*). The UN has markedly lower scores only in the Middle East (Egypt 7.8 percent, Iraq 18.3 percent, Turkey 41.5 percent). The figures for China (67.3 percent) and India (59.2 percent) are even higher than, for instance, those for the nine European countries included in the survey (48.9 percent).[10] In an earlier survey, when asked about the appropriate level of political responsibility for handling various issues (*Who should decide?*), a majority assigned decision-making powers on *peacekeeping* (48.9 percent) and *development aid* to the UN (52.6 percent; WVS Wave 5 2005–8). Also in the field of human rights, populations in the relative majority of countries are in favor of UN powers (41.6 percent), although this is seen differently in China (where 32.6 percent assign this competence to the UN), the US (35.5 percent), and India (22.7 percent) (WVS Wave 5 2005–8).[11]

---

[9] The World Values Survey, available at: http://www.worldvaluessurvey.org/ (status: Wave 6, 2010–14), is conducted regularly in ninety-seven countries to date, thus representing 90 percent of the world population. Importantly though, surveys are not conducted in all ninety-seven countries in every round.

[10] Germany, Estonia, Cyprus, Netherlands, Poland, Romania, Slovenia, Sweden, and Spain.

[11] The questions about "who should decide" were not included in the more recent sixth WVS Wave (2010–14).

These findings of the World Value Surveys are confirmed by a poll conducted by the Chicago Council on Global Affairs and the WorldPublicOpinion.org project in fourteen countries in 2007. There, too, a clear majority of respondents were in favor of a strong role for the UN in security policy. There was broad support, for instance, for a permanent Blue Helmet force, for the right of the UNSC to authorize the use of military force, and for UN regulation of the international arms trade.[12] A relative majority was even in favor of a UN tax.[13]

However, these data are ambiguous as regards a broad acceptance of UN supremacy in the sense of a minimal world state. On the one hand, an overwhelming majority of more than 72 percent agreed with the following statement: "For certain problems, like environmental pollution, international bodies should have the right to enforce solutions." A clear majority was in favor of this statement in all countries surveyed without exception (including the United States, Russia, and South Korea). The picture changes, however, when the statement is couched in different terms, as in the survey conducted by ISSP Research Group (2015): "In general, the country (we) should follow the decisions of international organizations to which it belongs, even if the government disagrees." Agreement then falls markedly to 38.3 percent, and in some countries there is even a majority against (albeit never an absolute majority). In short, acceptance of the authority, or even supremacy, of international institutions, although astonishingly high, can be remarkably ambivalent when the respondents' own country is at issue.

In spite of some support for UN's responsibility in the distribution of development aid and of the need for a UN tax, there is comparatively little support for redistribution. Elements of transnational solidarity are in evidence, but they seem to be limited in concrete terms to emergency aid in the event of humanitarian disasters, where it is, however, very strong (Radtke 2007). When it comes to the appropriate focus for social policy corrections to market results, hence the institutionalization of social rights, the nation state remains the prime address. According to a European Social Survey poll in 2002, an average 61 percent of respondents believe that the national level should be responsible for this policy area; 14 percent even assign competence to the local or regional level (Alber 2010). These data are supported by the skeptical views expressed during the Euro crisis, regarding the establishment of a "Transfer-Union." More recent research, however, points out that solidarity in Europe depends more on institutional schemes than on territorial issues (Kuhn 2015).

---

[12] Eighty-four percent of respondents were in favor of a standing UN peacekeeping force. Furthermore, a majority is in favor of the UNSC being authorized to use military force in certain cases, especially national defense (74 percent), to prevent the violation of human rights, in particular genocide (71 percent), and to dissuade countries from supporting terrorist organizations (69 percent) (WorldPublicOpinion.org 2007).

[13] An average of 47 percent agreed that the UN should be able to raise taxes on the international arms trade, oil, and the like (WorldPublicOpinion.org 2007).

Moreover, the view of broader segments of the populations, as indicated in representative surveys, is more skeptical about international institutions than that of the elites. While individual attitudes about international institutions are not as bleak for global governance as is often suggested and assumed, the gap between the elites and the overall population can hardly be denied (see Hooghe 2003). Based on the general findings that elites, on average, hold more liberal positions than the general population (see Holsti 2004; MacClosky and Brill 1983) and that the better educated are more internationally oriented (see Mau 2007), it has been argued that elites are more cosmopolitan (Calhoun 2003; Zürn 2014) and more in favor of post-national integration (Hooghe 2003). A recent survey of the elite within Germany carried out at the WZB Berlin Social Science Center, which integrated some questions from mass surveys, supports this view. Céline Teney and Marc Helbling (2014: 264) have shown the divide convincingly: "In other words, there are significant elite–mass positional discrepancies on the issues of immigration, international trade, and development aid that cannot be explained by elite–mass differences in education, age, gender, place of residence, and political orientation." Oliver Strijbis (2018, in preparation) shows, on the basis of a similarly designed elite survey sent to different elites (again in the United States, Germany, Poland, Mexico, and Turkey), that this mass–elite divide holds in all countries under question. The difference is explained by a combination of transnational living style, education, and economic interests.

In sum, these findings certainly contradict the view that the nation state continues, quasi-automatically and regardless of the problems involved, to be assigned ultimate political responsibility by the population. They also contradict the view of IOs as technical agencies that solve coordination problems on behalf of national governments without the population taking any interest in them. In effect, international institutions have established themselves as important addressees for expectations and demands, and are at the same time under critical scrutiny by broad sections of the population. This runs contrary to the empirical conditions necessary for the intergovernmental model of an international order and strengthens the different versions of institutional cosmopolitanism.

However, there is little sign of comprehensive transnational solidarity developing that would make it possible to shift redistributive policy in the sense of creating social rights to the global or even European level. This weakens the chances of the institutionalization of a cosmopolitan democracy model. There is only limited support for an interventionist capacity for the UN—an essential part of the minimal world state. Although the UN enjoys a remarkable level of acceptance and there is considerable willingness to endow it with the power of and capacity for enforcement, there is less willingness to comply with international decisions if one's own government

245

rejects them—raising some doubts about the contributory trends in favor of the minimal world state. The survey data currently available can thus be interpreted as being conducive to cosmopolitan pluralism.

9.5 Conclusion

The search for developments contributing to four models of a global order has produced some interesting results. The intergovernmental model of democratic states faces a number of empirical developments that call its applicability into question, especially if current trends continue. This is all the more remarkable given that the arguments that are advanced in justification of this model are largely instrumental, so that it depends particularly strongly on empirical backing. Conversely, the cosmopolitan democracy model faces the problem that no development conducive to transnational solidarity or to the acceptance of a far-reaching supremacy for international institutions is evident. There is much to suggest that this deficiency will not be overcome in the foreseeable future, especially given the emergence of new powers in world politics. Although the empirical conditions presupposed by cosmopolitan pluralism and the minimal world state are still far from being met, trends in their direction can be observed. This is particularly true for cosmopolitan pluralism. A major problem facing the minimal world state is the lack of acceptance of a coercive international institution charged with realizing fundamental rights. The last decade in particular saw a decline in support for the concept of a "responsibility to protect."

These findings alone do not, of course, reflect on the ultimate persuasiveness of the four models. Normative models cannot be rejected on empirical grounds alone. The normative appeal of cosmopolitan democracy for global redistribution remains just as convincing an ideal as the demand for an institution that can secure and enforce fundamental rights worldwide. Ultimately, only a "wide reflective equilibrium" (Daniels 2011) taking account of normative and empirical aspects can establish the validity of a model of global order. Still, any such attempt must take the empirical framework conditions into consideration. The development of models of global order is much more than a purely normative exercise.

A political theory of globality therefore requires interplay between the empirical and normative perspectives, which, however, can never quite merge. The best two witnesses for such a position are likely to be the two leading living proponents of the two disciplines. Jürgen Habermas (2010: 53), on the one hand, has never been tired of warning against the temptation "either to take sides idealistically but non-committedly with the superabundant moral content or to adopt the cynical pose of the so-called 'realists'."

On the other hand, Robert Keohane (2008: 714) calls for normative aspects to be taken into account in International Relations (IR): "[W]e need to think deeply about these issues so that we can articulate coherent normative points of view, and then connect these normative issues with practical problems. For me, as a student of institutions, the most pressing practical problem involves institutional design."

10

Conclusion

A New Paradigm in International Relations?

At the very beginning, I formulated the ambitions of this book: first, to reconstruct global governance as a political system founded on normative principles and reflexive authorities in order to identify the legitimation problems built into it; secondly, to explain the rise of societal politicization and counter-institutionalization via causal mechanisms pointing to the endogenous dynamics of that global governance system; and, finally, to explore the conditions under which the subsequent processes of legitimation or delegitimation lead to the system's decline or to a deepening of it. I wish now to recapitulate the major results of this study in light of these ambitions.

In addition, I submit in this conclusion that the arguments put forward in this book are in line with a newly emerging paradigm in International Relations (IR). A "global politics paradigm" is increasingly complementing the "cooperation under anarchy paradigm" which has been dominant in IR for around five decades. At the very end, I suggest some areas for further research within the realm of this paradigm building on the findings of this book.

10.1 The Global Governance System and its Legitimation Problems

The current global governance system emerged in the 1990s through the interaction between the institutional dynamics triggered by the post-Second World War order and the fall of the Soviet empire. In the historical-institutionalist account of the rise of the global governance system given in Chapter 5, the choice of the United Nations (UN) system and embedded liberalism in the 1940s started a path-dependent sequence that, for around three decades, strengthened these institutions through self-reinforcing processes. Yet, from a certain tipping point on, further liberalization undermined the concept of embedded liberalism by weakening its own shock absorbers. The nation states lost some degree of freedom to handle the risks of an integrated world market. As a consequence, resistance against neoliberalism pushed states to accept not only market-making but also some market-braking international institutions in issue areas such as human rights and environmental politics. In addition, most existing global governance institutions received more authority and became more intrusive, challenging Westphalian sovereignty irrevocably. This whole dynamic was strongly accelerated by an external shock, delivered when the Soviet empire faltered and functional differentiation developed its full potential. Consequently, the national political system lost even more grip on other societal subsystems, which were freed to follow their internal logic to go global. Even the political system globalized itself by developing normative principles and stronger international and transnational institutions. This happened partly in response to the needs and demands of world society and partly by following an internal logic in response to globalization. Together, these developments led to a global governance system. The steep rise of public authority as indicated in the International Authority Database (IAD) indicates a system change.

The global governance system is built on three pillars: general normative principles, a set of sector-specific institutions exercising at least some authority, and their interactions with each other. To begin with, the global governance system is based on *normative principles* that together are different from earlier international systems. Most importantly, justifications of global governance regimes address both state actors and non-state actors, including individuals. This indicates a recognition of non-state actors as subjects of the system, which thus has a double constituency that consists of states with conditional sovereignty as well as of societal actors. Also societal actors possess some rights, address international authorities, and are sometimes direct addressees of inter- and transnational authorities, not merely addressees reached via national governments. Justificatory communications from international authorities, for instance, are directed not only at governments, but also at societal actors and individuals. Moreover, international institutions open up for non-state actors in many respects. This is most tangible during global conferences.

Global governance also presupposes the existence of at least some global common goods. The reasons given for global regulations that reduce the autonomy of participating states and societal actors almost exclusively refer to global goals and public goods, as indicated, for instance, by the wording of many preambles to international treaties. While many of these justifications are merely strategic and hypocritical, the general practice would be meaningless if there were not a presupposition that a global common good exists. This presupposition is at the heart of the notion of a political system: Without the idea of common goods there is no such thing as a political system that is different from other societal systems. That this presupposition is utilized most often for other, much more parochial purposes is also not unknown in national political systems.

The presupposition of global goods and the recognition of non-state actors leads almost straightaway to yet another normative principle of the global governance system: the possibility of public authority in the global realm. Authority implies the notion of voluntary subordination of states and societies to institutions. Inter- and transnational institutions can then make competent judgments and decisions that are taken into account even when they run counter to others' own interests. When states respect obligations that may go against their own stated interests, and these duties are justified with reference to global common goods and individual rights, the international system is no longer anarchical. Then at least a rudimentary political system has developed that is different from other function systems and contains at least some pockets of authority and hierarchy. The double constituency, presupposition of common goods and recognition of the possibility of authority, together point to a system in which states are not the only bearers of rights, and rights and duties derive from a position in an emergent normative order rather than from membership in an international system of sovereign equals.

Besides general, sector-spanning normative principles, the global governance system also contains *specific political institutions encompassing patterns of authority and legitimation.* This second layer of the system is made up of international and transnational authorities that are recognized by direct and indirect addressees as being qualified to make competent judgments and decisions and to exercise public authority justified by reference to the normative principles.

These authorities however are characterized by features that are specific to the global governance system. First of all, they exercise a form of authority over state and non-state actors, including individuals. They formulate prescriptions and recommendations for them with the expectation that they will be deferred to. States and non-state actors take these requests seriously to the extent that they acknowledge the limitations of their local or partial rationality. In this sense, reflexive authority relies on reflexivity on the part of those who recognize the authorities. Second, inter- and transnational authorities work differently than imagined by traditional accounts of public authority. Those who defer in a reflexive authority relationship can—at their discretion—always decide when they want to put the authority under question. Constituencies can carefully explore the implications of deference, and can always ask for changes in the authority relationship. In this sense, reflexive authority is characterized by a permanent reflection by subordinates on the value of their subordination. Unlike traditional authority, therefore, reflexive authority is typically not internalized. It allows a scrutiny of the effects of the exercise of authority at any time, does not consist of commands only but also of demands or requests, and is embedded in sectoral knowledge orders. Inter- and transnational public authority comes not only in the conventional form of political authority, but often in that of epistemic authorities, which mainly produce interpretations with behavioral implications, but not necessarily decisions to which actors defer directly. Not least, epistemic authorities influence the process of interest formation within nation states.

Empirical assessment of patterns of authority in the global governance system shows that both political and epistemic authority beyond the nation state has risen generally over time since 1945, and rose especially steeply in the 1990s. At the same time, a specific type of public authority in the global governance system has gained especial relevance: politically assigned epistemic authorities (PAEAs). These are bodies to which states delegate the competence to gather and interpret politically relevant information. The Organisation for Economic Co-operation and Development (OECD), for instance, assesses the quality of different national policies in policy fields such as labor markets or education. Deference to these interpretations does not mean following a direct request or a command, but taking on an expectation that one will follow the recommendations implicit in these assessments. Although authority relationships in the global governance system are mostly reflexive, they can nevertheless be highly consequential and require legitimation.

The third layer of the global governance system resides in the *interplay between different spheres of authority* beyond the nation state, including their relationship with national authorities. These interactions testify to the systemic features of global governance. Measured from the perspective of constitutionalized rule, however, these features are marked by severe shortcomings and structural legitimation problems.

One central feature of the global governance system is that different spheres of authority within it are only loosely coupled with each other. Inter- and transnational authorities are most often sectorally defined and thus responsible for a limited set of issues only. Their scope ranges from being responsible for the management of one single species (the International Whaling Regime) to being responsible for the management of peace and security throughout the world (the United Nations Security Council (UNSC)). These different, sectorally defined spheres of authority are not fully integrated. The management of interface conflicts between different spheres (e.g. between trade and health institutions) is rudimentary at best. Whereas the constitutionalized nation state has established some sites of meta-authority, the global governance system only knows informal meta-authorities such as hegemons or the G7/20 summits, which are weak and highly exclusive at the same time. This feature of the current global governance system causes the first significant legitimation problem. Since spheres of authority are only loosely coupled, they are limited to sectoral justifications and thus introduce a technocratic bias into the patterns of legitimation. Most inter- and transnational authorities do indeed subscribe to a technocratic narrative of justification. The depth and type of authority that is exercised by many international and some transnational authorities, however, is increasingly overburdening such a narrative. Some of the decisions made within the global governance system cannot be plausibly based on technocratic grounds only—take, for instance, the austerity programs of the International Monetary Fund (IMF) or the military interventions authorized by the UNSC.

The other systemic feature of the global governance system is a weakly established separation of powers. The central decision makers in international authorities comprise the secretariats of the key international organizations involved and, more importantly, executive representatives of the most powerful nation states. The more an international institution exercises authority, the more, as a rule, powerful states care about their influence within it. As a result, the most authoritative international institutions such as the UNSC, the IMF, and the World Bank contain formal mechanisms that ensure that special consideration is given to great power interests. International institutions with authority, therefore, not only introduce a hierarchy between the global and the national level, but also stratification between different states— that is to say that they institutionalize inequality between them. This inequality sometimes goes so far that the representatives of the most powerful states combine legislative (setting the rules), executive (making decisions on the basis of the rules), and administrative (implementing the decisions) competencies in the absence of judicial supervision. The UNSC and its permanent members, for instance, assume legislative and executive functions at one and the same time, when they pass resolutions that extend the meaning of threats to international peace, authorize an intervention on this basis, and carry out that intervention—all this in the absence of a court that can effectively supervise them.

The absence of a separation of powers produces a second legitimation problem. It undermines the key grounds for belief in legitimacy: non-arbitrariness and impartiality in the exercise of authority. The exercise of international authority often leads to decisions and interpretations that violate the regulative idea according to which like cases should be treated alike. In this way, the integrity of law—and with it the most fundamental understanding of fairness—is often violated. This power bias, in combination with the technocratic bias, produces severe legitimation problems for the global governance system. Not surprisingly therefore, we are increasingly witnessing struggles in and about such a system.

10.2 Politicization and Counter-Institutionalization

The legitimation problems of the global governance system are part of the reactive sequences in which international authorities endogenously produce challengers and challenges. Reactive sequences, in general, consist of processes that are at least partially produced by the institution in question and that threaten to undermine the conditions necessary to maintain it. At the core of reactive sequences in the global governance system lies the "authority–legitimation link" (ALL), which simply states that when international institutions exercise authority, they need addressees to believe in their legitimacy. As long as the intergovernmental level was restricted to merely developing a *modus vivendi* for interaction, requiring the consent of each member state, and carried out in the mode of executive multilateralism, a two-stage process of legitimation was sufficient. Decisions taken on the level beyond that of the constituent members were legitimated through the legitimacy of the members' representatives. To the extent that international authorities undermine the consent principle, and, at the same time, become more intrusive and affect societies directly, they are evaluated against normative standards. As a result, legitimation problems arise leading to processes of delegitimation and re-legitimation. Two types of such processes can be distinguished: societal politicization and counter-institutionalization.

Politicization can be defined as moving something into the realm of public choice, thus presupposing the possibility that collectively binding decisions can be made on that matter. Full-scale politicization has three components: the growing *salience* of an issue, a *polarization of opinion* about this issue, and an *expansion of the actors and audiences* engaged in the debate. The politicization of international institutions can be pursued by transnational actors such as ATTAC or Occupy, who most often challenge specific policies, and by domestic actors such as right-wing populist parties questioning the transfer of authority to the international level in general. But the politicization of inter- and transnational authorities not only calls attention to resistance to global governance, but also to those processes in which international institutions are used by non-state actors to achieve specific political goals. Many transnational interest groups and transnational CSOs address inter- and transnational institutions directly, often with the goal of achieving stricter regulation at the global level.

Higher levels of authority lead to higher levels of politicization. This is a robust finding that has received support in different settings and for international institutions as well as the European Union (EU). The challenges put forward against international institutions with high levels of authority target not only their policies, but also their legitimacy. Institutions like the UNSC, the IMF, and the World Bank are especially criticized for the opaqueness of their decision making, their narrow technocratic justification, and their institutionalized inequality. Moreover, different types of authority lead to different methods and levels of politicization: The exercise of political authority is more strongly politicized than the exercise of epistemic authority, even if it is politically delegated epistemic authority. The reason is that international institutions with a mandate to make decisions (political authority) are more visible and offer more opportunity structures for politicization; the authority of transnational authorities and international authorities with a mandate to make interpretations (epistemic authority), by contrast, is less visible and offers fewer opportunities to mobilize. For similar reasons, public authority exercised by transnational institutions is less often politicized than that of international institutions.

The politicization of international institutions usually follows a path of four steps, as exemplified, for instance, by both the financial and the Eurozone crisis. In the first step, due to increased denationalization and trans-border externalities, international regulatory deficits are denounced. Transnational non-governmental organizations (NGOs), expert groups, or international organizations (IOs) identify the need for international regulation. In the second step, this leads—most often in a time of crisis—to a strengthening of the international authority with new and most often more intrusive competences. For instance, the immediate response to the debt crisis in southern European states was a significant strengthening of EU competences. This makes international authority tangible for broad sections of society in the third step, and provides a political opportunity structure for politicization. The Greek case may be extreme, but it is not the exception. Finally, the public authority of international institutions is challenged on grounds of insufficient legitimacy. The outcome of the subsequent legitimation struggle is open. Sometimes it leads to a deepening of global governance, as in the case of human rights protection mechanisms for IO policies; sometimes it leads to fragmentation and decline.

Contestation of inter- and transnational authority by states is the other form of legitimation struggle in the global governance system. It comes most often in form of *counter-institutionalization*. From the late 1990s on, the increase in the authority of international institutions slowed down and was accompanied by another significant development: rising powers. Some of those rising powers aimed to change the institutional landscape of the global governance system. If states are unhappy with a given international authority, they can give in, they can set up a blockade against decision making, they can opt for counter-institutionalization, or they can simply exit. In line with the notion of a global governance system, exit is very rarely chosen as an option. Instead, blockades, compromises, and counter-institutionalization prevail. Counter-institutionalization in particular is a strategy intended to change the global governance system instead of moving out of it. It refers to attempts to build and/or utilize other international institutions in order to change the institutional status quo—alternative institutions are brought into play, new ones are created, coalitions are formalized, and existing institutions are contested. Counter-institutionalization goes beyond routine changes within the system, but falls short of system change: It is a case of systemic change instead.

Counter-institutionalization comes in two forms. Counter-institutionalization by incumbent states means, above all, regime shifting and competitive regime creation. Established powers build and use parallel governance forums, especially when the targeted institutions exercise authority on the principle of "one-state, one-vote." The World Health Organization (WHO) is a case in point. Incumbents often insist on institutionalized inequality. They ask for a global governance system that gives them a privileged role and allows for double standards. The costs of this strategy are significant. Legitimation of international authority is increasingly difficult when inequality is institutionalized and like cases are treated in a discriminatory way.

Rising powers use strategies of counter-institutionalization as well. They aim to change existing institutions that privilege Western states. They do not want just to be included in global governance institutions, as the liberal order theory predicts; they want to reshape them. Nevertheless, the "distance" between the preferences of rising power states and the content of given international institutions is often less dramatic than expected by many, especially by power transition theorists. Rising powers do not aim to overhaul existing international institutions. Rather, they want to reform them from the inside. In essence, counter-institutionalization by rising powers aims at voice—not at exit or loyalty. At the same time, there is an ongoing suspicion that stronger international institutions are instruments of Western dominance and help to prolong an unequal distribution of benefits. This tension leads to ambiguous responses, bound together by the common struggle of rising powers against institutionalized inequality.

10.3 Decline or Deepening?

Moving on to the outcome and effects of legitimation struggles, an increased level of politicization seems to be leading to a broadening of the narratives that are referred to in the legitimation process. As a response to contestation, authority holders at least temporarily change their justificatory rhetoric. This temporary change in legitimation narratives is, however, not necessarily based on substantial reforms of the international authority under question, nor does it necessarily lead to them.

Whether an extension of legitimacy narratives leads to a deepening of global governance is contingent. It depends on how stubborn the institutional response of the authority holders to the delegitimation challenge is and whether it involves symbolic moves or substantial reforms. When the response insists on retaining the status quo, or when it remains symbolic and the legitimation narrative in the long run moves back to being mainly technocratic, then we can expect an ongoing authority–legitimacy gap. This gap most often leads to the fragmentation and decline of global governance. In contrast, substantial responses indicate a deepening of global governance inasmuch as they target the legitimation problems. The choice depends on certain scope conditions.

When is a deepening of global governance as a response to delegitimation to be expected? What are the scope conditions? The findings, taken together, suggest that institutional adaptation in favor of alleviating the deficits of the global governance system is most likely in three sets of circumstances. In the first, societal actors that aim for institutional adaptation are necessary to achieve successful policies, either for informational reasons or as partners in the implementation process. It can be stated that those international authorities that are most dependent on societal partners (e.g. the World Bank) are most open and most willing to change substantially. In the second, non-state challengers find strong coalition partners and the institution they are addressing can be attacked as openly inconsistent. The best coalition partners are those embedded in strong member states. National parliaments or constitutional courts are cases in point. If such internal coalition partners are not available, an external coalition of like-minded actors can sometimes also bring about substantial reforms. This situation, however, less often leads to success and is, in effect, dependent on the targeted authority being highly vulnerable to campaigns. In the third, substantial institutional reforms to integrate rising powers and their societies into the global governance system are likely when the new powers are needed to resolve urgent problems; i.e. when they possess "system significance." The establishment of the G20, essentially replacing the G7/8 architecture, and the reform of the IMF, which were both initiated during financial crises, are good examples.

If none of these sets of circumstances exists, authority holders may ignore demands for change. This often leads, however, to counter-institutionalization by rising powers or an increasing legitimacy gap, which, in turn, reduces the room for maneuver of the executives of member states in future negotiations. Moreover, if authority holders are confronted with demands for institutional changes from state challengers, they can sidestep the reforms by regime shifting and competitive regime creation. Additional fragmentation of the global governance system is thus a real danger. As a result, the reduction of transaction costs—a major reason for developing international institutions in the first place—evaporates. A complex institutional landscape, with many parallel opportunities to achieve ends is useful for the Western states in distributional terms. It is, however, detrimental to the collective costs of achieving a working global governance system.

In sum, deepening global governance institutions is possible, in spite of or, better, because of their contestation. Although it can lead to counter-institutionalization, fragmentation, and decline, it may also lead to re-legitimation efforts and, where successful, a deepening of global governance. To put it differently, reactive sequences are defined by self-undermining processes in the first place, at the end of the whole sequence though, the deepening of the institution in question remains a possibility.

It should be added that some of the underlying conditions of world society may improve over time and seem, in the mid-term, to allow for a global governance system that is less deficient than the current one. As argued in Chapter 9, in many societies there seems to be a general recognition of cosmopolitan ideas and the need for international authority. This tendency to think global, however, is limited and hardly includes a willingness to accept authorities with strong enforcement capacities or redistribution across national societies.

10.4 A Global Politics Paradigm on the Rise?

Since its founding after the First World War, IR as a discipline has successively developed three paradigms or research programs that partially built on one another and partially changed their fundamental assumptions (Deitelhoff and Zürn 2016). The founding period of the discipline of IR was dominated by the theme of war and peace. This "war and peace paradigm" remained dominant until the 1960s, when interdependence and cooperation gained importance and the "cooperation paradigm" became dominant. Both of these paradigms shared the view that the international system is anarchic. This has been challenged by a new "global politics paradigm."[1] From this perspective, we are in the process of moving from the cooperation paradigm that prevailed from the 1970s on to a global politics paradigm that began to take over at the end of the last century.

A paradigm, in the sense used here, does not refer to a well-developed and strongly formalized theory that dominates a field, as in Thomas Kuhn's (1962) seminal account of scientific revolutions. Given the state of theory building in IR, and given the highly reflective object of study, a paradigm rather points to a set of assumptions about, and perspectives on, world politics—it points,

---

[1] I owe thanks to Robert Keohane who suggested this term instead of global order paradigm.

in fact, to shared unobservables, to use a term from the realist theory of science. As used here, the term paradigm also has similarities with a research program as understood by Imre Lakatos (1976). It is broader, however, and includes a plurality of theories with partially incommensurable assumptions. Given its equidistance to two established terms, I use them interchangeably in the remainder of this chapter.

This book is part of the emerging global politics paradigm. While it builds on many insights produced by the cooperation paradigm, it goes beyond that by reconstructing a global governance system consisting of patterns of authority relationships which endogenously produce politicization, counter-institutionalization, and legitimation struggles. The term "global politics" is not bound to an understanding which equates global policies with consensus or at least peaceful conflict management within civilized and institutionalized channels. The term "global" does not refer to a fair representation of all parts of the planet.

What then does the global politics paradigm stand for? It refers to those political processes and policies which describe themselves as global and which indeed often have global effects. I use the term "global politics" to describe the general perspective according to which the international political realm is structured by normative principles and contains at least some pockets of hierarchy. Such an understanding incorporates serious conflicts and struggles as well as power asymmetries and, in doing so, gives them another meaning. The question then is not whether we see war and struggles as support for the realist imaginary, or peace and consensus pointing to the idealist one. The question is how to understand the parallelism of increasing levels of violence and deeper institutionalization, the concurrence of war and order, of integration and fragmentation, and how to relate them causally. In a recent review article, Janice Bially Mattern and Ayşe Zarakol (2016: 624–5) suggest that the concept of hierarchy is central for a new approach that is clearly different from approaches based on the notion of anarchy. They write: "Hierarchy-centered approaches to IR promise to deliver what anarchy-centered approaches have not: a framework for theorizing and empirically analyzing world politics as a *global system* rather than just an international one...: [T]he concept of hierarchy offers a basis for uniting fragmented insights into world politics."

In general, the study of governance without government (Rosenau and Czempiel 1992), global governance (Rosenau 1990), or global polity (Ougaard and Higgott 2002) is certainly part of the emerging global politics paradigm. This is also true for studies on international authority (see e.g. Hurd 2007; Lake 2010) and contested multilateralism (Morse and Keohane 2014). Parts of the debates on a new world order belong to the paradigm as well. While many theories of power transition focus on rising powers who want to bring in the realist imaginary again, others, like John Ikenberry (2011a: 6–7), put forward a global politics perspective that sees those competitors as remaining within the order. Of course, studies of the gap between demand and supply with respect to global governance are also part of the global politics perspective (Hale et al. 2013).

Moreover, parts of the study of order from the perspective of the English school (Hurrell 2007; Buzan 2010) or from the perspective of world society (Albert 2016) belong to the paradigm, as do some contributions from critical theory. The notion of global politics with inscribed values and hierarchies is compatible with some post-structuralist and post-Marxist theories (Cox 1987; Hardt and Negri 2004). In this critical view, global politics is not anarchic, but has institutionalized knowledge, values, and hierarchies that reproduce inequality, injustice, and resistance (Onuf and Klink 1989; Daase and Deitelhoff 2015). Practice-based approaches see hierarchies as intersubjectively organized inequalities (Adler-Nissen 2017; Pouliot 2016b; Sending 2015).

This plurality of approaches is typical of a research paradigm. Within each of the paradigms, different theories and approaches compete with each other. The development of the cooperation paradigm, for instance, was fueled by the debates between rational and sociological institutionalists. Yet both sides agreed essentially that, in a world of increasingly open borders and growing interdependencies, international institutions can and need to develop even in an anarchical system that does not know a public power beyond the state. Whether these international institutions are best understood as a function of constellations of state interests that stand in a relationship of strategic interaction (Keohane 1984; Snidal 1986; Koremenos et al. 2001) or as a function of transnational norm developments in which identity, persuasion, and the logic of appropriateness are decisive (Katzenstein 1996; Keck and Sikkink 1998; Wendt 1999; Risse 2000) was a question debated within this cooperation research program—different institutionalisms within one paradigm, so to speak.

Moreover, older research programs in IR do not die quickly, as in Kuhn's account of paradigms in the natural sciences. None of the paradigms that ever existed in IR is really dead. For this reason, the proponents of the cooperation program, for instance, have had to play a two-level game. In addition to the internal debates between rationalists and constructivists, there has been an ongoing exchange with the realist camp representing the old peace and war research program. Nevertheless, the relative weight of research programs changes over time.

Changes in research programs result from both developments within the academic discipline and developments in the object of study. Changes in the structure of world politics itself make the adoption of new themes, concepts, and theories likely. Changes in research programs are, therefore, associated with significant changes in world politics. For instance, the close connection between the founding of the discipline after 1918 and the peace and war issue is obvious. Peace and war between states was the theme that moved the founders of the discipline, international diplomats, and the people. The *intermezzo* between the wars was so short that no other IR theme could really develop, especially since the economic crisis after Black Tuesday in 1929 was framed as an issue that added to the competition between states and radical-ized their foreign policies. On the one hand, there were the early Idealists, who believed in the power of international law and good reason and may be symbolized by Woodrow Wilson's idea of making the world safe for democ-racies. The idealistic and legalistic twist of these early studies was countered by self-acclaimed Realists on the other hand, who emphasized the need to stand strong when aggressors showed up.

It took until the early 1960s for a new research program to take off in IR. The new paradigm pointed to the need for and possibility of cooperation in an anarchical system, even if cooperation partners have little in common. In the nuclear age, the impossibility of war and the need to find cooperative schemes to accommodate friends and foes—i.e. within the political blocs and between East and West—became obvious. The questions referred to the strategies required in order to prevail without war, ways in which cooper-ation can be induced, and the role IOs can play in making cooperation possible. It essentially started with the refinement of deterrence theory. The goal was to identify strategies and instruments that helped to avoid escalation and allowed for minimal cooperation in order to avoid the worst outcome: nuclear war (see, especially, Schelling 1960; also Snyder and Diesing 1977). Against this backdrop, a rethinking of nuclear deterrence took place. With the help of game theory, the credibility gap in the doctrine of mutually assured destruction (MAD) was detected.

In parallel, the development of the EU after the Treaty of Rome pointed to the possibility of achieving integration beyond the nation state without a decisionist act (which the early idealists asked for; see Haas 1958, 1964). Finally, the 1970s made "interdependence" and the management of inter-dependence a buzzword. It was against this background that the cooperation paradigm gained weight, without pushing the peace and war paradigm com-pletely aside. Cooperation under anarchy (Oye 1986) and after hegemony (Keohane 1984) became the core task for governments with an enlightened self-interest.

Rationalist cooperation theory, arguably the major theory of the coopera-tive system of states based on Westphalian sovereignty and intergovernmen-talism, provides a strong and plausible explanation for the emerging pattern of these international regimes in the decades after the Second World War.

Based on learning from the interwar period, it needed American leadership, plus the willingness of the European states to follow the lead, to establish institutions that reduced transaction costs and thus fostered cooperation (Keohane 1984). Thanks to US leadership, the low number of relevant players left at the table, and an increased need to recover quickly given the perceived Soviet threat, conditions were permissive for institution building. This made it possible to build international institutions not only in a constellation of interests that resembled coordination games (as with traffic and other standards), but also for interest constellations that resembled dilemma games (Snidal 1986; Zürn 1992). These institutions supposedly served state interests and functioned in the mode of executive multilateralism without significant societal participation.

Rationalist cooperation theory could explain both the institutional successes within the Western system and the initial failure of any institutionalized cooperation between East and West. It was also able to provide an explanation of the slow improvement of the difficult East–West relationship in the shadow of nuclear deterrence. The features of these institutions and their decisions were also largely in line with the expectations of rationalist cooperation theory. International institutions were ascribed little authority of their own and ran, to a large extent, in accordance with simple international rules, which were not, in the beginning, very intrusive. Self-interested state actors chose the institutionalization of cooperation because the costs of non-cooperation had grown. The logic even worked in the context of East–West relations where international regimes—i.e. East–West regimes—now emerged as well (Rittberger 1990; Haftendorn et al. 1999).

Partially in response to the deepening of international institutions, the rationalist theory expanded its scope by taking into account the interplay between domestic political processes and international cooperation (Putnam 1988; Moravcsik 1998), which is necessary for understanding parts of the self-reinforcing dynamics of embedded liberalism. Moreover, the deepening of institutionalization led to accounts that explained the variance in the institutional design of institutions (Koremenos et al. 2001), including higher levels of legalization (Goldstein et al. 2001), and the different degrees of autonomy of the IOs (Hawkins et al. 2006a).

These changes in the politics of international cooperation were accompanied by the rise of sociological-institutionalist reasoning about global norms. According to this view, it is not necessarily the constellation of given state interests that is decisive for understanding international institutions; rather, it is the formative role of global norms and the logic of appropriateness (March and Olsen 1996). The development of international norms then takes place as a result of processes of persuasion and arguing on the part of often non-state actors (Risse 2000; Deitelhoff and Müller 2005) and the rhetorical traps into which state leaders often fall, especially when there is a marked decoupling between rhetoric and behavior (Risse et al. 1999; Schimmelfennig 2003). So norm entrepreneurs (Liese 2006), the diffusion of norms (Keck and Sikkink 1998), as well as socialization (Checkel 2005) and internalization (Klotz 1995; Finnemore 1996) are what makes these norms effective.

This research moved further in the 1990s by conceptualizing governance without government (Rosenau and Czempiel 1992; Mayer et al. 1993) as a form of governing that takes place on the level beyond the nation state. With this shift from regime analysis to the concept of governance without government, the assumption of anarchy was transcended, which *de facto* laid the foundation for a new research program. The global politics paradigm thus moved beyond anarchy (Hurd 2007; Lake 2009). In this view, global politics, including a set of regional orders, has since emerged, full of hierarchical and asymmetric relationships that are institutionalized. Global politics then becomes a normative order that contains elements of institutional authority (Rosenau 1997) and hierarchy (Lake 2009). The rights and duties of states (and other actors) are derived from this normative order and not from their status as equal sovereigns. One may, therefore, speak of an international political system, a world polity, or a global governance system. Indeed, global governance is one of the buzzwords of this research program.

Although the rise of the global politics paradigm is, to a significant extent, a response to changes in world politics, it also reflects learned understandings about the role of IOs, the recognition of authorities, internalized knowledge systems, and the institutionalization of inequality. In this sense, the use of the concept of global governance is not necessarily restricted to the days after 1990. It can certainly be configured to understand the European system during the reign of popes and the functioning of empires. It may also be used to shed new light on the international system that emerged in the nineteenth century with the first IOs and developed until the heyday of the cold war in the early 1980s (see e.g. Murphy 1994; Weiss and Wilkinson 2014).

Publication indicators point to the development of IR paradigms as described (Figure 10.1). The Google Books Ngram Viewer reflects it almost perfectly. From 1918 on, "peace and war" was the dominant combination of terms in the titles of books. "International cooperation" as a concept took off only in the 1950s, but from the early 1960s it became the dominant term, and stayed that way until recently. It seems however that "global governance" (as the buzzword of the global politics paradigm) is now taking the lead.

A look at Google Scholar supports the assertion. While terms like "international cooperation" and "IO" are still leading on this count, the term "global

Figure 10.1. Changing paradigms and book titles

Source: Google Books Ngram Viewer

governance" is already ahead of "peace and war" and far surpasses all the others in terms of its growth rate.[2]

Theories associated with the global politics perspective need to shed new light on world politics, allowing its processes to be uncovered and criticized. In doing so, they look at tensions and struggles as functions of the features of a global system, instead of seeing global politics as an epiphenomenon of struggles between independent units with differing power capacities and interests. In order to prevail as a paradigm, the central task then is to develop hypotheses about the causes of conflicts and struggles, and the ongoing institutionalizations in world politics that are other and better than the theories linked with the anarchy premise.

10.5 Future Research

Research programs in IR blossom when they offer answers to questions relevant for current developments. Against this backdrop, I want at the end of this Conclusion to point to some issues and developments to which the global politics paradigm can contribute—and actually needs to contribute if

---

[2] The average growth rate of Google Scholar hits regarding pertinent IR terms (with "international cooperation," "peace and war," "international institution/s," and "international organization/s" being included) is mainly due to the rise of electronically available publications in general. It is 223 percent when comparing 1990 and 2000 and 110 percent when comparing 2000 and 2010. As "global governance" was basically not used in 1990 (only fifteen hits), growth rates are much higher (12,033 percent and 471 percent) than the aforementioned average growth rates of other IR terms. Thus, with some 10,400 hits in 2010, "global governance" has now surpassed "peace and war" (9,940) and is starting to catch up with "international organization/s" and "international institution/s" (author's calculations, October 5, 2014).

it wants to succeed the cooperation paradigm. Among the variety of issues and questions that arise, I limit myself to five themes, which are more directly associated with concepts and findings in this book.

Scope conditions: None of the causal mechanisms discussed in this book are deterministic. Since *reactive* sequences are at stake, agency and thus choice are necessarily built into these processes. Therefore, none of the steps identified in the different versions of the authority–legitimation link takes place necessarily or is invariant. Incumbent states that are dissatisfied, for instance, may still find formal or informal, old or new ways of projecting their power in existing institutions, or they may acquiesce in outcomes that they find suboptimal, but too costly to challenge. It is therefore interesting not only to study the scope conditions for the relative dominance of self-reinforcing dynamics and reactive sequences, but also to ask about the more specific scope conditions under which each step is taken in each of the causal mechanisms I have sketched. Under what conditions can insufficiently legitimated IOs be politicized? Under what conditions does politicization lead to a productive institutional response? When does the decoupling of power from outcome lead to the exit of the powerful and when do the weaker accommodate the positions of the powerful in order to maintain "their" institution? Future studies of reactive sequences in and across different institutions and issue areas should address these questions. This will allow our understanding of the global governance system to be enhanced.

Politically assigned epistemic authorities: The current global governance system knows both international and transnational authority. In my analysis, the focus was more on the international kind than the transnational. Yet transnational authorities are of growing relevance, especially within the type of PAEAs. Some of them work out interpretations in order to help democratically legitimated majoritarian institutions to make the right decisions. In other cases, interpretations become *de facto* decisions, as in the case of those made by central banks and courts. Pulling different features of PAEAs together (interpretation versus decision; rule-implementing versus rule-setting; intergovernmental versus transnational) would allow for differentiations and typologies that could be used to shed light on the working and dynamics of these central players in the global governance system.

Interface conflicts: The global governance system has been characterized as one with loosely coupled spheres of authority. This characterization is based on the somewhat simple notion that there are three different types of relationship between different spheres of authority: independent (no coupling), interdependent without meta-authorities (loose coupling), and interdependent coordinated by meta-authorities (constitutionalized system).

The interaction between loosely coupled spheres of authority can vary significantly, however. If collisions or conflicts between different spheres of authority arise, they can be managed in quite different ways. There may be some form of coordinated and norm-guided conflict management, but disputes can also lead to ugly power struggles between different institutions. It is clearly of interest for understanding the global governance system, how the interaction between different spheres takes place and what determines the different forms of conflict management at the interface. Different forms of it can, in turn, be expected to play a significant role in legitimation processes.

Hierarchy, stratification, and reflexive authority: In a review essay on "Hierarchy in World Politics," Janice Mattern and Ayşe Zarakol (2016) move hierarchy to the core of theorizing and analyzing the global system. They distinguish between a narrow version of hierarchy which focuses on authority as commands and a broader one defined as intersubjectively organized inequality. The notion of reflexive authority lies in between. On the one hand, it points to only a very weak, almost a halved, version of the narrow understanding of authority. At the same time, it takes elements of intersubjectively organized inequality into account, when it refers to the underlying knowledge order and points to authority as a means to institutionalize inequality and formalize stratification between states. Yet, the concepts used and developed in the global politics paradigm so far do not really sit very well together. Further work and thinking are required.

Cross-cutting cleavages: Regulatory conflicts and legitimation struggles in and about global governance arrangements are mirrored within national political systems as conflicts about open versus closed borders and/or the transfer of authority to levels above the nation state. By now, it can be compellingly demonstrated that these conflicts provide the impetus for a new cleavage in most Western democracies (Kriesi et al. 2012; Grande and Kriesi 2013). The conflict line between cosmopolitan frequent travelers and those communitarians stuck in their homelands increasingly complements, and partially replaces, the old cleavage between capital and labor. The first round of the Austrian presidential election demonstrated this in an exemplary way. While the two candidates of the traditional cleavage, between the Social Democratic Party (SPÖ) and the conservative People's Party (ÖVP), together received little more than 20 percent of the vote, the two candidates from the parties representing the new cleavage, the right-wing populist party (FPÖ) versus the Green Party, received over 60 percent. By now all party systems in Western Europe contain parties with cosmopolitan orientations and others who put forward communitarian arguments (Zürn and de Wilde 2016). This new cleavage has gained in importance over the last two decades, especially in recent years. Its emergence is the background condition that made Donald

Trump's ascendancy to the White House possible. Yet it also cuts across national borders (de Wilde et al. 2018, in preparation). On the one hand, the Western states are increasingly confronted with a coalition of authoritarian states led by *men* like Vladimir Putin, Viktor Orbán, and Recep Tayyip Erdoğan, who often refer to arguments that sound similar to the ones used by populist right-wing parties in Western countries. On the other hand, the parts of national governments and administrations that work in IOs are most likely the most radical cosmopolitans within their respective national political systems (de Wilde et al. 2016a). These constellations point to a close link between the new cleavage and the global governance system. The latter clearly helped bring the former about; at the same time it is being heavily affected by it. A closer analysis of this link between domestic structures and the global governance system is vital. It will tell us a lot about the future of national borders and the future of the global governance system.

References

Abbott, K. W. (2000), "Hard and Soft Law in International Governance," *International Organization*, 54/3: 421–56.

Abbott, K. W. (2009), "The Governance Triangle: Regulatory Standards Institutions and the Shadow of the State," in W. Mattli and N. Woods (eds.), *The Politics of Global Regulation* (Princeton: Princeton University Press), 44–88.

Abbott, K. W. (2011), "International 'Standards' and International Governance," *Journal of European Public Policy*, 8/3: 345–70.

Abbott, K. W., Genschel, P., Snidal, D., and Zangl, B. (2015), "Orchestration: Global Governance Through Intermediaries," in K. W. Abbott, P. Genschel, D. Snidal, and B. Zangl (eds.), *International Organizations as Orchestrators* (Cambridge: Cambridge University Press), 3–36.

Abbott, K. W., Green, J. F., and Keohane, R. O. (2016), "Organizational Ecology and Institutional Change in Global Governance," *International Organization*, 70/2: 247–77.

Abbott, K. W., Keohane, R. O., Moravcsik, A., Slaughter, A.-M., and Snidal, D. (2000), "The Concept of Legalization," *International Organization*, 54/3: 401–19.

Abbott, K. W., and Snidal, D. (1998), "Why States Act Through Formal International Organizations," *Journal of Conflict Resolution*, 42/1: 3–32.

Ackerman, B. (2000), "The New Separation of Powers," *Harvard Law Review*, 113/3: 633.

Adler, E., and Pouliot, V. (2011), "International Practices," *International Theory*, 3/01: 1–36.

Adler-Nissen, R. (2017), "Are We 'Lazy Greeks' or 'Nazi Germans'? Negotiating International Hierarchies in the Euro Crisis," in A. Zarakol (ed.), *Hierarchies in World Politics* (Cambridge: Cambridge University Press), 198–218.

Adorno, T. W., Frankel-Brunswik, E., Levinson, D. J., and Sanford, R. N. (1950), *The Authoritarian Personality* (New York: Harper).

Alber, J. (2010), "What—if Anything—is Undermining the European Social Model?" *WZB Discussion Paper*, SP I 2010–202 (Berlin).

Albert, M. (2016), *A Theory of World Politics* (Cambridge: Cambridge University Press).

Albert, M., Buzan, B., and Zürn, M. (2013) (eds.), *Bringing Sociology to IR: World Politics as Differentiation Theory* (Cambridge: Cambridge University Press).

Alexander, J. C. (1990), "Differentiation Theory: Problems and Prospects," in J. C. Alexander and P. Colomy (eds.), *Differentiation Theory and Social Change. Comparative and Historical Perspectives* (New York: Columbia University Press), 1–15.

Almond, G. A., and Powell, G. B. (1978), *Comparative Politics: System, Process, and Policy* (2nd edn, Boston: Little Brown and Co).

References

Alter, K. J. (2009), *The European Court's Political Power: Selected Essays* (Oxford: Oxford University Press).

Alter, K. J. (2011), "The Evolving International Judiciary," *The Annual Review of Law and Social Science*, 7: 387–415.

Alter, K. J. (2014), *The New Terrain of International Law: Courts, Politics, Rights* (Princeton: Princeton University Press).

Alter, K. J., Helfer, L., and Madsen, M. (2016), "How Context Shapes the Authority of International Courts," *Law and Contemporary Problems*, 79/1: 1–36.

Alter, K. J., and Meunier, S. (2009), "The Politics of International Regime Complexity," *Perspectives on Politics*, 7/1: 13–24.

Ambrose, S. E. (1983), *Rise to Globalism. American Foreign Policy since 1938* (New York: Penguin).

Amin, S. (1988), *L'Eurocentrisme. Critique d'une Idéologie* (Paris: Anthropos/Economica).

Amnesty International (1994), *Peace-keeping and Human Rights*, AI Index: IOR 40/01/94 <https://www.amnesty.org/en/documents/IOR40/001/1994/en/>.

Amnesty International (2004), *The Apparent Lack of Accountability of International Peacekeeping Forces in Kosovo and Bosnia-Herzegovina*, AI Index: EUR 05/002/2004 <http://www.amnesty.org/en/library/info/EUR05/002/2004/en>.

Amnesty International (2007), *Sudan. Arms Continuing to Fuel Serious Human Rights Violations in Darfur*, AFR 54/019/2007 <http://www.amnesty.org/en/library/asset/AFR54/019/2007/en/dom-AFR540192007en.pdf>.

Anderson, B. (1983), *Imagined Communities: Reflections on the Origin and Spread of Nationalism* (London: Verso).

Anderson, C. J., and Pontusson, J. (2001), *Welfare States and Employment Insecurity: A Cross-National Analysis of 15 OECD Countries*, 2001 Annual Meeting of the American Political Science Association, 2001 (San Francisco).

Anderson, J. E. (1975), *Public Policy-Making* (New York: Praeger).

Archibugi, D. (2004), "Cosmopolitan Democracy and its Critics: A Review," *European Journal of International Relations*, 10/3: 437–73.

Armingeon, K., and Ceka, B. (2014), "The Loss of Trust in the European Union During the Great Recession Since 2007: The Role of Heuristics From the National Political System," *European Union Politics*, 15/1: 82–107.

Armitage, D. (2007), *The Declaration of Independence: A Global History* (Cambridge: Harvard University Press).

Arthur, B. (1994), *Increasing Returns and Path Dependence in the Economy* (Ann Arbor: University of Michigan Press).

Avant, D. D., Finnemore, M., and Sell, S. K. (2010), "Who Governs the Globe?," in D. D. Avant, M. Finnemore, and S. K. Sell (eds.), *Who Governs the Globe?* (New York: Cambridge University Press), 1–34.

Bachrach, P., and Baratz, M. S. (1962), "Two Faces of Power," *American Political Science Review*, 56/4: 947–52.

Baines, E. K. (2007), "The Haunting of Alice: Local Approaches to Justice and Reconciliation in Northern Uganda," *The International Journal of Transitional Justice*, 1: 91–114.

Baldwin, D. (1979), "Power Analysis and World Politics: New Trends versus Old Tendencies," *World Politics*, 31/2: 161–94.

Barker, R. (2001), *Legitimating Identities: The Self-Presentations of Rulers and Subjects* (Cambridge: Cambridge University Press).

Barnett, M. (2004), *Rules for the World: International Organizations in Global Politics* (Ithaca: Cornell University Press).

Barnett, M., and Duvall, R. (2005) (eds.), *Power in Global Governance* (Cambridge: Cambridge University Press).

Barnett, M., and Finnemore, M. (1999), "The Politics, Power, and Pathologies of International Organizations," *International Organization*, 53/4: 699–732.

Barro, R. J. (1996), *Getting it Right: Markets and Choices in a Free Society* (Cambridge: MIT Press).

Bartelson, J. (1995), *A Genealogy of Sovereignty* (Cambridge: Cambridge University Press).

Bartley, T. (2007), "Institutional Emergence in an Era of Globalization. The Rise of Transnational Private Regulation of Labor and Environmental Conditions," *American Journal of Sociology*, 113/2: 297–351.

Beck, S. (2012), "From Trust to Trust: Lessons Learned from 'Climategate'," in K. Hogl, E. Kvarda, R. Nordbeck, and M. Pregernig (eds.), *Environmental Governance: The Challenge of Legitimacy and Effectiveness* (Cheltenham: Edward Elgar), 220–41.

Beck, U. (1996), "Das Zeitalter der Nebenfolgen und die Politisierung der Moderne," in U. Beck, A. Giddens, and S. Lash (eds.), *Reflexive Modernisierung. Eine Kontroverse* (Frankfurt a.M.: Suhrkamp Verlag), 19–112.

Beetham, D. (1991), *The Legitimation of Power* (Atlantic Highlands: Humanities Press International).

Beisheim, M., Dreher, S., Walter, G., Zangl, B., and Zürn, M. (1999), *Im Zeitalter der Globalisierung? Thesen und Daten zur gesellschaftlichen und politischen Denationalisierung* (Baden-Baden: Nomos).

Beisheim, M., and Liese, A. (2014), *Transnational Partnerships: Effectively Providing for Sustainable Development?* (Basingstoke, New York: Palgrave Macmillan).

Beisheim, M., Liese, A., and Ulbert, C. (2008), "Transnationale öffentlich-private Partnerschaften—Bestimmungsfaktoren für die Effektivität ihrer Governance-Leistungen," in G. F. Schuppert and M. Zürn (eds.), *Governance in einer sich wandelnden Welt (Sonderheft 41 der Politischen Vierteljahresschrift)* (Wiesbaden: VS Verlag für Sozialwissenschaften), 452–74.

Beitz, C. R. (1979), "Bounded Morality: Justice and the State in World Politics," *International Organization*, 33/3: 405–24.

Beitz, C. R. (1994), "Cosmopolitan Liberalism and the States System," in C. Brown (ed.), *Political Restructuring in Europe: Ethical Perspectives* (London: Routledge), 123–36.

Beitz, C. R. (1999), "Social and Cosmopolitan Liberalism," *International Affairs*, 75/3: 515–29.

Beitz, C. R. (2009), *The Idea of Human Rights* (Oxford: Oxford University Press).

Bennett, A., and Checkel, J. T. (2015) (eds.), *Process Tracing: From Metaphor to Analytic Tool* (Cambridge: Cambridge University Press).

Benvenisti, E., and Downs, G. W. (2007), "The Empire's New Clothes: Political Economy and the Fragmentation of International Law," *Stanford Law Review*, 60/2: 595–632.

Bergh, A., and Karlsson, M. (2010), "Government Size and Growth: Accounting for Economic Freedom and Globalization," *Public Choice*, 142/1: 195–213.

Bernstein, S. (2011), "Legitimacy in Intergovernmental and Non-State Global Governance," *Review of International Political Economy*, 18/1: 17–51.

Bernstein, S. (2014), "The Publicness of Non-State Global Environmental and Social Governance," in A. Gheciu and J. Best (eds.), *The Return of the Public in Global Governance* (Cambridge: Cambridge University Press), 120–48.

Bhagwati, J. N. (1977) (ed.), *The New International Economic Order: the North–South Debate* (Cambridge: MIT Press).

Bhaskar, R. (1978), *A Realist Theory of Science* (Hassocks, Sussex: Harvester).

Biermann, F., and Siebenhüner, B. (2009), *Managers of Global Change: The Influence of International Environmental Bureaucracies* (Cambridge: MIT Press).

Biersteker, T. J., and Hall, R. B. (2002) (eds.), *The Emergence of Private Authority in Global Governance* (Cambridge: Cambridge University Press).

Binder, M. (2009), "Humanitarian Crises and the International Politics of Selectivity," *Human Rights Review*, 10/3: 327–48.

Binder, M. (2013), "Die Politisierung internationaler Sicherheitsinstitutionen? Der UN-Sicherheitsrat und NGOs," in M. Zürn and M. Ecker-Ehrhardt (eds.), *Die Politisierung der Weltpolitik: Umkämpfte internationale Institutionen* (Berlin: Suhrkamp), 134–57.

Binder, M. (2017), *The United Nations and the Politics of Selective Humanitarian Intervention* (Palgrave Macmillan).

Binder, M., and Eisentraut, S. (2018, in preparation), "Negotiating the UN Human Rights Council. Rising Powers, Established Powers and NGOs," in M. D. Stephen and M. Zürn (eds.), *Contested World Orders: Rising Powers, Non-Governmental Organizations and the Politics of Authority Beyond the Nation-state.*

Binder, M., and Heupel, M. (2015), "The Legitimacy of the UN Security Council. Evidence from Recent General Assembly Debates," *International Studies Quarterly*, 59/2: 238–50.

Binder, M., and Lockwood Payton, A. (2018, in preparation), "Cleavages in World Politics. An Analysis of Rising Power Voting Behavior in the UN General Assembly," in M. D. Stephen and M. Zürn (eds.), *Contested World Orders: Rising Powers, Non-Governmental Organizations and the Politics of Authority Beyond the Nation-state.*

Black, J. (2017), "'Says Who?' Liquid Authority and Interpretive Control in Transnational Regulatory Regimes," *International Theory*, 9/2: 286–310.

Blake, D., and Payton, A. (2008), *Voting Rules in International Organizations: Reflections of Power or Facilitators of Cooperation?*, ISA's 49th Annual Convention, 2008 (San Francisco, CA).

Bodansky, D. (2013), "Legitimacy in International Law and International Relations," in J. L. Dunoff and M. A. Pollack (eds.), *Interdisciplinary Perspectives on International Law and International Relations: The State of the Art* (Cambridge: Cambridge University Press), 321–44.

Bothe, M., and Marauhn, T. (2000), "The United Nations in Kosovo and East Timor—Problems of a Trusteeship Administration," *Journal of International Peacekeeping*, 6/4–6: 152–6.

Botzem, S. (2012), *The Politics of Accounting Regulation: Organizing Transnational Standard Setting in Financial Reporting* (Cheltenham/Northampton: Edward Elgar Publishing).

Bourdieu, P. (1990), *The Logic of Practice* (Stanford: Stanford University Press).

Bourdieu, P. (1991), *Language and Symbolic Power* (Cambridge: Polity Press).

Bradley, C. A., and Kelley, J. (2008), "The Concept of International Delegation," *Law and Contemporary Problems*, 71/1: 1–36.

Brassett, J., and Tsingou, E. (2011), "The Politics of Legitimate Global Governance," *Review of International Political Economy*, 18/1: 1–16.

Breitmeier, H., Young, O. R., and Zürn, M. (2006), *Analyzing International Environmental Regimes. From Case Study to Database* (Cambridge: MIT Press).

Breuilly, J. (1994), *Nationalism and the State* (2nd edn, Chicago: The University of Chicago Press).

Brown, C. (1992), *International Relations Theory: New Normative Approaches* (Brighton: Harvester Wheatsheaf).

Brozus, L. (2002), *Globale Konflikte oder Global Governance? Kontinuität und Wandel globaler Konfliktlinien nach dem Ost-West-Konflikt* (Wiesbaden: VS Verlag).

Buchanan, A., and Keohane, R. O. (2006), "The Legitimacy of Global Governance Institutions," *Ethics & International Affairs*, 20/4: 405–37.

Bull, H. (1977), *The Anarchical Society. A Study of Order in World Politics* (Basingstoke/London: MacMillan).

Bunge, M. (1997), "Mechanism and Explanation," *Philosophy of the Social Sciences*, 27/4: 410–65.

Burgoon, B. (2009), "Globalization and Backlash: Polanyi's Revenge?," *Review of International Political Economy*, 15/2: 145–78.

Busemeyer, M. R. (2009), "From Myth to Reality: Globalization and Public Spending in OECD Countries Revisited," *European Journal of Political Research*, 48/4: 455–82.

Bush, George H. W. (1991), *Address before a Joint Session of Congress on the End of the Gulf War*, March 6, 1991.

Büthe, T. (2002), "Taking Temporality Seriously: Modeling History and the Use of Narratives as Evidence," *American Political Science Review*, 96/3: 481–93.

Büthe, T., and Mattli, W. (2011), *The New Global Rulers: The Privatization of Regulation in the World Economy* (Princeton: Princeton University Press).

Butler, J. P. (1996), *Excitable Speech: A Politics of the Performative* (New York: Routledge).

Buzan, B. (2004), *From International to World Society? English School Theory and the Social Structure of Globalisation* (Cambridge: Cambridge University Press).

Buzan, B. (2010), "Culture and International Society," *International Affairs*, 86/1: 1–25.

Buzan, B., Waever, O., and Wilde, J. de (1998), *Security: A New Framework for Analysis* (Boulder: Lynne Rienner).

BVerfG (2009), "2 BvE 2/08, June 30, Absatz-Nr. (1 - 421)" <http://www.bverfg.de/entscheidungen/es20090630_2bve000208.html>.

Calhoun, C. (2003), "The Class Consciousness of Frequent Travellers: Towards a Critique of Actually Existing Cosmopolitanism," in D. Archibugi (ed.), *Debating Cosmopolitics* (London: Verso), 86–116.

Caney, S. (2005), *Justice Beyond Borders: A Global Political Theory* (Oxford: Oxford University Press).

Caplan, R. D. (2004), "International Authority and State Building. The Case of Bosnia and Herzegovina," *Global Governance*, 10/1: 53–65.

Capoccia, G., and Kelemen, R. D. (2007), "The Study of Critical Junctures: Theory, Narrative, and Counterfactuals in Historical Institutionalism," *World Politics*, 59/3: 341–69.

Carlsnaes, W. (1992), "The Agent-Structure Debate in Foreign Policy Analysis," *International Studies Quarterly*, 36/3: 245–70.

Carothers, T. (2006), "The Rule-of-Law Revival," in T. Carothers (ed.), *Promoting the Rule of Law Abroad: In Search of Knowledge* (Washington: Carnegie Endowment for International Peace), 3–14.

Carr, E. H. (1964), *The Twenty Years' Crisis 1919–1939: An Introduction to the Study of International Relations* (New York: Harper Perennial).

Chakrabarty, D. (2000), *Provincializing Europe: Postcolonial Thought and Historical Difference* (Princeton: Princeton University Press).

Chakravartty, A. (2007), *A Metaphysics for Scientific Realism: Knowing the Unobservable* (Cambridge: Cambridge University Press).

Chalmers, A. W., and Dellmuth, L. M. (2015), "Fiscal Redistribution and Public Support for European Integration," *European Union Politics*, 16/3: 386–407.

Checkel, J. T. (2005), "International Institutions and Socialization in Europe: Introduction and Framework," *International Organization*, 59/4: 801–26.

Checkel, J. T. (2006), "Tracing Causal Mechanisms," *International Studies Review*, 8/2: 362–70.

Chesterman, S. (2004), *You, the People. The United Nations, Transitional Administration, and State-Building* (Oxford: Oxford University Press).

Chesterman, S. (2008), "An International Rule of Law?," *American Journal of Comparative Law*, 56/2: 331–62.

Cho, S. (2010), "The Demise of Development in the Doha Round Negotiations," *Texas International Law Journal*, 45: 573–601.

Chorev, N. (2012), *The World Health Organization between North and South* (Ithaca: Cornell University Press).

Christiano, T. (2012), "Is Democratic Legitimacy Possible for International Institutions?," in D. Archibugi, M. Koenig-Archibugi, and R. Marchetti (eds.), *Global Democracy: Normative and Empirical Perspectives* (Cambridge: Cambridge University Press), 69–95.

Clark, I. (2005), *Legitimacy in International Society* (Oxford: Oxford University Press).

Clarke, K. M. (2007), "Global Justice, Local Controversies: The International Criminal Court and the Sovereignty of Victims," in M.-B. Dembour and T. Kelly (eds.), *Paths to International Justice: Social and Legal Perspectives* (New York: Cambridge University Press), 134–60.

Claude, I. L. (1966), "Collective Legitimization as a Political Function of the United Nations," *International Organization*, 20/3: 367–79.

Coen, D., and Pegram, T. (2015), "Wanted: A Third Generation of Global Governance Research," *Governance*, 28/4: 417–20.

Coleman, J. S. (1990), *The Foundations of Social Theory* (Cambridge: Cambridge University Press).

Commission on Global Governance (1995), *Our Global Neighbourhood* (Oxford: Oxford University Press).

Coni-Zimmer, M., Flohr, A., and Wolf, K. D. (2018, in preparation), "Transnational Private Authority and its Contestation," in M. D. Stephen and M. Zürn (eds.), *Contested World Orders: Rising Powers, Non-Governmental Organizations and the Politics of Authority Beyond the Nation-state*.

Cooley, A. (2005), *Logics of Hierarchy: The Organization of Empires, States, and Military Occupations* (Ithaca: Cornell University Press).

Cooper, A. F. (2002), "Like-minded Nations, NGOs and the Changing Pattern of Diplomacy within the UN System. An Introductory Perspective," in A. F. Cooper, J. English, and R. C. Thakur (eds.), *Enhancing Global Governance. Towards a New Diplomacy?* (Tokyo: United Nations University Press), 1–18.

Cooper, A. F. (2008), *Celebrity Diplomacy* (Boulder: Paradigm Publishers).

Cooper, S., Hawkins, D. G., Jacoby, W., and Nielson, D. (2008), "Yielding Sovereignty to International Institutions: Bringing System Structure Back In," *International Studies Review*, 10/3: 501–24.

Corbey, D. (1995), "Dialectical Functionalism: Stagnation as a Booster of European Integration," *International Organization*, 49/2: 253–84.

Council of Europe (2002), *Kosovo: The Human Rights Situation and the Fate of Persons Displaced from their Homes. Report by Alvaro Gil-Robles, Commissioner for Human Rights for the Attention of the Parliamentary Assembly and the Committee of Ministers of the Council of Europe*, CommDH(2002)11 <https://wcd.coe.int/ViewDoc.jsp?id=982119&-Site=COE>.

Court of First Instance (2006), "Organisation des Modjahedines du Peuple d'Iran v. Council of the European Union [2006]" ECR II-4665.

Cox, R. W. (1979), "Ideologies and the New International Economic Order: Reflections on Some Recent Literature," *International Organization*, 33/2: 257–302.

Cox, R. W. (1987), *Production, Power, and World Order. Social Forces in the Making of History* (New York: Columbia University Press).

Cueto, M. (2004), "The Origins of Primary Health Care and Selective Primary Health Care," *American Journal of Public Health*, 94/11: 1864–74.

Culpepper, P. D. (2011), *Quiet Politics and Business Power: Corporate Control in Europe and Japan* (Cambridge, New York: Cambridge University Press).

Daalder, I. H. (1991), *The Nature and Practice of Flexible Response: NATO Strategy and Theater Nuclear Forces Since 1967* (New York: Columbia University Press).

Daase, C., and Deitelhoff, N. (2015), "Jenseits der Anarchie. Widerstand und Herrschaft im internationalen System," *Politische Vierteljahresschrift*, 56/2: 299–318.

Dahl, R. A. (1989), *Democracy and its Critics* (New Haven: Yale University Press).

Dahl, R. A. (2005), "Is International Democracy Possible?," in S. Fabbrini (ed.), *Democracy and Federalism in the European Union and the United States: Exploring Post-national Governance* (London: Routledge), 194–204.

Dai, X. (2007), *International Institutions and National Policies* (Cambridge: Cambridge University Press).

Dai, X., and Tokhi, A. (2015), "Depth, Participation, and International Human Rights Agreements," *Paper presented at the American Political Science Association, San Francisco, September 3–6*.

Daniels, N. (2011), "Reflective Equilibrium" <http://plato.stanford.edu/entries/reflective-equilibrium/>.

David, P. A. (1985), "Clio and the Economics of QWERTY," *The American Economic Review*, 75: 332–7.

David, P. A. (2007), "Path Dependence: a Foundational Concept for Historical Social Science," *Cliometrica*, 1/2: 91–114.

de Wilde, P., Junk, W. M., and Palmtag, T. (2016a), "Accountability and Opposition to Globalization in International Assemblies," *European Journal of International Relations*, 22/4: 823–46.

de Wilde, P., Koopmans, R., Strijbis, O., Wessels, B., and Zürn, M. (2018, in preparation) (eds.), *Struggle over Borders: The Political Sociology of Cosmopolitanism and Communitarianism*.

de Wilde, P., Koopmans, R., and Zürn, M. (2014), "The Political Sociology of Cosmopolitanism and Communitarianism: Representative Claims Analysis," *WZB Discussion Paper*, SP IV 2014-102 (Berlin).

de Wilde, P., Leupold, A., and Schmidtke, H. (2016b), "Introduction. The Differentiated Politicisation of European Governance," *West European Politics*, 39/1: 3–22.

de Wilde, P., and Zürn, M. (2012), "Can the Politicization of European Integration Be Reversed?," *Journal of Common Market Studies*, 50/S1: 137–53.

Deitelhoff, N. (2006), *Überzeugung in der Politik: Grundzüge einer Diskurstheorie internationalen Regierens* (Frankfurt a.M.: Suhrkamp).

Deitelhoff, N. (2009), "The Discursive Process of Legalization: Charting Islands of Persuasion in the ICC Case," *International Organization*, 63/1: 33–65.

Deitelhoff, N., and Müller, H. (2005), "Theoretical Paradise—Empirically Lost? Arguing with Habermas," *Review of International Studies*, 31/1: 167–79.

Deitelhoff, N., and Zürn, M. (2016), *Lehrbuch der Internationalen Beziehungen: Per Anhalter durch die IB-Galaxis* (München: C.H.Beck).

della Porta, D. (2007), *The Global Justice Movement: Cross-national and Transnational Perspectives* (Boulder: Paradigm).

della Porta, D. (2011), *"Transnational Social Movements and the Politicization of International Politics," WZB Discussion Paper* SP IV 2012-301 (Berlin).

della Porta, D., and Caiani, M. (2009), *Social Movements and Europeanization* (Oxford: Oxford University Press).

della Porta, D., and Tarrow, S. (2005), "Transnational Processes and Social Activism: An Introduction," in D. della Porta and S. Tarrow (eds.), *Transnational Protest and Global Activism* (Lanham: Rowman & Littlefield).

della Porta, D., and Tarrow, S. (2012), "Interactive Diffusion. The Coevolution of Police and Protest Behavior With an Application to Transnational Contention," *Comparative Political Studies*, 45/1: 119–52.

Dellmuth, L. M., and Tallberg, J. (2015), "The Social Legitimacy of International Organisations. Interest Representation, Institutional Performance, and Confidence Extrapolation in the United Nations," *Review of International Studies*, 41/3: 451–75.

Dellmuth, L. M., and Tallberg, J. (2018, in preparation), "Elite Communication and Popular Legitimacy in Global Governance."

Deutsch, K. W., Burrell, S. A., Kann, R. A., Lee, M., Lichtermann, M., Lindgren, R. E., Loewenheim, F. L., and van Wagenen, R. W. (1957), *Political Community and the North*

Atlantic Area: International Organization in the Light of Historical Experience (Princeton: Princeton University Press).

Dingwerth, K., Schmidtke, H., and Weise, T. (2018, in preparation), "Speaking Democracy: Why International Organizations Adopt a Democratic Rhetoric."

Down, I., and Wilson, C. (2008), "From Permissive Consensus to Constraining Dissensus. A Polarizing Union?," *Acta Politica*, 43/1: 26–49.

Doyle, M. W. (1986), *Empires* (Ithaca: Cornell University Press).

Dreher, A., Sturm, J.-E., and Ursprung, H. W. (2008), "The Impact of Globalization on the Composition of Government Expenditures: Evidence from Panel Data," *Public Choice*, 134/3–4: 263–92.

Drezner, D. W. (2011), "Sanctions Sometimes Smart. Targeted Sanctions in Theory and Practice," *International Studies Review*, 13/1: 96–108.

Drezner, D. W. (2013), "The Tragedy of the Global Institutional Commons," in M. Finnemore and J. Goldstein (eds.), *Back to Basics: State Power in a Contemporary World* (Oxford: Oxford University Press), 280–310.

Dryzek, J. S. (2006), *Deliberative Global Politics* (Cambridge: Polity Press).

Dryzek, J. S. (2008), "Two Paths to Global Democracy," *Ethical Perspectives*, 15/4: 469–86.

Dryzek, J. S., Bächtinger, A., and Milewicz, K. (2011), "Toward a Deliberative Global Citizens' Assembly," *Global Public Policy*, 2/1: 33–42.

Durkheim, É. (2012), "The Division of Labor in Society," in G. Simpson (ed.), *Émile Durkheim. The Division of Labor in Society* (Mansfield: Martino), first pub. 1883.

Eagleton-Pierce, M. (2014), "The Concept of Governance in the Spirit of Capitalism," *Critical Policy Studies*, 8/1: 5–21.

Easton, D. (1953), *The Political System: An Inquiry into the State of Political Science* (New York: Knopf).

Ecker-Ehrhardt, M. (2010), "Aid Organizations, Governments and the Media: The Critical Role of Journalists in Signaling Authority Recognition," in S. Koch-Baumgarten and K. Voltmer (eds.), *Public Policy and the Mass Media: The Interplay of Mass Communication and Political Decision Making* (London: Routledge), 106–24.

Ecker-Ehrhardt, M. (2017), "Self-Legitimation in the Face of Politicization: Why International Organizations Centralize Public Communication," *Review of International Organizations*, <https://doi.org/10.1007/s11558-017-9287-y>.

Ecker-Ehrhardt, M., and Weßels, B. (2013), "Input- oder Output-Politisierung internationaler Organisationen? Der kritische Blick der Bürger auf Demokratie und Leistung," in M. Zürn and M. Ecker-Ehrhardt (eds.), *Die Politisierung der Weltpolitik: Umkämpfte internationale Institutionen* (Berlin: Suhrkamp), 36–60.

Ecker-Ehrhardt, M., and Zürn, M. (2013), "Die Politisierung der Weltpolitik," in M. Zürn and M. Ecker-Ehrhardt (eds.), *Die Politisierung der Weltpolitik: Umkämpfte internationale Institutionen* (Berlin: Suhrkamp), 335–67.

Eckersley, R. (2007), "A Green Public Sphere in the WTO? The Amicus Curiae Interventions in the Transatlantic Biotech Dispute," *European Journal of International Relations*, 13/3: 329–56.

Eckstein, H. (1973), "Authority Patterns. A Structural Basis for Political Inquiry," *American Political Science Review*, 67: 1142–61.

Eisentraut, S. (2013), "Autokratien, Demokratien und die Legitimität internationaler Organisationen. Eine vergleichende Inhaltsanalyse staatlicher Legitimationsanforderungen an die UN-Generalversammlung," *Zeitschrift für Internationale Beziehungen*, 20/3: 3–33.

Elias, N. (1976), *Über den Prozeß der Zivilisation. Soziogenetische und psychogenetische Untersuchungen* (26th edn, Frankfurt a.M.: Suhrkamp).

Elkins, Z., Guzman, A. T., and Simmons, B. A. (2006), "Competing for Capital: The Diffusion of Bilateral Investment Treaties, 1960–2000," *International Organization*, 60/4: 811–46.

Elster, J. (1985), *Making Sense of Marx* (Cambridge, New York, Paris: Cambridge University Press).

Elster, J. (1986), *Ulysses and the Sirens: Studies in Rationality and Irrationality* (Rev. edn, Cambridge: Cambridge University Press).

Elster, J. (1995), "Strategic Uses of Arguments," in K. J. Arrow, R. H. Mnookin, L. Ross, and A. Tversky (eds.), *Barriers to Conflict Resolution* (New York: W.W. Norton), 236–57.

Elster, J. (1999), "Arguing and Bargaining in Two Constituent Assemblies," *University of Pennsylvania Journal of Constitutional Law*, 2: 345.

Enoch, D. (2014), "Authority and Reason-Giving," *Philosophy and Phenomenological Research*, 89/2: 296–332.

Eriksson, M. (2009), *In Search of a Due Process: Listing and Delisting Practices in the European Union* (Uppsala, Sweden, New York: Dept. of Peace and Conflict Resolution, Uppsala University; Mediation Support Unit, Dept. of Political Affairs, United Nations).

Esping-Andersen, G. (1990), *The Three Worlds of Welfare Capitalism* (Princeton: Princeton University Press).

Eurobarometer (2007), "Standard Eurobarometer 66. Public Opinion in the European Union/ Autumn 2006—TNS Opinion & Social" <http://ec.europa.eu/public_opinion/archives/eb/eb66/eb66_en.pdf>.

Eurobarometer (2015a), "Standard Eurobarometer (05/2015)" <http://ec.europa.eu/COMMFrontOffice/publicopinion/index.cfm/Chart/getChart/themeKy/41/groupKy/206>.

Eurobarometer (2015b), "Standard Eurobarometer (11/2015)" <http://ec.europa.eu/COMMFrontOffice/publicopinion/index.cfm/Chart/getChart/themeKy/26/groupKy/159>.

Eurobarometer (2016a), "Standard Eurobarometer (05/2016)" <http://ec.europa.eu/COMMFrontOffice/publicopinion/index.cfm/Chart/getChart/themeKy/50/groupKy/263>.

Eurobarometer (2016b), "Standard Eurobarometer (05/2016)" <http://ec.europa.eu/COMMFrontOffice/publicopinion/index.cfm/Chart/getChart/themeKy/19/groupKy/102>.

European Court of Justice (2008), "Yassin Abdullah Kadi and Al Barakaat International Foundation v. Council and Commission." Joined Cases C-402/05 P and C-415/05 P, 3 September 2008, *ECR I-6351*.

Fanon, F. (1961), *Les damnés de la terre* (Paris: Éditions Maspero).

Faude, B., and Parizek, M. (2018, in preparation), "'Contested Multilateralism' as Credible Signaling: How Strategic Inconsistency Can Induce Cooperation among States."

Faude, B., and Stephen, M. D. (2016), "After Western Hegemony: Rising Powers and International Institutional Change," *Working paper presented at the 112th APSA Annual Meeting & Exhibition in Philadelphia.*

Finkelstein, L. (1995), "What Is Global Governance?," *Global Governance*, 3/1: 367–72.

Finnemore, M. (1996), "Norms, Culture, and World Politics: Insights from Sociology's Institutionalism," *International Organization*, 50/2: 325–47.

Fioretos, O. (2011), "Historical Institutionalism in International Relations," *International Organization*, 65/2: 367–99.

Fioretos, O. (2016), "Retrofitting Financial Globalization: The Politics of Intense Incrementalism after 2008," in T. Rixen, L. A. Viola, and M. Zürn (eds.), *Historical Institutionalism and International Relations. Explaining Institutional Development in World Politics* (Oxford: Oxford University Press), 68–95.

Fioretos, O. (2017) (ed.), *International Politics and Institutions in Time* (Oxford, New York: Oxford University Press).

Fischer-Lescano, A., and Teubner, G. (2004), "Regime-Collisions: The Vain Search for Legal Unity in the Fragmentation of Global Law," *Michigan Journal of International Law*, 25: 999–1046.

Fischer-Lescano, A. (2006), *Regime-Kollisionen: Zur Fragmentierung des globalen Rechts* (Frankfurt a. M.: Suhrkamp).

Flemes, D. (2013), "Network Powers: Strategies of Change in the Multipolar System," *Third World Quarterly*, 34/6: 1016–36.

Follesdal, A. (1998), "Survey Article: Subsidiarity," *The Journal of Political Philosophy*, 6/2: 190–218.

Follesdal, A. (2012), "Global Distributive Justice? State Boundaries as a Normative Problem," *Global Constitutionalism*, 1/02: 261–77.

Follesdal, A., and Hix, S. (2006), "Why There is a Democratic Deficit in the EU. A Response to Majone and Moravcsik," *Journal of Common Market Studies*, 44/3: 533–62.

Ford, C. E., and Oppenheim, B. A. (2008), "Neotrusteeship or Mistrusteeship? The 'Authority Creep' Dilemma in United Nations Transitional Administration," *Vanderbilt Journal of Transnational Law*, 41/1: 55–105.

Forst, R. (1994), *Kontexte der Gerechtigkeit: Politische Philosophie jenseits von Liberalismus und Kommunitarismus* (Frankfurt a.M.: Suhrkamp).

Forst, R. (2001), "Towards a Critical Theory of Transnational Justice," *Metaphilosophy*, 32/1/2: 160–79.

Forst, R. (2010), "The Justification of Human Rights and the Basic Right to Justification: A Reflexive Approach," *Ethics*, 120/4: 711–40.

Forst, R. (2011), *The Right to Justification: Elements of a Constructivist Theory of Justice* (New York: Columbia University Press).

Forst, R. (2015), *Normativität und Macht: Zur Analyse sozialer Rechtfertigungsordnungen* (Berlin: Suhrkamp).

Forsythe, D. P. (1988), *Human Rights and U.S. Foreign Policy: Congress Reconsidered* (Gainesville: University Presses of Florida).

Foucault, M. (1982), *The Archaeology of Knowledge* (New York: Pantheon Books).

Franck, T. (1990), *The Power of Legitimacy Among Nations* (Oxford: Oxford University Press).

Franck, T. M. (1992), "The Emerging Right to Democratic Governance," *American Journal of International Law*, 86/1: 46–91.

Fraser, N. (2009), *Scales of Justice: Reimagining Political Space in a Globalizing World* (New York: Columbia University Press).

Frieden, J. A. (1999), "Actors and Preferences in International Relations," in D. Lake and R. Powell (eds.), *Strategic Choice and International Relations* (Princeton: Princeton University Press), 39–76.

Furedi, F. (2013), *Authority: A Sociological History* (Cambridge, New York: Cambridge University Press).

Furia, P. A. (2005), "Global Citizenship, Anyone? Cosmopolitanism, Privilege and Public Opinion," *Global Society*, 19/4: 331–59.

Gabel, M. (1998), *Interests and Integration: Market Liberalization, Public Opinion, and European Union* (Ann Arbor: University of Michigan Press).

Galtung, J. (1964), "A Structural Theory of Aggression," *Journal of Peace Research*, 1/2: 95–119.

Galtung, J. (1972), "Eine strukturelle Theorie des Imperialismus," in D. Senghaas (ed.), *Imperialismus und strukturelle Gewalt. Analysen über abhängige Produktion* (Frankfurt a. M.: Suhrkamp), 29–104.

Garrett, G. (1998), "Global Markets and National Politics: Collision Course or Virtuous Circle?," *International Organization*, 52/4: 787–824.

Gaus, D. (2013), "Rational Reconstruction as a Method of Political Theory between Social Critique and Empirical Political Science," *Constellations*, 20/4: 553–70.

Gehring, T., and Faude, B. (2014), "A Theory of Emerging Order Within Institutional Complexes: How Competition Among Regulatory International Institutions Leads to Institutional Adaptation and Division of Labor," *Review of International Organizations*, 9/4: 471–98.

Geis, A., Nullmeier, F., and Daase, C. (2012) (eds.), *Der Aufstieg der Legitimitätspolitik. Rechtfertigung und Kritik politisch-ökonomischer Ordnungen (Leviathan Sonderband 40/27)* (Baden-Baden: Nomos).

Gellner, E. (1983), *Nations and Nationalism* (Oxford: Blackwell).

Genschel, P. (2014), "State Transformations in OECD Countries," *Annual Review of Political Science*, 17/1: 337–54.

Genschel, P., and Jachtenfuchs, M. (2014), *Beyond the Regulatory Polity? The European Integration of Core State Powers* (Oxford: Oxford University Press).

Genschel, P., and Zangl, B. (2008), "Metamorphosen des Staates: Vom Herrschaftsmonopolisten zum Herrschaftsmanager," *Leviathan*, 36/3: 430–54.

George, A. L., and Bennett, A. (2005), *Case Studies and Theory Development in the Social Sciences* (Cambridge: MIT Press).

Gerhards, J., Offerhaus, A., and Roose, J. (2009), "Wer ist verantwortlich? Die Europäische Union, ihre Nationalstaaten und die massenmediale Attribution von Verantwortung für Erfolge und Misserfolge," in F. Marcinkowski and B. Pfetsch (eds.), *Politik in der Mediendemokratie (Sonderheft 42 der Politische Vierteljahresschrift)* (Wiesbaden: VS Verlag für Sozialwissenschaften), 529–58.

Gerring, J. (2008), "Review Article: The Mechanismic Worldview: Thinking Inside the Box," *British Journal of Political Science*, 38/1: 161–79.

Gerschenkron, A. (1962), *Economic Backwardness in Historical Perspective: A Book of Essays* (Cambridge: Belknap Press).

Giddens, A. (1985), *The Nation State and Violence. Volume II of a Contemporary Critique of Historical Materialism* (Berkeley: University of California Press).

Gilpin, R. (1981), *War and Change in World Politics* (Cambridge: Cambridge University Press).

Gilpin, R. (1988), "The Theory of Hegemonic War," *Journal of Interdisciplinary History*, 18/4: 591–613.

Glasius, M. (2008), "Global Justice Meets Local Civil Society: The International Criminal Court's Investigation in the Central African Republic," *Alternatives*, 33: 413–33.

Godlee, F. (1994), "WHO in Crisis," *British Medical Journal*, 309/6966: 1424–8.

Goertz, G., and Powers, K. (2014), "Regional Governance. The Evolution of a New Institutional Form," *WZB Discussion Paper*, SP IV 2014-106 (Berlin).

Goldmann, M. (2015), *Internationale öffentliche Gewalt: Handlungsformen internationaler Institutionen im Zeitalter der Globalisierung* (Heidelberg: Springer).

Goldstein, J., and Gulotty, R. (2017), "The Limits of Institutional Reform in the United States and the Global Trade Regime," in O. Fioretos (ed.), *International Politics and Institutions in Time* (Oxford, New York: Oxford University Press), 196–217.

Goldstein, J., Kahler, M., Keohane, R. O., and Slaughter, A.-M. (2001) (eds.), *Legalization and World Politics* (Cambridge: MIT Press).

Goldstein, J., and Martin, L. L. (2000), "Legalization, Trade Liberalization, and Domestic Politics: A Cautionary Note," *International Organization*, 54/3: 603–32.

Goodin, R. E. (2010), "Global Democracy: in the Beginning," *International Theory*, 2/02: 175–209.

Gourevitch, P. (1978), "The Second Image Reversed: The International Sources of Domestic Politics," *International Organization*, 32/04: 881–912.

Grande, E., and Hutter, S. (2016), "Beyond Authority Transfer. Explaining the Politicisation of Europe," *West European Politics*, 39/1: 23–43.

Grande, E., and Kriesi, H. (2013), "Das Doppelgesicht der Politisierung. Zur Transformation politischer Konfliktstrukturen im Prozess der Globalisierung," in M. Zürn and M. Ecker-Ehrhardt (eds.), *Die Politisierung der Weltpolitik: Umkämpfte internationale Institutionen* (Berlin: Suhrkamp), 84–108.

Grande, E., and Pauly, L. W. (2005) (eds.), *Complex Sovereignty: Reconstituting Political Authority in the Twenty-first Century* (Toronto: University of Toronto Press).

Grant, R. W., and Keohane, R. O. (2005), "Accountability and Abuses of Power in World Politics," *American Political Science Review*, 99/1: 29–43.

Gray, K., and Murphy, C. N. (2013), "Introduction: Rising Powers and the Future of Global Governance," *Third World Quarterly*, 34/2: 183–93.

Green, J. F. (2014), *Rethinking Private Authority: Agents and Entrepreneurs in Global Environmental Governance* (Princeton: Princeton University Press).

Green, J. F., and Colgan, J. (2013), "Protecting Sovereignty, Protecting the Planet: State Delegation to International Organizations and Private Actors in Environmental Politics," *Governance*, 26/3: 473–97.

Greenpeace International (2006), "Greenpeace New Study Reveals Death Toll of Chernobyl Enormously Underestimated" <http://www.greenpeace.org/international/en/press/releases/greenpeace-new-study-reveals-d/>.

Greif, A., and Laitin, D. D. (2004), "A Theory of Endogenous Institutional Change," *American Political Science Review*, 98/4: 633–52.

Greven, M. T. (1999), *Die politische Gesellschaft. Kontingenz und Dezision als Probleme des Regierens und der Demokratie* (Opladen: Leske + Budrich).

Grimm, D. (2012), *Die Zukunft der Verfassung II: Auswirkungen von Europäisierung und Globalisierung* (Berlin: Suhrkamp).

Grimmer, J., and Stewart, B. (2013), "Text as Data: The Promise and Pitfalls of Automatic Content Analysis Methods for Political Texts," *Political Analysis*, 21/3: 267–97.

Gronau, J. (2015), *Die Selbstlegitimation internationaler Institutionen: G8 und G20 im Vergleich* (Frankfurt a.M.: Campus-Verlag).

Gronau, J., Nonhoff, M., Schneider, S., and Nullmeier, F. (2009), "Spiele ohne Brot? Die Legitimationskrise der G8," *Leviathan*, 37/1: 117–43.

Gu, J., Humphrey, J., and Messner, D. (2008), "Global Governance and Developing Countries: The Implications of the Rise of China," *World Development*, 36/2: 274–92.

Guild, E. (2008), "The Uses and Abuses of Counter-Terrorism Policies in Europe: The Case of the 'Terrorist Lists'," *Journal of Common Market Studies*, 46/1: 173–93.

Haas, E. B. (1958), *The Uniting of Europe: Political, Social, and Economic Forces 1950–1957* (Stanford: Stanford University Press).

Haas, E. B. (1964), *Beyond the Nation-State. Functionalism and International Organization* (Stanford: Stanford University Press).

Haas, E. B. (1990), *When Knowledge is Power: Three Models of Change in International Organizations* (Berkeley: University of California Press).

Haas, P. M. (1992), "Introduction: Epistemic Communities and International Policy Coordination," *International Organization*, 46/1: 1–35.

Haas, P. M., and Haas, E. B. (1995), "Learning to Learn: Improving International Governance," *Global Governance*, 1/3: 255–84.

Haas, P. M., Keohane, R. O., and Levy, M. A. (1993), "The Effectiveness of International Environmental Institutions," in P. M. Haas, R. O. Keohane, and M. A. Levy (eds.), *Institutions for the Earth: Sources of Effective International Environmental Protection* (Cambridge: MIT Press), 3–24.

Habermas, J. (1985), *The Theory of Communicative Action. Reason and the Rationalization of Society* (Boston: Beacon Press).

Habermas, J. (1996), *Between Facts and Norms: Contributions to a Discourse Theory of Law and Democracy* (Cambridge: MIT Press).

Habermas, J. (2007), "Kommunikative Rationalität und grenzüberschreitende Politik: eine Replik," in P. Niesen and B. Herborth (eds.), *Anarchie der kommunikativen Freiheit—Jürgen Habermas und die Theorie der internationalen Politik* (Frankfurt a.M.: Suhrkamp), 406–59.

Habermas, J. (2010), "Das utopische Gefälle: Das Konzept der Menschenwürde und die realistische Utopie der Menschenrechte," *Blätter für Deutsche und Internationale Politik*, 8: 43–53.

Hadden, J. L. (2015), *Networks in Contention: The Divisive Politics of Climate Change* (New York: Cambridge University Press).

Hafner-Burton, E. M., Kahler, M., and Montgomery, A. H. (2009), "Network Analysis for International Relations," *International Organization*, 63/3: 559–92.

Haftel, Y. Z., and Thompson, A. (2006), "The Independence of International Organizations: Concepts and Applications," *Journal of Conflict Resolution*, 50/2: 253–75.

Haftendorn, H., Keohane, R. O., and Wallander, C. A. (1999) (eds.), *Imperfect Unions: Security Institutions Over Time and Space* (Oxford, New York: Oxford University Press).

Halberstam, D. (2009), "Local, Global, And Plural Constitutionalism: Europe Meets The World," *Public Law and Legal Theory Working Paper* No. 176.

Hale, T., and Held, D. (2011) (eds.), *Handbook of Transnational Governance: Institutions and Innovations* (Cambridge, Malden: Polity).

Hale, T., Held, D., and Young, K. (2013), *Gridlock. Why Global Cooperation is Failing When We Need it Most* (Cambridge: Polity Press).

Hall, P. A., and Soskice, D. (2001), *Varieties of Capitalism. The Institutional Foundations of Comparative Advantage* (Oxford: Oxford University Press).

Hall, P. A., and Taylor, R. C. R. (1996), "Political Science and the Three New Institutionalisms," *Political Studies*, 44/5: 936–57.

Halliday, T. C., and Shaffer, G. C. (2015) (eds.), *Transnational Legal Orders* (New York: Cambridge University Press).

Hamilton, A., Madison, J., and Jay, J. (1982), *The Federalist Papers* (Toronto, New York: Bantam).

Hanrieder, T. (2014), "Gradual Change in International Organizations: Agency Theory and Historical Institutionalism," *Politics*, 34/4: 324–33.

Hanrieder, T. (2015), *International Organization in Time: Fragmentation and Reform* (Oxford: Oxford University Press).

Hanrieder, T., and Zürn, M. (2017), "Reactive Sequences in Global Governance," in O. Fioretos (ed.), *International Politics and Institutions in Time* (Oxford, New York: Oxford University Press), 93–116.

Hardt, M., and Negri, A. (2004), *Multitude: War and Democracy in the Age of Empire* (London: Penguin Books).

Harteveld, E., van der Meer, T., and Vries, C. E. de (2013), "In Europe We Trust? Exploring Three Logics of Trust in the European Union," *European Union Politics*, 14/4: 542–65.

Hasenclever, A. (2001), *Die Macht der Moral in der internationalen Politik* (Frankfurt a.M.: Campus).

Hawkins, D. G., Lake, D. A., Nielson, D. L., and Tierney, M. J. (2006a) (eds.), *Delegation and Agency in International Organizations* (Cambridge: Cambridge University Press).

Hawkins, D. G., Lake, D. A., Nielson, D. L., and Tierney, M. J. (2006b), "Delegation Under Anarchy: States, International Organizations, and Principal-agent Theory," in D. G. Hawkins, D. A. Lake, D. L. Nielson, and M. J. Tierney (eds.), *Delegation and Agency in International Organizations* (Cambridge: Cambridge University Press), 3–38.

Hay, C. (2007), *Why We Hate Politics* (Cambridge: Polity Press).

Hayek, F. A. (1960), *The Constitution of Liberty* (London: Routledge & Kegan Paul).

Hazelzet, H. (2001), "Carrots or Sticks. EU and US Reactions to Human Rights Violations (1989–2000)," Ph.D. Thesis (Florence, Italy, European University Institute).

Hedström, P. (2005), *Dissecting the Social: On the Principles of Analytical Sociology* (Cambridge: Cambridge University Press).

Hein, W. (2016), "Intellectual Property Rights and Health—The Constraints of WHO Authority and the Rise of Global Health Governance as an Element of Contestation," *WZB Discussion Paper*, SP IV 2016-110 (Berlin).

Held, D. (1995), *Democracy and the Global Order. From the Modern State to Cosmopolitical Governance* (Cambridge: Polity Press).

Held, D. (2003), "Cosmopolitanism: Globalisation Tamed?," *Review of International Studies*, 29/4: 465–80.

Held, D. (2005), "Principles of the Cosmopolitan Order," in G. Brock and H. Brighouse (eds.), *The Political Philosophy of Cosmopolitanism* (Cambridge: Cambridge University Press), 10–27.

Held, D., and Koenig-Archibugi, M. (2005) (eds.), *Global Governance and Public Accountability* (Oxford: Blackwell).

Held, D., McGrew, A., Goldblatt, D., and Perraton, J. (1999), *Global Transformations: Politics, Economics and Culture* (Cambridge: Polity Press).

Helfer, L. R. (2009), "Regime Shifting in the International Intellectual Property System," *Perspectives on Politics*, 7/1: 39–44.

Helleiner, E. (1994), *States and the Reemergence of Global Finance: From Bretton Woods to the 1990s* (Ithaca: Cornell University Press).

Herschinger, E., Jachtenfuchs, M., and Kraft-Kasack, C. (2013), "Transgouvernementalisierung und die ausbleibende gesellschaftliche Politisierung der inneren Sicherheit," in M. Zürn and M. Ecker-Ehrhardt (eds.), *Die Politisierung der Weltpolitik: Umkämpfte internationale Institutionen* (Berlin: Suhrkamp), 190–212.

Herz, J. H. (1981), "Political Realism Revisited," *International Studies Quarterly*, 25/2: 182–97.

Heupel, M. (2017a), "EU Sanctions Policy and the Protection of Due Process Rights: Judicial Lawmaking by the Court of Justice of the EU," in M. Heupel and M. Zürn (eds.), *Protecting the Individual from International Authority. Human Rights in International Organizations* (Cambridge: Cambridge University Press), 129–51.

Heupel, M. (2017b), "EU Sanctions Policy and the Protection of Subsistence Rights: Learning From the Early Mover," in M. Heupel and M. Zürn (eds.), *Protecting the Individual from International Authority. Human Rights in International Organizations* (Cambridge: Cambridge University Press), 111–28.

Heupel, M. (2017c), "Human Rights Protection in World Bank Lending: Following the Lead of the US Congress," in M. Heupel and M. Zürn (eds.), *Protecting the Individual from International Authority. Human Rights in International Organizations* (Cambridge: Cambridge University Press), 241–72.

Heupel, M. (2017d), "UN Sanctions Policy and the Protection of Due Process Rights: Making Use of Global Legal Pluralism," in M. Heupel and M. Zürn (eds.), *Protecting the Individual from International Authority. Human Rights in International Organizations* (Cambridge: Cambridge University Press), 86–110.

Heupel, M. (2017e), "UN Sanctions Policy and the Protection of Subsistence Rights: Fighting Off a Reputational Crisis," in M. Heupel and M. Zürn (eds.), *Protecting the Individual from International Authority. Human Rights in International Organizations* (Cambridge: Cambridge University Press), 66–85.

Heupel, M., and Hirschmann, G. (2017), "Conceptual Framework," in M. Heupel and M. Zürn (eds.), *Protecting the Individual from International Authority. Human Rights in International Organizations* (Cambridge: Cambridge University Press), 40–65.

Heupel, M., and Zürn, M. (2017a) (eds.), *Protecting the Individual from International Authority. Human Rights in International Organizations* (Cambridge: Cambridge University Press).

Heupel, M., and Zürn, M. (2017b), "The Rise of Human Rights Protection in International Organizations. Results and Theoretical Implications," in M. Heupel and M. Zürn (eds.), *Protecting the Individual from International Authority. Human Rights in International Organizations* (Cambridge: Cambridge University Press), 297–331.

Hilgers, S. (2014), *Europe's Forgotten Institution—The Absent Politicization of the European Investment Bank: Master Thesis* (Berlin: Free University of Berlin).

Hinsley, F. H. (1986), *Sovereignty* (Cambridge: Cambridge University Press).

Hirschl, R. (2004), *Towards Juristocracy: The Origins and Consequences of the New Constitutionalism* (Harvard: Harvard University Press).

Hirschman, A. O. (1970), *Exit, Voice, and Loyalty: Responses to Decline in Firms, Organizations, and States* (Cambridge: Harvard University Press).

Hirschmann, G. (2015), *Guarding the Guards? Accountability in United Nations Peace Operations (doctoral dissertation)* (Berlin: Free University).

Hirschmann, G. (2017a), "NATO Peacekeeping and the Protection of Bodily Integrity Rights and the Rights Not to Be Enslaved: Domestic Channels for NATO Reform," in M. Heupel and M. Zürn (eds.), *Protecting the Individual from International Authority. Human Rights in International Organizations* (Cambridge: Cambridge University Press), 203–19.

Hirschmann, G. (2017b), "NATO Peacekeeping and the Protection of Due Process Rights: The OSCE and Council of Europe as Advocates for the Rights of Detainees," in M. Heupel and M. Zürn (eds.), *Protecting the Individual from International Authority. Human Rights in International Organizations* (Cambridge: Cambridge University Press), 220–35.

Hirschmann, G. (2017c), "UN Peacekeeping and the Protection of Due Process Rights: Learning how to Protect the Rights of Detainees," in M. Heupel and M. Zürn (eds.), *Protecting the Individual from International Authority. Human Rights in International Organizations* (Cambridge: Cambridge University Press), 186–202.

Hirschmann, G. (2017d), "United Nations Peacekeeping and the Protection of Physical Integrity Rights: When Protectors Become Perpetrators," in M. Heupel and M. Zürn (eds.), *Protecting the Individual from International Authority. Human Rights in International Organizations* (Cambridge: Cambridge University Press), 157–85.

Hoeglinger, D. (2016), "The Politicisation of European Integration in Domestic Election Campaigns," *West European Politics*, 39/1: 44–63.

Höffe, O. (1999), *Demokratie im Zeitalter der Globalisierung* (München: C.H.Beck).

Holsti, K. J. (1991), *Peace and War: Armed Conflicts and International Order 1648–1989* (Cambridge: Cambridge University Press).

Holsti, O. R. (2004), *Public Opinion and American Foreign Policy* (Ann Arbor: University of Michigan Press).

Hooghe, L. (2003), "Europe Divided? Elites vs. Public Opinion on European Integration," *European Union Politics*, 4/3: 281–304.

Hooghe, L. (2004), "Does Identity or Economic Rationality Drive Public Opinion on European Integration?," *Political Science and Politics*, 37/3: 415–20.

Hooghe, L. (2005), "Calculation, Community and Cues. Public Opinion on European Integration," *European Union Politics*, 6/4: 419–43.

Hooghe, L. (2009), "A Postfunctionalist Theory of European Integration: From Permissive Consensus to Constraining Dissensus," *British Journal of Political Science*, 39/1: 1–23.

Hooghe, L., and Marks, G. (2001), *Multi-level Governance and European Integration* (Lanham: Rowman & Littlefield Publishers).

Hooghe, L., Marks, G., Lenz, T., Bezuijen, J., Ceka, B., and Derderyan, S. (2017), *Measuring International Authority. A Postfunctionalist Theory of Governance, Volume III* (Oxford: Oxford University Press).

Hooghe, L., Marks, G., Schakel, A. H., Niedzwiecki, S., Osterkatz, S. C., and Shair-Rosenfield, S. (2016), *Measuring Regional Authority* (Oxford: Oxford University Press).

Hooghe, L., Marks, G., and Wilson, C. (2002), "Does Left/Right Structure Party Positions on European Integration?," *Comparative Political Studies*, 35/8: 965–89.

Höpner, M., and Schäfer, A. (2007), *A new Phase of European Integration. Organized Capitalisms in Post-Ricardian Europe*, MPIfG Discussion Paper 2007/4 (Köln).

Horkheimer, M. (1987a [1936]), "Allgemeiner Teil," in M. Horkheimer (ed.), *Studien über Autorität und Familie* (2nd edn, Lüneburg: Dietrich zu Klampen Verlag), 3–76.

Horkheimer, M. (1987b [1936]) (ed.), *Studien über Autorität und Familie* (2nd edn, Lüneburg: Dietrich zu Klampen Verlag).

Hurd, I. (1999), "Legitimacy and Authority in International Politics," *International Organization*, 53/2: 379–408.

Hurd, I. (2007), *After Anarchy: Legitimacy and Power in the United Nations Security Council* (Princeton: Princeton University Press).

Hurd, I. (2011), *International Organizations: Politics, Law, Practice* (Cambridge, New York: Cambridge University Press).

Hurd, I. (2015), "The International Rule of Law and the Domestic Analogy," *Global Constitutionalism*, 4/3: 365–95.

Hurrell, A. (2007), *On Global Order: Power, Values and the Constitution of International Society* (Oxford: Oxford University Press).

Hurrell, A., and Narlikar, A. (2006), "A New Politics of Confrontation? Brazil and India in Multilateral Trade Negotiations," *Global Society*, 20/4: 415–33.

Hutter, S., and Grande, E. (2014), "Politicizing Europe in the National Electoral Arena: A Comparative Analysis of Five West European Countries, 1970–2010," *Journal of Common Market Studies*, 52/5: 1002–18.

Hutter, S., Grande, E., and Kriesi, H. (2016) (eds.), *Politicising Europe: Integration and Mass Politics* (Cambridge: Cambridge University Press).

Ikenberry, G. J. (2001), *After Victory. Institutions, Strategic Restraint, and the Rebuilding of Order After Major Wars* (Princeton: Princeton University Press).

Ikenberry, G. J. (2009), "Liberal Internationalism 3.0: America and the Dilemmas of Liberal World Order," *Perspectives on Politics*, 7/1: 71–87.

Ikenberry, G. J. (2010), "The Liberal International Order and its Discontents," *Millennium—Journal of International Studies*, 38/3: 509–21.

Ikenberry, G. J. (2011a), *Liberal Leviathan: The Origins, Crisis and Transformation of the American World Order* (Princeton: Princeton University Press).

Ikenberry, G. J. (2011b), "The Future of the Liberal World Order. Internationalism after America," *Foreign Affairs*, 90/3: 56–68.

IMF (1998), *External Evaluation of the ESAF: Report by a Group of Independent Experts* <http://www.imf.org/external/pubs/ft/extev/index.htm>.

IMF (2003), *Evaluation Report: Fiscal Adjustment in IMF-Supported Programs. Report by the Independent Evaluation Office* <http://www.imf.org/external/np/ieo/2003/fis/>.

Imig, D., and Tarrow, S. (2001), *Contentious Europeans: Protest and Politics in an Integrating Europe* (Lanham: Rowman & Littlefield Publishers, Inc.).

ISSP Research Group (2015), *International Social Survey Programme: National Identity III - ISSP 2013*.

Jackson, R. H. (1987), "Quasi-States, Dual Regimes, and Neoclassical Theory: International Jurisprudence and the Third World," *International Organization*, 41/4: 519–50.

Jackson, R. H. (1990), *Quasi-States: Sovereignty. International Relations and the Third World* (Cambridge: Cambridge University Press).

Jacobs, A. M., and Weaver, R. K. (2015), "When Policies Undo Themselves. Self-Undermining Feedback as a Source of Policy Change," *Governance*, 28/4: 441–57.

Jaeger, H.-M. (2007), "'Global Civil Society' and the Political Depoliticization of Global Governance," *International Political Sociology*, 1/3: 257–77.

James, A. (2005), "Constructing Justice for Existing Practice: Rawls and the Status Quo," *Philosophy and Public Affairs*, 33/3: 281–316.

Jenkins, W. I. (1978), *Policy Analysis: A Political and Organizational Perspective* (New York: St. Martin's Press).

Jetschke, A., and Abb, P. (2018, in preparation), "The Devil Lies in the Details: The Positions of the BRICS Countries Toward R2P and UN Security Council Reform," in M. D. Stephen and M. Zürn (eds.), *Contested World Orders: Rising Powers, Non-Governmental Organizations and the Politics of Authority Beyond the Nation-state*.

Johansson, P. (2009), "The Humdrum Use of Ultimate Authority: Defining and Analysing Chapter VII Resolutions," *Nordic Journal of International Law*, 78/3: 309–42.

Jupille, J., Mattli, W., and Snidal, D. (2013), *Institutional Choice and Global Commerce* (Cambridge: Cambridge University Press).

Kahler, M. (1995), *International Institutions and the Political Economy of Integration* (Washington, DC: Brookings Institution).

Kahler, M. (2004), "Defining Accountability Up: the Global Economic Multilaterals," *Government & Opposition*, 39/2: 132–58.

Kahler, M. (2013), "Rising Powers and Global Governance: Negotiating Change in a Resilient Status Quo," *International Affairs*, 89/3: 711–29.

Kahler, M. (2016), "Complex Governance and the New Interdependence Approach (NIA)," *Review of International Political Economy*, 23/5: 825–39.

Kahler, M., and Lake, D. A. (2003) (eds.), *Governance in a Global Economy. Political Authority in Transition* (Princeton: Princeton University Press).

Kalter, F., and Kroneberg, C. (2014), "Between Mechanism Talk And Mechanism Cult. New Emphases in Explanatory Sociology And Empirical Research," *KZfSS Kölner Zeitschrift für Soziologie und Sozialpsychologie*, 66/1: 91–115.

Kappel, R. (2011), "The Challenge to Europe: Regional Powers and the Shifting of the Global Order," *Intereconomics*, 46/5: 275–86.

Karlsson Schaffer, J. (2012), "The Boundaries of Transnational Democracy: Alternatives to the All-Affected Principle," *Review of International Studies*, 38/2: 321–42.

Katzenstein, P. J. (1985), *Small States in World Markets. Industrial Policy in Europe* (Ithaca: Cornell University Press).

Katzenstein, P. J. (1996) (ed.), *The Culture of National Security. Norms and Identity in World Politics* (New York: Columbia University Press).

Keane, J. (2009), *Life and Death of Democracy* (London: Simon & Schuster).

Keane, J. (2014), *The New Despotisms of the 21st Century: Imagining the End of Democracy* (London: MEMO Publishers).

Keck, M. E., and Sikkink, K. (1998), *Activists Beyond Borders: Advocacy Networks in International Politics* (Ithaca: Cornell University Press).

Keck, M. E. (1999), "Transnational Advocacy Networks in International and Regional Politics," *International Social Science Journal*, 51/159: 89–101.

Kegley, C. W. J., and Wittkopf, E. R. (1989), *World Politics. Trends and Transformation* (New York: St. Martin's Press).

Kelley, J. (2004a), *Ethnic Politics in Europe: The Power of Norms and Incentives* (Princeton: Princeton University Press).

Kelley, J. (2004b), "International Actors on the Domestic Scene. Membership Conditionality and Socialization by International Institutions," *International Organization*, 58/03: 425–57.

Kelsen, H. (1944), *Peace through Law* (Chapel Hill: University of North Carolina Press).

Kennedy, P. (1989), *The Rise and Fall of the Great Powers. Economic Change and Military Conflict from 1500 to 2000* (London: Fontana Press).

Keohane, R. O. (1984), *After Hegemony. Cooperation and Discord in the World Political Economy* (Princeton: Princeton University Press).

Keohane, R. O. (2000), "Introduction," in J. S. Nye and J. D. Donahue (eds.), *Governance in a Globalizing World* (Washington, DC: Brookings Institution Press), 1–41.

Keohane, R. O. (2008), "Big Questions in the Study of World Politics," in C. Reus-Smit and D. Snidal (eds.), *The Oxford Handbook of International Relations* (Oxford: Oxford University Press), 708–15.

Keohane, R. O. (2012), "Twenty Years of Institutional Liberalism," *International Relations*, 26/2: 125–38.

Keohane, R. O., Macedo, S., and Moravcsik, A. (2009), "Democracy-Enhancing Multilateralism," *International Organization*, 63/01: 1–31.

Keohane, R. O., and Nye, J. S. (1977), *Power and Interdependence: World Politics in Transition* (Boston: Little, Brown and Company).

Keohane, R. O., and Nye, J. S. (2001), *Power and Interdependence* (3rd edn, New York: Longman).

Keohane, R. O., and Victor, D. G. (2011), "The Regime Complex for Climate Change," *Perspectives on Politics*, 9/1: 7–23.

Kindleberger, C. P. (1986), *The World in Depression, 1929–1939* (Rev. and enl. edn, Berkeley: University of California Press).

Kirton, J. J. (2013), *G20 Governance for a Globalized World* (Farnham, Burlington: Ashgate).

Kissinger, H. A. (1957), *A World Restored: Metternich, Castlereagh and the Problems of Peace 1812–22* (Boston: Houghton Mifflin).

Kitschelt, H. (1986), "Four Theories of Public Policy Making and Fast Breeder Reactor Development," *International Organization*, 40/01: 65–104.

Kitschelt, H. (1997), *The Radical Right in Western Europe: A Comparative Analysis* (Ann Arbor: University of Michigan Press).

Kleine, M. (2013), "Trading Control. National Fiefdoms in International Organizations," *International Theory*, 5/03: 321–46.

Klotz, A. (1995), *Norms in International Relations. The Struggle Against Apartheid* (Ithaca: Cornell University Press).

Koenig-Archibugi, M. (2011), "Is Global Democracy Possible?," *European Journal of International Relations*, 17/3: 519–42.

Koenig-Archibugi, M. (2012), "Fuzzy Citizenship in Global Society," *Journal of Political Philosophy*, 20/4: 456–80.

Kojéve, A. (1975), *Hegel: Eine Vergegenwärtigung seines Denkens* (Frankfurt a.M.: Suhrkamp).

Kojéve, A. (2014), *The Notion of Authority* (London: Verso).

Kolk, A., and van Tulder, R. (2005), "Setting New Global Rules? TNCs and Codes of Conduct," *Transnational Corporations*, 14/3: 1–27.

Kolko, J., and Kolko, G. (1972), *The Limits of Power: The World and United States Foreign Policy, 1945–1954* (New York: Harper & Row).

Koopmans, R., and Statham, P. (2010), "Theoretical Framework, Research Design, and Methods," in R. Koopmans and P. Statham (eds.), *The Making of a European Public Sphere: Media Discourse and Political Contention* (Cambridge: Cambridge University Press), 34–62.

Koremenos, B., Lipson, C., and Snidal, D. (2001), "Rational Design: Looking Back to Move Forward," *International Organization*, 55/4: 1051–82.

Koremenos, B. (2001), "The Rational Design of International Institutions," *International Organization*, 55/4: 761–99.

Koschorke, A. (2012), *Wahrheit und Erfindung: Grundzüge einer Allgemeinen Erzähltheorie* (Frankfurt a.M.: Fischer).

Krajewski, M. (2002), "Democratic Legitimacy and Constitutional Perspectives of WTO Law," *Journal of World Trade*, 35/1: 167–86.

Krasner, S. (1976), "State Power and the Structure of International Trade," *World Politics: A Quarterly Journal of International Relations*, 28/3: 317–47.

Krasner, S. D. (1988), "Sovereignty. An Institutional Perspective," *Comparative Political Studies*, 21/1: 66–94.

Krauthammer, C. (1991), "The Unipolar Moment," *Foreign Affairs*, 70/1: 23–33.

Kreuder-Sonnen, C. (2016), *Emergency Powers of International Organizations: Between Normalization and Containment* (Berlin: Dissertation, Free University Berlin).

Kriesi, H., Grande, E., Dolezal, M., Helbling, M., Hutter, S., Höglinger, D., and Wüest, B. (2012) (eds.), *Political Conflict in Western Europe* (Cambridge: Cambridge University Press).

Krisch, N. (2010), *Beyond Constitutionalism: The Pluralist Structure of Postnational Law* (Oxford: Oxford University Press).

Krisch, N. (2014), "The Decay of Consent. International Law in an Age of Global Public Goods," *The American Journal of International Law*, 108/1: 1–40.

Krisch, N. (2017), "Liquid Authority in Global Governance," *International Theory*, 9/2: 237–60.

Krugman, P. R. (1994), *Peddling Prosperity* (New York: Norton).

Kuhn, T. S. (1962), *The Structure of Scientific Revolutions* (Chicago: Chicago University Press).

Kuhn, T. (2015), *Experiencing European Integration: Transnational Lives and European Identity* (Oxford: Oxford University Press).

Kumm, M. (2009), "The Cosmopolitan Turn in Constitutionalism: On the Relationship Between Constitutionalism In and Beyond the State," in J. L. Dunoff and J. P. Trachtman (eds.), *Ruling the World? International Law, Global Governance, Constitutionalism* (Cambridge, New York: Cambridge University Press), 258–325.

Kurki, M. (2007), "Critical Realism and Causal Analysis in International Relations," *Millennium—Journal of International Studies*, 35/2: 361–78.

Lakatos, I. (1976), *Proofs and Refutations: The Logic of Mathematical Discovery* (Cambridge, New York: Cambridge University Press).

Lake, D. A. (2009), *Hierarchy in International Relations* (Ithaca: Cornell University Press).

Lake, D. A. (2010), "Rightful Rules: Authority, Order, and the Foundations of Global Governance," *International Studies Quarterly*, 54/3: 587–613.

Lake, D. A. (2017), *Madison's Dilemma and the Problem of Global Governance: The Organizational Ecology of Public and Private Authority: Prepared for the workshop "Beyond Anarchy"* (Frankfurt a.M.).

Layne, C. (1993), "The Unipolar Illusion: Why New Great Powers Will Rise," *International Security*, 17: 5–51.

Legg, A. (2012), *The Margin of Appreciation in International Human Rights Law: Deference and Proportionality* (Oxford: Oxford University Press).

Legro, J. W. (2005), *Rethinking the World. Great Power Strategies and International Order* (Ithaca: Cornell University Press).

Leibfried, S., and Zürn, M. (2005) (eds.), *Transformations of the State?* (Cambridge: Cambridge University Press).

Lenz, T., Bezuijen, J., Hooghe, L., and Marks, G. (2015), "Patterns of International Authority. Task Specific vs. General Purpose," in E. da Conceição-Heldt, M. Koch, and A. Liese (eds.), *Internationale Organisationen: Autonomie, Politisierung, interorganisationale Beziehungen und Wandel (Sonderheft 49 der Politischen Vierteljahresschrift)* (Baden-Baden: Nomos), 131–56.

Lesage, D., and Van de Graaf, T. (2015) (eds.), *Rising Powers and Multilateral Institutions* (Houndmills: Palgrave Macmillan).

Leupold, A. (2016), "A Structural Approach to Politicisation in the Euro Crisis," *West European Politics*, 39/1: 84–103.

Liese, A. (2006), *Staaten am Pranger. Zur Wirkung internationaler Regime auf innerstaatliche Menschenrechtspolitik* (Wiesbaden: VS Verlag für Sozialwissenschaften).

Linz, J. J. (1994), "Presidential or Parliamentary Democracy: Does It Make a Difference?," in J. J. Linz and A. Valenzuela (eds.), *The Failure of Presidential Democracy* (Baltimore: Johns Hopkins University Press), 3–91.

Luban, D. J. (2004), "Preventive War," *Philosophy & Public Affairs*, 32/3: 207–48.

Luhmann, N. (1984), *Soziale Systeme* (Frankfurt a.M.: Suhrkamp).

Lukes, S. (2005), *Power: A Radical View* (2nd edn, Houndmills: Palgrave Macmillan).

MacClosky, H., and Brill, A. (1983), *Dimensions of Tolerance* (New York: Russell Sage Foundation).

Macdonald, K., and MacDonald, T. (2017), "Liquid Authority and Political Legitimacy in Transnational Governance," *International Theory*, 9/2: 329–51.

MacDonald, T. (2012), "Citizens or Stakeholders? Exclusion, Equality and Legitimacy in Global Stakeholder Democracy," in D. Archibugi, M. Koenig-Archibugi, and R. Marchetti (eds.), *Global Democracy: Normative and Empirical Perspectives* (Cambridge: Cambridge University Press), 47–68.

MacIntyre, A. C. (1988), *Whose Justice? Which Rationality?* (Notre Dame, Indiana: University of Notre Dame Press).

Mahoney, J. (2000), "Path Dependence in Historical Sociology," *Theory and Society*, 29: 507–48.

Mahoney, J. (2012), "The Logic of Process Tracing Tests in the Social Sciences," *Sociological Methods & Research*, 41/4: 570–97.

Mahoney, J., and Thelen, K. (2010), "A Theory of Gradual Institutional Change," in J. Mahoney and K. Thelen (eds.), *Explaining Institutional Change: Ambiguity, Agency, and Power* (Cambridge: Cambridge University Press), 1–37.

Maier, M., Adam, S., and Maier, J. (2012), "The Impact of Identity and Economic Cues on Citizens' EU Support: An Experimental Study on the Effects of Party Communication in the Run-up to the 2009 European Parliament Elections," *European Union Politics*, 13/4: 580–603.

Majone, G. (1994), "Independence vs. Accountability? Non-Majoritarian Institutions and Democratic Government in Europe," in J. J. Hesse (ed.), *European Yearbook of Public Administration and Comparative Government* (Oxford: Oxford University Press).

March, J. G., and Olsen, J. P. (1996), "Institutional Perspectives on Political Institutions," *Governance*, 9/3: 247–64.

March, J. G. (1998), "The Institutional Dynamics of International Political Orders," *International Organization*, 52/4: 943–69.

Marchetti, R. (2012), "Models of Global Democracy: In Defence of Cosmo-Federalism," in D. Archibugi, M. Koenig-Archibugi, and R. Marchetti (eds.), *Global Democracy: Normative and Empirical Perspectives* (Cambridge: Cambridge University Press), 22–46.

Marcuse, H. (1991), *One-Dimensional Man: Studies in the Ideology of Advanced Industrial Society* (2nd edn, Boston: Beacon Press).

Marmor, A. (2011), "An Institutional Conception of Authority," *Philosophy & Public Affairs*, 39/3: 238–61.

Martens, K., and Jakobi, A. P. (2010) (eds.), *Mechanisms of OECD Governance: International Incentives for National Policy-Making?* (Oxford: Oxford University Press).

Mattern, J. B., and Zarakol, A. (2016), "Hierarchies in World Politics," *International Organization*, 70/03: 623–54.

Mattli, W., and Slaughter, A.-M. (1998), "Revisiting the European Court of Justice," *International Organization*, 52/1: 177–209.

Mau, S. (2007), *Transnationale Vergesellschaftung. Die Entgrenzung sozialer Lebenswelten* (Frankfurt a. M.: Campus Verlag).

Maus, I. (2007), "Verfassung oder Vertrag. Zur Verrechtlichung globaler Politik," in P. Niesen and B. Herborth (eds.), *Anarchie der kommunikativen Freiheit: Jürgen Habermas und die Theorie der internationalen Politik* (Frankfurt a.M.: Suhrkamp), 350–82.

May, J. V., and Wildavsky, A. B. (1978), *The Policy Cycle* (Beverly Hills: Sage Publications).

Mayda, A. M., and Rodrik, D. (2005), "Why Are Some People (and Countries) More Protectionist Than Others?," *European Economic Review*, 49/6: 1393–430.

Mayer, P., Rittberger, V., and Zürn, M. (1993), "Regime Theory. State of the Art and Perspectives," in V. Rittberger (ed.), *Regime Theory and International Relations* (Oxford: Clarendon Press), 391–430.

Mayntz, R. (2004), "Mechanisms in the Analysis of Social Macro-Phenomena," *Philosophy of the Social Sciences*, 34/2: 237–59.

Mayntz, R. (2014), "Die Finanzmarktkrise im Licht einer Theorie funktioneller Differenzierung," *KZfSS Kölner Zeitschrift für Soziologie und Sozialpsychologie*, 66/1: 1–19.

Mayntz, R., Rosewitz, B., Schimank, U., and Stichweh, R. (1988) (eds.), *Differenzierung und Verselbständigung—Zur Entwicklung gesellschaftlicher Teilsysteme* (Frankfurt a.M.: Campus).

Mazower, M. (2012), *Governing the World: The History of an Idea* (New York: Penguin).

McCarthy, J. D., and Zald, M. N. (1977), "Resource Mobilization and Social Movements. A Partial Theory," *American Journal of Sociology*, 82/6: 1212–41.

Mearsheimer, J. J. (2001), *The Tragedy of Great Power Politics* (New York: Norton).

Mendes, J. and Venzke, I. (2018, forthcoming), "Introduction: The Idea of Relative Authority in European and International Law," in J. Mendes and I. Venzke (eds.), *Allocating Authority: Who Should Do What in European and International Law?*

Mendlovitz, S. H. (1975) (ed.), *On the Creation of a Just World Order: Preferred Worlds for the 1990s* (New York: Free Press).

Messner, D., and Nuscheler, F. (2003), "Das Konzept Global Governance. Stand und Perspektiven," *INEF-Report*.

Metzges, G. (2006), *NGO-Kampagnen und ihr Einfluss auf internationale Verhandlungen* (Baden-Baden: Nomos).

Meyer, J. W. (2005), *Weltkultur. Wie die westlichen Prinzipien die Welt durchdringen* (Frankfurt a.M.: Suhrkamp).

Meyer, J. W., Boli, J., Thomas, G. M., and Ramirez, F. O. (1997), "World Society and the Nation-State," *American Journal of Sociology*, 103/1: 144–81.

Meyer, J. W., and Rowan, B. (1977), "Institutionalized Organizations: Formal Structure as Myth and Ceremony," *American Journal of Sociology*, 83/2: 340–63.

Milgram, S. (1974), *Obedience to Authority: An Experimental View* (London: Tavistock).

Milner, H. V. (1988), *Resisting Protectionism. Global Industries and the Politics of International Trade* (Princeton: Princeton University Press).

Milward, A. (1992), *The European Rescue of the Nation-State* (London: Routledge).

Mitchell, R. B., Clark, W. C., Cash, D. W., and Dickson, N. M. (2006) (eds.), *Global Environmental Assessments: Information and Influence* (Cambridge: MIT Press).

Modelski, G. (1987), *Long Cycles in World Politics* (Seattle: University of Washington Press).

Möllers, C. (2012), "Individuelle Legitimation: Wie rechtfertigen sich Gerichte?," in A. Geis, F. Nullmeier, and C. Daase (eds.), *Der Aufstieg der Legitimitätspolitik. Rechtfertigung und Kritik politisch-ökonomischer Ordnungen (Leviathan Sonderband 40/27)* (Baden-Baden: Nomos), 398–418.

Möllers, C. (2013), *The Three Branches: A Comparative Model of Separation of Powers* (Oxford: Oxford University Press).

Moore, B. (1966), *Social Origins of Dictatorship and Democracy* (Boston: Beacon Press).

Moravcsik, A. (1998), *The Choice for Europe: Social Purpose and State Power from Messina to Maastricht* (Ithaca: Cornell University Press).

Moravcsik, A. (2006), "What Can We Learn from the Collapse of the European Constitutional Project?," *Politische Vierteljahresschrift*, 47/2: 219–41.

Moravcsik, A. (2008), "The Myth of Europe's 'Democratic Deficit'," *Intereconomics: Journal of European Economic Policy*, 43/6: 331–40.

Morgenthau, H. J. (1967), *Politics Among Nations. The Struggle for Power and Peace* (4th edn, New York: Alfred A. Knopf).

Morse, J. C., and Keohane, R. O. (2014), "Contested Multilateralism," *The Review of International Organizations*, 9/4: 385–412.

Moschella, M., and Vetterlein, A. (2016), "Self-Reinforcing and Reactive Path Dependence. Tracing the IMF's Path of Policy Change," in T. Rixen, L. A. Viola, and M. Zürn (eds.), *Historical Institutionalism and International Relations. Explaining Institutional Development in World Politics* (Oxford: Oxford University Press), 143–64.

Mosley, P., Harrigan, J., and Toye, J. F. J. (1995), *Aid and Power: the World Bank and Policy-based Lending* (London: Routledge).

Moulin, C., and Nyers, P. (2007), "'We Live in a Country of UNHCR'—Refugee Protests and Global Political Society," *International Political Sociology*, 1/4: 356–72.

Mueller, J., and Mueller, K. (1999), "Sanctions of Mass Destruction," *Foreign Affairs*, 78: 43–52.

Müller, H., and Tokhi, A. (2018, in preparation), "The Contestation of the Nuclear Nonproliferation Regime," in M. D. Stephen and M. Zürn (eds.), *Contested World Orders: Rising Powers, Non-Governmental Organizations and the Politics of Authority Beyond the Nation-state*.

Müller, J.-W. (2016), *What Is Populism?* (Philadelphia: University of Pennsylvania Press).

Münkler, H. (2005), *Imperien. Die Logik der Weltherrschaft—vom Alten Rom bis zu den Vereinigten Staaten* (Berlin: Rowohlt).

Murphy, C. N. (1994), *International Organization and Industrial Change. Global Governance since 1850* (Cambridge: Polity Press).

Nagel, T. (2005), "The Problem of Global Justice," *Philosophy & Public Affairs*, 33/2: 113–47.

Narlikar, A. (2005), *The World Trade Organization: A Very Short Introduction* (Oxford: Oxford University Press).

National Intelligence Council (2008), "Global Trends 2025: A Transformed World," NIC 2008-003, <https://www.files.ethz.ch/isn/94769/2008_11_Global_Trends_2025.pdf>.

Neidhardt, F., Eilders, C., and Pfetsch, B. (2004), "Die 'Stimme der Medien'— Pressekommentare als Gegenstand der Öffentlichkeitsforschung," in C. Eilders, F. Neidhardt, and B. Pfetsch (eds.), *Die Stimme der Medien* (Wiesbaden: VS Verlag für Sozialwissenschaften), 11–36.

Nelson, P. (2009), "Political Opportunity Structures and Non-State Influence: Making the Case for Transparency at the World Bank," in J. M. Joachim and B. Locher (eds.), *Transnational Activism in the UN and the EU. A Comparative Study* (New York: Routledge), 61–75.

Neyer, J. (2012), *The Justification of Europe. A Political Theory of Supranational Integration* (Oxford: Oxford University Press).

Neyer, J. (2013), *Globale Demokratie: Eine Einführung* (Stuttgart: UTB).

Nielson, D. L., and Tierney, M. J. (2003), "Delegation to International Organizations: Agency Theory and World Bank Environmental Reform," *International Organization*, 57/2: 241–76.

Nolan, A., Porter, B., and Langford, M. (2007), *The Justiciability of Social and Economic Rights: An Updated Appraisal*, Working Paper No. 15/2007 (New York).

Nolte, G. (2016), "Introduction," in H. P. Aust and G. Nolte (eds.), *The Interpretation of International Law by Domestic Courts. Uniformity, Diversity, Convergence* (Oxford: Oxford University Press), 1–9.

Norris, P. (2000), "Global Governance & Cosmopolitan Citizens," in J. S. Nye and J. D. Donahue (eds.), *Governance in a Globalizing World* (Washington: Brookings Institution Press), 155–77.

Norris, P. (2009), "The Globalization of Comparative Public Opinion Research," in T. Landman and N. Robinson (eds.), *The SAGE Handbook of Comparative Politics* (London: Sage), 522–40.

Norwegian Social Science Data Services (2011), "European Social Survey Education Net" <http://essedunet.nsd.uib.no/>.

Nullmeier, F., Biegon, D., Nonhoff, M., Schmidtke, H., and Schneider, S. (2010) (eds.), *Prekäre Legitimitäten: Rechtfertigung von Herrschaft in der postnationalen Konstellation* (Frankfurt a.M.: Campus).

Nullmeier, F., Geis, A., and Daase, C. (2012), "Der Aufstieg der Legitimitätspolitik: Rechtfertigung und Kritik politisch-ökonomischer Ordnungen," in A. Geis, F. Nullmeier, and C. Daase (eds.), *Der Aufstieg der Legitimitätspolitik. Rechtfertigung und Kritik politisch-ökonomischer Ordnungen (Leviathan Sonderband 40/27)* (Baden-Baden: Nomos), 11–40.

Nye, J. S. J. (1990), "Soft Power," *Foreign Affairs*, 80/Fall: 153–71.

O'Brian, R., Goetz, A. M., Scholte, J. A., and Williams, M. (2000), *Contesting Global Governance: Multilateral Institutions and Global Social Movements* (Cambridge: Cambridge University Press).

OECD (2008), *Globalisation and Emerging Economies: Brazil, Russia, India, Indonesia, China and South Africa* (Geneva: OECD Publishing).

OECD (2010), *Perspectives on Global Development 2010: Shifting Wealth* (Paris: OECD Publishing).

OECD (2013), *Long-term Growth Scenarios. Economics Department Working Papers. No.1000. ECO/WKP(2012)77*.

Offe, C. (2002), "Wessen Wohl ist das Gemeinwohl?," in H. Münkler and K. Fischer (eds.), *Gemeinwohl und Gemeinsinn* (Berlin: Akademie Verlag), 55–76.

Offe, C. (2008), "Governance—'Empty signifier' oder sozialwissenschaftliches Forschungsprogramm?," in G. F. Schuppert and M. Zürn (eds.), *Governance in einer sich wandelnden Welt (Sonderheft 41 der Politischen Vierteljahresschrift)* (Wiesbaden: VS Verlag für Sozialwissenschaften), 61–76.

Olson, M. (1971), *The Logic of Collective Action* (Cambridge: Harvard University Press).

Onuf, N. G., and Klink, F. F. (1989), "Anarchy, Authority, Rule," *International Studies Quarterly*, 33: 149–73.

Operations Evaluation Department (2001), *OECD Review of the World Bank's Performance on the Environment* (Washington, DC) <http://documents.worldbank.org/curated/en/2001/06/1490093/oed-review-banks-performance-environment>.

Organski, A. F. K., and Kugler, J. (1981), *The War Ledger* (Chicago: University of Chicago Press).

OSCE (2002), *Review of the Criminal Justice System (September 2001–February 2002)*, OSCE Mission in Kosovo, Department of Human Rights and Rule of Law <http://www.osce.org/kosovo/13043>.

Ougaard, M., and Higgott, R. A. (2002) (eds.), *Towards a Global Polity* (London, New York: Routledge).

Overbeek, H., Dingwerth, K., Pattberg, P., and Compagnon, D. (2010), "Forum: Global Governance: Decline or Maturation of an Academic Concept?," *International Studies Review*, 12/4: 696–719.

Oye, K. A. (1986), "Explaining Cooperation under Anarchy: Hypotheses and Strategies," in K. A. Oye (ed.), *Cooperation under Anarchy* (Princeton: Princeton University Press), 1–24.

Park, S. (2010), *World Bank Group Interactions with Environmentalists. Changing International Organisation Identities* (Manchester: Manchester University Press).

Parson, E. A. (2003), *Protecting the Ozone Layer: Science and Strategy* (Oxford: Oxford University Press).

Parsons, T. (1967), *Sociological Theory and Modern Society* (New York: Free Press).

Patberg, M. (2016), *Usurpation und Autorisierung. Konstituierende Gewalt im globalen Zeitalter. Dissertation.* (Hamburg: Universität Hamburg).

Paul, T. V., Larson, D. W., and Wohlforth, W. C. (2014) (eds.), *Status in World Politics* (Cambridge: Cambridge University Press).

Pauly, L. W., and Grande, E. (2005), "Reconstituting Political Authority: Sovereignty, Effectiveness, and Legitimacy in a Transnational Order," in E. Grande and L. W. Pauly (eds.), *Complex Sovereignty: Reconstituting Political Authority in the Twenty-first Century* (Toronto: University of Toronto Press), 3–21.

References

Pauwelyn, J., Wessel, R. A., and Wouters, J. (2014), "When Structures Become Shackles: Stagnation and Dynamics in International Lawmaking," *European Journal of International Law*, 25/3: 733–63.

Pedersen, S. (2007), "Review Essay: Back to the League of Nations," *The American Historical Review*, 112/4: 1091–116.

Peters, B. (2000), "Normative Theorien und soziale Empirie," in S. Müller-Doohm (ed.), *Das Interesse der Vernunft. Rückblicke auf das Werk von Jürgen Habermas seit "Erkenntnis und Interesse"* (Frankfurt a.M.: Suhrkamp), 274–98.

Peters, B., and Karlsson Schaffer, J. (2013), "The Turn to Authority Beyond States," *Transnational Legal Theory*, 4/3: 315–35.

Peters, D. (2018, in preparation), "Exclusive Club Under Stress: The G7 Between Rising Powers and Non-state Actors After the Cold War," in M. D. Stephen and M. Zürn (eds.), *Contested World Orders: Rising Powers, Non-Governmental Organizations and the Politics of Authority Beyond the Nation-state*.

Pew Research Center (2013), *39-Nation Pew Global Attitudes Survey*.

Pianta, M., and Zola, D. (2005), *The Rise of Global Movements, 1970–2005*, ACI Meeting, 2005 (Paris).

Pierson, P. (1994), *Dismantling the Welfare State? Reagan, Thatcher, and the Politics of Retrenchment* (Cambridge: Cambridge University Press).

Pierson, P. (1996), "The New Politics of the Welfare State," *World Politics*, 48/2: 143–79.

Pierson, P. (2004), *Politics in Time. History, Institutions, and Social Analysis* (Princeton: Princeton University Press).

Pogge, T. (1994), "Cosmopolitanism and Sovereignty," in C. Brown (ed.), *Political Restructuring in Europe: Ethical Perspectives* (London: Routledge), 89–122.

Pogge, T. (2002a), "Kosmopolitismus und Souveränität," in M. Lutz-Bachmann and J. Bohman (eds.), *Weltstaat oder Staatenwelt? Für und wider die Idee einer Weltrepublik* (Frankfurt a.M.: Suhrkamp), 125–71.

Pogge, T. (2002b), "Moral Universalism and Global Economic Justice," *Politics, Philosophy and Economics*, 1/1: 29–58.

Pouliot, V. (2016a), *International Pecking Orders: The Politics and Practice of Multilateral Diplomacy* (New York: Cambridge University Press).

Pouliot, V. (2016b), "Hierarchy in Practice. Multilateral Diplomacy and the Governance of International Security," *European Journal of International Security*, 1/01: 5–26.

Pouliot, V. (2017), "Against Authority," in A. Zarakol (ed.), *Hierarchies in World Politics* (Cambridge: Cambridge University Press), 113–34.

Pouliot, V. (2018, in preparation), "Historical Institutionalism Meets Practice Theory. Renewing the Selection Process of the United Nations Secretary-General."

Pouliot, V., and Thérien, J.-P. (2017), "Global Governance in Practice," *Global Policy*, <https://doi.org/10.1111/1758-5899.12529>.

Pollack, M. A. (2003), *The Engines of European Integration: Delegation, Agency, and Agenda Setting in the EU* (Oxford, New York: Oxford University Press).

Prantl, J. (2005), "Informal Groups of States and the UN Security Council," *International Organization*, 59/3: 559–92.

Preuß, U. K. (1994) (ed.), *Zum Begriff der Verfassung* (Frankfurt a.M.: Fischer Taschenbuch Verlag).

Prys-Hansen, M., Hahn, K., Lellmann, M., and Röseler, M. (2018, in preparation), "Contestation in the UNFCCC: The Case of Climate Finance," in M. D. Stephen and M. Zürn (eds.), *Contested World Orders: Rising Powers, Non-Governmental Organizations and the Politics of Authority Beyond the Nation-state.*

Putnam, H. (1966), "What Theories are Not," in E. Nagel, P. Suppes, and A. Tarski (eds.), *Logic, Methodology and Philosophy of Science. Proceedings of the 1960 International Congress* (Amsterdam: North-Holland), 240–51.

Putnam, H. (1975), *Mathematics, Matter, and Method* (London, New York: Cambridge University Press).

Putnam, H. (1981), *Reason, Truth, and History* (Cambridge, New York: Cambridge University Press).

Putnam, R. D. (1988), "Diplomacy and Domestic Politics. The Logic of Two-Level Games," *International Organization*, 42/3: 427–60.

Radtke, K. (2007), "Ein Trend zu transnationaler Solidarität? Die Entwicklung des Spendenaufkommens für die Katastrophen- und Entwicklungshilfe in Deutschland," *WZB Discussion Paper*, SP IV 2007-304 (Berlin).

Rauh, C. (2016), *A Responsive Technocracy? EU Politicisation and the Consumer Policies of the European Commission* (Colchester: ECPR Press).

Rauh, C., and Bödeker, S. (2013), *The International Trade Regime in the Public Sphere, 1986–2012: Evaluating the Social Legitimacy of Global Governance with Semi-automated Text Mining Approaches*, 1st European Workshop on International Studies, 2013 (Tartu).

Rauh, C., and Zürn, M. (2014), "Zur Politisierung der EU in der Krise," in M. Heidenreich (ed.), *Krise der europäischen Vergesellschaftung?* (Wiesbaden: Springer Fachmedien Wiesbaden), 121–45.

Rauh, C., and Zürn, M. (2015), "Legitimation Dynamics in Global Governance: Civil Society Evaluations of the IMF, the World Bank, and the WTO in the International Business Press," *Paper presented at Legitimacy and Legitimation in Global Governance Workshop, April 16–17, Stockholm.*

Raustiala, K., and Victor, D. G. (2004), "The Regime Complex for Plant Genetic Resources," *International Organization*, 58/2: 277–309.

Rawls, J. (1971), *A Theory of Justice* (Oxford: Oxford University Press).

Rawls, J. (1999), *The Law of Peoples* (Cambridge: Harvard University Press).

Raz, J. (1990), "Introduction," in J. Raz (ed.), *Authority* (Oxford: Basil Blackwell), 1–19.

Raz, J. (2006), "The Problem of Authority: Revisiting the Service Conception," *Minnesota Law Review*, 90/4: 1003–44.

Raz, J. (2009), *The Authority of Law: Essays on Law and Morality* (2nd edn, Oxford, New York: Oxford University Press).

Reinold, T. (2012), *Sovereignty and the Responsibility to Protect: The Power of Norms and the Norms of the Powerful* (London: Routledge).

Reinold, T. (2017), "Human Rights Protection in IMF Lending: Organizational Inertia and the Limits of Like-Minded Institution-Building," in M. Heupel and M. Zürn (eds.), *International Organisations and Human Rights. Explaining Limitations of International Authority* (Cambridge: Cambridge University Press), 273–92.

Reinold, T., and Zürn, M. (2014), "'Rules About Rules' and the Endogenous Dynamics of International Law: Dissonance Reduction as a Mechanism of Secondary Rule-making," *Global Constitutionalism*, 3/2: 236–73.

Reus-Smit, C. (2013), *Individual Rights and the Making of the International System* (Cambridge: Cambridge University Press).

Richey, L. A., and Ponte, S. (2013), "Brand Aid: Values, Consumption, and Celebrity Mediation," *International Political Sociology*, 7/1: 107–11.

Rieger, E., and Leibfried, S. (1997), "Sozialpolitische Grenzen der Globalisierung. Wohlfahrtsstaatliche Gründe außenwirtschaftlicher Schließung und Öffnung," *Politische Vierteljahresschrift*, 38/4: 771–96.

Risse, M. (2012), *On Global Justice* (Princeton: Princeton University Press).

Risse, T. (2000), "'Let's Argue!'. Communicative Action in World Politics," *International Organization*, 54/1: 1–40.

Risse, T. (2013), "Transnational Actors and World Politics," in W. Carlsnaes, T. Risse-Kappen, and B. A. Simmons (eds.), *Handbook of International Relations* (London, Thousand Oaks: Sage Publications), 426–52.

Risse, T. (2015) (ed.), *European Public Spheres: Politics is Back* (Cambridge: Cambridge University Press).

Risse, T., Engelmann-Martin, D., Knopf, H.-J., and Roscher, K. (1999), "To Euro or Not to Euro? The EMU and Identity Politics in the European Union," *European Journal of International Relations*, 5/2: 147–87.

Risse, T., and Sikkink, K. (1999), "The Socialization of International Human Rights Norms into Domestic Practices. Introduction," in T. Risse, S. C. Ropp, and K. Sikkink (eds.), *The Power of Human Rights. International Norms and Domestic Change* (Cambridge: Cambridge University Press), 1–38.

Rittberger, V. (1990) (ed.), *International Regimes in East–West Politics* (London: Pinter).

Rittberger, V., Nettesheim, M., and Huckel, C. (2008) (eds.), *Authority in the Global Political Economy* (Basingstoke, New York: Palgrave Macmillan).

Rittberger, V., Zangl, B., and Kruck, A. (2013), *Internationale Organisationen* (4th edn, Wiesbaden: Springer VS).

Rittberger, V., and Zürn, M. (1990), "Towards Regulated Anarchy in East–West Relations," in V. Rittberger (ed.), *International Regimes in East–West Politics* (London: Pinter), 9–63.

Rixen, T., and Viola, L. (2016), "Historical Institutionalism and International Relations. Towards Explaining Change and Stability in International Institutions," in T. Rixen, L. A. Viola, and M. Zürn (eds.), *Historical Institutionalism and International Relations. Explaining Institutional Development in World Politics* (Oxford: Oxford University Press), 3–34.

Rixen, T., Viola, L. A., and Zürn, M. (2016) (eds.), *Historical Institutionalism and International Relations: Explaining Institutional Development in World Politics* (Oxford: Oxford University Press).

Rixen, T., and Zangl, B. (2013), "The Politicization of International Economic Institutions in US Public Debates," *The Review of International Organizations*, 8/3: 363–87.

Rocabert, J., Schimmelfennig, F., Winzen, T., and Crasnic, L. (2018, in preparation), "The Rise of International Parliamentary Institutions: Authority and Legitimacy."

Rodrik, D. (1997), *Has Globalization Gone too Far?* (Washington: Institute for International Economics).

Rohrschneider, R. (2002), "The Democracy Deficit and Mass Support for an EU-Wide Government," *American Journal of Political Science*, 46/2: 463–75.

Ronzoni, M. (2009), "The Global Order: A Case of Background Injustice? A Practice-Dependent Account," *Philosophy & Public Affairs*, 37/3: 229–56.

Rosenau, J. N. (1990), *Turbulence in World Politics. A Theory of Change and Continuity* (Princeton: Princeton University Press).

Rosenau, J. N. (1992), "Governance, Order, and Change in World Politics," in J. N. Rosenau and E.-O. Czempiel (eds.), *Governance Without Government: Order and Change in World Politics* (Cambridge: Cambridge University Press), 1–29.

Rosenau, J. N. (1995), "Governance in the Twenty-First Century," *Global Governance*, 1/1: 13–43.

Rosenau, J. N. (1997), *Along the Domestic–Foreign Frontier. Exploring Governance in a Turbulent World* (Cambridge: Cambridge University Press).

Rosenau, J. N., and Czempiel, E.-O. (1992) (eds.), *Governance Without Government: Order and Change in World Politics* (Cambridge: Cambridge University Press).

Rucht, D. (2013), "Globalisierungskritische Proteste als Herausforderung an die internationale Politik," in M. Zürn and M. Ecker-Ehrhardt (eds.), *Die Politisierung der Weltpolitik: Umkämpfte internationale Institutionen* (Berlin: Suhrkamp), 61–83.

Ruggie, J. G. (1975), "International Responses to Technology. Concepts and Trends," *International Organization*, 29/3: 557–83.

Ruggie, J. G. (1983), "International Regimes, Transactions, and Change: Embedded Liberalism in the Postwar Economic Order," in S. D. Krasner (ed.), *International Regimes* (Ithaca: Cornell University Press), 195–231.

Ruggie, J. G. (1992), "Multilateralism. The Anatomy of an Institution," *International Organization*, 46/3: 561–98.

Ruggie, J. G. (1993), "Territoriality and Beyond: Problematizing Modernity in International Relations," *International Organization*, 47/1: 139–74.

Ruggie, J. G. (1994), "Trade, Protectionism and the Future of Welfare Capitalism," *Journal of International Affairs*, 48/1: 1–12.

Ruggie, J. G. (2004), "Reconstituting the Global Public Domain—Issues, Actors, and Practices," *European Journal of International Relations*, 10/4: 499–531.

Russett, B. M., and Oneal, J. R. (2001), *Triangulating Peace. Democracy, Interdependence, and International Organizations* (New York: Norton).

Sabel, C. F., and Zeitlin, J. (2012), "Experimentalist Governance," in D. Levi-Faur (ed.), *Oxford Handbook of Governance* (Oxford: Oxford University Press).

Said, E. (1978), *Orientalism* (New York: Pantheon).

Sangiovanni, A. (2008), "Justice and the Priority of Politics to Morality," *Journal of Political Philosophy*, 16/2: 137–64.

Save the Children UK (2002), *Note for Implementing and Operational Partners by UNHCR and Save the Children-UK on Sexual Violence & Exploitation: The Experience of Refugee Children in Guinea, Liberia and Sierra Leone based on Initial Findings and Recommendations from Assessment Mission 22 October–30 November 2001* <http://www.savethechildren .org.uk/sites/default/files/docs/sexual_violence_and_exploitation_1.pdf>.

Scharpf, F. W. (1970), *Demokratietheorie zwischen Utopie und Anpassung: Konstanzer Universitätsreden 25* (Konstanz: Universitätsverlag).

References

Scharpf, F. W. (1987), *Sozialdemokratische Krisenpolitik in Europa* (Frankfurt a.M.: Campus).

Scharpf, F. W. (1991), "Die Handlungsfähigkeit des Staates am Ende des zwanzigsten Jahrhunderts," *Politische Vierteljahresschrift*, 32/4: 621–34.

Scharpf, F. W. (1996a), "Negative and Positive Integration in the Political Economy of European Welfare State," in G. Marks, F. W. Scharpf, P. C. Schmitter, and W. Streeck (eds.), *Governance in the European Union* (London: Sage), 15–39.

Scharpf, F. W. (1996b), "Politische Optionen im vollendeten Binnenmarkt," in M. Jachtenfuchs and B. Kohler-Koch (eds.), *Europäische Integration* (Opladen: Leske + Budrich), 109–40.

Scharpf, F. W. (1999), *Governing in Europe: Effective and Democratic?* (Oxford: Oxford University Press).

Scharpf, F. W. (2009), "Legitimität im europäischen Mehrebenensystem," *Leviathan*, 37/2: 244–80.

Scharpf, F. W. (2011), "Monetary Union, Fiscal Crisis and the Preemption of Democracy," *MPIfG Discussion Paper*, 11/11 (Cologne).

Schelling, T. C. (1960), *The Strategy of Conflict* (Cambridge: Harvard University Press).

Scherer, A. G., Palazzo, G., and Baumann, D. (2006), "Global Rules and Private Actors: Toward a new Role of the Transnational Corporation in Global Governance," *Business Ethics Quarterly*, 16/4: 505–32.

Scheuermann, M. (2014), "Die Weltorganisation im 21. Jahrhundert. Sicherheit, Entwicklung und Menschenrechte," in M. Scheuermann (ed.), *Die Vereinten Nationen* (Wiesbaden: Springer Fachmedien Wiesbaden), 147–92.

Scheve, K., and Slaughter, M. J. (2004), "Economic Insecurity and the Globalization of Production," *American Journal of Political Science*, 48/4: 662–74.

Schimmelfennig, F. (2003), *The EU, NATO and the Integration of Europe. Rules and Rhetoric* (Cambridge: Cambridge University Press).

Schimmelfennig, F. (2005), "Strategic Calculation and International Socialization: Membership Incentives, Party Constellations, and Sustained Compliance in Central and Eastern Europe," *International Organization*, 59/4: 827–60.

Schimmelfennig, F. (2012), "Zwischen Neo- und Postfunktionalismus: Die Integrationstheorien und die Eurokrise," *Politische Vierteljahresschrift*, 53/3: 394–413.

Schimmelfennig, F. (2015), "Efficient Process Tracing. Analyzing the Causal Mechanisms of European Integration," in A. Bennett and J. T. Checkel (eds.), *Process Tracing. From Metaphor to Analytic Tool* (Cambridge: Cambridge University Press), 98–125.

Schmalz-Bruns, R. (2007), "An den Grenzen der Entstaatlichung. Bemerkungen zu Jürgen Habermas' Modell einer 'Weltinnenpolitik ohne Weltregierung'," in P. Niesen and B. Herborth (eds.), *Anarchie der kommunikativen Freiheit: Jürgen Habermas und die Theorie der internationalen Politik* (Frankfurt a.M.: Suhrkamp), 269–93.

Schmelzle, C. (2015), *Politische Legitimität und zerfallene Staatlichkeit* (Frankfurt a.M.: Campus-Verlag).

Schmidt, V. A. (2013), "Democracy and Legitimacy in the European Union Revisited: Input, Output and 'Throughput'," *Political Studies*, 61/1: 2–22.

Schmidtke, H. (2014), *Politicizing International Institutions: The Case of Global Tax Governance* (Bremen: Dissertation, University of Bremen).

Schmidtke, H. (2016), "The Differentiated Politicisation of European Tax Governance," *West European Politics*, 39/1: 64–83.

Schmitter, P. C. (1969), "Three Neo-Functionalist Hypotheses about International Integration," *International Organization*, 23/1: 161–66.

Schmitter, P. C. (2009), "On the Way to a Post-Functionalist Theory of European Integration," *British Journal of Political Science*, 39/1: 211–15.

Schneider, C. J., and Urpelainen, J. (2013), "Distributional Conflict Between Powerful States and International Treaty Ratification," *International Studies Quarterly*, 57/1: 13–27.

Scholte, J. A. (2002), "Civil Society and Democracy in Global Governance," *Global Governance*, 8/3: 281–304.

Scholte, J. A. (2011) (ed.), *Building Global Democracy? Civil Society and Accountable Global Governance* (Cambridge: Cambridge University Press).

Schuppert, G. F. (2010), *Staat als Prozess: Eine staatstheoretische Skizze in sieben Aufzügen* (Frankfurt, a.M., New York: Campus).

Schuppert, G. F. (2012), "New Modes of Governance and the Rule of Law: The Case of Transnational Rule Making," in M. Zürn, A. Nollkaemper, and R. P. Peerenboom (eds.), *Rule of Law Dynamics. In an Era of International and Transnational Governance* (Cambridge: Cambridge University Press), 90–110.

Schweisfurth, T. (2006), *Völkerrecht* (Tübingen: Mohr Siebeck).

Schweller, R. L. (2011), "Emerging Powers in an Age of Disorder," *Global Governance*, 17/3: 285–97.

Schweller, R. L., and Wohlforth, W. C. (2000), "Power Test. Evaluating Realism in Response to the End of the Cold War," *Security Studies*, 9/3: 60–107.

Scott, J. M. (1997), "In the Loop. Congressional Influence in American Foreign Policy," *Journal of Political and Military Sociology*, 25/1: 47–75.

Sending, O. J. (2015), *The Politics of Expertise: Competing for Authority in Global Governance* (Ann Arbor: University of Michigan Press).

Sending, O. J. (2017), "Recognition and Liquid Authority," *International Theory*, 9/2: 311–28.

Senghaas, D. (1972) (ed.), *Imperialismus und strukturelle Gewalt. Analysen über abhängige Produktion* (Frankfurt a.M.: Suhrkamp).

Senti, M. (2002), *Internationale Regime und nationale Politik: Die Effektivität der Internationalen Arbeitsorganisation (ILO) im Industrieländervergleich* (Bern: Haupt).

Shapiro, M. (1981), *Courts: A Comparative and Political Analysis* (Chicago: University of Chicago Press).

Sharman, J. C. (2013), "International Hierarchies and Contemporary Imperial Governance. A Tale of Three Kingdoms," *European Journal of International Relations*, 19/2: 189–207.

Siebenhüner, B., and Biermann, F. (2009), "International Organizations in Global Environmental Governance: Epilogue," in F. Biermann, B. Siebenhüner, and A. Schreyögg (eds.), *International Organizations in Global Environmental Governance* (Abingdon: Routledge), 264–9.

Simma, B. (1994), "From Bilateralism to Community Interest in International Law (Volume 250)," in The Hague Academy of International Law (ed.), *Collected Courses of the Hague Academy of International Law*.

Simmel, G. (2009 [1908]), "Domination and Subordination," in A. J. Blasi, A. K. Jacobs, and M. J. Kanjirathinkal (eds.), *Sociology. Inquiries into the Construction of Social Forms* (Leiden, Boston: Brill), 129–226.

Simmerl, G., and Zürn, M. (2016), "Internationale Autorität. Zwei Perspektiven," *Zeitschrift für Internationale Beziehungen*, 23/1: 38–70.

Singer, P. W. (1979), *Practical Ethics* (Cambridge: Cambridge University Press).

Slaughter, A.-M., Tulumello, A. S., and Wood, S. (1998), "International Law and International Relations Theory: A New Generation of Interdisciplinary Scholarship," *American Journal of International Law*, 92/3: 367–97.

Snidal, D. (1986), "The Game Theory of International Politics," in K. A. Oye (ed.), *Cooperation under Anarchy* (Princeton: Princeton University Press), 25–57.

Snyder, G. H., and Diesing, P. (1977), *Conflict among Nations. Bargaining, Decision Making, and System Structure in International Crisis* (Princeton: Princeton University Press).

Soifer, H. D. (2012), "The Causal Logic of Critical Junctures," *Comparative Political Studies*, 45/12: 1572–97.

Sørensen, G. (2011), *A Liberal World Order in Crisis: Choosing between Imposition and Restraint* (Ithaca: Cornell University Press).

Spoerri, M., and Freyberg-Inan, A. (2008), "From Prosecution to Persecution: Perceptions of the ICTY in Serbian Domestic Politics," *Journal for International Relations and Development*, 11/4: 350–84.

Statham, P. (2010), "What Kind of Europeanized Public Politics?," in R. Koopmans and P. Statham (eds.), *The Making of a European Public Sphere: Media Discourse and Political Contention* (Cambridge: Cambridge University Press), 277–306.

Steffek, J. (2003), "The Legitimation of International Governance: A Discourse Approach," *European Journal of International Relations*, 9/2: 249–75.

Steffek, J. (2013), "Mandatskonflikte, Liberalismuskritik und die Politisierung von GATT und WTO," in M. Zürn and M. Ecker-Ehrhardt (eds.), *Die Politisierung der Weltpolitik: Umkämpfte internationale Institutionen* (Berlin: Suhrkamp), 213–39.

Steffek, J., and Hahn, K. (2010) (eds.), *Evaluating Transnational NGOs: Legitimacy, Accountability, Representation* (Houndmills, New York: Palgrave Macmillan).

Steffek, J., Kissling, C., and Nanz, P. (2007) (eds.), *Civil Society Participation in European and Global Governance: A Cure for the Democratic Deficit?* (Houndmills: Palgrave Macmillan).

Steinberg, R. H. (2002), "In the Shadow of Law or Power? Consensus-Based Bargaining and Outcomes in the GATT/WTO," *International Organization*, 56/2: 339–74.

Steinmo, S., Thelen, K., and Longstreth, F. (1992) (eds.), *Structuring Politics: Historical Institutionalism in Comparative Analysis* (Cambridge: Cambridge University Press).

Stephen, M. D. (2018, in preparation), "Contestation Overshoot: Rising Powers, NGOs and the Failure of the WTO Doha Round," in M. D. Stephen and M. Zürn (eds.), *Contested World Orders: Rising Powers, Non-Governmental Organizations and the Politics of Authority Beyond the Nation-state*.

Stephen, M. D., and Zürn, M. (2014), "Contested World Orders: Rising Powers, Non-State Actors, and the Politics of Authority Beyond the Nation-State," *WZB Discussion Paper*, SP IV 2014-107 (Berlin).

Stephen, M. D., and Zürn, M. (2018a, in preparation) (eds.), *Contested World Orders: Rising Powers, Non-Governmental Organizations and the Politics of Authority Beyond the Nation-state.*

Stephen, M. D., and Zürn, M. (2018b, in preparation), "Introduction," in M. D. Stephen and M. Zürn (eds.), *Contested World Orders: Rising Powers, Non-Governmental Organizations and the Politics of Authority Beyond the Nation-state.*

Stichweh, R. (2013), "The History and Systematics of Functional Differentiation in Sociology," in M. Albert, B. Buzan, and M. Zürn (eds.), *Bringing Sociology to IR. World Politics as Differentiation Theory* (Cambridge: Cambridge University Press), 50–70.

Stone, R. W. (2011), *Controlling Institutions: International Organizations and the Global Economy* (Cambridge: Cambridge University Press).

Stone Sweet, A. (2000), *Governing with Judges: Constitutional Politics in Europe* (Oxford: Oxford University Press).

Stone Sweet, A., and Thatcher, M. (2002), *Theory and Practice of Delegation in Non-Majoritarian Institutions*, Faculty Scholarship Series, Paper 74 <http://digitalcommons.law.yale.edu/fss_papers/74>.

Strange, S. (1996), *The Retreat of the State. The Diffusion of Power in the World Economy* (Cambridge: Cambridge University Press).

Streeck, W. (1995), "From Market Making to State Building? Reflections on the Political Economy of European Social Policy," in S. Leibfried and P. Pierson (eds.), *European Social Policy: Between Fragmentation and Integration* (Washington D.C.: Brookings Institution), 389–431.

Streeck, W., and Thelen, K. A. (2005) (eds.), *Beyond Continuity: Institutional Change in Advanced Political Economies* (Oxford: Oxford University Press).

Strijbis, O. (2018, in preparation), "Who is the Most Frequent Traveler? The Cosmopolitanism of National, European, and Global Elites," in P. de Wilde, R. Koopmans, O. Strijbi, B. Wessels, B., and M. Zürn (eds.), *Struggle over Borders: The Political Sociology of Cosmopolitanism and Communitarianism.*

Stromseth, J. E. (1988), *The Origins of Flexible Response* (Houndmills: Palgrave Macmillan).

Suchman, M. C. (1995), "Managing Legitimacy: Strategic and Institutional Approaches," *The Academy of Management Review*, 20/3: 571–610.

Tallberg, J. (2000), "Supranational Influence in EU Enforcement: The ECJ and the Principle of State Liability," *Journal of European Public Policy*, 7/1: 104–21.

Tallberg, J., Sommerer, T., Squatrito, T., and Jönsson, C. (2013), *The Opening Up of International Organizations: Transnational Access in Global Governance* (Cambridge: Cambridge University Press).

Tallberg, J., and Zürn, M. (2018, in preparation), "The Legitimacy and Legitimation of International Organizations."

Tamanaha, B. Z. (2004), *On the Rule of Law: History, Politics, Theory* (Cambridge: Cambridge University Press).

Tammen, R. L., Kugler, J., Lemke, D., Stamm, A. C., Abdollahian, M., Alsharabati, C., Efird, B., and Organski, A. (2000), *Power Transitions: Strategies for the 21st Century* (Washington: C.Q. Press).

Tarrow, S. (2001), "Transnational Politics: Contention and Institutions in International Politics," *Annual Review of Political Science*, 4/1: 1–20.

Tarrow, S. (2005), *The New Transnational Activism* (Cambridge: Cambridge University Press).

Tarrow, S. (2015), *War, States, and Contention: A Comparative Historical Study* (Ithaca: Cornell University Press).

Taylor, T. (1978) (ed.), *Approaches and Theory in International Relations* (New York: Longman).

Teney, C., and Helbling, M. (2014), "How Denationalization Divides Elites and Citizens," *Zeitschrift für Soziologie*, 43/4: 258–71.

Terlingen, Y. (2007), "The Human Rights Council: A New Era in UN Human Rights Work?," *Ethics & International Affairs*, 21/1: 167–87.

The Nobel Peace Prize (2005), *Nobelprize.org.: Nobel Media AB 2014. Web.* <http://www.nobelprize.org/nobel_prizes/peace/laureates/2005/>, accessed 14 November 2016.

Thelen, K. (1999), "Historical Institutionalism in Comparative Politics," *Annual Review of Political Science*, 2/1: 369–404.

Tilly, C. (1985), "War Making and State Making as Organized Crime," in P. B. Evans, D. Rueschemeyer, and T. Skocpol (eds.), *Bringing the State Back In* (Cambridge: Cambridge University Press), 169–91.

Tilly, C., and Tarrow, S. G. (2007), *Contentious Politics* (Oxford: Oxford University Press).

Tokhi, A. (2018, in preparation), "The Contestation of the IMF," in M. D. Stephen and M. Zürn (eds.), *Contested World Orders: Rising Powers, Non-Governmental Organizations and the Politics of Authority Beyond the Nation-state.*

Triepel, H. (1938), *Die Hegemonie. Ein Buch von führenden Staaten* (Stuttgart, Berlin: W. Kohlhammer Verlag).

Tsebelis, G. (2002), *Veto Players: How Political Institutions Work* (Princeton: Princeton University Press).

Tversky, A., and Kahneman, D. (1981), "The Framing of Decisions and the Psychology of Choice," *Science*, 211/4481: 453–58.

Tyler, T. R. (1990), *Why People Obey the Law* (New Haven: Yale University Press).

Tyler, T. R., Boeckmann, R. J., Smith, H. J., and Huo, Y. J. (1997), *Social Justice in a Diverse Society* (Boulder: Westview Press).

Uba, K., and Uggla, F. (2011), "Protest Actions against the European Union, 1992–2007," *West European Politics*, 34/2: 384–93.

Udall, L. (1998), "The World Bank and Public Accountability. Has Anything Changed?," in J. Fox and L. D. Brown (eds.), *The Struggle for Accountability. The World Bank, NGOs, and Grassroots Movements* (Cambridge: MIT Press), 391–436.

UN General Assembly (2005), *A Comprehensive Strategy to Eliminate Future Sexual Exploitation and Abuse in United Nations Peacekeeping Operations*, UN Doc. A/59/710, updated 2005.

UN Secretary General (1999), *Secretary-General's Bulletin: Observance by United Nations Forces of International Humanitarian Law*, UN Doc., ST/SGB/1999/13.

UN Secretary General (2003), *Secretary-General's Bulletin: Special Measures for Protection from Sexual Exploitation and Sexual Abuse*, UN Doc., ST/SGB/2003/13.

UN Security Council (2005), *Note by the President of the Security Council*, S/2005/841. 29 December 2005.

United Nations Department of Economic and Social Affairs (2009), "Introduction to ECOSOC Consultative Status" <http://esango.un.org/paperless/Web?page= static&content=intro>, accessed 14 October 2013.

UNMIK Ombudsperson (2000), *Special Report No. 1* <http://www.ombudspersonkosovo .org/repository/docs/E4010426a_874491.pdf>.

Urpelainen, J., and Van de Graaf, T. (2015), "Your Place or Mine? Institutional Capture and the Creation of Overlapping International Institutions," *British Journal of Political Science*, 45/04: 799–827.

Vabulas, F., and Snidal, D. (2013), "Organization Without Delegation: Informal Intergovernmental Organizations (IIGOs) and the Spectrum of Intergovernmental Arrangements," *The Review of International Organizations*, 8/2: 193–220.

Valentini, L. (2012), "Ideal vs. Non-ideal Theory: A Conceptual Map," *Philosophy Compass*, 7/9: 654–64.

van den Bossche, P. (2008), "NGO Involvement in the WTO: A Comparative Perspective," *Journal of International Economic Law*, 11/4: 717–49.

van der Pijl, K. (1998), *Transnational Classes and International Relations* (London: Routledge).

Venzke, I. (2013), "Understanding the Authority of International Courts and Tribunals: On Delegation and Discursive Construction," *Theoretical Inquiries in Law*, 14/2: 381–409.

Verdirame, G. (2011), *The UN and Human Rights: Who Guards the Guardians?* (Cambridge: Cambridge University Press).

Vernon, R. (2010), *Cosmopolitan Regard: Political Membership and Global Justice* (New York: Cambridge University Press).

Victor, D. G. (2004), *The Collapse of the Kyoto Protocol and the Struggle to Slow Global Warming* (Princeton: Princeton University Press).

Victor, D. G. (2011), *Global Warming Gridlock: Creating More Effective Strategies for Protecting the Planet* (Cambridge: Cambridge University Press).

Viola, L. A. (2013), "Institutioneller Wandel durch Wettbewerb: Wie die Zivilgesellschaft die Weltgesundheitsorganisation verändert hat," in M. Zürn and M. Ecker-Ehrhardt (eds.), *Die Politisierung der Weltpolitik: Umkämpfte internationale Institutionen* (Berlin: Suhrkamp), 287–311.

Viola, L. A., Snidal, D., and Zürn, M. (2015), "Sovereign (In)equality in the Evolution of the International System," in E. Huber, M. Lange, S. Leibfried, J. Levy, F. Nullmeier, and J. Stephens (eds.), *The Oxford Handbook of Transformations of the State* (Oxford: Oxford University Press), 221–36.

von Bogdandy, A. (2013), "Prinzipien von Staat, supranationalen und internationalen Organisationen," in J. Isensee and P. Kirchhof (eds.), *Handbuch des Staatsrechts der*

Bundesrepublik Deutschland (Vol. XI, Internationale Bezüge; 3rd edn, Heidelberg: C.F. Müller), 275–304.

von Bogdandy, A., Dann, P., and Goldmann, M. (2010a), "Developing the Publicness of Public International Law: Towards a Legal Framework for Global Governance Activities," in A. von Bogdandy, R. Wolfrum, J. von Bernstorff, P. Dann, and M. Goldmann (eds.), *The Exercise of Public Authority by International Institutions. Advancing International Institutional Law* (Heidelberg: Springer), 3–32.

von Bogdandy, A., Goldmann, M., and Venzke, I. (2017), "From Public International to International Public Law. Translating World Public Opinion into International Public Authority," *European Journal of International Law*, 28/1: 115–45.

von Bogdandy, A., and Venzke, I. (2012), "In Whose Name? An Investigation of International Courts' Public Authority and Its Democratic Justification," *European Journal of International Law*, 23/1: 7–41.

von Bogdandy, A., and Venzke, I. (2014), *In Whose Name? A Public Law Theory of International Adjudication* (Oxford: Oxford University Press).

von Bogdandy, A., Wolfrum, R., Bernstorff, J. von, Dann, P., and Goldmann, M. (2010b) (eds.), *The Exercise of Public Authority by International Institutions. Advancing International Institutional Law* (Heidelberg: Springer).

Wade, R. H. (1997), "Greening the Bank. The Struggle over the Environment. 1970–1995," in D. Kapur, J. P. Lewis, and R. C. Webb (eds.), *The World Bank. Its First Half Century* (Washington: Brookings Institution Press), 611–734.

Waldner, D. (2015), "Aspirin, Aeschylus, and the Foundations of Qualitative Causal Inference," unpublished paper.

Walker, R. B. J. (1992), *Inside/Outside: International Relations as Political Theory* (Cambridge: Cambridge University Press).

Wallensteen, P., Staibano, C., and Eriksson, M. (2003), *Making Targeted Sanctions Effective: Guidelines for the Implementation of UN Policy Options* (Uppsala: Department of Peace and Conflict Research, Uppsala University).

Wallerstein, I. (1974), *The Modern World-System I. Capitalist Agriculture and the Origins of the European World-Economy in the Sixteenth Century* (New York: Academic Press).

Wallerstein, I. (1980), *The Modern World-System II. Mercantilism and the Consolidation of the European World-Economy, 1600–1750* (New York: Academic Press).

Waltz, K. N. (1979), *Theory of International Politics* (Boston: McGraw-Hill).

Wapner, P. (1995), "Politics Beyond the State: Environmental Activism and World Civic Politics," *World Politics*, 47/April: 311–40.

Warleigh, A. (2001), "'Europeanizing' Civil Society. NGOs as Agents of Political Socialization," *Journal of Common Market Studies*, 39/4: 619–39.

Watson Institute (2001), *Targeted Financial Sanctions: A Manual for Design and Implementation. Contributions from the Interlaken Process* (Providence, RI) <http://www.watsoninstitute.org/tfs/TFS.pdf>.

Weber, M. (1968), *Wirtschaft und Gesellschaft. Grundriß der Verstehenden Soziologie* (Tübingen: Mohr Siebeck).

Weber, M. (1978 [1925]), "Chapter III. The Types of Legitimate Domination [Die Typen der Herrschaft]," in G. Roth and C. Wittich (eds.), *Max Weber. Economy and*

Society. An Outline of Interpretative Sociology (Vol. 1, Berkeley: University of California Press), 212–301.

Weber, M. (2013a), "Kapitel I. Soziologische Grundbegriffe," in K. Borchardt, E. Hanke, and W. Schluchter (eds.), *Max Weber Gesamtausgabe I/23. Wirtschaft und Gesellschaft: Soziologie* (Tübingen: Mohr Siebeck), 147–215.

Weber, M. (2013b), "Kapitel III. Typen der Herrschaft," in K. Borchardt, E. Hanke, and W. Schluchter (eds.), *Max Weber Gesamtausgabe I/23. Wirtschaft und Gesellschaft: Soziologie* (Tübingen: Mohr Siebeck), 449–591.

Weidner, H. (2013), "Politisierung als Prozess und Ergebnis: Weltbank, Bergbausektor und Nachhaltigkeit," in M. Zürn and M. Ecker-Ehrhardt (eds.), *Die Politisierung der Weltpolitik: Umkämpfte internationale Institutionen* (Berlin: Suhrkamp), 312–34.

Weingart, P. (1983), "Verwissenschaftlichung der Gesellschaft—Politisierung der Wissenschaft," *Zeitschrift für Soziologie*, 12/3: 225–41.

Weingart, P. (2008), *Die Stunde der Wahrheit? Zum Verhältnis der Wissenschaft zu Politik, Wirtschaft und Medien in der Wissensgesellschaft* (2nd edn, Weilerswist: Velbrück Wissenschaft).

Weiss, T. G., and Wilkinson, R. (2014), "Rethinking Global Governance? Complexity, Authority, Power, Change," *International Studies Quarterly*, 58/1: 207–15.

Wendt, A. (1999), *Social Theory of International Politics* (Cambridge: Cambridge University Press).

Wessel, J. (2006), "Judicial Policymaking at the International Criminal Court. An Institutional Guide to Analyzing International Adjudication," *Columbia Journal of Transnational Law*, 44/2: 377–452.

White House (2002), *National Security Presidential Directive NSPD-22* (Washington) <http://www.combat-trafficking.army.mil/documents/policy/NSPD-22.pdf>.

Wiener, A. (2014), *A Theory of Contestation* (Berlin, Heidelberg: Springer).

Williams, B. A. O. (2005), *In the Beginning was the Deed: Realism and Moralism in Political Argument* (Princeton: Princeton University Press).

Williamson, O. E. (1975), *Markets and Hierarchies: Analysis and Antitrust Implications* (New York: Free Press).

Wolfrum, R. (1984), *Die Internationalisierung staatsfreier Räume* (Berlin, Heidelberg: Springer-Verlag).

Woods, N., and Narlikar, A. (2001), "Governance and the Limits of Accountability: The WTO, the IMF and the World Bank," *International Social Science Journal*, 53/170: 569–83.

World Bank (2010), *Analyzing the Effects of Policy Reforms on the Poor: An Evaluation of the Effectiveness of World Bank Support to Poverty and Social Impact Analyses* <http://siteresources.worldbank.org/INTPSIA/Resources/IEG_psia_full.pdf>.

WorldPublicOpinion.org (2007), "World Publics Favor New Powers for the UN" <http://www.worldpublicopinion.org/pipa/pdf/may07/CCGA+_UN_article.pdf>.

WVS Wave 5 (2005–2008), *WORLD VALUES SURVEY Wave 5 2005–2008 OFFICIAL AGGREGATE v.20140429. World Values Survey Association* (www.worldvaluessurvey.org). *Aggregate File Producer: Asep/JDS, Madrid SPAIN.*

WVS Wave 6 (2010–2014), *WORLD VALUES SURVEY Wave 6 2010–2014 OFFICIAL AGGREGATE v.20150418. World Values Survey Association* (*www.worldvaluessurvey.org*). *Aggregate File Producer: Asep/JDS, Madrid SPAIN.*

Young, A. R. (2010), "Perspectives on the Changing Global Distribution of Power: Concepts and Context," *Politics*, 30/S1: 2–14.

Young, I. M. (2004), "Responsibility and Global Labor Justice," *Journal of Political Philosophy*, 12/4: 365–88.

Young, O. R. (1994), *International Governance: Protecting the Environment in a Stateless Society* (Ithaca: Cornell University Press).

Zangl, B. (2006), *Die Internationalisierung der Rechtsstaatlichkeit. Streitbeilegung in GATT und WTO* (Frankfurt a. M: Campus).

Zangl, B., Heußner, F., Kruck, A., and Lanzendörfer, X. (2016), "Imperfect Adaptation. How the WTO and the IMF Adjust to Shifting Power Distributions Among Their Members," *The Review of International Organizations*, 11/2: 171–96.

Zangl, B., and Zürn, M. (2003), *Frieden und Krieg. Sicherheit in der nationalen und postnationalen Konstellation* (Frankfurt a. M.: Suhrkamp).

Zaum, D. (2013), "International Organizations, Legitimacy, and Legitimation," in D. Zaum (ed.), *Legitimating International Organizations* (Oxford: Oxford University Press), 3–25.

Zemanek, K. (2007), "Is the Security Council the Sole Judge of its Own Legality? A Re-Examination," in A. Reinisch and U. Kriebaum (eds.), *The Law of International Relations. Liber amicorum Hanspeter Neuhold* (Utrecht: Eleven International Publishing), 483–505.

Zürn, M. (1992), *Interessen und Institutionen in der internationalen Politik. Grundlegung und Anwendungen des situationsstrukturellen Ansatzes* (Opladen: Leske + Budrich).

Zürn, M. (1997a), "Assessing State Preferences and Explaining Institutional Choice: The Case of Intra-German Trade," *International Studies Quarterly*, 41/2: 295–320.

Zürn, M. (1997b), "'Positives Regieren' jenseits des Nationalstaates. Zur Implementation internationaler Umweltregime," *Zeitschrift für Internationale Beziehungen*, 4/1: 41–63.

Zürn, M. (1998), *Regieren jenseits des Nationalstaats. Globalisierung und Denationalisierung als Chance* (Frankfurt a.M.: Suhrkamp).

Zürn, M. (1999), "The State in the Post-National Constellation: Societal Denationalization and Multi-Level Governance," *ARENA Working Paper*, 35 (Oslo).

Zürn, M. (2000), "Democratic Governance Beyond the Nation-State. The EU and Other International Institutions," *European Journal of International Relations*, 6/2: 183–221.

Zürn, M. (2002), "Societal Denationalization and Positive Governance," in M. Ougaard and R. A. Higgott (eds.), *Towards a Global Polity* (London, New York: Routledge), 78–103.

Zürn, M. (2004), "Global Governance and Legitimacy Problems," *Government & Opposition*, 39/2: 260–87.

Zürn, M. (2006), "Zur Politisierung der Europäischen Union," *Politische Vierteljahresschrift*, 47/2: 242–51.

Zürn, M. (2007), "Institutionalisierte Ungleichheit in der Weltpolitik. Jenseits der Alternative 'Global Governance' versus 'American Empire'," *Politische Vierteljahresschrift*, 48/4: 680–704.

Zürn, M. (2008), "Governance in einer sich wandelnden Welt—eine Zwischenbilanz," in G. F. Schuppert and M. Zürn (eds.), *Governance in einer sich wandelnden Welt (Sonderheft 41 der Politischen Vierteljahresschrift)* (Wiesbaden: VS Verlag für Sozialwissenschaften), 553–80.

Zürn, M. (2012a), "Autorität und Legitimität in der postnationalen Konstellation," in A. Geis, F. Nullmeier, and C. Daase (eds.), *Der Aufstieg der Legitimitätspolitik. Rechtfertigung und Kritik politisch-ökonomischer Ordnungen (Leviathan Sonderband 40/27)* (Baden-Baden: Nomos), 41–62.

Zürn, M. (2012b), "Global Governance as Multi-Level Governance," in D. Levi-Faur (ed.), *Oxford Handbook of Governance* (Oxford: Oxford University Press), 730–44.

Zürn, M. (2013), "Politisierung als Konzept der Internationalen Beziehungen," in M. Zürn and M. Ecker-Ehrhardt (eds.), *Die Politisierung der Weltpolitik: Umkämpfte internationale Institutionen* (Berlin: Suhrkamp), 7–35.

Zürn, M. (2014), "The Politicization of World Politics and its Effects: Eight Propositions," *European Political Science Review*, 6/1: 47–71.

Zürn, M. (2016a), "Historical Institutionalism and International Relations—Strange Bedfellows?," in T. Rixen, L. A. Viola, and M. Zürn (eds.), *Historical Institutionalism and International Relations. Explaining Institutional Development in World Politics* (Oxford: Oxford University Press), 199–228.

Zürn, M. (2016b), "Opening Up Europe. Next Steps in Politicisation Research," *West European Politics*, 39/1: 164–82.

Zürn, M. (2016c), "Survey Article. Four Models of a Global Order with Cosmopolitan Intent: An Empirical Assessment," *Journal of Political Philosophy*, 24/1: 88–119.

Zürn, M. (2017), "From Constitutional Rule to Loosely Coupled Spheres of Liquid Authority. A Reflexive Approach," *International Theory*, 9/2: 261–85.

Zürn, M., Binder, M., and Ecker-Ehrhardt, M. (2012a), "International Authority and Its Politicization," *International Theory*, 4/1: 69–106.

Zürn, M., Binder, M., Ecker-Ehrhardt, M., and Radtke, K. (2007), "Politische Ordnungs-bildung wider Willen," *Zeitschrift für Internationale Beziehungen*, 14/1: 129–64.

Zürn, M., Binder, M., Tokhi, A., Keller, X., and Lockwood Payton, A. (2015), *The International Authority Data Project*, Paper presented at the International Authority Workshop, December 10–11, Berlin.

Zürn, M., and Checkel, J. T. (2005), "Getting Socialized to Build Bridges: Constructivism and Rationalism, Europe and the Nation-State," *International Organization*, 59/4: 1045–79.

Zürn, M., and de Wilde, P. (2016), "Debating Globalization. Cosmopolitanism and Communitarianism as Political Ideologies," *Journal of Political Ideologies*, 21/3: 280–301.

Zürn, M., and Faude, B. (2013), "On Fragmentation, Differentiation, and Coordination," *Global Environmental Politics*, 13/3: 119–30.

Zürn, M., and Heupel, M. (2017), "Human Rights Protection in International Organizations: An Introduction," in M. Heupel and M. Zürn (eds.), *Protecting the Individual from International Authority. Human Rights in International Organizations* (Cambridge: Cambridge University Press), 1–39.

Zürn, M., and Neyer, J. (2005), "Conclusions—The Conditions of Compliance," in M. Zürn and C. Joerges (eds.), *Law and Governance in Postnational Europe* (Cambridge: Cambridge University Press), 183–217.

Zürn, M., Nollkaemper, A., and Peerenboom, R. P. (2012b) (eds.), *Rule of Law Dynamics: In an Era of International and Transnational Governance* (Cambridge: Cambridge University Press).

Index

Note: Page numbers in bold indicate areas of key interest.